W9-AZL-119

New York

5th Edition

Herbert Bailey Livesey

Prentice Hall Travel

New York • London • Toronto • Sydney • Tokyo • Singapore

THE AMERICAN EXPRESS ® TRAVEL GUIDES

Published in the United States by
Prentice Hall General Reference
A division of Simon & Schuster, Inc.
15 Columbus Circle
New York, NY 10023

PRENTICE HALL and colophon are
registered trademarks of
Simon & Schuster, Inc.

First published 1983 in the United
Kingdom by Mitchell Beazley
International Ltd, Michelin House
81 Fulham Road, London SW3 6RB as
*The American Express Pocket Guide
to New York.* Second edition 1986,
reprinted 1987. Third edition 1988.
Fourth edition 1991. This edition,
revised, updated and expanded,
published 1993.

Edited, designed and produced by
Castle House Press, Llantrisant
Mid Glamorgan CF7 8EU, Wales

Library of Congress Catalog Card
Number 92-082890
ISBN 0-671-84753-8

The editors thank Ruth Wicks of Hill
and Knowlton (UK) Ltd, Neil Hanson
of Lovell Johns, David Haslam,
Melanie Gould, Anna Holmes and
Andrea Thomas for their assistance
during the preparation of this edition.

FOR THE SERIES:
Series Editor:
  David Townsend Jones
Map Editor: David Haslam
Indexer: Hilary Bird
Gazetteer: Anne Evans
Cover design:
  Roger Walton Studio

FOR THIS EDITION:
Edited on desktop by:
  Sharon Charity
Art editor: Eileen Townsend Jones
Illustrators: Illustrated Arts,
  Sylvia Hughes-Williams,
  Coral Mula, David Evans
Cover photo: Andrew Levin/Colorific

FOR MITCHELL BEAZLEY:
Art Director: Tim Foster
Managing Editor: Alison Starling
Production: Matthew Batchelor

PRODUCTION CREDITS:
Maps by Lovell Johns, Oxford,
  England
Subway map by TCS, Aldershot,
  England
Typeset in Garamond and
  News Gothic
Desktop layout in Ventura
  Publisher
Linotronic output by
  Tradespools Limited, Frome,
  England

Contents

Culture, history and background

Basic information

Planning and walks

Sights and places of interest

Where to stay

Eating and drinking

Nightlife and entertainment

Shopping

Recreation

Excursions

Maps

How to use this book

Few guidelines are needed to understand how this book works:

- For the general organization of the book, see CONTENTS on the pages preceding this one.
- Wherever appropriate, chapters and sections are arranged alphabetically, with headings appearing in **CAPITALS.**
- Often these headings are followed by location and practical information printed in *italics.*
- As you turn the pages, you will find subject headers, similar to those used in telephone directories, printed in CAPITALS in the top corner of each page.
- If you still cannot find what you need, check in the comprehensive and exhaustively cross-referenced INDEX at the back of the book.
- Following the index, a LIST OF STREET NAMES provides map references for all roads and streets mentioned in the book that are located within the areas covered by the main city maps.

CROSS-REFERENCES
These are printed in SMALL CAPITALS, referring you to other sections or alphabetical entries in the book. Care has been taken to ensure that such cross-references are self-explanatory. Often, page references are also given, although their excessive use would be intrusive and ugly.

FLOORS
We use the American convention in this book: "first floor" means the floor at ground level.

KEY TO SYMBOLS

☎	Telephone	⦿	MasterCard
Ⓕ	Facsimile (fax)	VISA	Visa
★	Recommended sight	▤	Secure garage
⬅	Parking	⌂	Quiet hotel
🏛	Building of architectural interest	⬍	Elevator
▣	Free entrance	🐕	Dogs not allowed
▨	Entrance fee payable	≋	Swimming pool
▪	Entrance expensive	◁	Good view
𝙓	Guided tour	⚱	Gym/fitness facilities
▣	Cafeteria	⅄	Bar
♣	Special interest for children	≡	Restaurant
⚘	Hotel	▬	Simple restaurant
▆	Simple hotel	⌂	Luxury restaurant
🏛	Luxury hotel	⊓	A la carte available
♥	Good value	▰	Set (fixed-price) menu available
▢	Cheap		
▨	Inexpensive	▬	Good wines
▥	Moderately priced	⚘	Open-air dining
▦	Expensive	●	Disco dancing
▧	Very expensive	♫	Nightclub
AE	American Express	♪	Live music
◉	Diners Club	♥	Dancing

HOTEL AND RESTAURANT PRICE CATEGORIES

These are denoted by the symbols ▢ (cheap), ▨ (inexpensive), ▥ (moderately priced), ▦ (expensive) and ▧ (very expensive). They correspond approximately to the following actual local prices, which give a guideline **at the time of printing**. Naturally, prices tend to rise, but, with a few exceptions, hotels and restaurants will remain in the same price category.

Price categories	Corresponding to approximate prices	
	for **hotels** *double room with bath; singles are slightly cheaper*	for **restaurants** *meal for one with service, taxes and house wine*
▧ very expensive	over $240	over $110
▦ expensive	$190-240	$60-110
▥ moderately priced	$140-190	$40-60
▨ inexpensive	$100-140	$20-40
▢ cheap	under $100	under $20

About the author

After an early career in higher education culminating in the post of Director of Admissions at New York University, **Herbert Bailey Livesey** decided that he no longer wanted to get up early and wear suits. An exhibition of his sculptures had proved a modest critical success and a resounding financial flop, so he decided, with greater logic than might be apparent, to leave salaried employment for a full-time career in writing. A native New Yorker, he is the author of nine books on such subjects as education and sociology. *Tournament,* his only published novel, took as its backdrop the world of deep-sea game-fishing.

He has written two other titles in this series: *Toronto, Montréal & Québec City* and *Barcelona, Madrid & Seville,* and is currently writing the forthcoming *Boston and New England.* His work appears frequently in such magazines as *Travel and Leisure, Food and Wine* and *Playboy.* He and his wife Joanne share four grown children and one very new granddaughter, Juliana. They live in a house north of New York, overlooking the bay in which explorer Henry Hudson anchored his boat, the *Half Moon,* in 1609.

A message from the series editor

In designing *American Express New York* we aimed to make this brand-new edition simple and instinctive to use, like all its sister volumes in our new, larger paperback format.

The hallmarks of the relaunched series are clear, classic typography, confidence in fine travel writing for its own sake, and faith in our readers' innate intelligence to find their way around the books without heavy-handed signposting by editors.

Readers with anything less than 20:20 vision will doubtless also enjoy the larger, clearer type, and can now dispense with the mythical magnifying glasses we never issued free with the old pocket guide series.

Months of concentrated work by the author and our editors have been dedicated to ensuring that this edition is as accurate and up to date as it possibly can be at the moment it goes to press. But time and change are forever the enemies, and in between editions we very much appreciate it when you, our readers, keep us informed of changes that you discover.

As ever, I am indebted to all the many readers who wrote during the preparation of this edition. Please remember that your feedback is extremely important to our efforts to tailor the series to the very distinctive tastes and requirements of our sophisticated international readership.

Send your comments to me at Mitchell Beazley International Ltd, Michelin House, 81 Fulham Road, London SW3 6RB; or, in the US, c/o American Express Travel Guides, Prentice Hall Travel, 15 Columbus Circle, New York, NY 10023.

David Townsend Jones

New York

Rainbow on the Hudson

New York is not America. That sentiment wasn't even original to English author Ford Madox Ford, who used it as a title for a book more than sixty years ago. A world city — *the* world city, by most measures — it cannot be contained within geopolitical boundaries. Every language is spoken in New York, every cuisine prepared, every nation and race represented, every dream conjured, every depredation performed. If an idea, an object, a hope, a taste, a scent, a sin cannot be found here, the likely conclusion is that it does not exist. The only emotion New York cannot arouse is indifference. No other place created by man provokes such adoration and abhorrence, often at the same time, in the same individual. Few words applied to this city can be dismissed as hyperbole. It is an entity of exhilarating, numbing, horrifying, glorious excess.

ETHNIC STEW
Although among the greatest of cities, New York can no longer claim to be the largest. It covers nearly 300 square miles and has a population of more than 7.3 million people, barely a third that of Mexico City. The 1990 census recorded 3,827,088 Caucasians (which compared with 4,293,695 in 1980), 2,102,512 African-Americans (1,784,124 in 1980), 27,531 Native Americans (11,824), 512,719 Asians and Pacific Islanders (231,505), with a further 852,714 (749,882) regarded as racially unclassifiable. Little wonder that all pithy descriptions of the diversity of the populace — melting pot, mosaic, rainbow — fall short.

The largest ethnic minority is that of Hispanic origin, but from many nations. There is neither an ethnic nor a racial majority. People of Italian, Irish and Eastern European origins are present in influential numbers. Germans and other Northern Europeans were among the earliest immigrants and were quickly assimilated. Puerto Ricans, Dominicans, Greeks, and Chinese persist as largely unified groups in distinct residential and commercial communities. Refugees from Southeast Asia, the Caribbean, Central America and the Indian subcontinent have become increasingly apparent.

An estimated 2.6 million residents were born in another country. New arrivals tend to gather together and take care of each other, entering the vocations of those who preceded them. Hence the high proportions of former Israelis who own limousine companies, Koreans who are greengrocers, Indians who run service stations, Greeks who have coffee shops.

Antipathies persist, as evidenced by recent incidents in which innocent Blacks, Whites, Jews, Asians and others have been victimized by bigots and hoodlums. But it can be argued that no city of such ethnic diversity deals as sensibly and humanely with the conflicts that inevitably arise between people who share little but their place of residence and their dreams.

> If you can make it there, you'll make it anywhere
> (*New York, New York*)

CITY OF VILLAGES

Water-girt New York comprises five distinct divisions called boroughs, only one of which — The Bronx — is situated on the North American continent. The island of Manhattan is, of course, the central borough. Brooklyn (largest in population) and Queens (largest in area) take up the western tip of Long Island, which itself stretches 125 miles east into the Atlantic. Staten Island, to the south of its sisters, snuggles up to New Jersey.

When approached from the east through the outlying industrial dross, the famous Manhattan skyline appears somehow diminutive. At the southern tip of the island, the concrete spires and glass slabs of the Financial District are dominated by the twin pillars of the World Trade Center. The profile then dips to the lower heights of converted warehouses ("loft" buildings) and tenements, lifting gradually once more to midtown and the peaks of the instantly recognizable Empire State and Chrysler Buildings. After another two miles, the skyline dips again, nearly meeting the rising ground that continues for another six miles, terminating at the lip of the inky tidal course known as the Spuyten Duyvil.

Once you plunge into the street canyons, warring stimuli battle for attention. The noise of endless construction and millions of lurching vehicles is trapped between the rearing phalanxes of stone and steel and glass. In winter, clouds of steam billow from manholes as if from an inferno just below. Rivers of people press forward, set on apparently urgent tasks. Traffic jerks and clogs along congested arteries. All the senses are staggered, and continue to be bombarded even when the newcomer has begun to adapt to the pace.

But there are quiet places, too. Side streets end in shaded cul-de-sacs, more than 50 museums muffle the clamor beyond their thick walls, and there are nearly 37,000 acres of parks. The most important of these is Central Park, in the heart of Manhattan. Two Monacos could be contained within its borders, with room left over for a chunk of Nice.

A BRIEF HISTORY

The broad protected harbor was first discovered in 1524, but permanent settlement did not take place until a century later. The English took New Amsterdam from the Dutch in 1664, and the city was renamed New York. Resentment against British rule culminated in the War of Independence in 1775, and New York was for a time the capital of the infant nation.

The population was then slightly more than 30,000. It multiplied dramatically with the mass immigrations of the 19th century, and those who prospered moved uptown. In the 40 years following the Civil War (1861-65), Central Park was finished and the first skyscrapers erected. In 1898, the four outer boroughs were annexed to Manhattan, instantly fashioning the largest city in the world. The population was now more than 3 million.

Despite the Wall Street Crash of 1929, construction of the Empire State Building began. Twenty years later, the city's population reached eight million, and the United Nations moved into its new headquarters on the

East River. The city was at its zenith — the capital of the world, untouched by war.

Since then, the pattern has been one of decline followed by resurgences, which are in turn punctured by sharp descents into fiscal crises, deteriorating public services, accelerating crime rates and loss of industry and workers. Despair continues to mount over the hydra-headed pandemic of rampant crack cocaine use, the AIDS tragedy, and poverty brought to the doorstep by growing legions of homeless people. Crack emerged as a deadly drug of choice in the early 1980s, and, at about the same time, AIDS started worming its horrifying way into the public consciousness. The homeless have become more evident and immediately distressing, with an estimated 90,000 living on the streets, as squatters, or in city-run shelters. About a quarter of them suffer serious mental illness, and at least that many are drug addicts or alcoholics.

Still, reaction and proposals for remedies have been slow in coming, partly because New York in the mid-1980s enjoyed renewed prosperity after a brush with near-bankruptcy only a few years before. That euphoria evaporated when the stock market crashed in October 1987, signaling the end of the free-spending decade and the start of a recession that rippled across the country. The crippled economy, and consecutive administrations in Washington that have proved indifferent to the plight of the cities, especially New York, have stalled efforts to deal with the city's apocalyptic problems.

Tentative steps have been taken. Controversial campaigns have distributed condoms among schoolchildren and created shelters for the homeless that are smaller and less dangerous than the virtual warehouses so many of them refuse to use. While these measures fall far short of the Sisyphean labors that must yet be undertaken, history insists that New York's problems will be solved or at least made tolerable, as they have since Peter Minuit sat down to strike a bargain. They will, of course, be replaced by others as yet unimagined.

Visitors inclined to sigh in relief that such painful occurrences don't happen where they live are wise to remember that things have a way of happening first in New York... before they move on. How many travelers know, for two examples, that London has an estimated 75,000 illegal squatters and homeless people, and that Paris, with a core population of 2.2 million, has 15-20,000?

Turn the coin and realize that tourism continues to grow, as new generations of Americans and foreigners rediscover the pleasures that never left New York. The demise of Broadway has been proclaimed with tedious regularity since the Depression, yet it continues to flourish. Despite two decades of unprecedented construction, hotels fill up as soon as they open their doors. Every newly-shuttered restaurant is replaced by another, frisky and eager to please. New York remains the white-hot center of activity for those intent on careers in publishing, finance, advertising, ballet, opera and the visual arts. There are still free concerts and Shakespeare in the Park. And vigorous new neighborhoods. And jazz in the subway. And Miss Liberty is in her rightful place in the harbor, as bright and inviting as a new penny.

SAFETY FIRST

To avoid a visit to New York on the basis of out-of-proportion stories of crime is akin to denying oneself Venice because of rubbish in the canals. Several US cities are statistically more dangerous, but New York's status as a world media capital focuses international attention here. More than 4,500 members of the press work in the city, 1,000 of them for foreign newspapers, periodicals, and television networks. It is hardly surprising that they find it more convenient to cover a homicide in Brooklyn than one in Dallas or Atlanta or Chicago or Miami, all of which have significantly higher rates of violent crime than New York. One result of the saturation coverage is incalculable harm to the city's international image.

Still, prudence is in order. At the risk of instilling undue paranoia in visitors already inclined to expect the worst, there are a number of precautions that should be taken. First and foremost, always be aware of what is going on around you. At airports and railroad stations, carry your own luggage and don't surrender it until well inside your hotel. On the subways, buses, and on the street, avoid making direct eye contact with deranged or hostile people. Carry only the amount of money and the specific charge/credit cards needed for each excursion. Pickpockets are most often at work on crowded conveyances, including elevators and revolving doors. Those called "spitters" use diversions — "accidentally" spilling something on a victim and helping clean it up while an accomplice lifts cash and credit cards. Consider buying a cloth holster or money belt to wear under your clothes. Don't carry a wallet in the obvious places; put it in the left or right front trouser pocket with your hand over it. Hold purses like footballs, rather than letting them dangle from shoulders.

After dark, women and older people are wise to travel in groups, or with escorts. Although the odds are that a nightly walk across the nearest park or along deserted streets would be uneventful, there is no reason to tempt fate. Expensive-looking jewelry and clothing should be avoided when traveling on foot. Don't be embarrassed to make a commotion or a detour into a hotel lobby or shop if feeling threatened. When in the subway at night, wait in the designated section near the token booth and ride in the crowded central cars, not the empty ones at front and back. In a hotel room, use the peephole in the door to check out callers. If any are suspicious, call the front desk. If there is a safe in the room, use it.

All that said, don't jump at every sound and don't think that reading this book or looking up at a building will brand you as a tourist. Most New Yorkers already *know* you're from out of town.

NEW YORKERS

There are two million interesting people in New York —
and only 78 in Los Angeles.
(Neil Simon)

The reputation New Yorkers have earned for rudeness and pugnacity is not without foundation. Yet beneath their often brusque exterior lies an enviable openness to new experiences and relationships. There is no fad, art form, life-style or ideology that they will not sample, or at least tolerate. Outside of working hours — and, in a 24-hour city, that means any time — they can be seen jogging, cycling, flipping Frisbees, roller- or ice-skating, dancing in nightclubs, demonstrating at the UN, taking the sun on the Hudson piers or watching it set from Riverside Park. Of all the surprises of a first visit to this city, one of the most agreeable can be New Yorkers themselves.

New York is a city of dreams
(Isaac Bashevis Singer)

Culture, history and background

Landmarks in New York's history

DISCOVERY TO REVOLUTION

1524: Italian explorer Giovanni da Verrazano discovered New York Bay while searching for a NW passage. **1609**: Henry Hudson sailed his *Half Moon* up the river that was eventually given his name. **1623**: New Netherland became a province of the Dutch West India Company, and the cluster of huts at the s tip of Manhattan was called New Amsterdam. **1626**: Provincial Director-General Peter Minuit bought the island from the Algonquin Indians.

1643: Population grew to about 500 people, speaking 18 different languages. During the tenure of Governor Peter Stuyvesant, settlements were established in the areas eventually known as The Bronx, Queens, Brooklyn and Staten Island. **1664**: The Duke of York sent a fleet into the harbor. Abandoned by the burgomasters who chafed under his authoritarian rule, Stuyvesant surrendered the city to the English. It was renamed New York. **1674**: After extended hostilities between the English and Dutch — and one brief reoccupation by the Dutch — the city and province were ceded by treaty to the English.

1689: A German merchant, Jacob Leisler, led a revolt against oligarchic trade monopolies when he learned of the overthrow of James II. He was hanged for treason. **1712**: Slaves now constituted a substantial segment of the population. Despite ordinances denying them weapons and the right of assembly, a number of Blacks set fire to a building near Maiden Lane and killed nine Whites who attempted to stop the blaze. When soldiers arrived, six of the Blacks committed suicide; 21 others were captured and executed. **1725**: The *New-York Gazette* was founded. **1734**: John Peter Zenger, publisher of the *New York Weekly Journal,* was charged with libeling the Government. He was acquitted in the first test of the principle of press freedom in the colonies.

1754-63: Population now 16,000. King's College founded. Benjamin Franklin proposed union of the colonies for common defense during the French and Indian War, but was rejected. A force led by George Washington was defeated by the French at Fort Necessity in Pennsylvania. The conflict, which was part of the worldwide Seven Years War, ended with the Treaty of Paris. English sovereignty over the major part of explored North America was thereby conceded.

1764-70: Colonial grumbling over British rule escalated into sporadic demonstrations and protests, with the passage of the punitive Sugar,

Stamp, and Colonial Currency Acts. The Quartering Act permitted British troops to requisition private dwellings and inns, their rent to be paid by the colonies. At the Stamp Act Congress held in Manhattan, delegates of nine colonies passed a Declaration of Rights and Liberties. Skirmishes between soldiers and the insurrectionist Sons of Liberty culminated in January 1770 in the killing of a colonial and the wounding of a number of others. The Boston Massacre, in which British troops fired upon taunting protesters, occurred 7 weeks later.

1775-83: The American Revolution. The Continental Congress appointed Washington as Commander-in-Chief and, on July 4, 1776, adopted the Declaration of Independence. After early battles ranging from Manhattan to Long Island, most of which he lost, Washington withdrew. New York was occupied by the British for the remainder of the War. With the Treaty of Versailles in September 1783, the British troops left the city. **1789**: Washington was sworn in as first President at Federal Hall in New York, the first capital of the Federal Government. **1790**: An official census recorded the population at 33,000.

1807-09: Robert Fulton made a round trip from New York to Albany in his steamboat *Clermont*. In reaction to British and French seizure of American ships at sea, Congress prohibited export of most goods. This Act did more harm to New York and New England agriculture and commerce than to the other side, and was repealed. **1812**: War declared against Britain. New York blockaded. **1814**: Peace treaty signed at Ghent. **1825**: Erie Canal opened, enhancing New York's role as a port. **1832**: New York and Harlem railroad completed.

IMMIGRATION AND INTERNATIONALISM
1830-60: The influx of immigrants — largely German and Irish — rose to flood proportions. Epidemics of yellow fever and cholera followed, made worse by poor water supplies, insanitary conditions and the poverty of most of the newcomers. Yet, on the eve of the Civil War, the population neared 750,000. **1861-65**: Civil War, caused by growing differences between northern and southern states, notably the slavery issue. New York on the side of the Union (North) against the Confederates (South).

1863: Draft Riots, following a conscription law that permitted the rich to buy deferment. New Yorkers set fire to buildings, and looted shops and homes. More than 1,000 people died. **1868-98**: The first waves of Italian and Eastern European immigrants arrived, many of them working on the new elevated railroad, Brooklyn Bridge and early skyscrapers. The Statue of Liberty, a Franco-American project, was inaugurated in 1886. At the culmination of a period of annexation and expansion, New York assumed its present boundaries. There were now more than 3 million inhabitants, and New York was already the world's largest city.

1900-29: Immigration continued unabated, despite growing pressure for its curtailment. The railroad system was extended, now underground as well as above. The decade after World War I brought Prohibition, women's suffrage, economic prosperity, and a Federal Act cutting immigration (1924). **1929-39**: The Wall Street Crash and the start of the Great

Depression. The worst of the Depression was over by 1936, but it did not end until 1939, when the country began to prepare for war.

1941-45: Apart from rationing, blackouts and shortages, New York was not greatly affected by World War II. It grew more prosperous, as did the rest of the country. **1948**: Idlewild Airport opened in Queens (renamed after John F. Kennedy in 1963). **1952**: United Nations headquarters complex opened.

1973: World Trade Center opened. **1975-76**: American Bicentennial celebrations. **1989**: World Financial Center opened at Battery Park City. **1990**: Ellis Island was transformed into a museum. **1992**: The renovated Guggenheim Museum opened after a closure of almost three years, with a new annex.

Who's who

One of the most cosmopolitan of cities, New York has a history rich in memorable characters. What follows is a small, but representative selection.

Allen, Woody *(born 1935)*
The writer-actor-comedian-satirist-director is said to get the bends whenever he ventures beyond the city limits of New York. Nevertheless, by his own account, a Brooklyn childhood and an aborted career at New York University gave him little joy but much material for his *New Yorker* magazine essays and his many memorable movies, which include *Annie Hall* and *Hannah and Her Sisters*.

Beecher, Henry Ward *(1813-87)*
A minister, lecturer, author and firebrand abolitionist, he was also the older brother of Harriet Beecher Stowe, who wrote *Uncle Tom's Cabin*. His pulpit was the Plymouth Church on Orange St. in Brooklyn Heights.

Booth, Edwin *(1833-93)*
Often cited as the first important American actor, Booth made his permanent home in New York. His career was blighted after his brother, John Wilkes, killed Abraham Lincoln.

Bryant, William Cullen *(1794-1878)*
Best known as a poet, Bryant made his living as a reform-minded editor of the *Evening Post* (1826-78). He is credited with prodding the city into the development of Central Park.

Burr, Aaron *(1756-1836)*
In a checkered political career that saw him lose as many elections as he won, Burr's highest position was as Vice-President to Thomas Jefferson. The image of Burr as an amoral schemer gained strength from his shooting of Alexander Hamilton in a duel (see page 19), and from the plan, attributed to him, to establish an independent republic in the southwest. He was tried for treason and acquitted, but never re-entered public life.

Dinkins, David N. *(born 1927)*
The first Black mayor of New York worked his way quietly and diligently up through the ranks of the powerful local Democrat Party, finally assuming the City's highest office in 1990.

Fulton, Robert *(1765-1815)*
Talented and energetic, Fulton's curiosity led him to careers in painting, gunsmithing, civil engineering, and the invention of ambitious mechanical devices. Although he was not, as is widely believed, the creator of the steamboat, his *Clermont* (1807) was the first profitable version.

Greeley, Horace *(1811-72)*
After his arrival in New York at the age of 21, Greeley worked as a printer, editor and newspaper columnist. He founded *The New Yorker* (1834) and the *Tribune* (1841), and edited them, in various combinations, for more than 30 years.

Although initially considered a conservative, he advocated women's suffrage, the abolition of slavery, labor unions and experiments in communal living. These were all remarkably daring stands at that time.

Hamilton, Alexander *(1755-1804)*
Born out of wedlock in the West Indies, Hamilton came to New York to study at King's College in 1773. His anonymous writings on behalf of the Revolutionary cause drew much attention, as did his service on the battlefield and as General Washington's aide. An influential delegate to the Continental Congress at 25, he was one of the leading proponents of the Constitution drafted by Jefferson. Undeniably brilliant, he nevertheless made many enemies. One of them, Aaron Burr (see page 18), mortally wounded him in a duel in 1804.

Henry, O. *(1862-1910)*
The pen name of William S. Porter, a short-story writer noted for his tight plots and surprise endings, exemplified in *Gift of the Magi*. He began writing in prison, to which he was sentenced for embezzlement. Most of his literary production took place in the last 10 years of his life, which he spent in New York.

Hopper, Edward *(1882-1973)*
Born in a small town on the Hudson River, Hopper moved in young adulthood to Greenwich Village. The muted, melancholy cityscapes of this Realist painter began to gain favor in the 1920s, although they ran against Modernist trends. In later years, his studio was at 3 Washington Sq. North.

Irving, Washington *(1783-1859)*
Diplomat, biographer, satirist and author — of *Rip Van Winkle* and *The Legend of Sleepy Hollow* among other tales — Irving was born in New York. His estate in nearby Tarrytown is open to the public.

Koch, Edward *(born 1924)*
Child of immigrant parents, Koch narrowly won election as mayor of New York in 1977. Known for speaking his mind, he early on established himself as the most popular mayor since LaGuardia. He was elected to three terms, and although his later years in office were dogged by scandal, none of this attached directly to him.

LaGuardia, Fiorello Henry *(1882-1947)*
Probably the most beloved mayor in the city's history — serving from 1935-45 for an until-then unprecedented three terms — the "Little Flower" gave luster and color to an office that had become celebrated for the flamboyance and corruptibility of its previous incumbents.

Millay, Edna St Vincent *(1892-1950)*
The popular lyric poet was a leader of the Greenwich Village Bohemian group that founded the Provincetown Players.

Minuit, Peter *(1580-1638).*
The famous $24 purchase of Manhattan was negotiated by Minuit, who was then appointed Director General (1626-31) of the new colony by the Dutch West India Company.

Morgan, John Pierpont *(1837-1913)*
Beginning with the fortune accumulated by his father, J.P. used it as seed money to build a financial empire that is said to have exceeded even that of the first Rockefeller. Along the way, he bought out industrialists Andrew Carnegie and Henry Frick. All three of them spent their declining years in New York, where they engaged in a variety of good works and acts of philanthropy, and thereby formed New York's strong cultural foundation.

Morse, Samuel F.B. *(1791-1872)*
While a member of the arts faculty at New York University, Morse perfected his telegraph device and the code to be used with it. A demonstration was given at Castle Clinton in 1842. Morse was also a pioneer in the development of photography.

Olmsted, Frederick Law *(1822-1903)*
Travel writer and prolific landscape architect in the US and in Canada, Olmsted designed Central Park, Prospect Park (Brooklyn) and Riverside Park, all in collaboration with Calvert Vaux.

O'Neill, Eugene *(1888-1953)*
The work of the playwright who fashioned *The Iceman Cometh* and *Mourning Becomes Electra* is the standard against which all American dramatists must be measured. One of his finest plays, *Long Day's Journey into Night,* was discovered among his papers after his death. O'Neill was awarded the Nobel Prize in 1936.

Parker, Dorothy *(1893-1967)*
Renowned for the razor-sharp wit she directed as readily at herself as at others, Parker employed that gift in verse, plays, movies, essays and short stories. Much of her work appeared in *The New Yorker* magazine.

Perelman, S.J. *(1904-79)*
Brooklyn-born Perelman wrote for *The New Yorker* magazine from 1934 almost until his death. Essentially a humorist and satirist, his interests focused on the inanities of advertising and Hollywood. He also wrote movie scripts and plays in the 1930s and 1940s, often in association with such luminaries as the Marx Brothers, Ogden Nash and George S. Kaufman.

Poe, Edgar Allen *(1809-49)*
Impoverished for most of his adult life, having alienated his wealthy

foster father through his alcoholism and gambling, Poe moved to New York with his child bride in 1844. Their cottage in the Fordham section of The Bronx is now a museum. He finally achieved recognition for his poetry with *The Raven,* which led to fame for such mystery stories as *The Gold Bug* and *The Murders in the Rue Morgue.*

Pollock, Jackson *(1912-56)*
Although contemporaries were working in similar directions, the seminal work of this innovative artist heralded the explosion of postwar creativity known as the New York School. Inspired by Picasso and impatient with the academic techniques he mastered in his early years, he applied paint to vast canvases by splashing, dribbling, thrusting and pouring, in a method later labeled "action painting."

Porter, Cole *(1893-1964)*
The enduring sophistication of Porter's lyrics is remarkable. He penned both words and music of more than 400 songs, for such stage musicals as *Can-Can, Silk Stockings* and *Kiss Me, Kate.*

Pulitzer, Joseph *(1847-1911)*
Hungarian-born Pulitzer emigrated to the US in 1864 and became a journalist, editor, and publisher in short order. He bought the *New York World* in 1883, and in competition with William Randolph Hearst permitted it to plummet to the nadir of "yellow journalism." After the Spanish-American War (1898), his newspapers altered course to become relatively dignified. His will bequeathed money for the establishment of the Columbia University School of Journalism.

Rauschenberg, Robert *(born 1925)*
Rauschenberg first attracted attention with an exhibition of entirely black canvases, but then moved on to "combine-paintings" — assemblages of pigment, collage and such three-dimensional objects as stuffed goats and rubber tires. Born in Texas, he is nonetheless an exemplar of the New York School of painting.

Rockefeller, John D. Jr. *(1874-1960)*
The son of the incalculably wealthy oil magnate and financier was granted control of his father's interests at the age of 37. To a large extent, this involved philanthropic activities, many of which benefited New York. Among the projects he inspired or helped underwrite were Riverside Church, the Cloisters of the Metropolitan Museum of Art and the Rockefeller Center.

Rockefeller, Nelson Alrich *(1908-79)*
After able participation in both Democrat and Republican federal administrations during World War II and after, Nelson defeated W. Averell Harriman for the governorship of the State of New York in 1958. His subsequent bids for the Republican presidential nomination were unsuccessful, but he was re-elected governor three times and was appointed Vice-President for the brief term of Gerald Ford (1974-77). He made substantial contributions to New York's cultural and educational institutions, as did his siblings.

Roosevelt, Theodore *(1858-1919)*
The 28th and youngest President passed the first 15 years of his extraordinarily active life at 28 E 20th St., near Gramercy Park. Hunter and

environmentalist, rancher and author, statesman and chauvinist, peace-maker and militarist, explorer and politician, he pursued these contra-dictory interests vigorously until his death.

Runyon, Damon *(1884-1946)*
Born in Manhattan (the one in Kansas), this popular journalist came to New York, where he quickly mastered the patois of the criminal fringe and transferred that knowledge to a long string of evocative and hu-morous short stories, which provided the basis of the hit musical *Guys and Dolls*.

Ruth, George Hermon *(1895-1948)*
A near-legendary athlete, "Babe" Ruth played for the New York Yan-kees professional baseball team from 1920-35. Most of his pitching and batting records went unchallenged for decades, and some still stand.

Stuyvesant, Peter *(1610-72)*
A harshly autocratic man intolerant of religious and political dissent, this Director General of New Amsterdam held power from 1647-64. In 1664 he surrendered the colony to an English naval force and retired to his farm, near the present Lower East Side.

Tweed, William Marcy *(1823-78)*
The undisputed leader of Tammany Hall, which controlled the city and state Democrat Party, "Boss" Tweed ruled the city from 1857 until the early 1870s. He died in prison, having defrauded taxpayers and con-tractors of unaccounted millions in bribes, kickbacks and related schemes.

Warhol, Andy *(c.1930-1986)*
No one is certain when he was born (about 1930), or where (probably Philadelphia), but there is no question of his primacy in the Pop Art movement of the 1960s. Through repeated prints of commonplace ob-jects — cows, soup cans, movie stars — he endeavored to elevate the mundane and overexposed into subjects worthy of serious con-sideration. He went on to found a "factory" that produced films of elusive intent, and a magazine of celebrity interviews.

White, Stanford *(1853-1906)*
As the most celebrated partner of the architectural firm of McKim, Mead & White, he probably received more credit than his due for their collective achievements. Many of their buildings have been lost, but a rich heritage remains. These include Washington Arch, the Villard Houses (pictured on page 156), the portico of St Bartholomew's Church, three buildings at Columbia University and three more at the former Bronx campus of New York University, in all of which White had a hand.

Whitman, Walt *(1819-92)*
The innovative free verse of *Leaves of Grass* drew mostly negative reaction on its first appearance in 1855, but many 20thC scholars regard Whitman as America's finest poet.

Wolfe, Thomas Clayton *(1900-38)*
The haunted author of *Look Homeward, Angel* and *You Can't Go Home Again* joined the English faculty at New York University in 1924 and spent most of the last years of his life in the city.

The arts in New York

Creativity found a foothold as soon as the city emerged from the early settlement period. The first theater opened its doors on Maiden Lane in 1732, to be followed by dozens more. But New York was chiefly a commercial center, and artists who achieved prominence — painters Benjamin West and John Singleton Copley, for example — went off to Europe, setting a pattern that was to prevail for nearly two centuries.

Impressionism and the other "isms" that reverberated around Europe in the later 19thC had little influence across the Atlantic. The esthetic ferment did not spill over to the United States until the **New York Armory Show** of 1913, when Duchamp's *Nude Descending a Staircase* scandalized public opinion. By then, however, most of the men who were to form the first generation of post-World War II **Radical Abstractionists** were already alive. Encouraged by such artist-teachers as Hans Hofmann, who fled the gathering European tragedy in the 1930s, these artists champed under the restraints of the Depression and War, exploding after 1945 into what seemed to be a movement already mature at the instant of birth.

The controlled "splash-and-dribble" canvases of **Jackson Pollock** were no less shocking than the earlier Cubist fantasies, which now seemed sedate by comparison. Pollock died young, but compatriots Robert Motherwell, Clyfford Still, Mark Rothko, Willem de Kooning, Philip Guston, James Brooks, Jack Tworkov, Franz Kline and Sam Francis all contributed to the importance of the movement. All were associated with the city, and together they became known as the "**New York School**." They gathered in the same bars, summered on Long Island, and inspired a new row of galleries along E 10th St. It was a zesty era, enhanced, if not inhibited, by its coexistence with the conformist Eisenhower-McCarthy period.

New York, which had long regarded itself as an oasis on the edge of a cultural wasteland, was the natural wellspring of what proved to be a surge to international pre-eminence in the arts. As the only major city to emerge unscathed from the 1939-45 global conflict, it could indulge its artists with almost unlimited support. The **Guggenheim Museum**, Frank Lloyd Wright's only commission in the city (illustrated on page 115), was intended to serve as a repository for modern painting and sculpture. It was completed in 1959.

The **Lincoln Center for the Performing Arts** was conceived in 1955 to house the Metropolitan Opera, the Philharmonic Orchestra, the City Opera and Ballet companies, a repertory theater, a concert hall for small classical and popular groups, and the Juilliard School for actors, musicians and dancers. The five principal buildings were finished between 1962 and 1966. Additions to the **Metropolitan Museum** and the **Museum of Modern Art**, and the erection of a new home for the **Whitney Museum of American Art**, maintained the pace.

During the last couple of decades, creative endeavor in the visual arts has been highly experimental: Conceptual, Minimal, Neo-Constructivist, Optical — all executed in wildly mixed media: neon, ferro-concrete, forged metal, shaped canvas, boxes and heaps of earth... The descendants of Jackson Pollock are as unrestrained as he was, and every bit as provocative.

> Art, like life, should be free, since both are experimental.
> (George Santayana)

New York's architecture

From the earliest megalithic dolmens and post-and-lintel palaces of the Nile, architecture has been the single art form essential to the survival of its creators. A product of culture and commerce, it shapes air and space and the materials at hand to satisfy basic need and psychic want. Or at least it can. As in all matters, the architecture of New York both dismays and exalts, often in ways unexpected by those who have never walked these streets.

The city has been a laboratory of sorts, giving succor to native-born architects and drawing virtually every major American architect of the last century into its thrall, at least for a commission or two. The reason is clear enough. As the bank robber said, it's where the money is. And few tycoons and corporations have been able to resist the temptation to erect monuments to themselves. From Carnegie to Morgan to Woolworth to Chrysler, they have enriched the city nearly as often as they have blighted it. No easy feat, that, given the impulse to make saleable space out of every expensive cubic foot of ground and air.

Shelter was the first requirement of those who colonized Manhattan on behalf of Dutch traders. The Great Fires of 1776 and 1835 destroyed every last dwelling built in the 17thC. However, if the existing structures of the following century in New York were to be grouped together, they would constitute a sizeable and quite handsome village. As it is, the buildings are scattered throughout the city, largely neglected survivors of the conflagrations. Most are made of wood, in the **Georgian** or **Federal** styles inspired by those that were prevalent in England during the successive reigns of the four Georges.

Federal Hall National Memorial

Although the Georgian style was itself imitative of Classical Greco-Roman themes, the first half of the 19thC saw a heightened enthusiasm for **Greek** and **Gothic Revival**. These overlapping modes dominated from 1830-55, manifest in the Athenian "temple" that is the **Federal Hall National Memorial** (1842), perhaps the purest example of Greek Revival architecture in New York, and that tribute to medieval workmanship, **Trinity Church** (built in 1846 and pictured opposite). A landmark at the end of Wall Street, Richard Upjohn's church is the city's best-known example of Gothic Revivalism. In the attached town houses that became increasingly popular at this time, Greek Revival was largely confined to decorative facades.

After the Civil War, an unabashed enthusiasm for virtually all European styles took hold. Motifs ranged from Venetian Renaissance to French Second Empire to Tudor to Romanesque, not infrequently all on the same building. The result was often called "Kitchen Sink." The fashionable architectural firm of the time was **McKim, Mead and White**, whose fondness for the Italian Renaissance is best seen in the **Villard Houses** (1886, pictured on page 156).

Technology prompted fresh looks at old design assumptions. The **Brooklyn Bridge** (1883) employed Gothic granite

Trinity Church

towers, but also spidery cables of woven steel. No longer limited by the weight of masonry, and able to use steel and reinforced concrete,

Flatiron Building

architects capitalized on the presence of a sturdy bedrock known as "Manhattan schist." **Skyscrapers** rapidly became a reality. Fortunately, the hydraulic elevator was invented at the same time. By 1900, commercial buildings of 20 floors and higher were routine.

At first, architectural styles changed remarkably little, despite the new horizons that had been opened up by the introduction of *caisson* (steel pile) foundations. The **Flatiron Building** (1902), although constructed around a steel frame, was decked out with cornices reminiscent of the Florentine Renaissance style. The **Woolworth Building** (1913) has all the detail of a Gothic cathedral, complete with gargoyles.

Rowhouses persisted as the favored residential mode, but they were now embellished with Italianate carving around arched doors and pediments. The wide use of red sandstone as a facing material gave this style the generic name "**brownstone**." Blocks of brownstones remain throughout Manhattan and Brooklyn, lending a Parisian flavor to their neighborhoods.

Luxury high-rise apartments made their appearance with the **Chelsea** and the **Dakota** (see SIGHTS AND PLACES OF INTEREST) in 1884, but the wealthy resisted that innovation for decades. The turn of the century brought a flirtation with the voluptuous **Beaux-Arts** style and related neo-château fancies, which is best demonstrated in the

Metropolitan Museum of Art
(1902) and the **New York Public Library** on 5th Ave.

A measure of reason prevailed in 1916, when newly formulated zoning law created a regulation for the height of buildings in relation to the width of the street below. One side effect of this was the development of buildings that were tiered, and a number of "wedding cakes" emerged.

Meanwhile, commercial architecture was entering the **Modernist** phase with the form-follows-

**Metropolitan
Museum of Art**

function theories of **Louis Sullivan**, who proved to his successors that tall structures need not simulate stacked neo-Georgian or Romanesque tiers. Sullivan, sometimes described as the father of the skyscraper, was associated primarily with Chicago, and had only one commission in New York, the **Bayard Building** on Bleecker St. in Greenwich Village.

The next major influence was **Art Deco**, applied to spectacular effect in the steel-arched tower of the **Chrysler Building** (1930), the world's tallest building until it was overtaken by the Empire State in 1931. With the **Empire State Building** (1931) and **RCA Building** (built in 1932 and now renamed the GE Building), the Chrysler represents the apogee of the first phase of the skyscraper phenomenon. Many feel that this period in New York's architecture has never been surpassed.

Further developments were delayed until the peacetime economic recovery of the late 1940s. Then, a technique was developed in which walls of glass without a weight-bearing function were hung on the sides of steel skeletons. Among the first and most enduring realizations of this International Style were **Lever House** (1952) and the **Seagram Building** (1958).

**Chrysler
Building**

More recently, sculptural planes and masses have shaped both small and large buildings, such as the **Whitney Museum** (1966, pictured on page 157) and the **Waterside Houses** (1974). Those departures from the

Lever House

austerities of Bauhaus convention prompted the emergence of the so-called **Post-Modernist** style. That label is misleading, at least to the degree that it suggests a new evolutionary stage beyond the Modernism of Walter Gropius and Mies van der Rohe.

On the contrary, the Post-Modernist trend of the 1980s in many ways represents a look back, a revival in decorative interest and borrowings from eras before the Bauhaus invasion, as with the "Chippendale" cornice of Philip Johnson's **AT&T Building** (sold to the Sony firm in 1991).

A more successful product of this enthusiasm is the block-long **Equitable Center**, with a cream-and-brown exterior that recalls Art Deco. Its focal point is the 54-story **Equitable Tower**, designed by Edward Larrabee Barnes and built from granite, limestone and glass. About as tall as the AT&T, it manages not to loom quite as much.

On nearby Times Square, two hotels have been made even more playful, in keeping with the fun-seeking tone of the area. The **Holiday Inn Crowne Plaza** and **Embassy Suites** look like huge gaudy

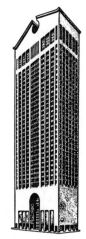

AT&T Building

jukeboxes, striped with primary colors and neon. Their builders were required to do this, as ongoing testament to the hub's status as the animated Great White Way. If residents and visitors are fortunate, this riotously eyefilling sub-category of Post-Modernism will be confined to that gaudy venue.

New York is Gershwin's "Rhapsody in Blue"... Majestic, hot, spicy, vulgar, stately, exquisite and overwhelming...
(Marilyn Michaels, actress and impressionist)

We say tomato

"Two great nations divided by a common language," intoned George Bernard Shaw. Despite the alleged homogenizing effect of shared movies, satellite television and international travel, the languages spoken in the United Kingdom and the United States bear less resemblance to each other than ever. British readers might therefore find the brief glossary offered on the following pages to be of assistance when deplaning on this side of the Pond.

They face an additional difficulty when staying in New York, however, and we refer not to muggers but communication. New Yorkers put their own spin on the mother tongue, nearly as distinctive as the Bostonese of Jack Kennedy or the drawl of Jimmy Carter.

New Yorkers, for example, don't "bump" into friends on the street, they "bunk" into them. Information that is contrary to their previous understanding doesn't "jive" (jibe), and they stand "on" line (in a queue), not *in* line as other Americans do. They aren't even New Yorkers, they're Noo Yawkers. Words containing "er" or "or" come out as grunts — the Hudson Riv*uh*, the neighb*uh*hood. On the other hand, the resident can't be found who actually says "Toity-toid and toid" (33rd Street and Third Avenue), as is widely believed even by other Americans.

No doubt due to their tendency to rush from task to task, New Yorkers frequently run their words together. Speakers of British English might find this the most baffling of many potential culture shocks. "Fuhgeddabowdit," says one native to another. That is, "forget about it." To add to the visitor's perplexity, the phrase can have different meanings, depending upon context and emphasis. It is said in lieu of "you're welcome." Or as an expression of pleasure. Or dismay. Disbelief. Humility. Even triumph, as in, "Didn't I tell you that would happen?"

Misunderstandings can go both ways. Some Britishisms will simply draw blank stares, as when the newly knighted Andrew Lloyd Webber said he had been "sent up rotten" by his friends. This means absolutely nothing to an American, nor do such formulations as "cocking a snook" or "winkle him out." Other phrases make sense, but not in the way intended. "He wouldn't wear that" will be taken literally, not to mean that the man in question wouldn't tolerate it.

It can get worse. The British man who has just met an attractive American woman and hopes to see her the next day will want to avoid declaring, "I'll knock you up tomorrow," as he conceivably might on his home turf, since that would mean he intended to get her pregnant. He will further want to avoid suggesting to a disappointed friend that he "keep his pecker up," or referring to a messy situation as a "cockup." Why? Hell, yaknowwadimean.

Either, either; neither, neither
Let's call the whole thing off.

British English-American English

TRAVELING AND VACATIONS

bonnet *hood*
boot *trunk*
bumper *fender*
bureau de change *foreign exchange*
campsite *campground*
car park *parking lot*
caravan *trailer*
coach *bus*
crossroads *intersection*
district *precinct*
dual carriageway *four-lane highway*
footpath *sidewalk*
give way *yield*
hire (noun) *rental*
holidaymaker *vacationer*
lorry *truck*
motoring association *automobile club*

overtake *pass*
package holiday *vacation package*
petrol *gasoline, gas*
post box *mailbox*
poste restante *general delivery*
puncture (noun) *flat tire*
queue *line*
rank (taxi) *taxi stand*
return (ticket) *round trip*
ring road *beltway*
roundabout *traffic circle*
saloon car *sedan*
single (ticket) *one-way*
subway *underpass*
underground, tube *subway*
windscreen *windshield*

LEISURE

bathing *swimming*
cinema *movie theater*
football *soccer*

horse-riding *horseback-riding*
paddle *wade*
rowing boat *rowboat*
sailing boat *sailboat*

SHOPPING

banknote, note *bill*
braces *suspenders*
chemist *drugstore, pharmacy*
cotton wool *absorbent cotton, cotton balls*
crisps *chips*
dummy *pacifier*
handbag *purse, pocket book*
jacket *coat*
mackintosh *raincoat*
nail varnish *nail polish*

nappy *diaper*
newsagent *newsstand*
precinct *mall*
pullover *sweater*
sanitary towel *sanitary napkin*
sticking plaster *Band-aid*
suspenders *garter belt*
sweet *candy*
trousers *pants*
vest *undershirt*
waistcoat *vest*

DINING

aubergine *eggplant*
barman *bartender*
bill *check*
biscuits *crackers*

book/booking *reserve/reservation*
chips *fries*
cockles *clams*

courgette   *zucchini*
draught   *draft*
lager   *beer*
lavatory   *bathroom*
lay the table   *set the table*
off-license   *liquor store*
serviette   *napkin*

spend a penny   *go to the bathroom*
spirits   *liquor*
takeaway   *takeout, to go*
whisky   *Scotch*
wholemeal   *wholewheat*

LODGING

3-pin (plug)   *3-prong (plug)*
bed-sitter   *studio, efficiency apartment*
call box   *telephone booth*
council housing   *housing projects*
dear   *expensive*

flat   *apartment*
homely   *homey*
lift   *elevator*
self-catering (apartment, cottage)   *housekeeping (apartment, cottage)*
terraced house   *rowhouse, brownstone (NY)*

And then there's zee (zed), zero (nought), on welfare (on the dole), hodge-podge (hotch-potch), home free (home and dry)... fuhgeddabowdit.

Basic information

Before you go

DOCUMENTS REQUIRED

British citizens except those from Northern Ireland, and citizens of New Zealand, Japan, and all Western European countries except Greece, no longer need a visa to visit the US, provided that their stay will last for 90 days or less and is for vacation or business purposes. If arriving by air or sea, the visitor must be traveling with an approved carrier (most are) and must have an **onward or return ticket**. (Open or standby tickets are acceptable.) If entering overland from Canada or Mexico, no visa is required. An unexpired **passport** is also essential.

British subjects will need to obtain a visa, as will any British citizen who wishes to stay more than 90 days for whatever reason, has a criminal record, has suffered from tuberculosis, is suffering from AIDS, is HIV-positive or has previously been refused a visa. The US embassy in London has a useful recorded message for all general visa inquiries (☎ *(0898) 200290)*. If you need a visa, it is wise to allow plenty of time.

You must show a valid **driver's license** and, unless you are a US citizen, a passport, in order to rent a car. An international driver's license is not required. Some firms ask to see your return ticket. Most rental companies will offer to sell you short-term insurance and it is wise to take it, unless your own policy gives adequate coverage. If you are arriving by private car from other states or countries, bring the **car registration document** and **certification of insurance** with you.

Senior citizens are eligible for a discount in some hotels but must be able to show **identification** in order to claim it.

TRAVEL AND MEDICAL INSURANCE

Medical care in the US is good to excellent, but costly. UK travel agents have the necessary forms, and tour operators frequently include **medical coverage** in their packages. Larger hotels have doctors on call, but visits are expensive. **Baggage insurance** is recommended in case of theft, which is distressingly common. American Express offers baggage insurance to card members, as do automobile clubs.

MONEY

The basic unit is, of course, the dollar ($). It is divided into 100 cents (¢). Coins are: the penny 1¢, nickel 5¢, dime 10¢, quarter 25¢ and half dollar 50¢. Bank notes (bills) in general circulation are in denominations of $1, $5, $10, $20, $50 and $100. A few $2 bills are in circulation. Any amount of money may be imported or exported, but when the total is in excess of $10,000 you are required to register with the US Customs Service.

It is wisest to carry cash in small amounts only, keeping the remainder in **travelers checks**. Travelers checks issued by American Express, Bank of America, Barclays, Citibank and Thomas Cook are widely recognized, and Mastercard and Visa have also introduced them. Make sure you read the instructions included with your travelers checks. It is important to note separately the serial numbers of your checks and the telephone number to call in case of loss. Specialist travelers check companies such as American Express provide extensive local refund facilities through their own offices or agents. Many shops are willing to accept dollar travelers checks.

Charge/credit cards are welcomed by nearly all hotels, airlines and car rental agencies, most restaurants and garages, and many shops. American Express, Diners Club, Mastercard and Visa are the major cards in common use. While **personal checks** drawn on out-of-town banks are not normally accepted, many hotels will cash small amounts in conjunction with a charge/credit card.

American Express has a **MoneyGram®** money transfer service that makes it possible to wire money worldwide in just minutes, from any American Express Travel Service Office. This service is available to all customers and is not limited to American Express Card members. See USEFUL ADDRESSES on page 43.

CUSTOMS

Returning US citizens and visitors first must clear passport control. They then collect their baggage and move on to a customs official. Although the process has been streamlined, the combination of three jumbo jets disgorging at once and government concern over smuggling can slow things down to a crawl. It may take no more than 30 minutes from plane to street, but an hour or more is not unusual.

Nonresidents can bring in any items clearly intended for personal use, duty-free, with the exceptions noted below.

Tobacco goods   200 cigarettes *or* 50 cigars *or* $4\frac{1}{2}$ lbs (2kg) tobacco. An additional 100 cigars may be brought in under your gift exemption (see below).

Alcoholic drinks   Adults over 18 are allowed up to 1 quart (1 liter) of spirits.

Other goods   Nonresidents may also import up to $100 in gifts without tax or duty if remaining in the US at least 72 hours. Returning residents are granted a duty-free allowance of $400, on goods brought back personally. Families traveling together can pool their allowances to cover joint purchases.

For more information on customs regulations, a brochure entitled *US Customs Hints* can be obtained from US embassies and consulates, or directly from the Department of the Treasury, US Customs Service, Box 7407, Washington, DC 20044.

TOURIST OFFICE

American visitors should make contact with the **New York Convention and Visitors Bureau** *(2 Columbus Circle, New York, NY 10019* ☎ *(212) 397-8200)*. Visitors from the UK can obtain much useful information from the **US Travel and Tourism Administration** *(P.O. Box 1EN, London W1A 1EN* ☎ *(071) 495-4466)*.

GETTING THERE

John F. Kennedy is the largest of New York's three **airports**, dealing primarily with international flights. Most national and some international airlines serve both the other airports — **LaGuardia**, which is the smallest and closest to the center (30 minutes), and **Newark**, which is on the other side of the Hudson River in New Jersey (45 minutes). Private planes can land at **Teterboro** in NE New Jersey.

Long-distance and commuter **trains** arrive at **Pennsylvania Station** *(7th Ave. and 32nd St., map* **5**P3*)*, while only commuter trains use **Grand Central Terminal** *(Park Ave. and 42nd St., map* **6**O4*)*.

All **buses**, both long-distance and commuter, arrive at the **Port Authority Bus Terminal** *(8th Ave. and 41st St., map* **5**O3*)*. The long-distance buses have their platforms below street level; passengers from local buses arrive at the upper stories.

From the W and S, **Interstate Highways I-78**, **I-80** and **I-95** connect with Manhattan via the **George Washington Bridge** (for upper Manhattan), the **Lincoln Tunnel** (for mid-Manhattan) and the **Holland Tunnel** (for lower Manhattan). From the N, **I-87** (Governor Thomas E. Dewey Thruway) and **I-95** (New England Thruway) lead to the **Triborough Bridge** and other Harlem River and East River crossings. Most of these funnel into the FDR Drive, which parallels the East River.

Tolls across the Hudson River are paid when entering the city, but not when leaving. There is a hefty toll charged on the Verrazano Bridge going from Brooklyn to Staten Island, however. Automobile clubs will suggest the best route from your point of departure.

CLIMATE

May, June, September and October are agreeable, incorporating the best days of the short and unpredictable spring and fall seasons. Extended periods of oppressive humidity and temperatures of 90°F (32°C) and more are characteristic in July and August. December through February feature cold rains, occasional snow, and readings at or near freezing point. True extremes are rare, however. Temperatures infrequently drop below freezing point or exceed 100°F (38°C), and a snowfall of more than four inches is unusual.

CLOTHES

A raincoat with a zip-out lining is a good investment for visits between October and April, as are collapsible rubber boots and a waterproof hat. The winds that accompany rain often turn umbrellas inside-out. High settings of interior heating and air conditioning mean that layering of clothes is advisable.

New Yorkers have grown less formal in dress in recent years. Men feel most comfortable with a jacket at medium-priced and luxury restaurants, but a tie is mandatory at only relatively few establishments. Trousers may be worn by women at all but a handful of the same places. Denim clothing is sometimes barred by the more exclusive discos and clubs.

GENERAL DELIVERY/POSTE RESTANTE

A letter marked "General Delivery," addressed to a specific post office, will be held there until collected. Identification is usually required when you collect your mail, and a fee may be charged. Some commercial firms also provide this service for their customers. The following are centrally located: **American Express** *(150 E 42nd St., New York, NY 10017, map 6 O4)*, **Central Post Office** *(42 8th Ave., New York, NY 10001, map 5 P3)*, **Thomas Cook** *(18 E 48th St., New York, NY 10017, map 6 O4)*.

Getting around

FROM THE AIRPORTS TO THE CITY

Carey Airport Express **buses** depart Kennedy and LaGuardia every 20-30 minutes between early morning and midnight, less frequently at other times. They stop at the Carey Ticket Office, across 42nd St. from **Grand Central Terminal**, and at the **New York Hilton**, the **Sheraton Manhattan**, and the **Marriott Marquis** hotels. The fare from Kennedy is slightly higher than that from LaGuardia, but neither is expensive. A similar service is provided by the Olympia Trails Airport Express buses, which travel between **Newark Airport** and **Penn Station**, the **World Trade Center**, and **Grand Central Terminal**. They leave Newark about every 20 minutes between 6.15am and midnight. New Jersey Transit express buses operate 24 hours a day every 15-30 minutes to Newark Airport, from the AirTrans Center of the **Port Authority Terminal** *(for further information ☎ 800-247-7433)*.

For not much more money, the **Gray Line Air Shuttle** operates 11-seat vans and 21-seat coaches from 52 midtown hotels to all three airports. The service operates daily from 7am to 10pm. Information is available at the ground transport desks at the airline terminals, or ☎757-6840. Some hotels provide their own transport from the airports, if advance arrangements are made. Plan on travel times of about 45 minutes-1 hour from JFK and Newark and 30-45 minutes from LaGuardia. Obviously, rush-hour traffic, accidents, and road repairs increase these times. To be safe when returning to the airports after a visit, leave at least 30 minutes earlier than might normally be expected.

Taxis from Kennedy (45-60 minutes) and LaGuardia (30-40 minutes) to destinations within the city are metered. From Newark (30-60 minutes), however, the fare is twice the amount shown on the meter. From New York *to* Newark, the fare is the amount on the meter plus $10. In all cases bridge and tunnel tolls are extra, and traveling in the rush hour can double the fare and time taken. Licensed yellow taxis from New York are not allowed to charge per passenger or for luggage. Non-metered car services provide transport *to* (but not necessarily from) the airports at somewhat lower rates than regular taxis. Two that have proved themselves to be reliable in the past are **Aviv** *(☎ 505-0555)* and **Sabra** *(☎ 410-7600)*.

Helicopters fly between the three airports and between Kennedy and the heliport at 34th St. and the East River. The flights between Kennedy and the Heliport take 10 minutes and leave every 30 minutes between 1.30-7.30pm, but cost twice as much as a taxi. Operations are sometimes suspended due to bad weather.

Private limousines are clean, comfortable and often cost little more than taxis, as they charge a flat rate and can be shared. You can arrange in advance to have one waiting for you (see OTHER TRANSPORT on pages 38-9).

Cars can be rented at all airports (see RENTING A CAR on page 37).

PUBLIC TRANSPORT

Subways and **buses** have improved significantly in recent years. Delays are less common, graffiti has been largely eliminated and a majority of subway cars are air conditioned. Panhandlers work their way through the trains, however, and stations are still dirty, littered, and often populated by homeless people.

For information on subways and buses ☎330-1234. Free maps are theoretically available at most token booths.

Trains operate 24 hours a day, with substantially reduced frequency between midnight-6am. A single fare lets you journey as far as you like along any one line. Peak rush hours, to be avoided if possible, are 8-9am and 5-7pm. A criticized recent decision to reduce the number of rush-hour trains has, inevitably, caused more crowding.

SUBWAYS

The system began as three privately-owned lines that went pretty much where they wished. They are still known as the **IRT** (running from N to S on the E and W sides of Manhattan), **IND** (running along 6th and 8th Aves.), and **BMT** (running roughly from lower Manhattan to Brooklyn and Queens). To use the subway, buy a token at the booth near the entrance. Free transfers can be made at 25 intersections with other lines.

In order to get on the right train going in the right direction, first note whether you must go uptown, downtown or crosstown, and whether your final station is a local or express stop (see the subway map at the end of the book). Insert the token into the turnstile, then follow directional signs to the correct platform. Once there, look for signs to indicate whether express and local trains stop on the same or on opposite sides of the platform. The front and sides of a train have signs indicating the route number, whether the train is express or local, and the last station on the route.

Platform loudspeakers give information about delays and re-routing of trains, but more often than not the announcements come out as indecipherable noise.

BUSES

Upon boarding, deposit a subway token or the equivalent in coins in the box next to the driver. He cannot give change, but can provide free transfers to intersecting lines. Routes roughly follow the major N-S avenues. E-W crosstown routes serve as connections between subway lines, which are primarily N-S. Buses operate on a 24-hour basis, but very infrequently between midnight and 6am. Route maps are sometimes available at subway token booths, but rarely on buses themselves. A better source is the **New York Convention and Visitors Bureau** on Columbus Circle.

TAXIS

There are only 11,787 taxicabs in operation. That total has been frozen since 1937, the reason an official medallion costs a new owner nearly $140,000. Licensed taxis are painted **yellow**. They can be hailed anywhere if the sign on the roof is illuminated. Taxi stands are also found outside major hotels.

Within the five boroughs there is a set rate for the first ninth of a mile and for every additional ninth. Bridge and tunnel tolls are extra. Drivers are required by the Taxi & Limousine Commission to take passengers to any destination in the city. This doesn't necessarily mean they actually will, particularly if a prospective passenger looks as if he or she might want to go to a dangerous or out-of-the-way neighborhood. Get in the cab before announcing where you wish to go.

The 40-hour training course for drivers falls well short of its objectives, especially when compared to London's demanding 2-year program. Its inadequacy is hardly surprising, considering that nearly 90 percent of the students are immigrants, most of them from countries where English is not the primary language. For that reason, it is wise to know the full address of your destination and the nearest cross street. Simply asking for a particular hotel or restaurant, no matter how well-known, may draw a blank stare from the driver. Despite this, he (and it is nearly always a "he") will expect a tip that is 20 percent of the total fare. Taxis have electronic digital meters that print out receipts if required.

For articles lost in taxis ☎825-0416.

GETTING AROUND BY CAR

Using a car in New York is not an entirely rational act. Street parking is often nonexistent, and garage parking is very expensive. Most large hotels have garages, but these are often expensive and a fee is usually charged every time a car is taken out and returned. If you must bring a car to New York, at least try to confine its use to evenings after 9pm and weekends, to get to such out-of-the way sights as THE CLOISTERS or Staten Island, or for touring the countryside. When parking, do not exceed the posted time limit, or your car could be towed away to a pound. If that happens, it costs a great deal of money and much time spent untangling red tape.

Most cross streets and many avenues are one-way, the direction alternating from one street or avenue to the next. In New York City, unlike the rest of the state, right turns are not permitted at red traffic lights unless stated. Speed limits are signposted, usually 35mph (55mph in New York State) or less.

For further details and information, contact the **American Automobile Association** *(Broadway and 62nd St.* ☎*586-1166),* or seek advice from your own automobile club.

RENTING A CAR
Car rental agencies are located at airline terminals and at offices throughout the city. See also Yellow Pages under *Automobile Renting* and *Leasing.* Most vehicles are equipped with radios, automatic transmission, and air conditioning at no extra charge. A charge/credit card can be presented in lieu of a deposit, in which case the driver can be as young as 18. Otherwise, a cash deposit is required, and the driver must be over 21. Rent-it-here-leave-it-there, weekend, and unlimited-mileage packages are available.

GETTING AROUND ON FOOT
See maps **1-8**.

The best, and most agreeable, way to cover short distances in Manhattan is on foot. Above 14th St., it is difficult to lose your way. Streets are laid out in a straight grid. Named and numbered avenues run N-S, from **1st Ave.** in the E to **11th Ave.** in the W. **5th Ave.** is the dividing line between E and W. Cross streets run E-W from **14th St.** in the S to **225th St.** in the N. Building numbers mount from one to the mid-hundreds to the E, and in the same way to the W. On the avenues, numbers increase as they proceed N.

Because the avenues and Broadway are so long, the nearest cross street is often mentioned when asking for a main avenue address. **Avenue of the Americas** is always spoken of as **6th Ave.**, although the grander name is still used for addresses.

The Manhattan grid is not perfect, of course. **Broadway** cuts diagonally across the island from **Park Ave.** and **14th St.** to the W of Central Park. Below **14th St.**, in the older part of the city, the grid goes awry. Down there, a good street map is essential. With some exceptions, odd street numbers are on the W side of avenues and on the N side of cross streets.

RAILROAD SERVICES
The Harlem, Hudson and New Haven commuter lines of the Metro North system feed into New York from up to 100 miles N, arriving at **Grand Central Terminal** *(Park Ave. and 42nd St., map 6O4).* **Pennsylvania (Penn) Station** *(7th Ave. and 32nd St., map 5P3)* is the terminus for the Long Island and New Jersey commuter lines, as well as for Amtrak trains from Canada, Boston, Chicago, Washington, Florida and intermediate points.

Amtrak   ☎736-3967 (Metroliners) ☎736-4545 (all others)
Metro North (commuter)   ☎532-4900 (Westchester County and Connecticut)

AIRLINES

Domestic flights leave from all three airports. The USAir Shuttle and the Delta Shuttle to Washington and Boston have separate terminals at LaGuardia. These two services have hourly flights during the day and early evening. The addresses below are for main Manhattan ticket offices, while the telephone numbers are for central reservation networks. The several offices listed at 100 E 42nd St. are on the 2nd floor of a building opposite Grand Central Terminal (entrance on 41st St.), map 6O4.

Air Canada   488 Madison Ave. ☎869-1900, map 6O4

American   100 E 42nd St. ☎800-433-7300

Continental   100 E 42nd St. ☎319-9494

Delta   100 E 42nd St. ☎239-0700

Northwest   299 Park Ave. (49th St.) ☎736-1220, map 6P4

TWA   100 E 42nd St. ☎290-2121

United   100 E 42nd St. ☎800-241-6522

US Air   100 E 42nd St. ☎800-428-4322

The following airlines offer flights to New York from the United Kingdom.

- **American Airlines** in the UK ☎(0800) 010151, in the US ☎800-433-7300
- **British Airways** in the UK ☎(081) 897-4000 (London), (0345) 222111 (elsewhere in the UK), in the US ☎800-AIRWAYS
- **Northwest Airlines** in the UK ☎(0345) 747800, in the US ☎736-1220
- **United Airlines** in the UK ☎(0800) 888555, in the US ☎800-241-6522
- **Virgin Atlantic Airways** in the UK ☎(0293) 562000, in the US ☎(800) 862 8621

FERRY SERVICES

America's favorite boat ride — the **Staten Island ferry** — is still the biggest bargain in town, serving up spectacular views and bracing breezes. It departs from the Whitehall St. pier at downtown Battery Park every 20-30 minutes, 24 hours a day, 7 days a week.

The **Statue of Liberty ferry** also leaves from Battery Park and follows a route stopping at ELLIS ISLAND. The price of the ride includes a guided tour of the museum (for more information, see NEW YORK FOR CHILDREN, page 272). Tickets for the Statue of Liberty and Ellis Island are sold inside the CASTLE CLINTON NATIONAL MONUMENT, near the piers. Still another ferry operates between **LaGuardia Airport** and piers at **34th St.** and **Wall St.** on the East River.

OTHER TRANSPORT

Hourly rates for **private limousines** are high, but there are special airport and theater/dinner flat rates that can total little more than taxi fares. Dozens of companies are listed in the Yellow Pages. Some are one- or two-car operations, others have entire fleets. These are a few of the reputable firms:

Dave-El   219 W 77th St. ☎645-4242, map **7L2**
London Towncars   40-14 23rd St. (Long Island City) ☎988-9700
Manhattan International   13-05 43rd Ave. (Long Island City)
☎718-729-4200
Sabra   326 2nd Ave. ☎777-7171, map **6Q5**
Silver Screen Limo   P.O. Box 4283, Sunnyside, NY 11104 ☎(718)
937-3808 or 937-3321
Tel-Aviv   139 1st Ave. ☎777-7777, map **4R5**

Rent a **rowboat** or **bicycle** at the 72nd St. boathouse in Central Park.
Bicycles and mopeds can be rented from the following:
A:Gene's   242 E 79th St. (2nd Ave.) ☎249-9218, map **8L5**
Metro Bicycles   9th Ave. & W 47th St. ☎581-4500, map **5O3**. Five
other branches around Manhattan. Open 7 days.
Pedal Pusher   1306 2nd Ave. (near 69th St.) ☎288-5592, map **8M5**
6th Ave. Bicycles   546 6th Ave. (15th St.) ☎255-5100, map **6Q4**

Rides in **horse-drawn hansom cabs** begin from near the 5th Ave.
and 59th St. corner of Central Park, day or night. Most of the rides take
30 minutes and are expensive. It is advisable to establish the rate in
advance.

On-the-spot information

PUBLIC HOLIDAYS
January 1; Martin Luther King Day, third Monday in January; President's
Day, celebrated on a 3-day weekend in mid-February; Memorial Day, a
3-day weekend at the end of May; Independence Day, July 4; Labor
Day, first Monday in September; Columbus Day, second Monday in
October; Election Day, first Tuesday in November; Veterans Day, No-
vember 11; Thanksgiving, last Thursday in November; December 25.

As in the rest of the country, shops, schools, banks, post offices and
most public services are usually closed on these days, although some
shops stay open on the 3-day weekends.

A number of other special days are observed with religious services,
parades, gift-giving, or other celebrations. These include: Chinese New
Year, January/February; St Patrick's Day, March 17; Easter and Passover,
April; Mother's Day, May; Puerto Rican Day, June; Rosh Hashanah,
September; Halloween, October 31; Chanukah, December.

TIME ZONES
New York is in the US Eastern Time Zone, 1 hour ahead of the Central
Time Zone, 2 hours ahead of the Mountain Time Zone and 3 hours
ahead of the Pacific Time Zone. All zones on Daylight Saving Time put
their clocks forward 1 hour April-October to benefit from extra daylight.

The US Eastern Time Zone is 5 hours behind Greenwich Mean Time
(GMT) in winter, or 4 hours behind GMT from the last Sunday in April to
the last Sunday in October during Daylight Saving Time.

Emergency information

EMERGENCY SERVICES
For **Police**, **Ambulance** or **Fire** ☎**911**. You will need a coin if using a phone booth.

HOSPITALS WITH EMERGENCY ROOMS
Ambulances called on 911 carry the patient to the nearest municipal hospital. Private hospitals are preferable, however, so if possible take a taxi to one of these:
Financial District　　Beekman Downtown Hospital, 170 William St. ☎312-5000, map **2T4**
Greenwich Village　　St Vincent's Hospital, 7th Ave. (11th St.) ☎790-7000, map **3R3**
Midtown East　　New York University Medical Center, 1st Ave. (30th St.) ☎340-7300, map **6P5**
Midtown West　　Roosevelt-St. Luke's Hospital, 9th Ave. (58th St.) ☎523-4000, map **5N3**
Upper East Side　　New York Hospital, York Ave. (68th St.) ☎746-5454, map **8M5**
Upper East Side and East Harlem　　Mount Sinai Hospital, 5th Ave. (100th St.) ☎241-6500, map **8J4**
West Harlem　　Columbia Presbyterian Medical Center, 622 W 168th St. ☎305-2500

OTHER EMERGENCIES
Doctors Emergency Service ☎570-2600
Dentists Emergency Service ☎679-3966 (9am-8pm) ☎679-4172 (8pm-9am)

LATE-NIGHT DRUGSTORE (PHARMACY)
Kaufman 557 Lexington Ave. (50th St.) ☎755-2266, map **6N4**

BANKS AND FOREIGN EXCHANGE
Customary banking hours are Monday to Friday 9am-3pm; some close at 4pm and some are open Thursday evenings or Saturday mornings. Travelers checks can be cashed at all banks, although most banks take hours to change foreign currencies. For this type of transaction, try one of Citibank's foreign exchange services, Bank Leumi Trust, or Deak-Perera. Otherwise, travel services such as American Express and Thomas Cook have exchange desks.
　　For US visitors, many banks have 24-hour automatic teller machines, allowing withdrawals from personal checking or savings accounts or cash

HELP LINES
Alcoholics Anonymous   ☎473-6200
Battered Women   ☎433-7297
Child Abuse   ☎800-342-3720
Crime Victim Hotline   ☎577-7777
Drug problems   ☎800-538-4840
Help line (personal counseling)   ☎481-1070
Poison   ☎340-4494 or 764-7667
Rape Help Line   ☎777-4000
Suicide Prevention   ☎532-2400
Traveler's Aid Society   ☎944-0013

AUTOMOBILE ACCIDENTS
- Call the police immediately
- If car is rented, call number in rental agreement
- Do not admit liability or incriminate yourself
- Ask witnesses to stay and give statements
- Exchange names, addresses, car details, insurance companies and 3-digit insurance company codes
- Remain to give your statement to the police

CAR BREAKDOWNS
Call one of the following from nearest telephone:
- Number indicated in car rental agreement
- Local office of AAA (if you are a member)
- Nearest garage or towing service.

LOST TRAVELERS CHECKS
Notify the local police immediately, then follow the instructions provided with your travelers checks, or contact the issuing company's nearest office. Contact **American Express** (☎*323-2000*) if you are stranded with no money.

advances against charge/credit cards. If your hometown bank is a member of the CIRRUS, PLUS, or NYCE networks, you should be able to find a participating local bank and machine. Do not use the machines late at night, when doing so will make you an obvious target for criminals.

OPENING HOURS
Department stores, clothes and sports equipment shops usually open between 9-10am and close at 6pm. Late-night shopping is on Monday and Thursday, usually until 9pm. Many department and electronics stores are open Sunday afternoon.

Although many fast-food stands, coffee shops and delicatessens open by 8am and don't close until 10pm or later, more formal restaurants confine themselves to noon-3pm and 6-11pm, with slight variations. Bars and discos do not have to close until 4am. In sections of the city where merchants are predominantly Jewish, shops often close from mid-afternoon Friday through Saturday and are open on Sunday. In Greenwich Village and SoHo, boutiques and galleries often do not get going until noon.

RUSH HOURS
Driving, or using public transport between 8-9am and 5-6.30pm, could be considered an exercise in masochism, and the situation is almost as bad for an hour before and after these times. Avoiding lunch between noon and 2pm is canny, as is making dinner reservations before 7.30pm or after 9pm.

POSTAL, TELEPHONE AND BUSINESS SERVICES
Post offices are open Monday-Friday 8am-5pm, Saturday 8am-noon. The **main post office** at 8th Ave. and 33rd St. is open 24 hours.

Telephones are everywhere. Try to use those in shops or public buildings — the ones installed on street corners are often out of order. Manhattan has its own area code: **212**. Local calls within the 212 area need only their 7-digit number. The Bronx, Brooklyn, Queens, and Staten Island use area code **718**. When calling an out-of-town number, or one of the other four boroughs from Manhattan, dial **1**, then the area code, and finally the 7-digit number. Direct dialing to all US numbers and many foreign countries is available, but calls are best made from hotel rooms, considering the amount of coins required for a pay phone. Remember that hotels typically add surcharges. Cheaper rates apply after 5pm and on weekends.

There are scores of independent shops specializing in copying, fax, telex and postal services; larger hotels also offer these services. Money can be wired from one Western Union office to another, and a mailgram might arrive sooner than a letter; see also **MoneyGram** on page 32. **ITT** is the primary international cable service (☎ 797-3311).

PUBLIC LAVATORIES (REST ROOMS)
These are to be avoided at all times in subway stations. Those in museums and public buildings are usually satisfactory. *In extremis,* duck into the nearest hotel. A promising experiment in self-cleaning public toilets has been conducted, and might result in widespread installation.

TIPPING
In restaurants tip the waiter at least 15 percent of the check before tax; 20 percent is more usual in luxury establishments, or if the service warrants it. An easy way to compute the minimum is to double the 8 percent sales tax. Some restaurants have taken to adding a service charge, so don't tip twice. Bellmen expect a dollar per bag. Doormen

get 50¢-$1 for hailing a taxi; tip chambermaids a similar amount for each night of a stay, too. Rest room/lavatory attendants should be given 50¢, to be left on the conspicuous plate. When there is a stated fee for checking coats and parcels, that will be sufficient. Otherwise give $1 per item. Tour guides expect $2-5, depending upon the length of the tour.

DISABLED TRAVELERS
Federal regulations have brought about improvements in access to most places. Many lavatories/rest rooms provide special facilities for the disabled, and about 90 percent of buses are now equipped with motorized platforms to lift people in wheelchairs. Most hotels have some specially converted rooms. Subways offer reduced fares for disabled passengers but only 20 stations have elevators or ramps, and the stairs are nearly impossible to negotiate without help. Seeing-eye dogs are permitted everywhere in New York. For further information, contact **Rehabilitation International USA** *(1123 Broadway, NY 10010* ☎ *420-1500, map 6 P4).* Disabled travelers from the UK should contact **RADAR** *(25 Mortimer St., London W1N 8AB* ☎ *(071) 637-5400).*

LOCAL PUBLICATIONS
Special arts and leisure sections appear on Friday and Sunday in the *New York Times* and in the weekly magazines *New York* and *The New Yorker.* They provide useful reviews and listings of current plays, concerts, films, exhibitions, ballets and operas; The *New York Times* includes ticket availability. *The Village Voice* is a weekly that emphasizes the offbeat arts and presentations. The *Daily News, New York Newsday,* and *New York Post* have extensive sports coverage.

Useful addresses

TOURIST INFORMATION
American Express Travel Service   150 E 42nd St. ☎687-3700, map 6O4; a valuable source of information for any traveler in need of help, advice or emergency services.
NY Convention and Visitors Bureau   2 Columbus Circle ☎397-8200, map 5N3.

MAIN POST OFFICES
8th Ave. (33rd St.), map 5P3 or Lexington Ave. (45th St.), map 6O4.

TELEPHONE SERVICES
International calls   Dial operator
New York Convention & Visitors Bureau   ☎397-8222
Sportsphone   ☎C1976-1313 or ☎976-2525
Telephone information   ☎555-1212
Time and temperature   ☎976-1616

Traffic report (during rush hours)   ☎976-2323
Wake-up call   ☎540-9253 (WAKE)

TOUR OPERATORS
As in most cities, the aptitudes and personalities of tour guides are highly variable. Too often, their *spiels* are tangled nests of opinion, half-digested facts, irrelevancies and failed attempts at humor. Some guides compound their deficiencies by imagining they are the main attraction of the trip. The presence of a tour operator on the list below doesn't imply that such a person won't lead a given group. Since there is no way to predict in advance the ability of an assigned guide, the best advice is to enjoy the views, use the tour to get the lay of the land and filter their declarations through a fine net of skepticism.

Adventure on a Shoestring   300 W 53rd St. ☎265-2663, map **5**N3. Walking tours. Call to reserve and to learn starting points, which are changed from tour to tour.

American Sightseeing International/Short Line Tours   166 W 46th St. ☎354-4740, map **5**O3. 2-8 hour bus tours.

Circle Line   Pier 83, end of W 43rd St. ☎563-3200, map **5**O2. 3-hour boat cruises around Manhattan, April-November, and 2-hour nighttime cruises of the harbor.

Gray Line Tours   900 8th Ave. (near 53rd St.) ☎397-2600, map **5**N3. 26 tours of 2 hours to a full day, some conducted in foreign languages.

Harlem, Your Way! Tours Unlimited   129 W 130th St. ☎690-1687.

Harlem Spirituals   1697 Broadway ☎757-0425, map **5**N3. Four different itineraries through Harlem, in five languages.

Island Helicopter   Heliport at end of E 34th St. ☎683-4575, map **6**P5. Daily flights, all year, minimum of two passengers.

Landmark Tours   151 1st Ave. ☎979-5263, map **4**R5. Walking tours April-October.

Liberty Helicopter Tours   Hudson River, end of W 30th St. ☎465-8905, map **5**P2. Three flight plans, with a minimum of three passengers.

Manhattan Sightseeing Bus Tours   150 W 49th St. ☎869-7866, map **5**O3.

New York Big Apple Tours   203 E 94th St. ☎410-4190, map **8**K5.

Seaport Line   Pier 16, South Street Seaport ☎385-0791, map **2**U5. 90-minute cruises of the harbor on a 19thC paddlewheeler and a steamboat. In summer, additional cocktail and music cruises.

Spirit of New York   Pier 9, foot of Wall St. ☎742-7278, map **2**U5. Lunch, brunch, dinner and late-night party cruises, lasting 2-3 hours.

MAJOR PLACES OF WORSHIP IN MIDTOWN MANHATTAN
Baptist   Calvary Baptist, 123 W 57th St., map **5**N3
Catholic   St Patrick's Cathedral, 5th Ave. (51st St.), map **6**N4
Episcopal   St Thomas' Church, 1 W 53rd St. (Entrance on 5th Ave.), map **6**N4

Jewish Temple Emanu-El, 5th Ave. (65th St.), map **8**M4
Lutheran Holy Trinity, Central Park West (65th St.), map **7**M3
Methodist Lexington United Methodist Church, 150 E 62nd St., map **6**N4
Presbyterian Presbyterian Church, 5th Ave. (55th St.), map **6**N4

LIBRARIES
American Bible Society 1865 Broadway ☎581-7400, map **5**N3
Donnell Library Center 20 W 53rd St. ☎790-6463, map **6**N4
Library for the Blind and Physically Handicapped 166 Ave. of the Americas ☎925-1011, map **3**S4
Lincoln Center Library (music, theater) 11 Amsterdam Ave. ☎799-2200, map **5**N2
Mercantile Library (contemporary books) 17 E 47th St. ☎755-6710, map **6**O4
New York Public Library 5th Ave. (42nd St.) ☎790-6262, map **6**O4
Schomburg Center (Black studies) 103 W 135th St. ☎862-4000

CONSULATES
Australia 636 5th Ave. ☎245-4000, map **6**N4
Canada 1251 Ave. of the Americas ☎768-2442, map **6**O4
Ireland (Eire) 515 Madison Ave. ☎319-2555, map **6**N4
Japan 299 Park Ave. ☎371-8222, map **6**O4
New Zealand 650 5th Ave. ☎698-4650, map **6**N4
United Kingdom 845 3rd Ave. ☎745-0200, map **6**N5

Planning
and walks

When to go

Not long ago, the conventional advice was to avoid New York in its relentlessly humid summer. Probably for that reason, the theater and concert season did not begin until October, when most of the new plays opened. That is still one of the best months to visit, when the gathering energy of the city is palpable. But the widespread availability of air conditioning makes July bearable, and major new musicals and dramas now hold their premières throughout the year.

While affluent New Yorkers still flee to summer cottages by the sea or in the New England hills, there is never that impression of an abandoned city given by, say, Paris in August. Some of the de luxe restaurants lock up for 2-3 weeks, but most remain open for business, as do the museums and landmark buildings. Concerted efforts under the "New York is a Summer Festival" rubric have brought about a full schedule of established cultural events, as a glance at the CALENDAR OF EVENTS below reveals. Many of these events feature front-rank performing groups at little or no cost — which is decidedly not the case from October to May. There is a marked shirt-sleeved looseness in New Yorkers themselves in the hot months, a departure from their inclination toward dressier formality during the rest of the year. Visitors devoted to art should note that most galleries are closed in July and August.

April-May and September-October are the best months in terms of weather. For that reason, hotels are heavily booked then. Demand slackens in January-February, but although there will be some bone-chilling days, winters are usually not too severe and snowfalls of more than four inches are rare.

Those intent on a shopping vacation will encounter large crowds and frayed tempers in the weeks between Thanksgiving and Christmas. The biggest sales are in January-February. Sports enthusiasts find that the seasons of the eight major professional teams overlap in early fall. Allowing for these few caveats, little will be missed no matter what time of year you choose.

Calendar of events

See also RECREATION, pages 272-87 and PUBLIC HOLIDAYS, page 39.

JANUARY
• Early Jan: one-day **Winter Festival in Central Park,** on the Great Lawn, near 81st St. Festivities include snow sculpture contest, cross-country skiing demonstrations and winter fashions. Snow is provided by machine if nature is uncooperative (☎408-0100 *for exact date and information).* • Mid-Jan for 2 weeks: **Boat Show.** Javits Convention Center. Same motives and same lavish display as the Auto Show, but the subject is pleasure craft, both power and sail. • Between mid-Jan and early Feb: **Chinese New Year.** Chinatown, lower Manhattan. Ten days of fireworks and celebrations feature silk lions and a fearsome dragon that snakes and dances along Mott St. to frighten evil spirits away (☎397-8222 *for details).* • Late Jan: **Winter Antiques Show.** 7th Regiment Armory, Park Ave. and E 67th St. This exhibition of superior antiques is also an excuse to see the grand interiors by Stanford White and Louis Comfort Tiffany, usually closed to the public.

FEBRUARY
• Feb is designated **Black History month:** Libraries, schools, universities, TV stations and neighborhood associations sponsor a wide range of events highlighting the contributions of African-Americans to American history and culture. Newspapers carry daily specifics (☎397-8222 *for information).* • Feb 12-22: **Lincoln and Washington Birthday Sales.** On the days around these national holidays, the large department stores mount enormous sales. • Mid-Feb: **Westminster Dog Show.** Madison Square Garden, 7th Ave. and 33rd St. Two days of intense competition. • Mid-Feb for 1 week: **National Antiques Show.** Madison Square Garden, 8th Ave. and 32nd St. Perhaps the largest show of antiques and related objects in the world (☎564-4400 *for dates).* • Late Feb: **Lantern Day.** Chinatown and City Hall, lower Manhattan. On the night of the 15th day of the Chinese Lunar New Year, children form a parade to present paper lanterns to the Mayor. There are martial arts demonstrations, dancing and singing (☎397-8222 *for details).*

MARCH
• For **Easter** events, see APRIL. • Early Mar: **International Cat Show.** Madison Sq. Garden. • Mar 17: **St Patrick's Day Parade.** 5th Ave. from 44th St. to 86th St. All New Yorkers are Irish on this day. Beer is green, clothing is green, even the line down the middle of 5th Ave. is green. Irish taverns and St Patrick's Cathedral are the centers of activity. • Mid-Mar: **International Auto Show.** Javits Convention Center. A vast, glittery exhibition of foreign- and American-made cars: antique, classic, custom and brand new. • Mid-Mar for a week: **New York Flower Show** Pier 92, on the Hudson River at 51st St. More than 15,000 square yards of gardens and landscapes, free lectures. • Late

Mar for 2 months: **Ringling Brothers and Barnum & Bailey Circus**. Madison Square Garden, 7th. Ave. and 33rd St. A small parade of elephants and wagons heralds the opening.

APRIL

• 2 weeks preceding Easter: **Easter Egg Exhibition**. Ukrainian Museum, 2nd Ave. (12th St.). A specially mounted display of hand-painted eggs, a staple of this small museum (☎ *228-0110 for details)*. • Week before Easter: **Easter Flower Show**. Macy's Department Store, Herald Sq. The largest department store in the US blooms on several floors. • Week before Easter: **Easter Lilies display**. Channel Gardens, Rockefeller Center. • Easter Sun: **Easter Parade**. 5th Ave., from 49th St. to 59th St. Not an organized parade at all, but a promenade of celebrants showing off their spring finery, some of it extraordinary.

MAY

• Weekend in mid-May: **Ninth Avenue International Festival**. 9th Ave. from 36th St. to 59th St. Once known as "Paddy's Market," this stretch of 9th Ave. specializes in prosaic and exotic foods. The festival is a gustatory orgy of *kielbasa,* quiche, *falafel, knishes, tacos,* Belgian waffles, *zeppoli, baklava, souvlaki* and every fast food conceived by man. Crafts, merchandise and entertainment. • May 20: **Martin Luther King Jr. Memorial Parade**. 5th Ave. above 59th St. • Around mid-May: **Greek Independence Day Parade**. 5th Ave. above 59th St. Less widely celebrated than St Patrick's Day. The growing Greek population nevertheless provides a substantial parade each year, with floats and bands. • Last weekend in May: **Memorial Day Weekend; official opening of city beaches; antiques show** at 7th Regiment Armory; **women's 10,000m Advil Mini-Marathon**. • Late May-early June: **Washington Square Outdoor Art Exhibition**. Washington Sq. and adjacent streets. Artists, amateur and otherwise, fill walls and fences with paintings (landscapes, tigers and Elvis on velvet, sedate nudes), metalwork, tooled leather and wire jewelry. Everything is for sale, and bargaining is expected. Repeated in early September.

JUNE

• All month: **music and other cultural events**, many of them free. There is dance, Shakespeare, opera, jazz, pop and folk music. Leading groups and companies perform outdoors, in Central Park, at the Rockefeller Center, in the Sculpture Garden of the Museum of Modern Art, at the South Street Seaport and at the World Trade Center. • Sun in mid-June: **Puerto Rican Day Parade**. 5th Ave. above 59th St. Colorful, well-attended, sprightly celebration associated with the patron saint of the Puerto Rican capital, San Juan. • Early June for ten days: **Festival of St Anthony**. Little Italy, lower Manhattan. Sullivan St. below Houston St. is lined with booths selling games of chance, sizzling sausages, *calzone,* pizza and flavored ices. Religious observances dominate during the day; secular entertainments take over after dusk. Go hungry, for the aromas are irresistible. • Early June: **Rose Day Weekend**. New

York Botanical Garden, The Bronx. Stunning demonstration of the horticulturist's craft, with tours and lectures. • Mid-June: **Salute to Israel Parade**. 5th Ave. above 59th St. • Late June-early July: **JVC Jazz Festival**. Concert halls and outdoor locations around Manhattan. Jazz in all its permutations, from Dixieland to atonal, takes over from noon-midnight. Some events are free. Check newspapers for details. • Also late June: **Lesbian and Gay Pride Day**. Parade down 5th Ave. to Greenwich Village.

JULY
• July 4th: **Independence Day Festivities**. Battery Park, lower Manhattan. **Old New York Harbor Festival** takes place in the afternoon and evening, with patriotic ceremonies, food, music and performers. South Street Seaport, downtown Manhattan. This is one of the best vantages for the spectacular **fireworks over the East River**, sponsored by Macy's Department Store. The display starts around 9.30pm, but check newspapers. **Tall ships and sailing vessels** from other nations and ports often visit. **Street festival** has music, crafts and food. • July-Aug: **Summer Festival**. Snug Harbor Cultural Center, Staten Island. Music and art exhibitions on weekends throughout the summer. • Mid-July through Aug: **Mostly Mozart Festival**. Lincoln Center, West Side Manhattan. This treasured event commences with a free outdoor concert, then carries on through the rest of the summer indoors, primarily in Avery Fisher Hall. Tickets are unusually inexpensive (☎875-5030 *for details*). • Late July to mid-Aug: **New York Philharmonic Parks Concerts**. Park locations in all boroughs. The famed symphony orchestra performs beneath the stars, free (☎875-5000). Also July-Aug: **Summergarden Concerts**. Free performances at the Museum of Modern Art by students of thefamed Juilliard School.

AUGUST
• Aug: **Greenwich Village Jazz Festival**. • Mid-Aug to early Sept: **Lincoln Center Out-of-Doors**. Lincoln Center, West Side Manhattan. Free live entertainment on the plaza from noon-sunset (☎875-5400 *for details*). • Late Aug-Sept: **US Open Tennis Championships**. National Tennis Center, Flushing Meadows, Queens (☎(718) 271-5100).

SEPTEMBER
• Early Sept for 2 weeks: **Washington Square Outdoor Art Exhibition**. Washington Sq. and adjacent streets. A duplicate of the spring event (see MAY). • Sun in mid-Sept: "**New York is Book Country**" street fair. 5th Ave. from 48th St. to 57th St. and adjacent blocks. More than 160 publishers and booksellers set up booths. • Mid-Sept: **Steuben Day Parade**. 5th Ave. from 59th St. to Yorkville. Exuberant small-scale commemoration of the German officer who aided the Revolutionary cause. • Late Sept: **Festa di San Gennaro**. Little Italy, lower Manhattan. Blocks of gaming- and eating-booths tantalize with the possibility of sudden modest riches and the certainty of excessive

calorie consumption. It is becoming an increasingly intercultural event, Sicilian sausages being augmented by Cantonese egg rolls. • Mid-Sept to early Oct: **New York Film Festival**. Alice Tully Hall, Lincoln Center. Serious film buffs revel in 3 weeks of afternoon and evening showings, with no need of questionable awards and overheated publicity.

OCTOBER

• On or about Oct 5: **Pulaski Day Parade**. 5th Ave. The Polish community takes its turn. • Weekend in early Oct: **Brooklyn Heights Art Show**. The Promenade. Arts and crafts from scores of local artists compete with spectacular vistas of lower Manhattan. From about noon-6pm. • Early Oct: **Columbus Day Parade**. 5th Ave. Second only to the St Patrick's Day Parade in intensity and numbers, and along the same route. • Late Oct for 1 week: **Fall Antiques Show**. W 52nd St. and Pier 92 *(☎ 777-5218)* Fair featuring Americana. Also, the more important **International Antique Dealers Show** Seventh Regiment Armory, Park Ave.& 66th St. • Oct 31: late afternoon. **Halloween Parade**. Greenwich Village, lower Manhattan. Villagers in outlandish costumes wind through the streets of their district, with ghoulish happenings along the route, and a party at Washington Sq.

NOVEMBER

• First Sun in Nov: **New York City Marathon**. From Staten Island to Central Park. Not the oldest, but the biggest marathon, with more than 24,000 runners following a route from the w end of the Verrazano Narrows Bridge through all five boroughs. • Early Nov for 6 days: **National Horse Show**. Madison Square Garden. Equestrian competition of jumping and dressage. • Last Thurs in Nov: **Macy's Thanksgiving Day Parade**. Broadway, 77th St. to 34th St. Traditional 3-hour morning event with bands, celebrities and huge helium-filled balloons in the shapes of such folk as Bugs Bunny, Snoopy, Superman and Mickey Mouse. • Nov 26-Jan 6: **Star of Wonder Show**. Hayden Planetarium. The night sky of Bethlehem is vividly reproduced, with music and commentary *(☎ 873-8828)*. • Thanksgiving-New Year's Day: **Lord & Taylor Christmas Windows**. 424 5th Ave. (39th St.). All the big stores vie with each other in Christmas decorations, but this one is the perennial champion, managing to outdo itself every year.

DECEMBER

• Late afternoon in early Dec: **Rockefeller Center Tree-Lighting Ceremony**. 5th Ave. between 50th St. and 51st St. The huge tree that rises above the ice-skating rink and the gilded statue of *Prometheus* is illuminated, by dignitaries and celebrities, to the accompaniment of Christmas carols. Extravagantly **decorated trees** are also set up in the American Museum of Natural History and the Metropolitan Museum of Art. • First night of Chanukah: **Lighting of Chanukah Candles**. City Hall, lower Manhattan, and 92nd St. YM-YWHA, 1395 Lexington Ave. • Dec: **Nutcracker Ballet**. Lincoln Center. Traditional performance by the New York City Ballet *(☎ 870-5570)*. • The two Suns before Christmas: 11am-3pm. **Fifth Avenue** Holiday Mall. 5th Ave., 34th St. to 57th St. The Ave. is **closed to traffic**, and public entertainments draw shoppers past sublime and gaudy windows. • Dec 31: **New Year's Eve**. All over the city. A "Big Apple" slides down a flag pole above Times Sq., reaching the bottom at the first second of the New Year to the cheers of thousands of witnesses. Cars sound their horns, boats in the harbor blow their whistles, and celebrants kiss each other in the ballrooms of dozens of hotels. There is also a 5-mile run in Central Park, which commences at midnight and is accompanied by fireworks.

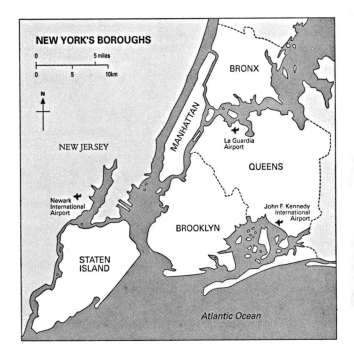

Orientation

New York is an island city, with four of its five administrative units, called boroughs, separated by water from the North American continent. They are linked with each other, and the mainland, by 65 bridges and 19 tunnels. Every likely tourist destination is within reach of the extensive public transport system — by subway, bus, or a combination of the two. Many out-of-town locations can be reached by rail or bus as well, although a car is often preferable.

At the spiritual and geographical center is **Manhattan**. Even residents of the other boroughs refer to it as "The City," a reality made official by the Postal Service: all addresses in Manhattan are given as "New York, NY," while the others are designated **Brooklyn, Queens, The Bronx** and **Staten Island**. Nearly all visitors to New York stay in Manhattan. The major hotels are there, as are approximately 17,000 restaurants and most of the theaters, concert halls, art galleries, landmarks, corporation headquarters, libraries, universities and best-known churches and department stores.

The outer boroughs, although largely residential and industrial, are by no means bereft, however. The Bronx has its zoo and **Yankee Stadium;** Queens has **Shea Stadium** and the **Aqueduct Racetrack**; Brooklyn has its beaches and a fine museum; and Staten Island has golf courses, a zoo, and two complexes of restored architectural treasures.

New York's neighborhoods

MANHATTAN
Manhattan is 12 miles along its N-S axis and about 3 miles across at its widest point. The roll of history and fashion flows northward, for development started with a Dutch settlement at the s tip and spread in the only direction available.

FINANCIAL DISTRICT *(map 1 U4)*. This neighborhood long ago assumed the role evident in its present name, and now bristles with concrete and glass monuments to capitalism, among which are a few public buildings surviving from the late Colonial and early Federalist periods. They constitute a captivating history lesson, enhanced by vistas of New York's rivers and harbor. Despite the frenetic business activity, there were no hotels of consequence and few first-class restaurants, until recently. That situation is being rectified, with three large hotels now open and several good-to-excellent new restaurants.

CHINATOWN AND LITTLE ITALY *(maps 3 & 4)*. When space began to run out in the Financial District, corporation rulers transferred their building mania to midtown. In doing so, they leapfrogged a band of small residential communities, former villages that still cling to very specific identities. While neither Chinatown, s of Canal St., nor Little Italy, a block or two to the N, are postcard-pretty, their ethnic vitality persists.

LOWER EAST SIDE *(map 4 R5)*. This lies to the E of Greenwich Village and historically was the first landfall of impoverished immigrants. A dreary area of rubbish-filled streets and sagging tenements — then and now — its only touristic significance is the frenetic Sundays shopping along Orchard St., when startling bargains in high-style apparel can be plucked from heaps of used and poorly-made clothing and shoes.

SOHO AND TRIBECA *(map 3 S4)*. In the 1960s, the warehouses and lofts of SoHo were "discovered" by artists seeking larger spaces at lower rents. Inevitably, they drew gallery owners and restaurateurs, until boutiques and stockbrokers began to supplant the painters and sculptors. So the artists moved on to nearby TriBeCa, where a similar, but slower, transformation is under way.

GREENWICH VILLAGE *(map 3 R4)*. This area also knows the cycle well. After a period as an upper-middle-class suburb, it too became an artist's enclave. Experimental theaters, art galleries and the new Bohemia flourished here in the early 20thC, and some theaters remain. Elegant brownstones and carriage-house mews alternate with slovenly commercial streets. Restaurants here and in SoHo blanket the entire field of price and achievement. New York University occupies buildings N, E and S of Washington Square.

Washington Square

> I should have been born in New York, I should have been born in the Village, that's where I belong.
> (John Lennon)

CHELSEA AND THE FLATIRON DISTRICT *(maps 5 Q3 & 6 Q4)*. North of 14th St., the planned gridwork of streets and avenues takes hold. On the W is Chelsea, undergoing spotty gentrification, with growing numbers of antique stores and trendy bars and eateries. That process has been swifter in the Flatiron District, S of the eponymous landmark building, aided by the renovation of Union Square Park and the relocation from midtown of many advertising and publishing houses.

GRAMERCY PARK AND MURRAY HILL *(map 6 P4)*. East of Park Ave. and S of 19th St. are the contiguous neighborhoods of Gramercy Park and Murray Hill, where pockets of 19thC elegance persist. Quiet and relatively small hotels provide alternatives to the flashy behemoths farther N, and the restaurants and nightspots give fair value without sacrifice of elbow room.

MIDTOWN DISTRICT *(maps 5-6)*. This area, from 42nd St. to 59th St. and Hudson River to East River, and particularly MIDTOWN EAST, contains a disproportionate share of the attractions for which New York is known. Most of the major hotels, theaters, shops and world-class restaurants are within its elastic boundaries, as well as the UNITED NATIONS HEADQUARTERS, **Times Square**, ROCKEFELLER CENTER, ST PATRICK'S CATHEDRAL, the MUSEUM OF MODERN ART, GRAND CENTRAL TERMINAL, and dozens of examples of New York's most renowned contribution to architecture, the skyscraper. The pace is swifter here, crowds thicker, rooms and meals more costly, aggravations greater.

UPPER EAST SIDE *(map 8)*. By comparison, this is relatively tranquil. Along 5th Ave., its western border, are most of the major museums of art and history, dominated by the METROPOLITAN MUSEUM OF ART. Mingled with the private townhouses of the side blocks are eclectic galleries and shops; and toward the East River, upwardly mobile young married couples and single people, who favor the postwar highrises, keep the many pubs and discos full.

UPPER WEST SIDE *(map 7)*. This is an area in transition. It is not as sleek as the Upper East Side, and has large concentrations of low-income families, but is enjoyed by professionals who find the area and its people less superficial. The LINCOLN CENTER FOR THE PERFORMING ARTS and the AMERICAN MUSEUM OF NATURAL HISTORY are the centerpieces. Between the Upper East and Upper West Side is CENTRAL PARK.

HARLEM. The area stretches river to river immediately to the N of the preceding two neighborhoods. Despite its substandard housing, poverty, and attendant ills, it boasts a number of important cultural institutions, especially the four specialized museums of AUDUBON TERRACE.

The high, narrow neck of land at the NW corner of Manhattan Island has the sanctuary of FORT TRYON PARK, and a remarkable assemblage of medieval chapels and gardens from European monasteries, known as THE CLOISTERS.

Even in combination, the other four boroughs cannot match this panoply, although each has its charms.

THE BRONX
The only borough on the mainland. A full day can be profitably spent at the BRONX ZOO AND NEW YORK BOTANICAL GARDEN, with a side trip to the VAN CORTLANDT MANSION AND MUSEUM.

BROOKLYN
Had it resisted annexation in 1898, Brooklyn would now be the fourth largest city in the United States. It is still self-contained, with its own civic and cultural centers, concert halls, downtown shopping district, beaches, colleges, and residential neighborhoods both elite and prosaic. Among its inducements are the BROOKLYN MUSEUM, NEW YORK AQUARIUM, BROOKLYN HEIGHTS and the promenade that overlooks an extraordinary panorama of the Manhattan skyline from the STATUE OF LIBERTY to the EMPIRE STATE BUILDING.

QUEENS
This largely residential borough has both **LaGuardia** and **JFK airports**. Sports fans take the subway to the **Aqueduct Racetrack** for thoroughbred racing, and to **Shea Stadium** for Mets baseball games. (See SPORTS, page 283.)

STATEN ISLAND
Despite the 1964 VERRAZANO NARROWS BRIDGE, which connects it with Brooklyn, Staten Island remains somewhat isolated from the other boroughs. Those who take the time to look around, however, will discover golf courses, beaches, country clubs, even a wildlife refuge. Among the pockets of bucolic solitude: RICHMONDTOWN RESTORATION, a village of Colonial and 19thC homes and shops; SNUG HARBOR CULTURAL CENTER, a living museum of buildings in every 19thC style; the TIBETAN MUSEUM; and the small but remarkable STATEN ISLAND ZOO.

Walks in New York

Many parts of Manhattan, and Brooklyn Heights across the East River, have a surprisingly intimate character, which can be best appreciated on foot. The following walks serve as samples.

WALK 1: AN INTRODUCTION TO NEW YORK

Allow 1hr. Map 6N4. Subway: 47th-50th St./Rockefeller Center

Tourists and natives alike find themselves passing through ROCKEFELLER CENTER and its immediate surroundings repeatedly. They come for the shopping along 5th Ave., to watch the iceskaters, for shows at Radio City Music Hall, to see the city's tallest Christmas tree, and to join the Easter Parade.

Begin at the **Channel Garden** entrance on the w side of 5th Ave. between 49th St. and 50th St., perhaps after a visit to ST PATRICK'S CATHE-DRAL, one block N. The Channel itself, with, appropriately, **La Maison Française** on the s and the **British Empire Building** on the N, has long, raised flower beds, where the plantings are changed with seasons. At the end of this walkway, a golden statue of *Prometheus* hovers above a sunken rectangular plaza, which is an outdoor café from April to September and an ice-skating rink from October to March.

Go around the plaza, which is usually encircled by the fluttering flags of many nations. The narrow limestone slab on the far side is the **GE Building**. It was originally called the RCA Building, after the previous corporate owners, and has muted Art Deco details over and around the high portals. Inside, José Maria Sert painted the heroic murals in sepia tones depicting muscular workers striding across walls and ceilings. Unhappily, the rooftop observation deck that once drew thousands of visitors every day is now closed to the public. Part of that space, however, is taken up by the lounge of the revamped **Rainbow Room**, so much of the panoramic vista can be seen from inside. Drinks and snacks in the lounge are not too expensive, but men must be dressed in jacket and tie, which are not the usual sightseeing garb.

Alternatively, descend to the subterranean concourse by the stairs or escalators at either side of the lobby, one floor beneath ground level. A village of small shops thrives down there, along arcades that connect buildings from 6th Ave. to 5th Ave., and from 48th St. to 53rd St. Directly ahead, bordering the sunken plaza, is a new open-sided café and takeout shop called **Savories**. It serves tempting salads and primarily American dishes. Also flanking the plaza are the more formal **American Festival Café** (to the left) and the **Sea Grill** (right).

Return to Rockefeller Plaza at the front of the GE Building and turn right, s, then right again, w, into 48th St. Continue w to Ave. of the Americas (known to all as 6th Ave.). The wall of intimidating skyscrapers on the opposite side is technically part of the Rockefeller Center, although the buildings were erected in the 1960s. Cross the Ave. and walk N. Note the gray 19thC building at the NE corner of 49th St., a defiant hold-out against the monoliths that surround it. Its ground floor is a bar-restaurant, **Hurley's**. There are usually several food carts at the next corner. If they tempt, take your snack to the marble bench around the fountain in front of the **Time-Life Building** at the corner of 6th Ave. and 50th St. Directly opposite is the **Radio City Music Hall**. For 50 years it featured big Hollywood "family" movies interspersed with stage shows that focused on the precision dance troupe known as The Rockettes. Business fell off in the 1970s and the hall nearly closed, but was saved by a new policy of special events, rock and pop concerts, and limited-run revues. The ornate **vaulted interior** must be seen to be believed.

NBC maintains **studios** in Rockefeller Center, in which are produced such popular TV shows as *Saturday Night Live, Donahue* and *Late Night with David Letterman.* Tickets for guided tours of the studios *(about every 15mins, Mon-Sat 9.30am-4.30pm)* may be purchased at the GE Building. Tours of Radio City Music Hall are also available *(☎632-4041 for information).*

WALK 2: FINANCIAL DISTRICT

Allow 2-3hrs. Map 1U4 and map on page 57. Subway: World Trade Center
From the day the first Dutch settlers crept into hastily constructed bark shelters, the foremost business of New York was commerce. Gradually, merchants became financiers, increasingly distant from the commodities they bartered, and as ever greater space was needed to contain the people who administered the system, so the present thicket of skyscrapers emerged, a 20thC metropolis built to the edges of a 17thC street plan.

By 1850, few people actually lived below Chambers St. and the BROOKLYN BRIDGE, the approximate northern border of what was "Little Old New York" and is now the FINANCIAL DISTRICT. From Monday to Friday 8am-6pm the streets teemed with millions of workers, then at dusk and on weekends the dark canyons heard only the sigh of winds and the rustle of blown refuse. That is less true today, for New Yorkers have started to move back, with restaurateurs and retailers following close behind them. So whether a Friday or a Saturday is chosen for a look around depends on the tastes of the visitor. Most buildings of note are open both days, but most eating places, except for those at SOUTH STREET SEAPORT, lock up as soon as the last commuter has downed his Martini and headed for home.

A walking tour logically begins with the observation deck of the s (#2) tower of the **World Trade Center**, the easiest structure to find in New York City. Exit onto Liberty St. Turn left, to the E, then right, s, on Broadway. Three blocks down is **Trinity Church**, the Gothic Revival third version (1846) of a 1696 original. Once so black with grime it almost glistened, it has now been scoured down to the red sandstone. After a stroll through the surrounding graveyard, continue s on Broadway to **Bowling Green**, a fenced pocket park guarded by a large sculpture of a snorting bull. Directly beyond the green is the **Custom House**, often cited as one of the city's best examples of the florid Beaux Arts style popular at the turn of the century. The four **sculptures** in front are by Daniel Chester French, best known for his monumental renderings of Abraham Lincoln. They represent the continents of Africa, America, Asia

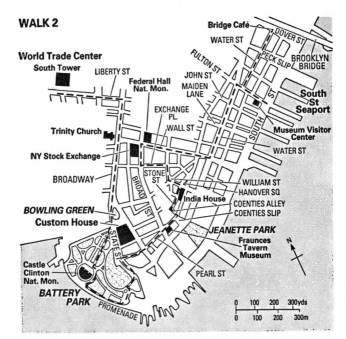

WALK 2

and Europe. Across the sixth floor cornice stand twelve **statues** symbolizing historical trading centers — from left to right, Greece, Rome, Phoenicia, Genoa, Venice, Spain, Holland, Portugal, Denmark, Germany, England and France. (The "Germany" designation was changed to "Belgium" in 1917 in reflection of the anti-German sentiments of the time.)

Bear right, SW, into **Battery Park**, following the main path to the semicircular **Castle Clinton National Monument**. An 1807 fortress that never fired on an enemy ship, it served instead as a concert and exposition hall, an immigrant processing center, and an aquarium. There are historical exhibits inside, and booths sell tickets for the Statue of Liberty and Ellis Island ferries. Walk through the castle onto the promenade at the water's edge, for a panorama that includes ELLIS ISLAND, the STATUE OF LIBERTY, **Governors Island** (a military base) and BROOKLYN HEIGHTS.

Passing the ferry docks, turn inland opposite the sign that reads "Gangway 1," keeping the park on the left. There is a refreshment stand on the right. Walk straight ahead, to the opposite side of the park. Directly across State St. is a **Georgian-Federal mansion** (#7), with an inset columned porch. Completed in 1806, it is the last of a row of such homes that once bordered this avenue. Turn left (N) and cross over at the next intersection, Pearl St. The narrow byway is now hemmed in by looming glass towers. After the first building is a grouping of benches and the entrance to **New York Unearthed** (☎ 363-9372 ▣ *open Mon-Sat* *noon-6pm),* a project of the SOUTH STREET SEAPORT MUSEUM. On display are objects discovered in archeological digs around lower Manhattan, and explanations of their significance. Continue along Pearl St. In three short blocks, at the corner of Broad St., is the **Fraunces Tavern Museum**, a re-creation of a Colonial Georgian residence. It has a museum of Revolutionary War artifacts upstairs, a pleasant restaurant down. Breakfast is the best meal served, and there is afternoon tea.

Proceed along Pearl St. The next corner is Coenties Slip, so named because it was once a docking bay for merchant ships. It was filled in long ago. Cross the street into what looks to be a small plaza with herringbone brick paving, flanked by a block of convenience stores and the upstairs **Grazio's Ristorante**. The "plaza" is actually the refurbished Coenties Alley. Pass the shops and turn right, into narrow Stone St. This was the first paved pathway in the Dutch colony. It isn't much to look at now, but ends shortly in Hanover Sq. To the right is the 1854 **India House**, Italian Renaissance in style to serve the merchant princes who were its earliest occupants. It is now a private club, but members of the public are welcome to use the restaurant, **Harry's at Hanover Square**. Its food is fairly inexpensive, if unremarkable, and the bar is packed with brash young brokers and office workers at the end of the working day.

Turn left, curving N along William St., then left, to the W, into Exchange Pl. Turning right, N, into Broad St., watch for the **New York Stock Exchange** (#8) on the left. It is readily identified by the Greco-Roman facade. The seemingly inchoate frenzy in the pit of the main floor can be observed, if not necessarily understood, from the **visitor's center** *(Mon-Fri 9.30am-4pm)*. Reach it through the building at 20 Broad St., taking the express elevator to the 3rd floor.

At the next corner, glance left down Wall St., its concrete canyon framing **Trinity Church**. The Greek Revival "temple" directly across the street is **Federal Hall National Memorial** (both of these buildings are illustrated in ARCHITECTURE). On that site, in an earlier structure, George Washington took the oath of office as the first president of the United States.

Continue E down Wall St., named for the wood stockade erected there in 1653 to protect the Dutch colonists from attack by Indians or the British. Turn left, N, on Water St., crossing Maiden Lane, where young women once washed their laundry in a brook. At John St., glance right for a startling view of the **four-masted bark** *Peking,* one of the floating exhibits of an unusual maritime museum. Continue to Fulton St., and turn right, E. This is the heart of the **South Street Seaport** restoration district, a fetching amalgam of early 19thC architecture and artifacts and late 20thC merchandising and recycling techniques. From here to the East River, Fulton St. is a pedestrian mall, the buildings to either side filled with boutiques, fast food stalls, informal cafés and restaurants, and branches of such upmarket chains as Laura Ashley, Caswell-Massey, Ann Taylor and Abercrombie & Fitch. On sunny days, every weekend, and most evenings, it is awash with locals and out-of-towners alike.

The row of buildings on the right, one block E, is **Schermerhorn Row**. Built around 1812 as a block of warehouses, it has now been restored to its Federalist origins. At #12 is the museum's **visitor center** *(open daily 10am-5pm)*. Upstairs at #2 is **Sweet's** seafood restaurant, opened in 1842 and, by some accounts, resting on its laurels since 1900. That doesn't stop the files of customers who dutifully line up for unadorned seafood lunches every weekday. At the end is the **North Star**, a persuasive imitation of a British pub, serving Guinness and Watney's brews. Just round the corner is the entrance to **Sloppie Louie's**, another historic spot that treats its patrons as cavalierly as its competitors but produces somewhat better fish. Sailing vessels of a more romantic era are moored at the piers of the SOUTH STREET SEAPORT across the way. In good weather, there are concerts, puppet shows, street musicians, and chairs in which to sit and admire the view of the Brooklyn Bridge.

Leave along the N side of Fulton St., turning right, N, into Water St. A restored stationer's store is followed by the **Seaport Gallery**, with maritime exhibits and helpful maps of the neighborhood. New shops open (and close) frequently with the ongoing development of the area. At the corner with Peck Slip, look toward the river at the amusing *trompe-l'oeil* **mural** that covers the entire side wall of a brick building, complete with a reproduction of a bridge tower duplicating the real one just beyond. At the end of these last shabby blocks of Water St. is a forerunner of the sprightly new bar-restaurants that have sprung up in the district, the **Bridge Café**. It serves lunch, dinner and Sunday brunch.

WALK 3: CIVIC CENTER-CHINATOWN-LITTLE ITALY
Allow 2-3hrs. Map 2T4 and map on page 60. Subway: Park Place

Contrasts are endemic to New York, sometimes jarring, sometimes poignant. They tumble over each other, person by person, structure by structure; overweening power and grinding need, harsh modernity and mellowed history, optimism and despair, cosmopolitanism and parochialism. This walk is an illustration.

Start at the junction of Broadway, Park Row and Vesey St., at **St Paul's Chapel** (illustrated on page 146). Completed in 1766, it is the oldest church and public building in Manhattan. Back on Broadway, turn left, to the N. Two blocks up is the WOOLWORTH BUILDING, whose cathedral-like lobby deserves a detour.

Cross Broadway to **City Hall Park**, with the approaches to the BROOKLYN BRIDGE in the background. Municipal architecture is more often dreary than inspired, but the 1811 CITY HALL is exceptional. Its elegant facade faces S, an evocation of the palaces of the Sun King. Pass City Hall on the right, continuing to the NE corner of the park. Behind City Hall is the former **New York County Courthouse**, known less for its Italianate Victorian architecture than for the scandal that swirled around it following completion in 1878. At that time, it was dubbed the "Tweed" courthouse. The infamous Democratic party boss and his cronies diverted an estimated $9 million from its heavily padded final cost. Renovation currently in progress will cost more than Tweed stole. Pass in front of the statue of Horace Greeley, founder of *The New York Tribune*.

Across Chambers St. is the marvelously Baroque **Hall of Records** (the sign above the door reads "Surrogate's Court"), and to the right is the

WALK 3

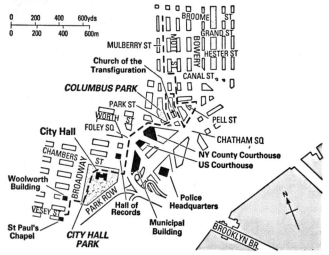

towering **Municipal Building**. An agglomeration style that was the hallmark of the McKim, Mead & White firm, it employs a concave facade, a forest of Corinthian columns before a triumphal arch that pierces the base, and 34 stories of statues, carvings and embellishment that owe debts to every European architectural fancy of the last 600 years. Glimpsed through the arch is a monumental steel sculpture, painted bright red, that announces the entrance of the aggressively contemporary **Police Headquarters**. Cross Chambers St., keeping right of the Hall of Records. The street opens into Foley Sq. On the E is an odd structure that can be said to signal the end of the Classical vogue in Federal architecture. Somber and intimidating, the 1936 **United States Courthouse** has a "temple" base, but an incongruous tower looming overhead. It is on the National Register of Historic Sites, for some reason. Pass in front of it and its more graceful sister, the **New York County Courthouse**, still bearing right, then walk E along Worth St. to the small Columbus Park on the opposite side. Cross over and walk to the far side of the park, turning left, N, on Mulberry St.

This, it will be instantly apparent, is CHINATOWN. A Cantonese enclave for more than 100 years, it is home to at least 150,000 Chinese, and spiritual center for ten times as many relatives who have scattered along the East Coast. Evenings and weekends, they all seem to have returned. The musty sterility of the Civic Center is instantly replaced by a barrage of visual and olfactory stimuli (most of them agreeable or at least intriguing).

Stroll along Mulberry until it intersects with Bayard St. Turn right, then right again on Mott St., where shades of crimson and yellow flare against the dark backdrop of the upper stories of grimy brick. In just these short blocks, window displays and maddening aromas inspire an irresistible urge to eat. At #22, for example, is the well-regarded **Peking Duck House** and, next door, the popular **20 Mott Street**.

But before you snatch up the nearest egg roll, a short investigation of the **Chinatown Fair** game arcade *(8 Mott St., map 2 T5)* will be worthwhile. Inside, among bleeping and clanging pinball and video machines, are two of Chinatown's longest-running attractions. First is "Birdbrain," a live chicken that plays tick-tack-toe with all comers. He will win. Second, at the end of the room, is another cage, with a chicken that dances on command.

Returning to Mott St., continue to the corner and then turn left into Chatham Sq., which soon blends into **The Bowery**. At the corner of Pell St. is a **restored brick house** dating from the Revolutionary War era. Turn left, w. In the midst of all the Far Eastern uproar, near the corner of Pell St. and Mott St., is the Georgian-Gothic **Church of the Transfiguration**.

Turn right, N, into Mott St., shortly passing a **Buddhist temple** on the right. Tucked between grocery stores and restaurants are shops offering satin shoes, kites, jade, fans, woks, kimonos, medicinal herbs, paper lanterns, embroidered silks, chopsticks, candles, cricket cages and Buddha figurines — often all together. Narrow staircases lead up to clubrooms, whence sometimes can be heard gongs and drums and the clack of *mah-jong* tiles. Telephone booths have pagoda roofs, and banners flutter overhead. By now, hunger may be stronger than any other impulse. See RESTAURANTS for suggestions.

At Canal St., turn left, w, one block, crossing over, N, at Mulberry St. For many years, Canal St. was an unofficial *cordon sanitaire* between Chinatown and **Little Italy**, but the former community is expanding N and E, the latter shrinking. Little Italy persists, however, and despite the advancing age of its remaining inhabitants, it is still a Neapolitan-Sicilian bubble of trattorias and cafés and fervent allegiances to church and family.

As in Chinatown, uptown and suburban relatives stream back to Little Italy for every native celebration and holiday. There, the big one is **Chinese New Year** *(mid-Jan to early Feb);* here, it's the **Festa di San Gennaro** *(Sept).* Try to be there, for floats, parades, dancing, and miles of sizzling sausage and *calzone.*

During the rest of the year the preservation of ethnicity is the draw, largely as regards food, although neighborhood *ristoranti* rarely surpass Italian eateries in other parts of the city. Nevertheless, fair value is given by **Il Cortile** *(125 Mulberry St., map 3 S4),* **Puglia** *(corner of Hester St. and Mulberry St., map 3 S4),* **Angelo's** *(146 Mulberry St., map 3 S4)* and **Grotta Azzurra** *(corner of Broome St., map 3 S4).* All are open for lunch and dinner, Tuesday to Sunday. Afterwards, or instead, turn right, E, along Grand St., for a *cappuccino* and a pastry at **Ferrara's** (#195). It has sidewalk tables in summer. A similar treat can be had at **Café Roma**, on the corner of Mulberry and Broome St. From here, it is only a few blocks w on Broome St. into the creative ferment of **SoHo**.

WALK 4

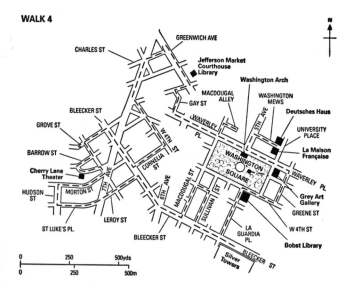

GREENWICH AVE

CHARLES ST

Jefferson Market
Courthouse
Library

Washington Arch

MACDOUGAL
ALLEY

GAY ST

WASHINGTON
MEWS

Deutsches Haus

BLEECKER ST

WAVERLEY
PL.

5TH AVE

UNIVERSITY
PLACE

GROVE ST

W 4TH ST

CORNELIA
ST

La Maison
Française

BARROW ST

WASHINGTON
SQUARE

WAVERLEY PL.

Cherry Lane
Theater

7TH AVE

6TH AVE

MACDOUGAL ST

SULLIVAN ST

HUDSON
ST

MORTON ST

Grey Art
Gallery

GREENE ST

LEROY ST

W 4TH ST

ST LUKE'S PL.

LA
GUARDIA
PL.

Bobst Library

BLEECKER ST

Silver
Towers

BLEECKER ST

0   250   500yds
0   250   500m

WALK 4: GREENWICH VILLAGE

Allow 2-3hrs. Map 3R4 and map above. Subway: Astor Place or 8th St.

"The Village isn't the same," say those who have prospered, matured and moved away. They are correct, but it doesn't matter. The neighborhoods of New York are not static. They shrink, expand, divide, deteriorate, adjust, or rally. Next year, or tomorrow, The Village will have changed again, but the past and provocative present remain.

Begin a tour at the University Pl. end of Washington Mews, one-half block N of the NE corner of WASHINGTON SQUARE. To the left is **La Maison Française**, to the right, **Deutsches Haus**. Both are units of NEW YORK UNIVERSITY, which owns much of the property in this area, as proclaimed by its ubiquitous purple-and-white banners. Proceed down the cobblestoned Mews. Once servant quarters and stables for the grand houses on Washington Sq. North and 8th St., most of the buildings are now private homes.

Turn left into 5th Ave., toward **Washington Arch**. A wooden version of the monument was first erected in 1886 to commemorate the centennial of George Washington's inauguration. It became an instant landmark, so the architect Stanford White designed this marble rendition, completed in 1892. **Washington's statue** on the left was carved by A. Stirling Calder, father of Alexander Calder.

Turn left along Washington Sq. North. This block of Greek Revival row houses was built in the 1830s, and **#16** was the site of Henry James's novel, *Washington Square*. Note the bronze lions bracketing the steps of **#6**, which now houses university offices and seminar rooms. Painter

Edward Hopper maintained a studio at #3, but the upper floors burned away in the early 1970s. Continue along as the street becomes Waverly Pl., turning right into Greene St.

One block down, at the corner of Washington Place, is the site of the infamous **Triangle Fire**, where in 1911, 146 garment workers lost their lives. The tragedy led to major legislation governing factory working conditions and fortified the then-weak labor movement. A plaque commemorates the event. At the foot of Greene St. is **Tisch Hall**, with its flower- and tree-filled plaza. It is the second of Philip Johnson's commissions for the university, now being shouldered into the background by a cylindrical addition to the adjacent **Shimkin Hall**. Turn right into W 4th St., which soon becomes Washington Square S.

The reddish building looming on the left is the **Bobst Library**, Johnson's first design for N.Y.U. Those who wish can step inside to see the 12-story balconied **atrium**. Outside, turn left, then left again on LaGuardia Pl., and walk s as far as Bleecker St. Turn left, E, to see the three high-rise apartment houses on the right, the university-owned **Silver Towers**. In the plaza at their base is a monumental rendering of Picasso's *Silvette,* one of only two exterior sculptures by the influential artist in North America.

Return to Bleecker St., now heading w, and continue to Sullivan St. This intersection is the center of the long-established Italian community of the South Village. Walk N, on Sullivan. Once a block of poultry stores and dim cafés, it is now undistinguished. Press on to the next intersection and turn left on W 3rd St. for a short block, then left again into MacDougal St. The **Café Reggio** *(119 MacDougal St., map 3 R4)* is an authentic throwback to the legendary Bohemian and beatnik days of The Village, as dark as always but less smoky than it used to be, with a well-used espresso machine hissing at one side. Continue s. At the next corner, across the street, is another famous old coffee house, **Le Figaro**. Turn right into Bleecker St., crossing 6th Ave. and picking up Bleecker St. again on the other side.

Turn left into Leroy St., which becomes St Luke's Pl. on the other side of 7th Ave. The houses on the right-hand side of this peaceful tree-shaded block date from the 1860s. Turn right into Hudson St., right again into Morton St., then left into Bedford St. (**#75½**), where Edna St Vincent Millay, the poet and actress, resided for a time. Only 8 feet wide, it is the narrowest house in The Village. The oldest is probably **#77**, next door, built in 1799.

Just beyond, turn left into Commerce St. At the end of the short block is the **Cherry Lane Theater**, one of several in which the energetic Ms. Millay had a hand. Turn right into Barrow St., bearing right again until you are back on Bedford St. Turn left. After one more block on Bedford, at the corner of Grove St., is a squarish wooden clapboard house of obvious age. It dates back to 1820, as does the much smaller frame house behind it, which was probably the kitchen and servant quarters for its larger neighbor. And behind the cookhouse are the double-gabled houses known as the "Twin Sisters," reputedly built by a seafaring father whose daughters would not live under the same roof. Turn left into Grove

St. In a few paces, look for the iron gate marked "private." Peer into the courtyard beyond. Among the bordering houses, built in the 1840s, are some of the few surviving **wood houses** in Manhattan.

Turn around, walk back along Grove St. and turn right into Bleecker St., a commercial artery, dominated by abundant displays of foodstuffs. Turn left into Cornelia St., and left again into W 4th St. for more shops of even greater diversity. Make a right turn at 7th Ave. and continue as far as Charles St., then turn right again and walk to Greenwich Ave. Turn left, window-gazing, then cut across and backtrack down the other side. The **triangular garden** between 10th St. and 6th Ave. was made possible by the demolition of the unlamented Women's House of Detention. The adjacent structure with the fanciful **brick tower** is the **Jefferson Market Courthouse Library**, a mouthful that describes its sequential uses.

Turn right into Christopher St., walking away from 6th Ave., then left into Gay St., which was home (at **#14**) to two sisters from Ohio, one of whom wrote *My Sister Eileen*. In a classic case of cultural recycling, her novel begat a play that was transformed into a musical that started the whole thing over again, complete with remakes and a television series. At the end of this crooked street, turn left into Waverly Pl. and follow it to the NW corner of Washington Square. Make one last detour — a half-block to the left. On the right is **MacDougal Alley**, a quaint relic of the privileged past. It is a deceptively ramshackle variation of Washington Mews, its former carriagehouses now serving as expensive residences.

Return to the square. It is one of the most used parks on the island, for both benign and malignant purposes, but recently has had a pronounced police presence. At the NW corner is a fenced section set aside as a dog run. Two blocks s, chess and domino players and *kibitzers* form knots around the cement games tables installed there. Cyclists, joggers, skaters, and skateboarders swerve along the paths. At and around the central fountain, which is intended more for splashing than beauty, and functions on an unpredictable schedule, several musical groups and individuals are bound to be performing, at least on fine days.

Farther E is a **statue of Garibaldi**. Consistent with campus legends everywhere, *Il Signore* is said to unsheathe his sword whenever a virgin passes. Finally, stroll over to the GREY ART GALLERY on the E side; this is another university facility, featuring exhibitions more lively than the name suggests *(open Tues,Thurs, Fri 11am-6.30pm; Wed 11am-8.30pm; Sat 11am-5pm)*.

WALK 5: CENTRAL PARK
Allow 2hrs. Maps 7&8 and map on page 65. Subway: 77th St.

An amenity without which life in New York is unimaginable, the park is a product of mid-19thC vision and expediency. At that time, the land N of 59th St. was a place of mosquito-infested swamps, malodorous meat-rendering factories, and the festering hovels of thieves and the homeless. Prompted by poet-journalist William Cullen Bryant and his supporters, the city authorities launched a design competition that was won by landscapist Frederick Law Olmsted and the British architect Calvert Vaux. The squatters were evicted, the swamps drained or re-

WALK 5

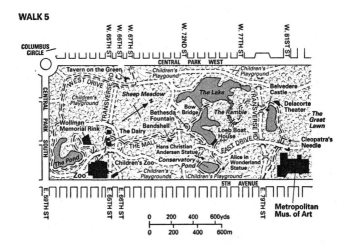

shaped into lakes, 100,000 trees planted and tons of rock and earth pushed about to supplement existing topographical features and create new ones. After 20 years it was complete, with gravel carriageways, bridle paths, playing fields, secluded glades and lakes for boating and fishing. Most of these remain, despite the trampings of generations of New Yorkers, periods of neglect, vandalism, and intrusions both well-intentioned and profane.

Olmsted and Vaux envisioned a people's park, a place of refuge for poor and privileged citizens alike, not an enclosed chunk of ersatz wilderness. To enhance circulation and fantasy, they incorporated bridges, fountains, promenades, and even a castle. Ever since they completed their commission, however, would-be benefactors and entrepreneurs have proposed "improvements." Most are turned away before the predictable firestorms of protest, but over the decades a number of projects both grand and irrelevant have squeezed through the screen. As a result, there are more structures and monuments within the park than even natives can enumerate, constituting an agreeable walking tour of surprising diversity.

One reluctant caveat, however: the stories about Central Park at night are overblown, but true enough to mandate caution. Apart from those frequent evening occasions — concerts and plays — that provide the security of large crowds, it is statistically unwise to visit after dusk.

Enter the park at 79th St. and 5th Ave., walking w along the path to the N of the Transverse Rd. This hugs the s wing of the METROPOLITAN MUSEUM OF ART, continues over a low rise and heads down under an arched stone bridge. Go through, bearing right, N. A few steps farther on is **Cleopatra's Needle**, an Egyptian obelisk given to the city and erected in 1881. Turn about, taking the first footpath to the right. It soon bears left. The level green to the N called **The Great Lawn** was once a reservoir, drained and filled in the 1930s and now busy much of the year with softball and football players. Above the small lake on the left, s, is **Belvedere Castle**.

At the end of the lake is the open-air **Delacorte Theater** *(check newspapers for current performances or ☎861-7277)*. Bear left around the back of the theater and up the hill to the castle. Paths at the back cross over the Transverse Rd. Take the one on the left, down the stone stairs, proceeding sw, then se. Eventually, it winds past the **Loeb Boat House** *(☎517-2233, open Sat & Sun 10am-5pm)*. Bicycles and rowboats are available for rent between April and October. A café with patio serves lunch and dinner on a seasonal schedule. Reservations are required for parties of six or more *(☎517-3623)*.

Follow the same pathway due e, crossing the nearby East Drive, until it soon reaches the concrete oval of **Conservatory Pond**. At its n end is a statue of *Alice in Wonderland,* and on the w, one of **Hans Christian Andersen**. Children clamber all over them, especially when stories are told at the Andersen monument on Saturday mornings *(May-Sept)*.

Take the walkway that goes w from the s end of the pond, under the Park Drive, up the stairs, and along the bank of the lake. **Bethesda Fountain** is just ahead, the most grandiose element of the Vaux contributions. A winged angel surmounts a gaggle of cherubim and, when New York is not having a water crisis, there is pretty splashing in the pool at the base. The terrace surrounding the fountain has tables with umbrellas in summer; Peruvian instrumental groups, jugglers and other performers often set up shop there.

Take the exit path leading w along the lake shore to the lovely cast-iron **Bow Bridge**. Another Vaux design, it was restored in 1974, and crosses the lake into **The Ramble**, a cat's cradle of footpaths that curl through low trees, patches of grass and plantings of bush and flower. The section is favored by serious birdwatchers, for more than 200 species of birds reside in or visit the park, and they find these thickets hospitable. Return across the bridge to the Bethesda Fountain, go up the stairs and cross the roadway. Walk s along **The Mall**.

Continue s on The Mall, a wide straight walk beneath a canopy of ancient trees. Off to the right, runners, skate-boarders, eaters and musicians compete for space on a parallel road. At the end of the mall are **bronze statues** of Walter Scott, Robbie Burns, Shakespeare and Christopher Columbus. Continue past Columbus, crossing the road. After about 20 yards, there is a walk on the right down to **The Dairy** *(open Tues-Thurs and Sat, Sun 11am-5pm; Fri 1-5pm, until 4pm in winter, closed Mon)*. Recent restoration of the building was faithful to its Victorian Gothic origins, and a loggia that was removed in the 1950s has been re-created. The vaulted interior is now an information center, with exhibitions and a slide show, and walking tours depart from there.

Return to the nearby road and turn right, s. An entrance to **Central Park Zoo** is about 100 yards down on the left, e, and it might be time to have a snack in one of its cafeterias, near the front gate. That can be the end of a tour, but if energy and curiosity remain, leave the zoo through the s gate, emerging briefly from the park into Doris C. Freedman Plaza.

Turn right (w), cross the road, turn right again, then go down the path on the left. Bear left at the lake encountered there. At the road that enters the park from Central Park South, head w, following the Park Drive as it curves N along the w side of the park. This is the final leg of the New York Marathon in November, with the finish line at about 66th St. A detour E along the Transverse Rd. soon arrives at the **Friedsam Memorial Carousel** (☎ *879-0244, open daily 10.30am-4.30pm, weather permitting)*. The expanse of lawn to the N is the **Sheep Meadow**. To its w is the **Tavern On The Green** restaurant (which until the 1930s was the barn for the sheep that grazed on the Meadow). The road in front of the restaurant exits on Central Park West.

Children's playgrounds, 22 of them, are located at intervals along the E and w borders of the park (see NEW YORK FOR CHILDREN). From May to October, park roads are closed to vehicular traffic, Monday to Friday 10am-3pm, Monday to Thursday 7-10pm, Friday 8pm until Monday 6am, holidays 7pm until 6am in the morning of the next working day. From November to April only, weekend closing times apply. Horse-drawn carriages can be hired for rides through the park; they gather at stands near the **Plaza Hotel**, at the corner of Central Park s (59th St.) and 5th Ave. For a recorded announcement of weekly events in the park ☎427-4040.

WALK 6: UPPER EAST SIDE
*Allow 2hrs. Map **8** and map on page 68. Subway: 68th St./Hunter College*

The wealthy and super-rich made the Upper East Side their habitat in the late 19thC, pushing aside the squatters and farmers who were then in residence. They erected Italo-Franco-Anglo châteaux and *palazzi* one after the other, each grander than its neighbor. Those were the last decades before enactment of income tax, however, and even these privileged folk couldn't maintain their 50-room retreats long after that blow. The rest of us profited, for many of those mansions now serve the public as schools and museums. The result is "**Museum Mile**," along 5th Ave., bordering Central Park, a string of public repositories of arts and antiquities of astonishing diversity, stretching from 70th St. to 103rd St. This suggested walk links many of those museums, which are described in detail in SIGHTS AND PLACES OF INTEREST. The walk can be broken off at any point and returned to, another day, as interest and energy dictate.

Start at the headquarters of the ASIA SOCIETY, at the NE corner of Park Ave. and 70th St. Opened in 1981, the handsome red granite structure houses galleries of Far Eastern artifacts. Exhibits are changed 2-3 times a year. Cross Park Ave. continuing w on 70th St. Several buildings along the next two blocks are interesting. The **Explorer's Club** (#46) reflects the waning Gothic Revival enthusiasm of the pre-World War I years, and #32 has Florentine detailing of the same period.

This district bordering Madison Ave. is home to at least a third of the city's important art galleries, and **Knoedler & Co.** (#19), dealing in 20thC moderns and some earlier masters, is one of the most influential. Keeping to the N side of the street, watch for the entrance to the **Frick Collection**

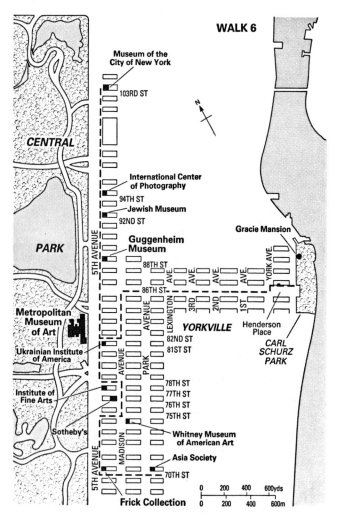

WALK 6

Museum of the City of New York

103RD ST

CENTRAL

International Center of Photography

94TH ST

Jewish Museum

92ND ST

Gracie Mansion

PARK

Guggenheim Museum

5TH AVENUE

88TH ST

86TH ST.

LEXINGTON AVE.

3RD AVE.

2ND AVE.

1ST AVE.

YORK AVE.

Metropolitan Museum of Art

MADISON AVENUE

PARK AVENUE

YORKVILLE

Henderson Place

CARL SCHURZ PARK

Ukrainian Institute of America

82ND ST

81ST ST

Institute of Fine Arts

78TH ST
77TH ST
76TH ST
75TH ST

Sotheby's

Whitney Museum of American Art

5TH AVENUE

MADISON

Asia Society

70TH ST

Frick Collection

| 0 | 200 | 400 | 600yds |
| 0 | 200 | 400 | 600m |

on the right. Industrialist Henry Clay Frick intended to have his 1914 mansion converted to a museum upon his death, and with that prospect in mind, he filled it with Renaissance and French and English 18thC paintings.

After completing your visit, exit by the front door and turn right, w, into 70th St., then right, N, into 5th Ave., where it forms one of the grand boulevards of the city, the green of CENTRAL PARK to the left and placid apartment blocks to the right. At 75th St., turn right, E. On the N side is a **Romanesque mansion** surrounded by an unusual iron fence, formerly the Harkness House, now a foundation headquarters. Continue to Madison Ave. The striking cantilevered structure on the SE corner is the **Whitney Museum Of American Art** (pictured on page 157), suggesting a fortress, complete with moat and fixed bridge. The leafy restaurant on the glassed-in sub-street level provides a welcome place to sit down and relax, in full view of an outdoor sculpture garden.

Walk N on Madison Ave., intimate by contrast with Park Ave. and 5th Ave., with shoulder-to-shoulder art and antiques galleries and compact, idiosyncratic shops. At 76th St. is the exclusive **Carlyle** hotel, choice of John F. Kennedy when he was in town. Opposite the hotel is the famed auction house, **Sotheby's** (#980), where estate treasures and fabulous artworks routinely fetch millions of dollars. On the same side, at #1000, is the Italianate gelati/pastry/espresso shop, **Sant Ambroeus**. A cappuccino at the zinc-topped bar hits the spot on a chilly day, as might a dish of sorbet in July. In either case, continue afterwards to 78th St. and walk W to 5th Ave., to the family home that tobacco heiress Doris Duke bequeathed to New York University. It now houses the highly regarded **Institute of Fine Arts**. At 5th Ave., turn right, N, once again. A cultural annex of the **French Embassy** is housed within the building at #972, which was designed by McKim, Mead & White (see Stanford White, in WHO'S WHO). Note the vigilant iron owl perched atop the second door.

The Gothic Revival house (1899) at the next corner is the **Ukrainian Institute of America** *(open Tues-Fri 2-6pm)*, which shelters a collection of contemporary Ukrainian paintings, folk art and costumes. The choices here are to spend the next 2-3 hours in the METROPOLITAN MUSEUM OF ART, just across 5th Ave.; to pick up the Central Park walk (see WALK 5) along the pathway at the S end of the Met; or to continue N along 5th Ave. to visit, in sequence, the GUGGENHEIM MUSEUM, the JEWISH MUSEUM, the INTERNATIONAL CENTER OF PHOTOGRAPHY and the MUSEUM OF THE CITY OF NEW YORK.

Should those alternatives seem daunting, have a coffee at the sidewalk café *(summer only)* of the **Stanhope Hotel** *(81st St.)*, then go to 82nd St. and turn right. This tree-lined, unblemished block of town houses serves as a fitting approach to the Met, seen to good advantage from Madison Ave. Turn left, N, into Madison, then right, E, into 86th St. The latest occupant of #80 is **Demarchelier**. A pretty replication of a Parisian bistro, with marble-topped tables and lace curtains in the windows, it's an agreeable possibility for a reasonably priced lunch. Crossing Lexington Ave. you are in **Yorkville**. Once a village of Germans and Slavic immigrants, little is now left to lend any middle-European distinction, apart from a bierstube or two. Exceptions are the **Café Geiger** and **Kleine Konditorei** on the S side of 86th St. between 3rd and 2nd Ave., which evoke something of the atmosphere of Viennese pastry shops.

For the most part, this welter of fruit stands, fast food stores, fifth-rate hotels and banal apartment buildings is in stark contrast to the relative serenity of 5th Ave. that preceded them. Appreciate its liveliness instead, and continue E on 86th St. After York Ave., cross to the N side. Near the end of the block is **Henderson Place**, a rear-entry mews for a block of

1882 row houses that has thus far survived encroaching development. Continue to the corner of East End Ave. and turn left, N. This provides a close look at the red-brick and black-trimmed structures. They would be as much at home in London as here, and this has now been declared an official historic district. At the next corner, cross East End Ave. and walk through the entrance to CARL SCHURZ PARK. Strolling E, the building at the N end of the park is **Gracie Mansion**, erected at the turn of the 19thC and now the home of the mayor. End the walk by pausing on a bench at the lip of the East River. On the opposite bank is the borough of Queens; to the right is Roosevelt Island; and to the left, the Triborough Bridge. The nearest subway station for your round trip is back at 86th St. and Lexington Ave.

WALK 7: BROOKLYN HEIGHTS
*Allow 1-2hrs. Map **4**U6 and map on page 71. Subway: Court St. or Borough Hall*
Manhattan's first suburb and the first neighborhood to come under the protection (in 1965) of the Landmarks Preservation Commission, Brooklyn Heights is meant for leisurely meandering. Smaller than GREENWICH VILLAGE, which it resembles in part, it is less flawed by commercial shabbiness and modern architectural intrusions. Street after street is lined with restored brownstone houses, with hardy plane trees in front and gardens at the back. Lovingly maintained details of cast-iron fences, chandeliered vestibules and flower boxes on the windows are contrasted with the spectacular panorama of harbor and skyline provided by the pedestrian esplanade that hangs above the East River docks.

Start from the BMT or IRT subway stations at Court St. or Borough Hall, and walk w on nearby Remsen St. After passing St. Francis College on the left and crossing Clinton St., the first prominent building encountered is the brick-faced **Brooklyn Bar Association** (#123). Dating from 1855, it has now been elegantly restored. Turn left, s, into Henry St. In the middle of the block, on the left, is **Hunt's Lane**, a forlorn alley of carriage houses converted to residences. Continue along Henry St. to Joralemon St., turn right, then right again into Hicks St. After a few steps, wander into **Grace Court Alley** on the right. It is far more handsomely preserved than Hunt's Lane, with tubs of flowers and small trees beside the front doors. A true mews, its upper-story hay cranes are still in place, above the stables where horses were once kept. Go N again along Hicks, then left, w, into Remsen, and right, N, into **Montague Terrace**. Unlike the houses already seen, commissioned individually by their first owners, the grouping of attached residences on the right was designed as a set in 1886 and retains much of its original look. Author Thomas Wolfe lived a while at **#5**, a fact attested to by a bronze plaque. At the next corner, glance right for a tantalizing glimpse of the lower Manhattan skyline. We'll come back to that.

For the moment, turn right, E, into Montague St. proper. This, the main commercial and eating street of the community, has known its ups and downs during the gentrification of Brooklyn Heights. Once abloom with craft stores, boutiques, bookstores and gourmet and health food emporia,

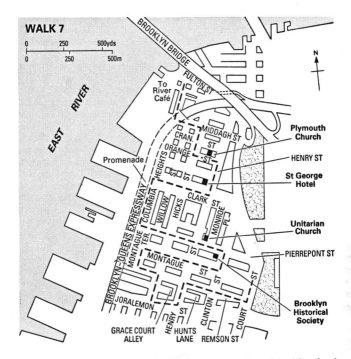

the direction in which it is now headed is uncertain. Franchised fast-food stands now intrude, and a number of buildings have fuzzy futures. One notable success, at least on the outside, is a former welfare hotel, the Bossert, now graciously remodeled for apartments. At #114 is **Lassen & Hennings Delicatessen**, its window filled with tempting arrays of cheeses and pâtés.

None of the eating places along Montague is likely to attract the attention of highbrow Manhattan restaurant critics, but they cover a range of ethnic proclivities; some have sidewalk tables. Consider **Teresa's** (#80), **FujiSan** (#130), **La Traviata** (#139) or **Rugantino** (#155).

After three blocks along Montague St. turn left, N, into Clinton St., then left again, W, into Pierrepont St. **The Brooklyn Historical Society** building on the corner, erected in 1880, shows the Classical influences in vogue at the time. Exhibits of books, paintings and artifacts related to the heritage of Long Island and New York are open to the public. Continue W along Pierrepont St. The **Unitarian Church** at the corner of Monroe Place was designed by the influential early 19thC architect Minard Lafever. Look up at the imposing turret on **#114**. It is hard to believe that the Renaissance Revival pile beneath it was once the duplicate of the Greek Revival mansion next door at **#108**.

Follow Pierrepont St. to the end. Until 1950, it ran downhill to the river's edge. A plan to run the Brooklyn-Queens Expressway through the heart of the Heights was resisted by residents, and the compromise that evolved was to stack the highway in two tiers and divert it along the westerly edge of the neighborhood. As a final fillip, it was roofed over, smothering traffic noises and exhaust fumes, and providing a 5-block promenade that bestows a glorious, unobstructed vista from the STATUE OF LIBERTY northward, past the spires of lower Manhattan, to the BROOK-LYN BRIDGE and Manhattan Bridge, and all the way to the EMPIRE STATE BUILDING.

Take it all in while strolling N, noting the trellised gardens and balconies of the narrow houses along the promenade. Near sunset is a good time, for the heavens blaze behind that famous skyline in a manner that cannot be duplicated on film. Tugboats surefootedly push barges up and down the East River, ferries glide back and forth, helicopters skim the tops of skyscrapers. The masted tall ships just s of the Manhattan end of the Brooklyn Bridge are exhibits of the SOUTH STREET SEAPORT MUSEUM.

Take the next exit right, E, into Clark St., glancing both ways as you cross Columbia Heights and then Willow St., for you might be drawn to explore them further. Down on the right on Columbia Heights, for example, is a rare clapboard house of considerable age. Beyond Hicks St., pass the once fashionable but now largely derelict **St George Hotel**, turning left, N, on Henry St., then left again, W, into Orange St. **Plymouth Church** is in mid-block, a chunky 1847 edifice. Its importance lies with its founder and first preacher, Henry Ward Beecher. An ardent opponent of slavery, he attracted the attention of Abraham Lincoln, who worshiped here, as did Charles Dickens and Mark Twain. His sister, Harriet Beecher Stowe, was the author of *Uncle Tom's Cabin.* In the fenced garden next to the church is a statue of the preacher, with a relief sculpture of the president in the wall to his right.

Proceed to Hicks St. and turn right, N. At Middagh St., named after a local burgher of the early 18thC, turn left, W. Most of the buildings along this block have been altered beyond recognition, but the splendid 1829 Federalist clapboard house at **#24** is an exception, its streetside fence enclosing a garden with a willow tree and connecting with a former servants' cottage. Step up to examine the carvings and leaded windows around the main door.

Continue to Columbia Heights. From here, you may wish to turn left (S), down to Clark St., and left again to reach the subway station at Clark and Henry Sts. Or, turn right, N, on Columbia Heights, as it dips toward the base of the **Brooklyn Bridge**, framed beneath a walkway connecting two sections of the Watchtower Building. This passage leads down to Old Fulton St. From 1814-1924 this Fulton St. was linked to the one in Manhattan by ferry.

Turn toward the river. A former fireboat house stands on the site of the old ferry terminal. For a short time, it was a modest maritime museum, now closed and falling into disrepair. Opposite it is the **Harbor View** restaurant *(1 Old Fulton St.),* which is an agreeable possibility for lunch or a drink.

But for a truly grand finale, walk N past the fireboat house to the **River Café**, in the white building at water's edge. Its staples are good-to-memorable food and an unimprovable vista. Reservations are usually necessary, but there might be a free table on the outside terrace in good weather. They'll call a taxi for the return to your hotel.

Something's always happening here.
If you're bored in New York, it's your own fault.
(Myrna Loy)

Sights and places of interest

Introduction

Few cities can rival New York for its sheer diversity — at every level of consciousness. Its monuments, theaters, galleries, and museums of art, history and technology have reputations that resound throughout the civilized world, offering visitors and residents an endless choice of cultural experiences. For a balanced picture of what the city has to offer, be sure to try to see some of the more specialized centers as well as the star attractions.

MUSEUMS AND ART GALLERIES

Many galleries and museums are expanding their collections, and some are modernizing their halls. These frequent reorganizations can mean that rooms — even entire wings — can be closed for long periods, their contents moved to other floors or into storage. Individual art-works can be withdrawn from display, perhaps to be lent to traveling exhibitions, for restoration, or even to be sold.

Complicating things further, the economic recession of the early 1990s has forced many museums to put opening hours for some wings and galleries on staggered schedules. Savings are thus made on utilities and personnel costs, but the practice can mean disappointment for visitors interested in particular exhibits. For all these reasons, detailed cataloging is impossible, and the descriptions on the pages that follow are intended to convey a general impression. Fortunately, organization in most museums and galleries is excellent, with clear labeling and helpful floor plans.

Most of the museums listed on these pages are non-profit institutions, receiving at least some public funding, which cannot, therefore, require admission fees. They get around this by asking visitors for "donations" of "suggested" amounts. This can be expensive, especially for families, so it should be remembered that paying less than the suggested donation is entirely legal. (But do pay a reasonable amount — they need the money.) Discounts are usually given to persons over 62 or 65 and to students, and many museums welcome visitors without charge for a few hours one day or night a week.

> Our admiration of the antique is not admiration of the old
> but of the natural.
> (Emerson, *Essays, First Series: History*)

OTHER SIGHTS

The pleasures of New York are not confined to its museums and monuments. It is a very walkable city, as is demonstrated by the routes suggested on the preceding pages. There are few slopes to climb, let alone hills, and many distinctive neighborhoods to explore. Some of these — Chinatown and Little Italy, for two examples — are villages complete in themselves, while others — SoHo, TriBeCa, the Flatiron District — are recycled areas once dormant, alive with the new and respectful of the old.

The favorite stories that every visitor takes home are invariably of happy accidents and chance meetings. There was that young man on Times Square with a pet python draped around his neck, the worker unloading a piano in Greenwich Village who sat down to play a little ragtime right there on the sidewalk. Take advantage of the stroll from subway to obligatory sight to note the smaller details — the windows on the **New York Yacht Club** on W 44th St., carved to resemble the sterns of ancient galleons; the row of painted iron jockeys on the veranda of the **21 Club**; the mimes who work the crowds on the steps of the METROPOLITAN MUSEUM OF ART and the fiddlers and rappers in Washington Square Park.

HOW TO USE THIS SECTION

If you wish to find a quiet retreat from the madding crowds of Manhattan, consult OASES, for some suggestions on free resting places. Comprehensive lists are given, which will allow you an at-a-glance view of the number and type of sights, and districts, that are described in detail on the following 81 pages.

Look for the ★ symbol next to the most important sights and ▥ for buildings of great architectural interest. Good views (◀€) and places of special interest for children (✿) are also indicated. Many, but not all museums are closed on Monday. The MUSEUM OF MODERN ART, one of the most important, is closed on Wednesday instead. Check the listings below or call ahead before making special trips.

Sights classified by type

BRIDGES AND TUNNELS
Brooklyn-Battery Tunnel
Brooklyn Bridge 🏛 ★ ◁€
George Washington Bridge
Holland Tunnel
Queensboro Bridge
Queens-Midtown Tunnel
Verrazano Narrows Bridge
CHURCHES AND SYNAGOGUES
Cathedral Church of St John The
Divine 🏛
Central Synagogue
Church of the Ascension 🏛
Church of the Transfiguration
Grace Church 🏛
Judson Memorial Baptist Church
🏛
Marble Collegiate Church 🏛
Riverside Church 🏛
St Bartholomew's Church 🏛
St Mark's-In-The-Bowery 🏛
St Patrick's Cathedral 🏛 ★
St Paul's Chapel 🏛
Temple Emanu-El
Trinity Church 🏛
COLLEGES AND UNIVERSITIES
Columbia University 🏛
Cooper Union
New York University 🏛
Yeshiva University
DISTRICTS
The Bowery
Brooklyn Heights 🏛 ◁€
Chelsea
Chinatown
Coney Island
East Side ★
Financial District ★
Flatiron District
Garment Center
Gramercy Park 🏛
Greenwich Village 🏛 ★
Harlem
Little Italy
Lower East Side
Midtown East
Murray Hill
Pomander Walk
SoHo ★

Theater District
TriBeCa
Turtle Bay
Upper West Side
Yorkville
EXHIBITION HALLS
AT&T InfoQuest Center ♣
Forbes Magazine Galleries ♣
Guinness World Records Exhibit
Hall ♣
IBM Gallery of Science and Art
Jacob K. Javits Convention Center
Seventh Regiment Armory
HISTORIC BUILDINGS
Abigail Adams Smith Museum 🏛
Bouwerie Lane Theatre
Castle Clinton Monument 🏛
City Hall 🏛
Dakota Apartments 🏛
Dyckman House 🏛
Ellis Island ★
Federal Hall National Memorial
🏛
Gracie Mansion 🏛
Grand Central Terminal 🏛
Morris-Jumel Mansion 🏛
Old Merchant's House
New York Stock Exchange
Richmondtown Restoration 🏛 ★
Snug Harbor Cultural Center 🏛
Theodore Roosevelt Birthplace
Van Cortlandt Mansion and
Museum 🏛
Villard Houses 🏛
LIBRARIES
American Bible Society
New York Public Library
Pierpont Morgan Library 🏛
MONUMENTS
Cleopatra's Needle
General Grant National Memorial
Hall of Fame for Great Americans
Statue of Liberty ★
MUSEUMS OF ART
American Academy and Institute
of Arts and Letters
American Craft Museum
Americas Society
Asia Society

Audubon Terrace
The Cloisters ⅏ ★ ◁€
Cooper-Hewitt Museum
Frick Collection ★
Guggenheim Museum ⅏ ★
International Center of
  Photography
Metropolitan Museum of Art
  ⅏ ★ ❀
Museo del Barrio
Museum of American Folk Art
Museum of American Illustration
Museum of Modern Art ★
National Academy of Design
New Museum of Contemporary Art
Queens Museum of Art
Studio Museum in Harlem
Whitney Museum of American Art
  ⅏ ★

MUSEUMS OF HISTORY AND CULTURE
American Museum of the Moving
  Image ❀
American Museum of Natural
  History ⅏ ★ ❀
American Numismatic Society
Aunt Len's Doll and Toy
  Museum ❀
Brooklyn Museum
China Institute
Fraunces Tavern Museum
French Institute
Goethe House
Hispanic Society of America
Jacques Marchais Center of
  Tibetan Art
Japan House
Jewish Museum
Museum of the City of New York
  ★ ❀
National Museum of the American
  Indian
New York City Fire Museum ❀
New-York Historical Society
Police Academy Museum
South Street Seaport ⅏ ★ ❀
Spanish Institute
Ukrainian Museum
Yeshiva University Museum

**MUSEUMS OF SCIENCE AND
TECHNOLOGY**
AT&T InfoQuest Center ❀
Children's Museum of Manhattan ❀

Hayden Planetarium ❀
Intrepid Sea-Air-Space Museum ❀
Museum of Television & Radio ❀

MUSIC AND SPORTS HALLS
Carnegie Hall
Lincoln Center ⅏
Madison Square Garden

PARKS AND GARDENS
Battery Park
Bowling Green
Brooklyn Botanic Garden
Bryant Park
Carl Schurz Park
Central Park ★
Fort Tryon Park
Greenacre Park
New York Botanical Garden
"Oases"
Paley Park
Prospect Park
Riverside Park
Union Square
Washington Square ⅏
Wave Hill Center for
  Environmental Studies

**SKYSCRAPERS AND MODERN
ARCHITECTURE**
AT&T Building ⅏
Chrysler Building ⅏
Citicorp Center
Empire State Building
  ⅏ ★ ❀ ◁€
Equitable Center
Ford Foundation Building ⅏
Flatiron Building ⅏
GE (RCA) Building ⅏
Lever House ⅏
Lipstick Building
News Building
Pan Am Building
Rockefeller Center ⅏ ★
Seagram Building ⅏
Trump Tower
United Nations Headquarters
Woolworth Building ⅏
World Financial Center ⅏
World Trade Center ⅏ ◁€

ZOOS AND AQUARIUM
Bronx Zoo ★ ❀
Central Park Zoo ❀
New York Aquarium ❀
Staten Island Zoo ❀

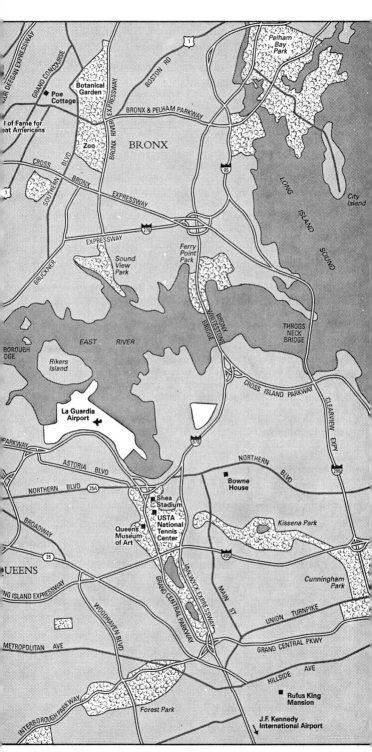

New York sights A to Z

ABIGAIL ADAMS SMITH MUSEUM 血
421 E 61st St. (1st Ave.), NY 10021 ☎*838-6878. Map 6N5* ☒
✗compulsory. Open Mon-Fri noon-4pm; Sun 1-5pm. Closed Sat, Aug ◙*for children under 12.*

An unexpected retreat amid the feverish pace of the East Side, this 1799 carriage house sits on a slope behind stone retaining walls, a fetching remnant of the Federalist era. The estate it served was owned by William Stephens Smith, but the titular tenant was his wife, the daughter of the eventual second President of the United States. She didn't stay long. After dismemberment of the property, it became a residence in 1826.

The house remained in private hands until its purchase in 1924 by the Colonial Dames of America. That organization still has its headquarters here, and maintains several exhibition rooms. Most of the furnishings are of the early 19thC, although they have not been traced to the original owners.

AMERICAN ACADEMY AND INSTITUTE OF ARTS AND LETTERS   Part of the AUDUBON TERRACE museum complex, this is primarily a society of prominent artists and thinkers. Exhibitions of an eclectic nature are laid on at certain times.

AMERICAN BIBLE SOCIETY
1865 Broadway (61st St.), NY 10023 ☎*406-1200. Map 5N3* ◙ *✗for groups. Open Mon-Fri 9am-5pm. Closed Sat, Sun.*

More than 38,000 volumes are on permanent display, including scraps of the Dead Sea Scrolls, pages from the 15thC Gutenberg Bible, and Braille editions once owned by Helen Keller.

AMERICAN CRAFT MUSEUM ☆
40 W 53rd St. (6th Ave.), NY 10019 ☎*956-3535. Map 6N4* ☒ *Open Wed-Sun 10am-5pm; Tues 10am-8pm. Closed Mon. Half-price entry for senior citizens and students* ◙ *under 12s.*

Wit, panache, and impeccable workmanship mark the ever-changing displays of antique and contemporary works, the latter often blurring the line that once separated crafts from pure art. The handsome new three-level building is opposite the MUSEUM OF MODERN ART. There is a library branch at 77 W 45th St.

AMERICAN MUSEUM OF THE MOVING IMAGE ☆
35th Ave. and 36th St., Astoria (Queens), NY 10006 ☎*718-784-0077* ☒ *✗ ♣ Open Tues-Fri noon-4pm; Sat, Sun noon-6pm. Closed Mon. Subway R or G train to Steinway St.*

Film-making in America began not in the Hollywood Hills but in and around New York City. Much of it took place here in Astoria, continuing from the earliest days of the silents to the first talkies. The Marx Brothers, Gary Cooper, and Claudette Colbert were only a few of the stars who appeared before the cameras of the Astoria studios. The old sound stages have now been refurbished, and a three-floor studio building has been set aside for this fascinating museum.

Movies, television shows, and videos are the featured attractions, but are by no means the extent of the 70,000-item collection. Memorabilia and artifacts are as ephemeral as old fan magazines, tin lunch boxes with inept portraits of actors, Disney toys, posters, costumes, and Cher dolls; as nostalgic as bulky models of 1940s TV receivers, and complete stage sets. A wide net is cast, including an amusing send-up by artist Red Grooms of extravagantly ornate old-time movie palaces, and a hi-tech theater capable of screening both ancient nitrate prints and the latest 70-millimeter spectacles.

AMERICAN MUSEUM OF NATURAL HISTORY 🏛 ★

Central Park W (79th St.), NY 10024 ☎ 769-5100. Map 7L3 🖼 (🔲Fri, Sat 5-9pm) 𝒦 ⚿ ☀ Open Sun-Thurs 10am-5.45pm; Fri, Sat 10am-8.45pm (but budgetary considerations may cause earlier closing).

Beloved by generations of schoolchildren for its realistic animal dioramas and models of Indian villages, the museum interprets its mission in the broadest terms. Appealing as the exhibits of mounted Alaskan bears and African lions unquestionably are, adults are drawn to the halls highlighting the crafts, costumes, jewelry, masks, and artifacts of the peoples of Asia, Mexico, and pre-colonial North America. The collections, begun in 1874, include 34 million items, from a 94-foot (29m) model of a blue whale to the fabled Star of India.

Calvert Vaux, who shared credit for Central Park, worked with Jacob Wrey Mould on the first building (1877). So many additions were made from then until 1933, however, that only a portion of it is still visible, and that from the rear. Critics cite the southern red granite facade as a superior example of the Romanesque Revival. Perhaps so, if one's notion of romantic architecture derives from ponderous Teutonic fortresses. The main entrance, dominated by a 1939 equestrian statue of President Theodore Roosevelt, is even less graceful. Yet in spite of the forbidding exterior, this great museum qualifies as an obligatory stop.

For maximum impact, choose the W 77th St. entrance rather than the one on Central Park W. Directly beyond the door leading to the first (ground) floor is an impressively scaled ocean-going canoe of a British Columbian tribe. (Adjoining rooms are devoted to North American mammals, birds and invertebrates, meteorites and gems.) The prow of the canoe points at a staircase, which you should ascend to the second (main) floor. On the left is the **Hall of Asian Peoples**, one of the most ambitious sections of the museum. In a masterful mix of scholarship and showmanship, its displays chart the progress of Eurasian cultures from prehistory to the recent past, employing every imaginable device to delineate the evolutionary stages of religion, commerce, language, art and science.

Returning to the main hall, pass beneath the sign for the **Birds of the World** hall and you soon come to the galleries of **African Peoples**, on the right. Covering societies of desert and bush, veldt and jungle, the museum uses models of irrigation systems, examples of fishing techniques, dance and worship, and tribal government, all to the strains of appropriate recorded music. Make a counter-clockwise loop of the rooms, returning to the "Birds" hall. Turn right, and walk straight ahead into an area of exhibits concerned with the arts and histories of the pre-Columbian Indian societies of Mexico and Central America. The first space is dominated by a huge Olmec head, carved from a single stone and weighing 20 tons. Along the walls are examples of pottery, ceramic sculptures and ornaments from specific cultures, primarily Mayan, Aztec and Olmec.

At the far end is the museum's newest addition, opened in 1988: the **Hall of South American Peoples**. Children are certain to take grisly delight in the assembled shrunken heads and blowpipes of the Amazon rainforest, in the gallery at the far end of the hall. Their parents may prefer to veer toward the archeological artifacts of the Andes. Layout and display methods are similar to those used in the preceding African and Asian halls.

After visiting these rooms, return again to the main hall and ascend the staircase immediately on the left, to the third floor. At the top of the stairs, bear right. The first rooms are concerned with Indians of the American woodlands and plains, followed by a gallery of aboriginal cultures of the Pacific, where homage is paid to the work of anthropologist Margaret Mead. Return to the main hall, which is devoted to primates. Straight ahead is one of the museum stores, followed by galleries allocated for temporary exhibitions.

Beyond that are the reptiles and amphibians, then, bearing left, the **African Hall**. Circle the mezzanine, gazing down upon the herd of elephants on the floor below. Most of the animal exhibits are mounted in large glass cases, with replicas of their habitats, executed with considerable ingenuity and artistry.

Exiting from the same door, turn right and go up the stairs on the left to the fourth floor. Here are the famous reassembled **dinosaur skeletons**, a children's favorite. The awesome *Tyrannosaurus Rex,* which figures in so many Grade B fantasy movies, is a particular star. Unfortunately, extensive renovations are underway, scheduled to take several years, and many of the dinosaur exhibits are behind closed doors. The museum promises to rotate fossils into view throughout the long process, however.

In addition to the basement cafeteria, there is a cocktail lounge in the lobby on certain days, and tables set around hot-dog carts on the front steps in summer. **Nature Max** (☎ *769-5650)* is a theater with one of the two largest screens in New York, for the showing of relevant films. Traveling shows, lectures, and music and dance programs augment the permanent exhibitions.

Hayden Planetarium
Central Park W (81st St.), NY 10024 ☎ *769-5920* ■■ ✚ *Open Mon-Fri 12.30-4.45pm; Sat 10am-5.45pm; Sun noon-5.45pm. Laser show (extra ▨) Fri, Sat 7.30pm, 9pm and 10pm. Special shows Mon-Fri 1.30pm and 3.30pm; Sat, Sun 1pm, 2pm, 3pm and 4pm. Extra shows during holiday weeks and July-Sept. Admission includes AMERICAN MUSEUM OF NATURAL HISTORY, which has an entrance on the first floor.*

Since 1935, the artful technology of the Hayden Planetarium has reproduced on its domed ceiling the movements of constellations, planets, and meteor showers. Seasonal shows focus on the "Star of Wonder," nebulae and stellar formations, and the projected end of the world through astronomical accident. Music and commentary supplement the one-hour presentations, and there are "cosmic laser concerts" (☎ 769-5921 for times and prices).

Saturday mornings are set aside for programs designed for preschoolers and children aged 7-12, but they might be just as enthralled by the regular shows. Just observing the $2\frac{1}{2}$-ton projector in action is worth the admission.

AMERICAN NUMISMATIC SOCIETY   Housing a large collection of coins and medals, this is part of the AUDUBON TERRACE complex.

AMERICAS SOCIETY
680 Park Ave. (68th St.), NY 10021 ☎ *249-8950. Map 8M4* 🖼 ✘ *by appointment. Open Tues-Sun noon-6pm. Closed Mon.*
The architectural firm of McKim, Mead & White was responsible for many notable buildings of the late 19th and early 20thC in New York, and a substantial number of them still exist. Perhaps because the third and most famous partner, Stanford White (see WHO'S WHO, page 22), died at the hands of a jealous husband in 1906, this 1909 structure is a Neo-Georgian departure from the Italianate preferences of their earlier projects.

After a period as home for the Soviet Delegation to the United Nations, one of the many Rockefellers bought the building and gave it to the Center for Inter-American Relations, which is now known as the Americas Society. Although arts and crafts of every country and age of the Western Hemisphere are exhibited in the gallery, the emphasis is on Latin America.

ASIA SOCIETY
725 Park Ave. (E 70th St.), NY 10021 ☎ *288-6400. Map 8M4* 🖼 ✘ *Open Tues-Sat 11am-6pm; Sun noon-5pm. Closed Mon.*
A striking addition to a bland stretch of Park Ave., the 1981 headquarters of the Asia Society echoes imperial palaces of India, with its facing of alternately polished and textured red granite. The gallery floors house one of the many benefactions of the Rockefeller family: in this case, the collection of Nepalese and Chinese artifacts assembled by John D. III. That is not the extent of the holdings, however, and there are supplementary loan exhibitions 3-4 times a year, as well as films, lectures and recitals.

This is not a formal museum, operating within the strictures of scholarship, and the objects on display reflect the individual tastes of the contributors. Fortunately, however, those predilections are disciplined and educated. Sculptured metal and polychromed ceramics mingle with ancient many-armed buddhas from Kampuchea and fierce feline temple guardians.

AT&T BUILDING 𝔐

*550 Madison Ave. (56th St.), NY 10022. Map **6N4***

The monolithic American Telephone & Telegraph Company commissioned this building (pictured on page 27) as their world headquarters in 1978. Philip Johnson and John Burgee were responsible for the design, widely regarded as the first major reaction to the austerity of the long-dominant "International Style." It was heralded (or decried) as a Post-Modernist leap backwards to the use of decorative details inspired by the various architectural revivals of the last century.

The principal departure from dogma was the broken pediment cap, said to resemble that atop a Chippendale secretary or chest of drawers. The base of the building is open, the wind swirling through columns and arches intended to evoke a classical grandeur. It is, instead, empty, echoing, and inhospitable. SONY Corporation, the new owner, has proposed modifications that would enclose the open spaces with glass and create a shopping arcade.

AT&T Infoquest Center

AT&T Building ☎*605-5555* 🖾 ✽ *Open Tues 10am-9pm; Wed-Sun 10am-6pm. Closed Mon.*

A glass elevator zips to the fourth floor, where each visitor receives a specially-programed "access card" to the exhibits. As might be expected of the corporate sponsor, these are concerned with all aspects of telecommunications. The presentations demonstrate the workings of photonics, video, fiberoptics, microelectronics, and computer software, but are hardly dry or stuffy. They are slick displays, blinking, chattering, beeping, gleaming. Children, who understand these things better than their elders, gleefully punch messages into keyboards, manipulate robot arms, and talk to computers.

AUDUBON TERRACE

Broadway at 155th St. See ORIENTATION MAP on pages 78-9. Subway 1 to 157th St.; AA, B to 155th St.

Gathered around a Neoclassical plaza in a NW precinct of Harlem is a remarkable complex of four museums and associated societies. While they are not all individually of great importance, as a group they rival all but a handful of the city's cultural repositories. Only their location has denied them the recognition they deserve. Unfortunately, it is soon to lose its centerpiece, the *Museum of the American Indian,* and the complex is likely to have even lower attendance figures.

Ornithologist John James Audubon owned this property at the crest of the slope above the Hudson River and intermittently lived here from 1825 until his death in 1851. It was purchased by a speculator, who was convinced that the steady northward thrust of the city would eventually make him rich. When it became clear that growth had stabilized at a point 5 miles s, the tract changed hands. A master plan was drawn up in 1908, and the present buildings were completed by 1926. They can be characterized as of the Beaux Arts mode, with a typical Greco-Renaissance mix. All the buildings are clustered in the block abutting Broadway between W 155th St. and W 156th St.

Museum of the American Indian

☎ 283-2420 ▨ *Open Tues-Sat 10am-5pm; Sun 1-5pm. Closed Mon.*
The largest repository of Native American artifacts anywhere, with more than one million items on display and in storage, this museum is of particular interest to overseas visitors who plan to go no farther w than Manhattan. Even three large, crammed (if skillfully organized) floors can contain no more than a small portion of the acquisitions. By 1993 (or thereabouts), part of this collection is to be moved to the United States Customs House, downtown near Battery Park, where it will become the **National Museum of the American Indian**. The rest will go to the Smithsonian Institution in Washington, DC.

Hispanic Society of America

☎ 926-2234 ▣ *Open Tues-Sat 10am-4.30pm; Sun 1-4pm. Closed Mon.*
The entrance is marked by an equestrian bronze of *El Cid,* the 11thC Spanish hero — a fitting choice for a museum that concerns itself with Iberian rather than Latin American culture and history. At the very minimum, step into the splendid main hall and savor the rosy blush of terracotta Renaissance arches and ornamentation. During certain hours, light through the two-story skylight heightens the play of intricate shadow on carved scrollwork and panels.

Of conventional interest are the canvases and drawings of El Greco, Velázquez and Goya. But the Spain of the Catholic kings is upstaged by that of the earlier Moors, with tiled chambers and relics of exquisite workmanship. The Roman and Visigothic occupations are represented as well, and there is a substantial library of pre-1700 books.

American Numismatic Society

☎ 234-3130 ▣ *Open Tues-Sat 9am-4.30pm; Sun 1-4pm. Closed Mon. Ring bell for entry.*
The first floor is given over to a large display of coins, medals and banknotes, the second floor to a specialist library.

American Academy and Institute of Arts and Letters

☎ 368-5900 ▣ *Open Tues-Sun 1-4pm. Closed Mon. Telephone first to confirm hours and exhibitions.*
Primarily an association of celebrated artists and intellectuals, not unlike its French counterpart, this institution mounts exhibitions on a range of subjects, from ancient manuscripts to architectural themes.

AUNT LEN'S DOLL AND TOY MUSEUM

6 Hamilton Terrace (W 141st St.), NY 10031 ☎ *281-4143. See ORIENTATION MAP on pages 78-9* ▨ *𝄪 ✤ Advance appointment essential. Subway 1 to 137th St.*
An enthusiasm for collecting has a way of getting out of hand — in this case, to the delight of parents and children alike. "Aunt Len" was a local schoolteacher who gathered more than 5,000 dolls, miniature houses with scale furniture, mechanical and clockwork toys, dolls' carriages and accessories. When Leon Holder Hoyte saw what she had done, she decided to give everyone else a chance to share it. Every corner and surface is crowded with her acquisitions, and the effect is magical. A visit might be combined with a trip to the several museums of AUDUBON TERRACE, some 14 blocks to the N.

BATTERY PARK

Battery Pl. and State St. (foot of Broadway). Map 1V4.

Named for a rank of cannon that defended the old town from uncertain foes — presumably British — after the Revolution, the present 21 acres of Battery Park occupy the w rim of the extreme s tip of Manhattan. Financial District workers eat their packed lunches in view of the STATUE OF LIBERTY, ELLIS ISLAND and the now diminished but no less beguiling harbor traffic.

Other attractions are the **Verrazano Memorial**, commemorating the Italian explorer who first saw New York Bay in 1524, and the CASTLE CLINTON NATIONAL MONUMENT, once on an islet but later joined by landfill to what is now the park. The **ferries** taking passengers to the Statue of Liberty and Ellis Island depart from piers at the edge of the park, and the ferry to Staten Island is nearby.

BOUWERIE LANE THEATRE

330 Bowery (Bond St.). NY 10012 ☎ *677-0060. Map 3R4* ☒ *Open for theatrical performances.*

Vaguely resembling a set of stacked Greek temples, at least in its five floors of cast-iron columns with Ionic and Corinthian capitals, the building was commissioned by a bank in 1874. It was converted into an off-Broadway theater in 1963, and at last look was the home of the Jean Cocteau Repertory Company.

THE BOWERY

Map 3R4-4T5.

A country road, dating from the time of the original Dutch colony, the "Bouwerie" retained its bucolic status into the 19thC. It went downhill from there — apart from a brief revival in the 1890s as a place for bawdy music halls — and rapidly slid into utter despair. It remains a grimy concentration of dosshouses and bars, the most visible inhabitants of which are men and women made homeless by alcoholism, drug addiction, madness and misfortune.

Since manifestations of those grim phenomena are now painfully apparent all over the city, The Bowery no longer ranks as a tourist attraction, a status that was always a mystery. There are, however, a handful of useful discount kitchenware, lighting and home furnishing stores at the CHINATOWN end of the street.

BOWLING GREEN

Battery Pl. (foot of Broadway). Map 1U4.

This oval green once hosted early Colonial bowlers, under the eyes of a statue of George III. It was the city's first park, leased in 1733 at a rent of one peppercorn per year. True to revolutionary tradition, the monument to the king was pulled down in 1776; the fence that still encloses the green dates from then. For a long time, it was the only lingering element of even minor historical or visual interest, but the green and its benches have been restored, and a fountain and circular pool have been added.

BRONX ZOO ★

Southern Blvd. (185th St.), Bronx, NY 10460 ☎*367-1010. See ORIENTATION MAP on pages 78-9* ➥ 🔲 *Wed* 🔳 *Fri-Tues. Modest extra charges for a few special sections; also for tractor train, aerial tram and monorail* ✗ *free by appointment* ☎*220-5141* 💺 ✦ ➥ 🌿 *Open Mon-Fri 10am-5pm; Sat, Sun, holidays 10am-5.30pm (4.30pm in winter). Most outdoor exhibits, and all rides, closed in winter (roughly Nov-Apr). Subway 2 to Pelham Parkway.*

Many New York attractions are as engaging as ever, others are in decline, but few have actually improved in recent years. The Bronx Zoo falls into this last felicitous category. Along with the NEW YORK BOTANICAL GARDEN, it is one of the best reasons to venture over the Harlem River. Known as the New York Zoological Park when it was inaugurated in 1899, it is now the largest urban zoo in the US, with more than 4,000 animals of 800 species, deployed in imaginative settings carved out of the hills and meadows of 265 acres. Because such diversity can cause indecision, the management have provided the means to obtain overviews and thereby make choices.

In addition to free **walking tours** on Saturday and Sunday (☎*220-5141),* and the **Zoo Shuttle** tractor tram, the **Skyfari aerial tram** glides over the African Plains section, and the **Bengali Express monorail** meanders about **Wild Asia**, where tigers and elephants roam free.

To proceed in an orderly manner on foot, begin at the **Fordham Rd.** entrance, called the Rainey Gate. This leads to the earliest part of the zoo, the formal Baird Court, centering on the **Seal Pool**, around which are arranged the **Aquatic Birds, Carnivores, Monkeys, Elephants**, and a giant bird enclosure called the **Flying Cage**. Pause by the 3-acre **Bison Range** for a look at the beasts that once roamed over thousands of square miles of the Old West. Beyond that is the 1972 **World of Birds**, through which you can pass in the company of more than 500 birds, with no interceding screens.

The 1908 Beaux-Arts Elephant House has been transformed into the **Zoo Center**, with audio-visual displays. To the s is a popular group of buildings sheltering the **Reptiles, Penguins** and **Gorillas**. Nearby is the fascinating **World of Darkness**, where a variety of nocturnal creatures are fooled by artificial lighting into believing that day is night.

Apart from these necessary structures, animals are at liberty in much of the park, in simulated habitats. Cleverly camouflaged moats keep them apart and protect the public. The Skyfari aerial tram carries observers above the remarkably convincing veldt of the **African Plains**, and you can look down on moving lion prides, antelope and deer.

The park embraces a stretch of the Bronx River, wide enough here to be called a lake. Most exhibits are to the w, but **Wild Asia** takes up the E bank. The concept is similar to the African Plains area, but the Bengali Express monorail follows a looping route around the perimeter and across the river. Fences separating clusters of rare animals from the Asian Subcontinent are the only element detracting from the carefully staged natural environment.

Throughout the park are specimens no longer found in the wild. In the **Children's Zoo**, young and gentle animals are available for petting

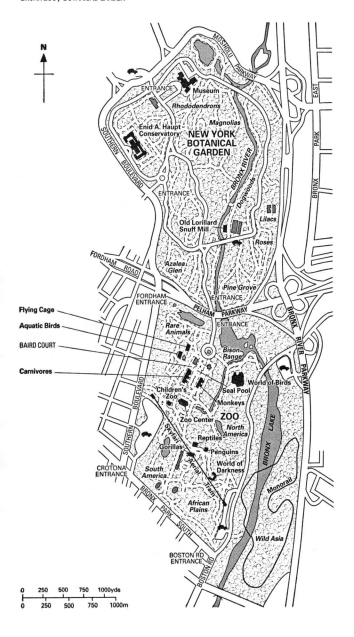

and feeding. Watching animals eat is inexplicably fascinating to most people. Here, they can witness the feeding of the sea lions at 3pm daily, the penguins at 11am and 3.45pm and, on Monday and Thursday at 2pm, the crocodiles, who take longer to digest.

BROOKLYN-BATTERY TUNNEL
Map 1V4 ⊠

Master builder Robert Moses intended an overwater span at this site, just s of the BROOKLYN BRIDGE, to connect lower Manhattan with the Belt Parkway, which skirts the edge of Long Island on the way to JFK Airport. Despite his clout as the most powerful city planner of his time — from the early 1930s into the 1960s — he bowed to public pressure and settled for a tunnel. At nearly 2 miles, it is the longest vehicular tunnel in the US.

BROOKLYN BOTANIC GARDEN
1000 Washington Ave. (Eastern Parkway), Brooklyn, NY 11225 ☎622-4433.
See ORIENTATION MAP on pages 78-9 ⊡ for grounds ⊠ for Japanese Garden and Steinhardt Conservatory ✘ Open Apr-Sept Tues-Fri 8am-6pm; Sat and Sun, public holidays 10am-6pm and Oct-Mar Tues-Fri 8am-4.30pm; Sat and Sun, public holidays 10am-4.30pm. Closed Mon. Subway 2 or 3 to Eastern Parkway-Brooklyn Museum.

Although much smaller than its big brother in the Bronx (see NEW YORK BOTANICAL GARDEN) a visit to the Brooklyn Botanic Garden is nonetheless worthwhile, especially in concert with a visit to the neighboring BROOKLYN MUSEUM. Specialized gardens include one with fragrances for the blind, another exclusively of roses, one of herbs, three authentic Japanese settings supplemented by a superb bonsai display, and an ebullient horticultural tribute to Shakespeare, incorporating 80 plant species mentioned in his plays.

The restrained Victorian conservatory was designed by the McKim, Mead & White firm in 1918, and was restored in 1989 and incorporated into the new **Steinhardt Conservatory**. That grand 55,000 square-feet facility has three octagonal pavilions that echo but improve upon the designs of their forerunners and are devoted to collections from tropical, temperate, and desert zones. They make the Garden a more compelling attraction than ever.

BROOKLYN BRIDGE ⋔ ★
Map 4T5-U6 ⊡ ⫷

Perhaps the most spectacular engineering achievement of its time, the enduring grace of the 486m (1,595-foot) span has inspired paeans by painters and poets. John Roebling conceived it in 1857, but construction did not begin until 1869. There was skepticism about its feasibility, the need for a bridge across a river well-served by ferry lines, and the projected expense. In the manner of public projects, those costs routinely multiplied, eventually totaling the then-stunning sum of nearly $16 million. Since construction paralleled the reign of one of New York's most corrupt political regimes, it is assumed that undetermined portions of the budgeted funds were diverted to the accounts of the notorious Boss Tweed and his cronies.

Roebling died in the first year of construction, contracting tetanus after his foot was crushed by a docking ferry. His son Washington took over. While rising from an underwater chamber, he suffered an attack of the bends and was permanently disabled. Although confined to a wheelchair, he oversaw the project to its conclusion, employing his wife Emily as a go-between. Thousands of new immigrants, largely Irish and Italian, labored 14 years on the project. Uncounted numbers died, many of them victims of the hazards associated with the nascent technology.

Six days after the opening on May 24, 1883, a rumor that the bridge was collapsing raced through the festive crowd of sightseers. There were 12 fatalities in the ensuing panic. Since then, the 133-foot (40m) height of the span has proved tempting to the foolhardy and suicidal. At least 34 jumpers have not survived the fall.

Despite early doubts about its stability, there is every reason to believe that the *grande dame* of New York bridges will be there when today's youngest pedestrians bring their grandchildren. There are incomparable **vistas** of East River traffic and the lower Manhattan skyline from the elevated walkway.

BROOKLYN HEIGHTS ⛫
Map 4U6.

In 1646, a handful of Dutch families decided to give official status to their settlement on the bluffs overlooking the juncture of the Hudson and East rivers and the larger village at the toe of Manhattan Island. They called their new home "Breuckelen" ("broken land"). The establishment of a regular steam ferry service in 1820 transformed the rural community into a suburb. Shipping magnates and wealthy merchants chose to move in, insulated from the traumas of the troubled city and yet in a position to monitor river traffic. Their terraced row houses and mansions competed in harbor vistas and luxury of appointments. A substantial number persisted into the 20thC, but by the 1950s, Brooklyn Heights was in decline.

A plan to ram a highway through the neighborhood was narrowly averted, and the resulting community spirit signaled its renaissance. Now designated an Historic District, it is the most desirable residential enclave in the borough. (See WALK 7 on pages 70-3.)

BROOKLYN MUSEUM
188 Eastern Parkway (Washington Ave.), Brooklyn, NY 11238 ☎ 638-5000. See ORIENTATION MAP *on pages 78-9* ⛫ **𝒓** ⬛ *Open Wed-Mon 10am-5pm. Closed Tues. Subway 2, 3 to Eastern Parkway-Brooklyn Museum.*

Despite a history of fiscal uncertainty, this fine institution has launched a massive expansion project that probably won't be completed until the year 2030. This ambitious undertaking will double the size of what is already one of the largest museums in the US. It has long been the keystone of the borough's cultural and recreational complex, which includes the adjacent BROOKLYN BOTANIC GARDEN, PROSPECT PARK and ZOO, and the **Brooklyn Public Library**. The museum must be ranked among the most important in the city, and it might have challenged even the nonpareil METROPOLITAN MUSEUM OF ART, if the initial plans of the architectural firm of McKim, Mead & White had been carried out. As it is, the scaled-down scheme that was erected at the turn of the century is an imposing Neoclassical pile, flawed only by a misguided 1930s modernization that removed the noble exterior staircase. Some compensation for this desecration is provided by the two 1916 Daniel Chester French **statues**, which were moved outside onto pedestals in 1963.

Inside are five floors of arts and antiquities spanning centuries and continents from Egypt to Oceania. Exhibits are grouped essentially along geographical or societal lines. The planned expansion will bring with it many upheavals, and the precise location of some parts of the collection may not always be as given below. However, for the lifetime of this edition, what follows is likely to remain true.

The first floor is devoted to the **arts and crafts of the primitive** (or at least pre-colonial) **peoples of the Americas, Africa and the South Pacific**. Totem poles of the NW tribes loom over cases of New Guinean ceremonial masks, Columbian ritual urns, Inca jewelry, Hopi and Zuni dolls, African fetishes and weapons. Adjacent rooms house a gallery reserved for art shows drawn from the Brooklyn community, a cafeteria, and a museum shop that purveys a remarkable array of crafts from around the world at reasonable prices.

On the second floor are **arts of Asia and Islam**, spotlighting ceramics, rugs, textiles, paintings, metal and jade secular and religious objects from India, China, Persia, Japan, Tibet and Indochina. A separate print room encompasses European and American graphic arts from the 14th-20thC.

The pride of the museum is the collection of **relics of Dynastic and Coptic Egypt** on the third floor, with sarcophagi mingling with alabaster figurines and an ebony sphinx. Of particular interest are the **Assyrian reliefs** in the Kevorkian Gallery, just beyond the elevator vestibule. The wall sculptures, some from the Palace of Ashurnasirpal II, depict winged deities and griffin-headed genies. With them are ceremonial vessels, partly animal-shaped, and engraved silver bowls.

Enter, then, into an unexpectedly dramatic inner court ringed with shallow cases of exquisite objects ranging from Egyptian to Cypriot and Greek: amulets, amphoras, glass bottles as fragile as paper, beakers, fragments of textiles, busts of monarchs. Additional rooms are given to still more jewelry, pottery and funerary pieces.

The fourth floor is devoted to **furniture and decorative arts**, largely of the 17th and 18thC, but also including the early Colonial period and some Manhattan Art Deco. The **Jan Martense Schenck House**, a Dutch 2-room dwelling of New York c.1675, is reconstructed and fully furnished with authentic pieces. There is also a costume institute. Near the fifth floor entrance is a lush **landscape** by the 19thC American Albert Bierstadt, overpowering the viewer with its rolling thunderclouds, shafts of light, alpine cascades and snowy peaks. The smaller canvases of the Hudson

River School that follow are pale by comparison, but are momentarily diverting. The first doorway leads into the East Galleries, reserved for **European painting**. After the glories of the first and third floors, these are disappointingly minor works by important artists. The supposed highlight is *Mlle. Fiorre in the Ballet La Source,* a very early (1866) Degas that looks merely half-finished and gives barely a hint of the off-center composition that was to become his hallmark. Next to it are two minor Corots.

The rest of the room holds portraits of modest distinction and some bucolic scenes by Millet. A small room of preliminary studies in pastels and gouache includes an appealing Toulouse-Lautrec, alongside drawings by Manet, Gauguin, Degas and Pissarro. They and their compatriots Renoir, Monet and Cézanne are represented in the last room by larger oils that demand little attention. In the **Cantor Gallery**, however, are a number of robust Rodin bronzes, recently reinstalled after years in storage. On the way out of this section, note the 15th and 16thC Italian religious paintings on wood. The rest of the floor is normally used for special exhibitions, often of an Americana theme.

An unusual **outdoor court** at the rear of the building preserves ornamental fragments that have been scavenged from such lamented buildings as the razed Penn Station. Jazz concerts are held there in the summer. Lectures, films and gallery talks are regular features in the museum's program.

BRYANT PARK
*Ave. of the Americas and 42nd St. Map **604**.*

Most midtown blocks have supported disparate functions over the last 150 years of development, but few as profound as this site. In the early 19thC, it was a potter's field. Two decades later, a fortress-like reservoir was completed, and in 1853, an imitation of London's Crystal Palace was erected on an adjacent strip of land. That was destroyed by fire in 1858, and the scorched earth was designated a park, dedicated to poet and journalist William Cullen Bryant (1794-1878).

At the turn of the century, the reservoir was drained and filled and the NEW YORK PUBLIC LIBRARY and park extension took its place. A pink granite **fountain** was installed in 1912 in tribute to charity organizer Josephine Lowell; it is the only one in the city to honor a woman.

The six-acre park's basic French design has been enhanced by lavish plantings of shrubs and flowers and two restored small Beaux Arts buildings, one of which is a public lavatory with a guard and attendant. A lush four-acre lawn roofs over new underground stacks for the library. The half-price music-and-dance booth on 42nd St. remains, and there will eventually be two restaurants at the back of the library.

For the present, office workers drop by to enjoy the sun and snacks from one of the two kiosks. Concerts of live and recorded music have been re-introduced. During recent renovations, high fences around the park served the added purpose of depriving drug dealers of one of their favorite gathering places. The city has vowed to keep them out. Whether it will be successful remains to be seen.

CARL SCHURZ PARK
Map 8L5.

Schurz was a German-born immigrant who became a US senator. The park in his name is at the E end of 86th St., which is the central artery of the formerly German community known as YORKVILLE. The official residence of the mayor, GRACIE MANSION (pictured on page 113), is at the N edge of the green.

CARNEGIE HALL
154 W 57th St. (7th Ave.), NY 10019 ☎247-7459. Map 5N3 ✗ Mon, Tues, Thurs at 11.30am, 2pm and 3pm ☎247-7800 for tour information.

It was feared that the 1891 hall would be demolished along with the old Metropolitan Opera House after the completion of the LINCOLN CENTER. Preservationists scored a too-infrequent victory, however, and funds were raised to renovate the interior, and, in a second stage, the exterior. The acoustics are still superb and the concert schedule is full, with artists and groups clamoring for dates.

CASTLE CLINTON NATIONAL MONUMENT ⋔
Battery Park (foot of Broadway), NY 10004 ☎344-7220. Map 1V4 ▣ ✗ Open 9am-5pm.

Concern over a possible second conflict with the English prompted initial plans for the battery of 28 cannon on the rocky outcrop 200 feet (60m) off the SW tip of Manhattan. The eventual reality of British impressment of crews of American merchant ships lent credence to the fear, and additional fortifications were thrown up. The intention was to discourage hostile ships attempting to enter the East River, in concert with crossfire from a similar installation on nearby Governor's Island (which is still a military post). Perhaps it worked, for the fort never loosed a volley.

When the lingering hatreds of the 1812 War faded, the circular sandstone structure was given to New York City. It was transformed into an entertainment center, hosting concerts, fireworks, balloon ascensions and recitals. In 1850, impresario P.T. Barnum presented Jenny Lind, the legendary "Swedish Nightingale" in her American debut. By then, the island had been joined with Manhattan, and in 1855 it became an immigrant processing center. That function was assumed in 1892 by ELLIS ISLAND, and the fort was converted into a public aquarium, a role it held until 1941.

After World War II, it was restored to its original status, and since 1975 has been a Federal landmark run by the National Park Service. Tickets for the ferries to the STATUE OF LIBERTY and ELLIS ISLAND are sold at booths inside. The boats leave from docks on the promenade to the W of the Castle.

CATHEDRAL CHURCH OF ST JOHN THE DIVINE ⋔
1047 Amsterdam Ave. (112th St.), NY 10025 ☎316-7400. Map 7l3 for information ☎662-2133 for tickets for special events ▣ ✗ Open 7am-5pm.

Work on the cathedral started in 1892. By the year 2000, they hope to have the two towers completed. That will still leave the transepts and other additions to be undertaken — perhaps somewhere around 2050? Even now, the interior space is second only to St Peter's in Rome, and the combined floor space of Chartres Cathedral and Notre-Dame de Paris would fit within the 146x601 feet (44x183m) area. The measured pace of construction is due to the determination to use methods that reach back to the Middle Ages. English master masons instruct American apprentices in the **stonecutting yard** *(open to the public Mon-Fri 8.45am-3.45pm).*

Religious and secular works have been donated to the cathedral over the last 100 years and offhandedly stored for future display. A recent inventory revealed the surprising scope of the collection, which includes 13th-16thC tapestries and paintings of the Italian Renaissance. They are on view on a circulating basis in the **Museum** *(* ▣ *Mon-Sat 11am-4pm; Sun noon-5pm* ✗ *Mon-Sat 11am, 2pm; Sun 12.30pm).* Many secular musical events are held, from classical to folk.

CENTRAL PARK ★
Maps 7&8.

Throughout its history, pragmatic visionaries have tempered the city's headlong rush to squeeze every penny of profit from the limited available land. In 1844, most of Manhattan N of 50th St. was a wasteland, supporting only squatters. Poet William Cullen Bryant prodded City Hall into acquiring 840 acres between what were to become 5th Ave. and 8th Ave. and 59th St. and 110th St. Frederick Law Olmsted and Calvert Vaux submitted the winning landscaping scheme in 1857.

Its execution required 20 years, but the results are cherished by every New Yorker, whether cyclist, jogger, stroller, lover, picnicker or baseball player. There are lakes, bridges, ponds, glades, hillocks, meadows, fountains, zoos, boat houses, playgrounds, bandstands, bridle paths, sculptures, terraces, a skating rink and an outdoor theater for summer Shakespeare. In a real sense, it is New York's greatest single achievement. (See WALK 5 on pages 64-7.)

A new service, which was introduced in 1992, is a two-hour **Trolley Tour** (▨) of the park. A motorized streetcar drives into some of the least-known nooks and crannies as well as past such landmarks as the ZOO and **Bethesda Fountain**. It leaves from Grand Army Plaza, at 60th St. and 5th Ave., three times a day from Monday to Friday in July and August *(* ☎ *360-2766).*

Central Park Zoo
5th Ave. and 64th St., NY 10021 ☎*439-6500. Map 8M4* ▨ ▣ ✦ *Open 11am-5pm.*

Relatively small and often crowded, the zoo is a handy alternative for those without the time or inclination to travel to the far larger BRONX ZOO. Mid-afternoon feeding time for the seals is a major draw, but the red pandas, monkeys, penguins, and polar bears are nearly as diverting. The zoo was closed in 1983 for desperately needed renovation. The grand reopening didn't take place until 1988, three years late and at triple the original estimated cost.

It was worth the wait. The former prison-like atmosphere was modified to provide more space and natural habitats for the animals, and more gardens and plantings were introduced, to help integrate the zoo into the surrounding park. Using the sea lion pool as the focal point, an open-sided **pavilion** serves to separate the outlying exhibits into three **climatic zones** — polar, temperate, and tropic — in which the appropriate animals are given replicas of their natural homes. The polar bears, for example, have their plunge pool, but with a glass wall so that they can be seen underwater.

A minor disappointment is the absence of such larger animals as elephants, too big to be comfortably housed on the 5½-acre property. At the N end of the zoo is the **Delacorte Clock**, with statues of dancing bears and elephants and two monkeys with hammers that bang a bell, rather timidly, on the hour and half hour. Beyond it, an archway leads under the Transverse Rd. to the separate **Children's Zoo**. It was closed in 1992 for a reconstruction that presumably won't take as long as that for the main facility. When open, it has cuddly farm animals to be fed and scratched behind the ears. Until the uncertain date of its reopening, the larger zoo has many educational programs for children of different age groups.

CENTRAL SYNAGOGUE
652 Lexington Ave. (55th St.), NY 10021 ☎*838-5122. Map 6M4* ▣

Down the centuries Sephardic Jews have carried the memory of Spain at the time of their expulsion, in the same year Columbus discovered America. This synagogue, one of the oldest in continuous use in the city, reflects that period and the subsequent dispersal of the Sephardim throughout Arab Africa and the Middle East. Designed by Henry Fernbach, one of the first successful Jewish architects in New York, the exterior is in a rather clumsily realized Moorish style, with horseshoe-shaped windows and two bulbous cupolas. It was completed in 1872 for a congregation formed 40 years earlier.

CHELSEA
Map 5Q3.

The genesis of the neighborhood known as Chelsea (pronounced "chell-see") is attributed to an unlikely creator. Writer Clement Clark Moore inherited the land and drew up plans for its streets and buildings. Many of his blocks of brownstone row houses remain, albeit often scarred by 20thC so-called improvements, but all too frequently they have been displaced by uninspired residential and industrial buildings.

Spotty gentrification has taken place of late, with antique stores, off-off Broadway experimental theaters, music pubs, art galleries, and nightclubs sufficiently chic to entice uptowners into long taxi rides.

The principal landmark is the **Chelsea Hotel**. Constructed in 1884 as one of the first luxury apartment houses, it failed to attract the wealthy tenants for which it was intended, and became a hotel in 1905. Writers, artists, and composers found it irresistible, and Thomas Wolfe, Sarah

Bernhardt, Tennessee Williams and Jackson Pollock are but a few of those who lived there. Less well known is the **General Theological Seminary**: enter the door at 175 9th Ave. and emerge in an unexpected square of trees and lawns. Boundaries of the district are 14th St. to 23rd St., and 7th Ave. to the Hudson River.

CHILDREN'S MUSEUM OF MANHATTAN ☎721-1234. Map **7L2** 📷 ✱ Open

*212 W 83rd St. (near Broadway), NY 10024 ☎721-1234. Map **7L2** 📷 ✱ Open June-Aug Tues-Sun 10am-5pm and Sept-May Mon, Wed-Fri 1-5pm; Sat, Sun 10am-5pm.*

The new home of a museum that occupied cramped quarters on 54th St. for 12 years is four stories high, with a total of 36,000 square feet of exhibition space. It endeavors, successfully, to walk the narrow line between instruction and play, with interactive exhibits full of sound, light and color.

The **Brainatarium**, to take one example, is a 20-foot-high domed theater, a kind of cerebral planetarium that glories in the wonders of the human mind, with a short film and a rap song describing its functions. A **communications center** on the second floor has a **television studio** where children can pretend to be news reporters, camera operators and actors; and the more serious "**Magical Patterns**" exhibition zone explains by demonstration the types of patterns that appear in both nature and the arts.

Behind the main building is the even newer **Sussman Environmental Center**. This "Urban Tree House," as it is also known, is intended to introduce children to environmental issues through serious play, rather than overt instruction. Judging by the way young visitors eagerly run from the water-cycle display to the composting corner (with its 4,000 earthworms), its approach works. Each child's photo and fingerprints are taken and presented later in a one-page "newspaper," with the picture and an account of the day's activities.

CHINA INSTITUTE

*125 E 65th St. (Park Ave.), NY 10021 ☎744-8181. Map **8M4** 📷 Open Mon-Sat 10am-5pm.*

Ferocious carved dogs at the entrance, twice-yearly exhibitions of art from the mother country (usually held in spring and late fall), and cooking and language classes, help satisfy (and arouse) curiosity about things Chinese.

The China Institute has, however, had a longer life and different sponsorship than might be expected. The parent institute was created in 1926 to aid Chinese-Americans and foster cultural relations with the West. In 1945, a grand East Side house was donated by publisher Henry Luce to serve as its headquarters. Luce was co-founder of the Time-Life magazine empire and had been born in China of missionary parents.

The institute makes available a range of educational and cultural offerings to citizens of Chinese origin and the larger public, including films, lectures, courses in calligraphy, opera, and vocational training for newly-arrived immigrants.

CHINATOWN
Map 2T4.

Traditionally defined as eight square blocks between THE BOWERY and Mulberry, Worth, and Canal Sts., Chinatown long ago spilled over those boundaries. From 1882, when a Federal law specifically excluded Chinese immigrants, until the 1960s, when such clearly racial restrictions were lifted, the population of the community was relatively stable. Since then, it has grown dramatically, threatening to swallow up Little Italy, to the N. The core of the neighborhood is gratifyingly exotic, the air heavy with dialects and enticing aromas. Every other restaurant is hung with golden ducks, and even the telephone booths have pagoda roofs. (See WALK 3 on pages 59-61.)

CHRYSLER BUILDING 🏛
405 Lexington Ave. (42nd St.), NY 10017 ☎682-3070. Map 604 ▣ Open Mon-Fri 9am-5pm. Closed Sat, Sun.

For a flicker of time after its completion in 1930, this was the highest structure in the world at 1,048 feet (320m), the first to surpass the Eiffel Tower. But that was a period of intense speculative competition, and the EMPIRE STATE BUILDING soon took the title. More than 60 years later, however, the Chrysler is still in the top ten, and it remains the most satisfying esthetic result of the skyscraper mania. Art Deco arches of stainless steel surmount the tower, flaring in the sun and illuminated at night, the base for a slender spire that thrusts 123 feet (37m) into the clouds. Abstract representations of automobile parts inform friezes and other decorative details, in deference to the first owner's business. There is no observation floor, but step inside for a look at the Cubistic assemblages of grained marble and chrome in the lobby.

See illustration in ARCHITECTURE.

CHURCH OF THE ASCENSION 🏛
36 5th Ave. (10th St.), NY 10003 ☎254-8620. Map 3R4. Open Mon-Sat noon-2pm, 5-7pm.

The first church on lower 5th Ave. (when upper 5th was still country), this was also the first to be executed in the Gothic Revival mode then sweeping through Europe. Brownstone was used for the facing, a material that was to become a favorite of the well-to-do for their row houses. In 1889, McKim, Mead & White remodeled parts of the interior and the parish house, hiring Louis Comfort Tiffany for the design of some of the stained glass and John LaFarge for the altar mural.

CHURCH OF THE TRANSFIGURATION
1 E 29th St. (5th Ave.), NY 10016 ☎684-6770. Map 6P4. Open 8am-6pm.

It is said that when an actor asked to be married, he was firmly dispatched to this "Little Church Around the Corner," an institution presumably not as fastidious as others about the dubious professions and social status of its parishioners. Another story claims the referral was of friends seeking a funeral for a deceased thespian. Either way, the church, built around 1850, has a long association with show folk.

CITICORP CENTER
153 E 53rd St. (Lexington Ave.), NY 10022 ☎*559-4259. Map 6N4* ☒ *Open 8am-midnight.*

Posterity has yet to render its verdict on this building. Its distinctive sloping roofline moves it into the Post-Modernist category of sky-scraper design, away from the rectangular glass boxes of the Bauhaus school. The roof was intended to house solar energy collectors, a good intention sacrificed to the gods of cost accounting. Quibbles aside, the 1978 building brought life to a dreary block, and accommodated into its design the modest but striking **St Peter's Lutheran Church**. Office floors begin at 127 feet (39m), clearing the church steeple and provid-ing a public atrium embracing 22 shops and restaurants. The interior plaza is filled with trees and tables, and live music is sometimes played there.

CITY HALL ▥
City Hall Park (Broadway and Murray St.), NY 10007 ☎*566-5200. Map 2T4* ☒ *Open Mon-Fri 10am-4pm. Closed Sat, Sun.*

Both dwarfed and enhanced by the taller buildings that enclose it on three sides, the third and present City Hall (1811) is a Georgian-Federal-Renaissance gem that even the Sun King might have accepted (at least as a summer cottage). (See WALK 3, page 59.)

CLEOPATRA'S NEEDLE
Central Park. Map 8L4.

One of only four obelisks outside Egypt, it was erected in CENTRAL PARK in 1881, behind the METROPOLITAN MUSEUM OF ART. The red granite spire is covered with hieroglyphics from the time of Thutmose III (c.1600BC). Regrettably, the change in climate, plus air pollution, has worn them down.

THE CLOISTERS ▥ ★
Fort Tryon Park, NY 10040 ☎*923-3700. See ORIENTATION MAP on pages 78-9* ▨ *Ticket includes same-day admission to METROPOLITAN MUSEUM OF ART* ✗ ➡ *Open Mar-Oct 9.30am-5.15pm; Nov-Feb 9.30am-4.45pm. Closed Mon, some holidays. Subway A to 190th St.*

Save The Cloisters for a day when the freneticism of the Big Apple becomes overbearing. This far-uptown unit of the METROPOLITAN MU-SEUM OF ART is a wondrous sanctuary in FORT TRYON PARK, overlooking the Hudson River from the northern heights of the island. On the crest of a hill banked by woodland and meadows, parts of several European monasteries and chapels have been blended in a unified edifice of blissful serenity. The collection was founded by George Grey Barnard, who gathered vast amounts of superb medieval sculpture on his many visits to Europe. It was first opened to the public in 1914, and moved to its present home in 1938, following a donation by the Rockefeller family.

MAIN FLOOR (N and W)   Approach is made up a curving driveway from the bus stop and parking lot, and entry is past nine arches from

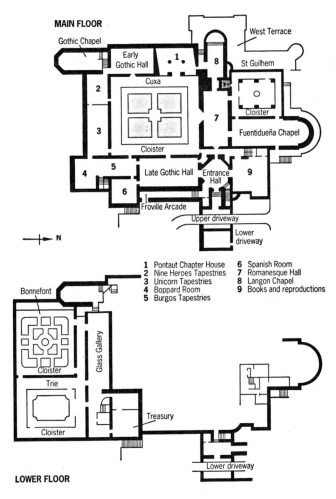

MAIN FLOOR

Gothic Chapel
Early Gothic Hall
1
8
West Terrace
St Guilhem
2
Cuxa
Cloister
7
Fuentidueña Chapel
3
Cloister
5
Late Gothic Hall
Entrance Hall
9
4
6
Froville Arcade
Upper driveway
Lower driveway

← N

1 Pontaut Chapter House
2 Nine Heroes Tapestries
3 Unicorn Tapestries
4 Boppard Room
5 Burgos Tapestries
6 Spanish Room
7 Romanesque Hall
8 Langon Chapel
9 Books and reproductions

Bonnefont
Glass Gallery
Cloister
Trie
Cloister
Treasury
Lower driveway
LOWER FLOOR

the **15thC Benedictine friary of Froville**. Walk through the French 12thC archway into the **Romanesque Hall** and turn right into the **Fuentidueña Chapel**. The low black stone baptismal font just inside is from Belgium, the barrel-vaulted apse from Segovia, the fresco above the altar from Catalonia. All are believed to be of the 12thC. On the left is a 16thC painted limestone sculpture from Zamora. The grinning hyena-like creature was meant to be a lion, and is surmounted by a headless Christ figure placing a crown on Mary's head. Return to the

99

Romanesque Hall and turn into the **St Guilhem Cloister**. Perhaps because of the delicacy of the ornamentation on the ancient pillars, this is the only indoor cloister. A glass ceiling permits boxed plants to grow in winter. Paired capitals and columns feature stylized leaves, flowers, and human figures. No two pairs are the same. As in the other rooms, a plan on the wall shows which portions are authentic.

Return to the Romanesque Hall once more and turn into the **Langon Chapel**. Note the thick oak doors banded with ironwork that serves both decorative and support functions. Much of the stonework is from an 11thC church in Langon, near Bordeaux, and the carved faces of the capital high on the right of the nave are often alleged to be Henry II and Eleanor of Aquitaine. The centerpiece of the chapel is the marble ciborium or tabernacle, a roofed structure on four pillars that shelters an altar and a 12thC Burgundian *Virgin and Child* carved from birch. Leave the chapel through the door on the left and turn sharply right to the **West Terrace**, a belvedere overlooking the usually placid Hudson and the high bluffs on the opposite shore called the Palisades. Apart from the GEORGE WASHINGTON BRIDGE to the S, there is little to detract from the impression that this was the way the riverscape looked when the first European settlers arrived. Go back inside, turning right at the end of the short corridor.

The Pontaut Chapter House is from a Benedictine abbey in Gascony, probably dating from the late 12thC. Because the room is nearly all original, it conveys the strongest sense of place of anywhere in The Cloisters. Ribbed, vaulted ceilings hint at early Gothic influences, but the rounded arches, somber capitals, and massive walls are clearly Romanesque. Bands of brick alternate with crudely shaped stone, all of which was once covered in plaster. Walk out in the **Cuxa Cloister**, in which the monastic mood is usually enhanced by recorded Gregorian chants and other sacred music of the Middle Ages and Renaissance. This is the largest of the cloisters, open to the sky, its four-sided colonnade enclosing a garden. It covers approximately half the area of its original 12thC site, a monastery in the French Pyrénées. Look closely at the capitals of the rose-streaked marble columns, for each is different, depicting simple leaf motifs, lions, complex hunting scenes and mythical animals. Circle the courtyard, looking for the mermaid capital in the E arcade, the best decorative work in the group.

Continue past the Chapter House and enter the **Early Gothic Hall** to examine the ecclesiastical figures, then move on to the **Gothic Chapel**. Distinctions from the Romanesque style predominating to this point are evident in the pointed arches and ribbed vaulting, the 14thC stained glass, and the greater delicacy of the stonework, especially at the tops of the window openings. Large effigies and sarcophagi are dotted about. Their origins are French and Catalan, while most of the glass is Austrian. Take the stairs down to the lower floor.

LOWER FLOOR   In the **Glass Gallery**, pause to study the 15th-16thC stained glass from which it takes its name. At the end is a large section of intricately carved woodwork, which once enclosed the staircase of a house in Abbeville, France. Although holy figures are duly depicted, the effect is of secular Gothic exuberance. The room straight ahead houses 37 carved wood panels, again from Abbeville, but this time they convey a distinctly religious impression.

Turn left into the **Treasury**, which features liturgical fans and combs, a silver reliquary in the shape of an arm, and exquisite chalices of silver and gold, one from the 4thC. This route leads back past the Abbeville woodwork to a door opening into the **Trie Cloister**. Off the main traffic lanes of the museum, this secluded spot encourages the contemplative frame of mind for which it was intended. Each capital varies from the others, the scenes more literal than those so far encountered, and the slender double pillars are of differently colored marble. The plants surrounding the fountain are examples of those found in the Unicorn Tapestries (see below).

Leave by the doorway at the NW corner, walking along the arcade modeled on the cloister of the abbey at Bonnefont-en-Comminges. Here, the attraction is not the architecture but the **garden**, which is heady with lemon thyme, marjoram, mace and woodruff. Brick paths separate beds of violets and forget-me-nots, dominated by four quince trees. A low wall affords views of the park to the S, and birdwatchers are often surprised by the variety of species attracted to the garden. When ready, re-enter the Glass Gallery and return upstairs.

MAIN FLOOR (S and E)   From the Gothic Chapel, turn into the **Nine Heroes Tapestries** room. The late 14thC hangings show five of the heroes who featured in this popular theme, among them Alexander the Great, Charlemagne and Julius Caesar. Understandably faded and fragmented, the tapestries provide a foretaste of the splendid 16thC **Unicorn Tapestries** in the next hall.

Scholarly consensus ranks this set of seven superbly executed panels among the finest in existence. That assessment may be restrained, for in concept, detailing and craftsmanship, they are peerless. The remarkable petal-by-leaf renderings of plants and flowers make it possible to identify many of the live specimens seen in the Trie Cloister (see above). Beyond such surface delights, however, is the telling of a tale with deep symbolic undercurrents. Christ is seen as a Unicorn, Gabriel as a hunter with a horn, Satan as a snake; pagan beliefs are mingled with Christian convictions; fruits and blossoms represent purity, lust or fertility. Baronial German furnishings and a flamboyant French Gothic fireplace suggest the surroundings in which the tapestries would for a long time have been viewed.

The **Boppard Room** is named after the German town from which its six 15thC stained-glass panels originate. Go past the late 15thC **Burgos Tapestries**, which were executed to the glorification of Charles VIII of France, and then turn into the **Spanish Room** to see Robert Campin's *Annunciation* triptych (c.1425). The altarpiece is remarkable for the choice of setting: a simple Flemish interior rather than the traditional ecclesiastical or historical environment. The painted Gothic red pine ceiling in this room is also worthy of attention. Leave the museum through the **Late Gothic Hall**, noting the fine 15thC Spanish retable on your way out.

COLUMBIA UNIVERSITY ⏛

Broadway (116th St.), NY 10027 ☎ *280-1754. See ORIENTATION MAP on pages 78-9* 🚇 *Campus open 24hrs. Subway 1 to 116th St.-Columbia University.*

Established in 1754 as King's College, and fueled by more than two centuries of alumni bequests and gifts, Columbia is one of the wealthiest universities in the US. As a member of the prestigious Ivy League, which includes Harvard, Yale and Princeton, it is also one of the most distinguished. With the end of the Revolution, "King's" College became "Columbia," and after an intermediate move to Madison Ave. and 49th St., settled here at Morningside Heights in 1897.

Over the years, the original men's college has joined with a teacher's college and Barnard College for women, and courses now include business administration, law, medicine, dentistry, librarianship, journalism, social work and public health. Founding father Alexander Hamilton graduated from here, and Dwight Eisenhower was the university's president for a time after World War II, before he moved on to a somewhat higher office.

The original layout of the campus and two of the first buildings were products of McKim, Mead and White. Fortunately, their design was opened up to permit larger pedestrian plazas, which in turn lent greater drama to the most prominent building, **Low Library**. Its style is Neoclassical, with a surmounting dome and a portico with ten columns and coffered ceiling. The elevated site makes the most of the building's monumentality. Halfway up the wide front steps is a statue of *Alma Mater* by Daniel Chester French, who is best known for his sculptures of Abraham Lincoln. Low Library is essentially an administration building. **Butler Library**, to the s, is the main repository of the university's five-million-volume collection.

The **Terrace Restaurant** *(* ☎ *666-9490)* on the top floor is open to the public. Given its situation, the food and service are quite good, and it affords excellent views of lower Manhattan.

CONEY ISLAND

Brooklyn. Subway B, D, F, M, N, QB to Stillwell Ave.-Coney Island.

For generations of working-class New Yorkers, Coney Island was Riviera-on-the-Subway, a wide strip of powdery sand that gave surcease from the steaming streets and tenements of the city. It has fallen on hard times, the shattered and burned-out housing inland occupied primarily by pensioners and the poor, the Steeplechase Park amusement center a wasteland.

Still, the beach has been cleaned up and sand added to make it wider, the better to accommodate the hundreds of thousands of people who show up every hot summer weekend. They crowd around the original **Nathan's Famous**, which serves up thousands of hot dogs and fried clams daily. Teenagers pair off and sneak into the shadows beneath the refurbished boardwalk as they have for generations. Before and after, they squeal through roller coaster dips on the 1927 "Cyclone" at **Astroland** *(* 📷 *entrance* 🎢 *rides).* Families gape at the sharks and dolphins of the NEW YORK AQUARIUM). The district is on the Atlantic Ocean in s

Brooklyn, along Surf Ave. between W 37th St. and Ocean Parkway. Thousands of Soviet immigrants have made nearby Brighton Beach a virtual Little Odessa.

COOPER-HEWITT MUSEUM

2 E 91st St. (5th Ave.) ☎ *860-6868. Map 8K4* 🚇 *(📷 Tues 5-9pm)* ✗ *Open Tues 10am-9pm; Wed-Sat 10am-5pm; Sun noon-5pm. Closed Mon.*

In this pricey venue at the top of the 5th Ave. "Museum Mile," even millionaires built their mansions flush with their property boundaries, foregoing lawns and gardens. But in that lamented time before the imposition of income taxes, Scottish-born Andrew Carnegie was more than simply rich. He had just sold his steel company (1901) for more than $250 million, which was serious money at the time. When he built this 64-room house in the same year, he left himself a green buffer all around and transplanted mature trees from upstate. Only a friend and business associate such as Henry C. Frick could indulge himself in a similar fashion (see the FRICK COLLECTION).

If pressed, an art historian might describe the Carnegie house as Georgian, but it really defies classification. Despite the unfortunate facade, there is a pleasant garden behind the cast-iron fence and a marvelous stained-glass canopy over the entrance. Within are the decorative art acquisitions of Peter Cooper (founder of COOPER UNION) and his granddaughters Eleanor and Sarah Hewitt. It has long been the only New York branch of the Smithsonian Institution, a circumstance to be changed when the new NATIONAL MUSEUM OF THE AMERICAN INDIAN opens in 1993.

The Cooper-Hewitt Museum's mission is to explore the historical development of design in all its guises, and its 165,000 objects span 14 centuries. Samplings include: wallpapers and leather wallcoverings, gilded and bronze-edged furniture, Iranian glassware and Greek pottery, antique locks and keys, candlesticks and doorknockers, hatboxes and copper food molds and birdcages in the shapes of cathedrals, chalets and Venice's Rialto Bridge. These are contrasted with contemporary chairs by Marcel Breuer and his compatriots and witty lamps by Milanese designers of the 1980s. Also on hand are more than 30,000 drawings, including works by Dürer, Rembrandt and Winslow Homer.

Passing through the mansion, visitors are accorded revealing looks at how the rich of a hundred years ago lived. The lobby has a deeply carved and coffered ceiling and parquet floors, and the plant-filled **Conservatory** mingles Victorian opulence with Art Nouveau and Deco fixtures.

COOPER UNION

Cooper Sq., NY 10003 ☎ *254-6300. Map 3R4. Open 8am-10pm.*

Peter Cooper became a millionaire through participation in the key 19thC industries of railroads and iron-making. In the benevolent if paternalistic manner of his fellows, he founded this college for the training of artists and engineers, and built the somber pile (1859) that still houses part of the institution. The Foundation Building rather resembles a railroad station of the time — dark, brooding, ponderous.

Still, Cooper made provision for a free-tuition curriculum for talented persons of any race, sex, creed or economic status, at a time when such notions were deemed dangerous to the natural order of things. That policy persists, and has profited tens of thousands of Americans who might not otherwise have had the chance of higher education. The Great Hall within hosted many celebrated 19thC speakers, among them suffragette Susan B. Anthony, abolitionist Henry Ward Beecher, Mark Twain and, in a rare New York appearance, Abraham Lincoln.

DAKOTA APARTMENTS ▥

*1 W 72nd St., NY 10023. Map **7**M3.*

Until 1884, members of New York's establishment would not have considered living in anything but a private house. This luxury ten-floor apartment building changed their minds, even though it was so far uptown that wags said it was in Dakota Indian territory. Its capacious rooms, high ceilings, thick-walled quiet, and offbeat Bavarian fortress exterior ensure its continued cachet with celebrities and other privileged folk. *Rosemary's Baby* was filmed inside. John Lennon, who lived here, was murdered outside the entrance in 1980.

DYCKMAN HOUSE ▥

4881 Broadway (204th St.), NY 10543 ☎923-8008 (Morris-Jumel Mansion) for information ▣ Open Tues-Sun 11am-4pm. Closed Mon. Subway 1 to 217th St.

The original owner of the property was Jan Dyckman. He came to New Amsterdam in 1661 and swiftly assembled the substantial estate he was to pass on to his descendants. For no recorded tactical reason, the house built here in 1748 was burned to the ground by British troops, toward the end of the Revolutionary War. The existing replacement was erected in 1783, before they left Manhattan. The estate was once thick with fruit trees and was tilled by tenant farmers well into the 19thC. Parts of the orchard still bloomed past 1900. Brick and flagstone form portions of the lower sections of the house, with weatherboarding rising to a low gambrel roof. The effect is appropriately Dutch Colonial, and some of the furnishings are authentic not only to the period but to the original family.

Although it is a long subway ride N to the Inwood district, the tranquil setting and park-like grounds smooth nerve ends frayed by the clamor of midtown.

EAST SIDE ★

*Map **8**L4.*

From 5th Ave. to the East River and 59th St. to 92nd St., this chic precinct (also known as the Upper East Side) harbors most of the city's major museums, upmarket single people, and resident millionaires, foreign and domestic. Tree-shaded cross streets near 5th Ave. are lined with attractive townhouses, the owners of which have succeeded in fending off the blandishments of developers. Commercial interlopers tend to be low-profile boutiques and art and antique galleries. Near the river are the luxury enclaves of **Beekman Place** and **Sutton Place**.

Along the avenues, beautiful people swirl in a fickle flow from this month's bistro to the bar-of-the-moment and meet each other in lines for the latest movie. (See WALK 6 on pages 67-70.)

ELLIS ISLAND ★

New York Harbor, NY 10004 ☎*269-5755. See* ORIENTATION MAP *on pages 78-9* ▣ *entrance* ▣ *ferry* ◄≡ ✗ *Open daily in winter 9.30am-5pm; summer 9.30am-5.30pm. Circle Line ferry from Battery Park and Liberty State Park in Jersey City.*

These echoing, gloomy halls must have seemed forbidding to the 12 million immigrants who passed through this bureaucratic purgatory between 1892 and 1954. Most were processed in a day, but some were held for weeks and months before being permitted entry to the tantalizing city in sight across the bay.

Restoration of the principal buildings — of more than 30 on the island — was completed in 1990, at a cost nearing $150 million. Chandeliers were rehung in the Great Hall of the Beaux Arts **Main Building**, and its four copper domes were laboriously cleaned to their original condition. Rubble was cleared, and the grime of decades of neglect was scoured away. Graffiti left by the immigrants has been preserved, however. The **Registry Room** is easily the most impressive, with a tiled, domed, two-story ceiling and three of those chandeliers. Patrons of the **Oyster Bar** (see WHERE TO EAT) in GRAND CENTRAL TERMINAL experience *déjà vu* with good reason — the same firm did the tile work in both places.

Now the bad news: the restoration effort has taken more than 5 years, and public interest in the reopening continues to be very high. The storied phrase, "huddled masses yearning to breath free," has renewed meaning for anyone embarking on this excursion. There are long waits at both ends of the ferry ride and for entrance to the various parts of the building, so plan on a total of *at least* three hours — five, if also visiting the STATUE OF LIBERTY.

For even a remote chance of avoiding crowds, arrive by 9am to catch the first ferry, and don't make firm lunch plans. The ticket booth for both the Statue of Liberty and Ellis Island is inside CASTLE CLINTON NATIONAL MONUMENT.

EMPIRE STATE BUILDING 血 ★

350 5th Ave. (34th St.), NY 10118 ☎*736-3100. Map* **6P4** ▣ *for observatory* ✗ ▣ ♣ *Observatory floors open 9.30am-midnight. Last ticket sold at 11.30pm. Check visibility notice before buying tickets.*

From its inception, the Empire State Building attracted superlatives — in achievement and in tragedy. Designated a national historic landmark, it is still the third highest building in the world, after the Sears Building in Chicago and the downtown WORLD TRADE CENTER, and it remains the foremost symbol of New York. It does, after all, stand 1,472 feet (448m) high, including TV mast. By comparison, the Eiffel Tower is 984 feet (300m).

King Kong swatted at biplanes from his perch in the 1931 movie classic, a plane crashed into the 79th floor in 1945, and at least 17 people have flung themselves to their deaths off parapets and down elevator shafts. The distinctive stepped cap was sketched in during one of the later design stages. It was to have been a mooring mast for airships. One attempt to bring that fanciful notion to reality resulted in some celebrated citizens nearly being blown away, and the idea was discarded. Without the rounded cap, the original 86 stories were only 2 feet (61cm) higher than the CHRYSLER BUILDING. With it, another 200 feet (61m) and a second public observatory were added. Perhaps as remarkable as its height was the fact that the Empire State came in under schedule and under budget.

Twice a month, 6,500 windows must be washed. There are 60 miles of water pipes within the walls and 60,000 tons of structural steel. For reasons best known to the participants, an annual race is run *up* the 1,575 steps to the 86th floor. The facing is limestone, fashioned in modified Art Deco. The observatory on the 86th floor has both a glass-enclosed area and an outdoor promenade around four sides of the building; while the one on the 102nd floor is fully enclosed.

Over 2.5 million people visit the observatories every year. Go during the day or at night, and save the other time for another of Manhattan's aeries.

EQUITABLE CENTER
787 7th Ave. (between 51st and 52nd Sts.), NY 10010. Map **5N3** ▣ ═ *Open Mon-Sat 9am-6pm.*

A continuation of the post-modernist trend in skyscraper architecture that began with the AT&T BUILDING, the Center incorporates the Equitable Tower and the Paine Webber Building. While attractive enough by those standards, with its arches and cream-and-brown exterior, it is more notable for what it contains than the visage it presents to the street. Within its walls are several good-to-excellent restaurants, including **Le Bernardin** and **Sam's**, both described in WHERE TO EAT.

In the lobby off 7th Ave. is a mural by Roy Lichtenstein, nearly four stories high, and down one corridor is a panoramic vision of America executed by Thomas Hart Benton. Its branch of the Whitney Museum has been closed, however.

FEDERAL HALL NATIONAL MEMORIAL �
26 Wall St. (Nassau St.), NY 10005 ☎ *264-8711. Map* **2U4** ▣ ✗ *by appointment. Open Mon-Fri 9am-5pm. Closed Sat, Sun.*

Paradigm of the early 19thC enthusiasm for the Greeks, Federal Hall (pictured in ARCHITECTURE) is not the building in which Washington took his oath of office in 1789, as is inferred by many. The **statue of George Washington**, outside, stands where the first President did indeed make those vows, but the building behind was not completed until 1842. It housed government offices from then until 1955, when it was converted to its present use as a museum. Now grandly labeled the **Museum of American Constitutional Government**, a permanent exhibit employs interactive video terminals to inform visitors on a variety of historical and contemporary issues. There are also artifacts of the Revolutionary War period, including a railing from the porch on which Washington repeated those famous words, and the clothes he wore that day.

Architects Town & Davis resisted the impulse to slap on sculptured friezes and ornate capitals, opting for fluted Doric columns and an unadorned pediment, all of marble quarried a few miles N of the city. Their only major deviation from their Greek inspiration was the interior rotunda, but the dramatic space works, which is ample justification. All in all, it is a trimlined Parthenon of disciplined stolidity and the finest example of Greek Revival in Manhattan. Free concerts are occasionally given at the Hall.

FINANCIAL DISTRICT ★
Map 1U4.

Bits and scraps of "Little Old New York" remain, but the southern end of Manhattan has long shuddered beneath the thrusting monoliths of international commerce and the machinations taking place within. The world eavesdrops on every whisper at the **Stock Exchange**, and conglomerates eye each other from their steel and concrete aeries.

Not long ago, the restaurants closed in this district in the evenings and on weekends, and Sunday afternoons drew only a few strollers down ghostly windswept canyons. Now people are moving back to live in rehabilitated warehouses and middle-aged skyscrapers, and visitors come for sun and nautical history to the SOUTH STREET SEAPORT. (See WALK 2 on pages 56-9.)

FIREFIGHTING MUSEUM   See NEW YORK CITY FIRE MUSEUM.

FLATIRON BUILDING 🏛
175 5th Ave. (23rd St.), NY 10010. Map 6Q4.

There are two reasons to seek out the Flatiron Building (pictured on page 25); its status as the first true skyscraper (a disputed claim), and its odd triangular shape (dictated by its plot at the confluence of 5th Ave. and Broadway). In the earliest tall buildings, made possible by the invention of the electric elevator, metal cages supported floors while masonry facings bore their own weight. In the decade before the Flatiron, new techniques allowed riveted steel frames to bear both floors *and* facing. That sort of steel skeleton was employed here, 286 feet (87m) high and only 6 feet (2m) wide at its narrow end.

To calm the conservative citizenry, a rusticated limestone facade imitated a stacked Italianate palace. Nevertheless, many were convinced that the building would collapse in the high winds characteristic of the area. It didn't. A thorough steam cleaning has made it gleam as it has not in over fifty years. You can enter the lobby during business hours, but there is no compelling reason to do so.

FLATIRON DISTRICT
Map 6Q4.

Officially, this most recent of re-emergent neighborhoods in lower Manhattan is called the Ladies' Mile Historic District. That designation refers to the department stores and retail shops along 5th Ave. that catered to women's needs in the decades around the turn of the century. When those enterprises moved farther uptown, clothing manufacturers and other light industries took their place, in a historical progression comparable to that of SOHO. But artists transformed that district, while the renaissance of this area can be credited in large measure to the book publishers and modeling and advertising agencies that began moving down here from midtown Madison Ave. in the 1970s.

They were looking for more space and lower rents, and their growing presence was noted early on by alert entrepreneurs. Smart shops, restaurants and nightspots have returned in profusion. They have elbowed their way into the blocks from 23rd to 14th Sts. and 7th Ave. and Broadway, also dubbed **SoFi** (for SOuth of FlatIron). Among SoFi attractions are the thrice-weekly **farmer's market** in renovated Union Square, the FLATIRON BUILDING and such hot eateries as **Lola** and the **Union Square Café**.

FORBES MAGAZINE GALLERIES

62 5th Ave. (12th St.), NY 10011 ☎*206-5548. Map 6R4* 📷 ✳ *Open Tues, Wed, Fri, Sat 10am-4pm.*

The late Malcolm Forbes was America's favorite millionaire. Many saw the immensely successful publisher as an ebullient man who enjoyed every dollar of his vast wealth, from his motorcycling tours and hot-air ballooning to his sumptuous yachts and lavish parties.

Forbes was also an inveterate collector, most noticeably of bejeweled **Fabergé Eggs**. There were 12 in his possession, of only 54 ever made. They are on view here, along with flotillas of model warships and ocean liners, legions of toy soldiers (more than 12,000), and a gallery of presidential papers and memorabilia. They are a delightfully playful array, the joyous accumulations of a man who must have left this mortal coil with a smile on his face.

FORD FOUNDATION BUILDING 🏛

320 E 43rd St. (2nd Ave.), NY 10016 ☎*573-5000. Map 605* 📷 *Open Mon-Fri 9am-5pm. Closed Sat, Sun.*

Atriums have become a cliché as pervasive as sunken plazas in contemporary New York commercial architecture — sops to planning boards and environmental groups. The resulting spaces are often bleak and inhuman. The Ford Foundation presented a gift to the city, however, not a burden, with its 1967 headquarters. The interior contains a third of an acre of mature trees and shrubs. A brook, hushed and clear, curls through the garden. Passers-by are welcome to step inside for a moment's respite.

The offices above the greenery are for the staff of the Foundation, which was created by Henry and Edsel Ford. It is the largest philanthropic trust in the world, concerning itself with a broad spectrum of human welfare issues, although it is best known for its contributions to education and the arts.

FORT TRYON PARK

See ORIENTATION MAP on pages 78-9 ◀ 🚇 🚃 *Subway A to 190th St.*

While THE CLOISTERS museum is the prime motive for taking the long subway ride to this tranquil pastoral sanctuary close to the northern tip of Manhattan. Other attractions here, however, are hills, woodlands, meadows, a small but fascinating botanical garden, a children's playground with wading pool, and staggering vistas of the Hudson River from the site of the namesake fortification. During the week, only an occasional cyclist or jogger is likely to interrupt the solitude.

FRAUNCES TAVERN MUSEUM

54 Pearl St. (Broad St.), NY 10004 ☎*425-1778. Map 2U4* 🔲 *✗ by appointment* 🚃 *Open Mon-Fri 10am-4pm. Closed Sat, Sun.*

This is a 20thC approximation of the tavern in which George Washington bade farewell to his troops. Constructed on the site of the original, it incorporates parts of the remaining walls. The first building was a three-story mansion, which was converted into a tavern in 1762 by Samuel Fraunces. A West Indian, he became steward to Washington when the English took New York in 1776. The General returned on December 4, 1783 for lunch with his officers and delivered the famous address.

Downstairs is now a restaurant; upstairs and in adjacent buildings there is a collection of Revolutionary musketry and mementoes, and two period rooms. Changing exhibitions and occasional lectures and entertainments focus on American history, especially as it unfolded in lower Manhattan. Washington's Birthday and the 4th of July are especially festive.

FRENCH INSTITUTE/ALLIANCE FRANÇAISE

22 E 60th St., (Madison Ave.), NY 10022 ☎*355-6100. Map 6N4* 🔲 *Open Mon-Thurs 10am-8pm; Fri 10am-6pm; Sat (Sept-June) 10am-1.30pm. Closed Sun.*

In a spectrum of activities to gladden the heart of every Francophile, the institute offers language and cooking classes, recent and venerable films, concerts, recitals, lectures — all of which relate to the mother country. Students and homesick expatriates can find French magazines and newspapers, and perhaps a new friend, in the small gallery and library.

FRICK COLLECTION ★

1 E 70th St. (5th Ave.), NY 10021 ☎*288-0700. Map 8M4* 🔲 🎏 *Open Tues-Sat 10am-6pm; Sun 1-6pm. Closed Mon, major holidays. Children under 10 not admitted; 10-16s only with adult.*

From the 1890s onward the part of 5th Ave. facing lower Central Park has been a millionaires' row. Now the privileged live in duplex penthouses, for not even the very wealthy can afford to maintain the palatial residences built by their antecedents. Most of those mansions have been demolished, a few converted to institutional use. The Andrew Carnegie residence, for example, is now the COOPER-HEWITT MUSEUM. All this makes the Frick Collection even more special, for the house is

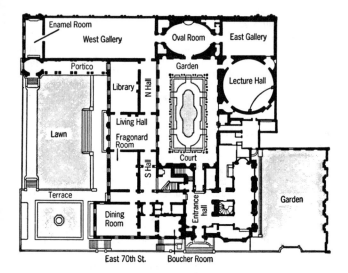

Enamel Room
West Gallery
Oval Room
East Gallery
Portico
Garden
Library
Lecture Hall
N Hall
Living Hall
Fragonard Room
Lawn
Court
S Hall
Terrace
Garden
Entrance hall
Dining Room
East 70th St.   Boucher Room

much the way that it was left by the first and only owner — filled with paintings, furniture, clocks and Persian carpets.

Carnegie and industrialist Henry C. Frick were business associates who parted company over policy disputes. Frick chose to build his house (in 1914) only 20 blocks s of his former friend's 64-room residence. Although bearing allegiance to no particular style, its low roofline and front lawn are a welcome visual break in the prevailing wall of high-rises. And there is no more gracious oasis in the city than the interior court with its splashing fountain and flowering plants. After Frick's death, a harmonious addition doubled the floor space. The house was opened to the public in 1935.

Entrance is made from E 70th St. The first important room on your left is the **Boucher Room**, with eight panels representing the Arts and Sciences that François Boucher painted for one of Madame de Pompadour's legendary Rococo bedrooms. Next is the corner **Dining Room,** which is perhaps the most striking room in the mansion, with its French furniture and 18thC paintings by Hogarth, Gainsborough and Reynolds. To the N is the **Fragonard Room**, where four paintings known as *The Progress of Love,* once owned by Madame du Barry, celebrate the different stages of love. The other seven panels were also executed by Jean-Honoré Fragonard, a disciple of Boucher and a favorite at the court of Louis XV. Furnishings in the room are consistent with the period. The high point of the **Living Hall** is the El Greco portrait of *St Jerome* over the fireplace. It is flanked by two Hans Holbein paintings, and there are also works by Titian and Bellini. On the center table is a bronze by Pollaiuolo. Leading off from this room are the **South Hall,** notable for Vermeer's

Officer and Laughing Girl, and **North Hall**, which has Ingres' portrait of *La Comtesse d'Haussonville*. The **Library** concentrates on English painting, with a George Romney portrait of *Lady Hamilton* and a luminous early Turner. Priceless Chinese vases add to the authentic appeal of this paneled room.

Largest of the chambers is the **West Gallery**, its imposing chilliness offset by the splendor of the masterpieces within. They deserve a methodical clockwise examination. (On the way, make sure you turn into the small **Enamel Room** for a look at Limoges painted enamels of the 15th-17thC.) Among the treasures of this trove are a trio of Rembrandts, two works by Van Dyck, a Velázquez, a Goya and an El Greco. Turner was a progenitor of the Impressionist revolution that followed his death in 1851, and his vivid cityscape of Dieppe is particularly significant in this respect.

Pass through the **Oval Room**, with its Whistlers and terracotta *Diana,* into the **East Gallery**, where Goya, Gainsborough and Van Dyck are featured. Finally, there is the **Garden Court**, with its glass roof and fountain. Chamber music concerts take place on occasional Sundays. Inquire at the entrance desk for detailed information.

GARMENT CENTER
Map 5P3.
Neither steel nor automobiles nor their ilk are fabricated in New York so, by default, people in suits conjuring advertising jingles and peddling stocks describe themselves as "industries." As that word is commonly understood, however, the primary manufacturing enterprise of the city is clothing.

Somewhere between 80,000 and 300,000 citizens are employed in the rag trade today, depending upon how a statistician tots up the legions of cutters, shippers, salesmen, suppliers, designers, messengers, models, packers, deliverymen, buyers, union organizers and sewing machine operators who ply their trades here. Between breakfast and dinner, every one of them seems to pour through the streets of this scruffy district along 7th Ave. between 34th and 40th Sts., dodging handcarts, gulping coffee from paper containers, grabbing lapels, scuttling to appointments, making deals. The fashions they produce often rival the best of Paris and Milan.

GE BUILDING (formerly RCA Building)
30 Rockefeller Plaza (between 5th Ave. and Ave. of the Americas and 49th and 50th Sts.), NY 10017. Map 6O4.
Long known as the RCA Building, the new owners, General Electric, have imposed this name. As fast as Manhattan real estate changes hands, there is no certainty it won't soon be changed again. By whatever label, it remains the centerpiece of the 19-building ROCKEFELLER CENTER complex, at 850 feet (259m) and 70 stories. Completed in the Depression years, its first-floor murals are in the heroic Social Realist mode. Unfortunately, the observation deck is now closed. (See WALK 1 on pages 55-6.)

GENERAL GRANT NATIONAL MEMORIAL

Riverside Drive (122nd St.), NY 10027 ☎*666-1640. See ORIENTATION MAP on pages 78-9* ▣ ✗ *Open Wed-Sun 9am-5pm. Closed Mon, Tues.*

Popularly known as Grant's Tomb, it is no accident that the official designation honors the Civil War service of Ulysses S. Grant rather than his scandal-ridden tenure as the 18th US President. The mausoleum is fashioned after the style of a 4thC Greek tomb, and was financed by private contributions rather than by Congress. After its completion in 1897, both Grant and his wife were interred within, behind impressive bronze doors. A gallery shows photographs and memorabilia from both careers.

The exuberant free-form **mosaic benches** that surround the somber structure on three sides are the work of Chilean artist Pedro Silva, who was inspired by the iconoclastic Catalan architect Antoni Gaudí. They are entirely inappropriate to the site, but are a lot more fun than the monument itself.

GEORGE WASHINGTON BRIDGE

See ORIENTATION MAP on pages 78-9.

Dreamers of the 19thC insisted that the broad Hudson River could be spanned, but it took the capitalistic euphoria of the late 1920s to bring together the necessary funds and determination to make it a reality. The bridge was completed in 1931, within months of the EMPIRE STATE, CHRYSLER and GE (FORMERLY RCA) BUILDINGS, and, like them, was defiant of the economic desolation of the Great Depression.

For a time, the 3,500 feet (1,067m) between its main towers made it the world's longest suspension bridge. Budgetary considerations and public opinion fortunately prevented plans to sheath the open steel framework in concrete and granite, as envisioned by architect Cass Gilbert. A second deck for trams and trains was planned by engineer Othmar H. Ammann, but was not added until 1962, when it was given over to general road traffic. There are eight lanes on the upper deck, six below.

GOETHE HOUSE

1014 5th Ave. (82nd St.), NY 10028 ☎*972-3960. Map **8L4** ▣ Open Wed, Fri, Sat noon-5pm; Tues, Thurs noon-7pm. Closed Sun, Mon.*

Films, lectures, art exhibitions and research materials fill this cultural repository, one of dozens that are sponsored by Germany around the world.

GRACE CHURCH ▥

802 Broadway (10th St.), NY 10003 ☎*254-2000. Map **3R4**. Open Mon-Fri 9am-5.45pm; Sat noon-4pm; Sun for services.*

Although a practicing engineer, James Renwick took advantage of the mid-19thC tolerance for professional generalism to design this fine Episcopal church. Its success led to commissions for ST PATRICK'S CATHEDRAL and the Smithsonian Institution in Washington, all in the Gothic Revival style then in favor. The wealthy congregation already had a church downtown, but opened a competition in 1843 for a new one closer to their homes. Renwick won, although he was only 25, and construction began in the same year. The **marble steeple**, with its delicate filigrees and curls, replaced the wooden original in 1884. There is a lovely **English garden** to the N, in front of the rectory, a later Renwick accomplishment.

The parishioners were virtually all from fashionable society, but propriety was briefly cast aside when circus promoter P.T. Barnum wangled a wedding of his stellar attraction, Tom Thumb, to a lady midget who was also in his employ.

GRACIE MANSION 血

*East End Ave. (E 88th St.), NY 10028. Map **8**K5 ▣ ✗compulsory. Visit by appointment only (write to: Tour Program, Gracie Mansion, East End Ave., NY 10128).*

Now the residence of the mayor of New York City, the mansion is named after Archibald Gracie, the merchant and shipowner who built it in 1799. Prominent details are the encompassing **veranda** and lattice railings at porch and roof levels. It is hard to believe that the house once served as a public lavatory in CARL SCHURZ PARK, in which it is still located.

The wealth that permitted Gracie to erect this stately Federalist mansion evaporated when two of his ships were seized by the French in 1807. His family was forced to sell in 1823, but the families that subsequently owned and lived in the house kept it up. The same couldn't be said of the City, however, which purchased it in 1887 and largely ignored it until the 1930s. At that time, the powerful master builder Robert Moses restored the mansion and persuaded the City's popular mayor, Fiorello LaGuardia, to make it his official residence. LaGuardia moved in during World War II.

Tours of Gracie Mansion are difficult to arrange and tourists without reservations are fenced off at some distance, so the best way to view the house is from the deck of a Circle Line **tour boat** (see USEFUL ADDRESSES on page 44).

GRAMERCY PARK 🏛 ★
Map 6Q4.

A small community forever battling against the dreary commercial en-
croachments nibbling at its edges, these few square blocks evoke
19thC residential elegance as no other area in Manhattan can. The focal
point is the rectangular park from which the district takes its name. The
park is protected by a high fence, and only people living in the surrounding houses have keys to the gate. Edwin Booth is represented by
a statue inside; by all accounts, he was a better actor than his brother
John Wilkes Booth, the assassin of Lincoln. Another president, Theodore Roosevelt, lived nearby. Gramercy Park is part of an official Historic District, a designation which has been awarded to many areas of
the five boroughs by the city's Landmarks Preservation Commission.

GRAND CENTRAL TERMINAL 🏛
Park Ave. and 42nd St., NY 10017. Map 6O4 🖵 ⇌ ☗ *Open 6am-2am.*

An attempt to level the terminal to make way for yet another speculative office tower was thwarted in the late 1970s. Grand Central was
therefore saved from the fate of Penn Station, over on the West Side.
The conservationist effort was worthwhile. Straddling Park Ave., the
main facade looks s, toward what was, in 1913, fast becoming the
center of population and commerce. Its Beaux Arts adornment includes a heroic sculpture group comprised of Mercury, Athena and
Hercules draped around a clock, but this is masked from street level by
the second-story flyovers that encircle the terminal and join lower and
upper Park Ave.

Inside, a vast vaulted space 125 feet (38m) wide, and more than twice
as long, arcs over rush-hour throngs of 190,000 daily commuters. Despite
their headlong rush, not even those who have accumulated 20 years of
workday arrivals and departures are unaware of the grandeur of this main
concourse. Line paintings depict the celestial constellations against the
pale blue ceiling, and light streams through high arched windows.
Musicians of varying persuasions and aptitudes often perform in the great
hall, some with official sanction.

The latest in a series of laudable renovations has removed the famous
giant Kodak photograph at the E end and the large clock above the
corridor to the 42nd St. exit. Take it all in from the open bar inside the
Vanderbilt Ave. entrance, or wend down to the **Oyster Bar and Restaurant** (see WHERE TO EAT) between the main and lower levels. Despite
the unlikely location, this is one of the top seafood restaurants in town.

GRANT'S TOMB   See GENERAL GRANT NATIONAL MEMORIAL.

GREENACRE PARK
51st St. (2nd Ave.). Map 6N5.

Private benefactors have contributed a number of public "pocket"
parks that bestow touches of grace and greenery upon otherwise congested neighborhoods. This is a somewhat ostentatious example, its
open space cluttered up with a semisculptural arrangement of rough-

hewn sentinels, but it is an agreeable retreat from the exhaust fumes and noise.

GREENWICH VILLAGE 🏛 ★
Map 3R3.

Those who could afford it fled the disease, fires and squalor of the city to the s to build homes in what was then this rural village of the late 18thC. The pastoral serenity was short-lived, for the northward sprawl of the metropolis soon swamped it. The rich moved farther uptown, and artists took their places, turning brownstone row houses into apartments and studios. Henry James, Winslow Homer, Edgar Allen Poe and, later, Edna St Vincent Millay and Edward Hopper were among the luminaries who lived here, and "The Village" became America's Left Bank.

Although present-day rents are beyond the means of most poets and painters, *laissez-faire* life-styles pertain, and eccentricity remains in evidence. WASHINGTON SQUARE is the focal point of the neighborhood, which is usually delineated by Houston St., 14th St., 4th Ave. and the Hudson River (see WALK 4 on pages 62-4.)

GUGGENHEIM MUSEUM 🏛 ★
1071 5th Ave. (89th St.), NY 10028 ☎860-1313. Map 8K4 ☒ ✗ ⇌ Open Fri-Wed 10am-8pm. Closed Thurs.

Curmudgeonly genius Frank Lloyd Wright detested New York — he suggested that it be razed and begun again — and the Solomon R. Guggenheim Museum was his only completed commission in the city.

To say that the result was controversial falls well short of the truth. Along a boulevard characterized by conservative apartment houses and Neoclassical public buildings, the exterior of the Guggenheim resembles a flower pot teetering on the edge of a coffee table. The circular central gallery with its spiral stripe of glass is smaller at the base than at the top and squats off-center on a floating horizontal slab. Wright wanted a marble facing; the concrete used instead had an unfortunate yellow cast.

Reaction was predictably divided, even before the 1959 opening. Scornful perplexity was perhaps the most common response, not unlike that accorded to the mostly nonobjective and abstract works of art

The **Guggenheim Museum**, designed by Frank Lloyd Wright

displayed inside. By then, however, Wright was unable to counter-attack, as he was dead.

There was equally vigorous argument over the interior design of the core structure. Logic insists that the best way to view a museum's exhibits is to begin at the top and work down, not exhausting yourself with thoughts of missing rooms and finding elevators. That's how it is here. Take the elevator to the top and slowly descend along the spiral ramp, past bays of paintings and sculptures. Illumination comes from the glass dome and continuous window band, supplemented when necessary by artificial lighting.

Many viewers, though, including an influential group of artists whose works are displayed at the Guggenheim, felt that the ramp made it uncomfortable to consider a painting for more than a moment or two, that it hurried patrons along and made pictures appear lopsided. The furor was stoked anew when the entire museum was closed for over two years to permit the construction of a nine-floor limestone **annex** and a rooftop **sculpture garden**, as well as a complete overhaul of the original building, including floor-by-floor access to the annex.

After the usual delays, it reopened in 1992. Many of the structural modifications made over the last three decades have been cleared away, largely restoring Wright's vision. The small rotunda N of the larger spiral structure once housed offices, but has been re-formed to provide additional exhibition space. With the new floors in the annex, gallery space has been increased by over 60 percent. Many more works are now on view, and the Guggenheim is being reassessed in a new light — one every bit as factious as in 1959.

Architectural arguments aside, the collections and loan exhibitions concentrate on the fathers of modern art — Picasso, Cézanne, Mondrian, Braque, Klee, Chagall, Kandinsky — and Establishment exponents of the New York School of Abstract Expressionism and their successors. Younger experimental artists provide spice.

A branch of the Guggenheim Museum was opened at the same time in a renovated cast-iron building at the corner of Broadway and Prince St. in SoHo.

GUINNESS WORLD OF RECORDS

Empire State Building (350 5th Ave.-34th St.) ☎*947-2335. Map* **6**P4 ▣ ✻
Open daily 9am-8pm.
Trafficking in predictable astonishments presented through video, film and replicas, the hall is an understandable favorite with those suffering a surfeit of profundity from other exhibitions. Compare yourself with life-sized photographs of the tallest, fattest, fastest humans, all under the rubric of the famous encyclopedia of trivia published by the Anglo-Irish brewer. It's fun, for a quick circuit.

HALL OF FAME FOR GREAT AMERICANS

Bronx Community College, 181st St., Bronx, NY 10453 ☎*220-6187. See*
ORIENTATION MAP *on pages 78-9* ▣ *Open daily 10am-5pm.*
This neglected national monument was designed by Stanford White

and dedicated in 1901, when the land it stood on was part of the new uptown campus of NEW YORK UNIVERSITY. To attract the prestige coveted by its administration, the university decided to invent a memorial to Americans who had made substantial contributions to the arts, sciences, statesmanship and pedagogy.

White conceived a semicircular Neoclassical loggia, to curve around his Gould Memorial Library, with busts of national heroes such as Lincoln, Benjamin Franklin, Edison, Booker T. Washington, Thomas Paine and Alexander Graham Bell. A total of 97 are on display. To be considered for inclusion, candidates must have been dead for at least 25 years. The campus is now Bronx Community College, part of the City University of New York.

HARLEM
See ORIENTATION MAP on pages 78-9.
At the turn of the century, Harlem was still a semirural district, shrinking farms alternating with the summer homes of residents of the city to the s. Blocks of tenements were spreading out from the main streets, however, and shortly before World War I, they began to fill with American Blacks migrating from the harshly segregationist South. Their lot improved little, but despite unspeakable poverty, there existed a number of lively music halls and nightclubs.

During the 1920s and early 1930s, Whites from downtown engaged in the social ritual of dancing to jazz and drinking bathtub gin at such places as the Cotton Club (in which Blacks worked and entertained but could not be patrons). Many foreigners still cherish that romantic image, as unreal today as that of cowboys pushing cattle herds through downtown Dallas. It is necessary to stress, therefore, that much of Harlem is uninviting, with addicts and desperate unemployed posing a constant threat to residents and outsiders alike. With notable exceptions, it is emblematic of the failures of American society, and is of interest primarily to visiting sociologists.

That having been said, there are a number of isolated streets and institutions that deserve the attention even of casual tourists. Among these are the museums of the AUDUBON TERRACE complex, the MUSEO DEL BARRIO, AUNT LEN'S DOLL AND TOY MUSEUM, the **Schomburg Center for Research in Black Culture** *(515 Lenox Ave. near 135th St.* ☎ *862-4000),* the restored **Apollo Theater** *(253 W 125th St.* ☎ *749-5838),* and the STUDIO MUSEUM. Architectural restorations of note include the Victorian cottage row of **Sylvan Terrace** near the MORRIS-JUMEL MANSION and the 1890s **St Nicholas Historic District**, which is popularly known as Strivers' Row. The safest ways to see these are by taxi, chauffeured car, or as part of conducted tours such as those offered by **Harlem Renaissance Tours** *(* ☎ *722-9534)* and **Harlem, Your Way!** *(* ☎ *690-1687).*

The district is bounded, roughly, by 96th St., 165th St., Broadway and the East and Harlem rivers. Spanish Harlem, called El Barrio by its Hispanic residents, is the subdivision from 5th Ave. to the East River and N to 125th St. Remnants of Italian Harlem are found in the vicinity of the intersection of 116th St. and 2nd Ave.

HAYDEN PLANETARIUM   Part of the AMERICAN MUSEUM OF NATURAL HISTORY complex, the Planetarium features "cosmic laser concerts," as well as the more usual heavenly explorations.

HISPANIC SOCIETY OF AMERICA   Part of the complex known as AUDUBON TERRACE, this museum focuses on the culture and history of the Iberian Peninsula rather than the Spanish and Portuguese colonies of America.

HISTORICAL SOCIETY   See NEW-YORK HISTORICAL SOCIETY.

HOLLAND TUNNEL
Map 3S2 🖾
The first road tunnel (1927) under the Hudson River, and therefore something of a technological feat, it links Jersey City and Canal St. in Manhattan. The longer, westbound tube is more than $1\frac{1}{2}$ miles in length. Even though the air is changed by giant fans every $1\frac{1}{2}$ minutes, few drivers envy the guards who take turns inside. The tunnel is named after the chief engineer.

IBM GALLERY OF SCIENCE AND ART
590 Madison Ave. (57th St.), NY 10022 ☎ *745-6100. Map 6N4* 🖾 *Open Tues-Sat 11am-6pm.*
Corporations understandably consider it good business to throw a bone or two to the community when they decide to erect yet another giant headquarters skyscraper. A few do this with considerable grace and thoughtful beneficence, as here. Attached to the otherwise conventional main structure is a glassed atrium with trees, snack bars, tables, a stage for luncheon musical performances and a gift store of the New York Botanical Garden.

One level down are two sets of galleries, one with interactive exhibits concerning the results of recent research by (who else?) IBM scientists. The other series of rooms are apt to be of greater interest, containing traveling art shows. These are typically gathered around common themes — "Sport in Art" was one — and feature artists working in styles from photographic realism to thoroughly nonobjective. They are rarely less than illuminating, and are often compelling. Complementary films are often shown.

INTERNATIONAL CENTER OF PHOTOGRAPHY
1130 5th Ave. (94th St.), NY 10028 ☎ *860-1777. Map 8K4* 🖾 *✗ Open Tues noon-8pm; Wed-Fri noon-5pm; Sat, Sun 11am-6pm. Closed Mon.*
One of New York's younger (1974) museums is housed in a 1914 Georgian-Federal house, its brick face and shutters made more attractive by the contrast they make to the grandiose mansions that are customary along this stretch of 5th Ave.

As the only museum in the city devoted solely to photography, its expanding collection focuses on 20thC luminaries Ansel Adams, Irving Penn, Henri Cartier-Bresson, Weegee, and Robert Capa, and is supplemented by as many as 15 special-theme and one-person shows every year. Lectures, audiovisual presentations, workshops, and a book-and-print store contribute to the generally lively atmosphere. There is a smaller midtown branch *(77 W 45th St. ☎536-6443 ⊡ map 6 O4).*

INTREPID SEA-AIR-SPACE MUSEUM
Pier 86 Hudson River, end of W 46th St. ☎245-0072. Map 502 ▨ ✱ Open Wed-Sun 10am-5pm. Closed Mon, Tues.

The *Intrepid* is an aircraft carrier that first saw active service in the Pacific in World War II, with subsequent duty off Vietnam and as a recovery ship for space vehicles. Now decommissioned and permanently moored in the Hudson, it displays weaponry, warplanes and space hardware. These are hardly dainty, dust-free exhibits in glass cases. One is an entire guided missile submarine, no less, and there are more than three dozen aircraft, among them one of the first to ever land on an aircraft carrier.

Most of the exhibits are under cover, so while the flight deck is bone-chillingly windswept much of the year, *Intrepid* can be visited in winter. Short films show the ship in action, and tours include the impressive control room and bridge.

JACQUES MARCHAIS CENTER OF TIBETAN ART
338 Lighthouse Ave., Staten I sland, NY 10306 ☎(718) 987-3500 ▨ ✗ by appointment. Open Apr-Nov Wed-Sun 1-5pm; other months by appointment. Closed Mon, Tues. Staten Island Ferry from Manhattan. Near Richmondtown Restoration. Take a taxi or S113 bus from ferry terminal.

The Staten Island Ferry is worth taking just for the breathtaking views it affords. But if an additional excuse is required, this museum might head the list. It did for the Dalai Lama, who visited it in 1991 during a tour of the US. Within the relatively accurate replica of a Buddhist temple (1947) are exquisite bronzes, scrolls, painted silks, and religious books. Some objects are carved from human bones. Many of them are Tibetan in origin, but China, Nepal, and adjacent regions are also represented.

Linger a moment in the terraced gardens dotted with Oriental deities and animal sculptures. Jacques Marchais, the founder, was in fact a female (and American) art dealer, but in the 1940s a male (and French) name was a business asset.

Special events are scheduled for many Sundays at 2pm, such as recitals of traditional Chinese dance and demonstrations of Buddhist sand painting.

JAPAN HOUSE
333 E 47th St. (1st Ave.), NY 10017 ☎832-1155. Map 605 ▨ ✗ by appointment. Open Tues-Sun 11am-5pm. Closed Mon. Longer hrs during exhibitions.

The contemplative and ordered *shibui* tradition flourishes in this otherwise electric neighborhood, with frequent loan exhibitions of such delicacies as *Noh* masks, decorated paper screens, scrolls, and diverse Shinto and Buddhist objects. Founded in 1907 to promote understanding between the two countries, the parent Japan Society has grown even more relevant with the influx of Japanese businessmen and their families, and the attendant adjustment problems. Conferences and other outreach efforts attempt to address ongoing tensions between the US and Japan.

While classes in Japanese, films, recitals, and lectures are major features of the society's agenda, the **art gallery** is of greater interest to tourists. Frequently changed shows focus on everything from ceremonial swords and kimonos to contemporary photography and art films.

JACOB K. JAVITS CONVENTION CENTER

655 W 34th St. (12th Ave.), NY 10001 ☎*216-2000. Map 5P2.*

A center for extra-large meetings and expositions was sorely needed by the city, and this contemporary crystal palace facing the Hudson was the solution. Designed by the noted I.M. Pei firm, its two main halls are the size of 15 football fields, and the lobby is high enough to shelter the Statue of Liberty. It is the venue of choice for such events as conventions and auto shows. The only deficiency is its somewhat isolated location and the resultant difficulty in finding transport.

JEWISH MUSEUM

1109 5th Ave. (92nd St.), NY 10028 ☎*860-1888. Map 8K4* 🖾 (🔳 *Tues 5-8pm)* ✗ *Open Mon, Wed, Thurs noon-5pm; Tues noon-8pm; Sun 11am-6pm. Closed Fri, Sat.*

Within this conventional 1908 château, with its bland 1963 wing, is an important collection of Judaica that is of interest to people of all faiths. Special exhibitions of contemporary painting and sculpture are mounted on the same premises as a reproduction of a Persian synagogue and displays of prayer-holding *mezuzahs* and 8-candle *menorahs.*

On view are a variety of ceremonial objects, both intricately wrought and stunningly simple: wedding rings, Torah headpieces and crowns, circumcision instruments, spice boxes, and amulets. Especially poignant are reminders of the poverty of Lower East Side immigrants and the incomprehensible tragedy of the Holocaust. A diorama of Israel, created by schoolchildren, is both charming and enlightening.

A major renovation of the museum was scheduled for completion in late 1992, but given the spotty track record of such projects, call ahead to make sure the museum has reopened *(temporary information number* ☎*399-3344).*

JUDSON MEMORIAL BAPTIST CHURCH 🏛

55 Washington Sq. S (Sullivan St.), NY 10012 ☎*477-0351. Map 3R4. Open Mon-Fri 9am-5pm. Closed Sat, Sun except for services; July-Aug closed Mon.*

More than merely supportive of the cultural and political concerns of its GREENWICH VILLAGE constituency, Judson initiates. Parishioners and ministers carry forth energetic programs in the arts and community affairs. Architects McKim, Mead and White designed a Venetian variation on their customary predilection for the Romanesque, and the 1892 facade continues to brighten the hodgepodge of Washington Sq. South. The adjacent campanile is now part of a NEW YORK UNIVERSITY residence hall. A fundraising campaign is underway to enable urgently needed repairs of the roof, plumbing, and marble exterior.

LEVER HOUSE 🏛
390 Park Ave. (53rd St.), NY 10022. Map 6N4.
In its way as difficult to miss as ST BARTHOLOMEW'S CHURCH two blocks s, Lever House was in the forefront of the Bauhaus-influenced third phase of skyscraper fever that seized the imagination of developers in the post-World War II years. The builders embraced the new glass-and-steel curtain wall technology, but with important variations. For one, they broke the unvarying high-rise canyon of Park Ave. by the astonishing decision not to use every bit of available air space. The wide side of the unadorned slab tower is turned s, at a right angle to the avenue, permitting air and sun to circulate. For another, the color is an unusual blue-emerald. In its totality, Lever House fulfils the promise of the International Style that was to be denied its descendants. Even architects Skidmore, Owings and Merrill infrequently matched their achievement in subsequent efforts.

LIBERTY ISLAND   See STATUE OF LIBERTY.

LINCOLN CENTER 🏛 ★
140 W 65th St. (Columbus Ave.), NY 10023. Map 7M3 ▣ 𝑥 ▣ ⇒ 𝑥 daily 10am-5pm ⴲ Open 10am-5pm; theaters various times and prices.
An ambitious conglomeration of six concert halls and theaters, the Lincoln Center for the Performing Arts is the home of the **Metropolitan Opera Company**, **New York Philharmonic Orchestra**, **American Ballet Theater**, and the **New York City Opera** and **Ballet**. It also hosts a variety of visiting ballet and repertory companies, symphony orchestras, film festivals, and popular and classical performing artists and events.

No project of such magnitude, especially one concerned with the arts, could hope to sail from conception to realization without conflict. Lincoln Center provoked dismay, outrage, and a chain reaction of second-guessing that is only now fading before the recognition that this is a cultural resource of monumental importance.

It happened that in the post-World War II years, several of the city's premier performing arts organizations were seeking new premises. This need coincided with planners casting about for ways to arrest the decline of various Manhattan neighborhoods. The new United Nations Headquarters accomplished that on the EAST SIDE, helping to establish New York as a world capital of statesmanship. It seemed that the proposed Lincoln Center might do the same for the arts. On balance it has, allowing for quibbles over interior decor and acoustics. Admittedly, the architectural whole is more impressive than its parts, despite the participation of Eero Saarinen and Philip Johnson.

Approach is customarily made from Columbus Ave., up long, low steps into the main plaza. Most impressive at night, when the center fountain and facades are lit, the **New York State Theater** is on the left, **Avery Fisher Hall** on the right, and the rounded arches of the **Metropolitan Opera House** directly ahead. To reach the **Vivian Beaumont Theater** and **Mitzi Newhouse Theater**, cut between the Opera House and Avery Fisher Hall. The Beaumont building incorporates the research **Library and Museum of the Performing Arts**, a branch of the public library system *(Ⅹ Thurs 11am)*.

On the N side of 65th St., **Alice Tully Hall** adjoins the **Juilliard School**, a prestigious performing arts college. There, too, is the new **Walter Reade Cinema**, which shows art- and revival films. To the s of the Opera House is **Damrosch Park** with its **Guggenheim Bandshell**. In warmer months, the pedestrian spaces are enlivened by outdoor cafés, ice cream kiosks and wandering street musicians.

To greater or lesser degree, the buildings reveal Classical inspiration informed by Modernist sensibilities, from austere to romantic in interpretation according to the predilections of their designers. Each enjoys the presence of large-scale artworks by notable painters and sculptors. Avery Fisher Hall, with the New York Philharmonic in residence, has Richard Lippold's *Orpheus and Apollo;* the Opera House, two Marc Chagall murals; the New York State Theater, a Lee Bontecou and a Jasper Johns, among others.

Among the four restaurants at the center are the **Allegro Café** *(noon-8pm)* and **Fountain Café** *(noon-midnight)* in Avery Fisher Hall, and the **Grand Tier** *(open to ticketholders 2hrs before performances)* in the Opera House. Guided tours of the Center last for approximately 1 hour *(☎877-1800 ext. 516)*. Backstage tours of the Opera House are also available *(☎582-3512, Oct-June only)*. Box office telephones are listed by theater under NIGHTLIFE AND ENTERTAINMENT.

LINCOLN TUNNEL
Map 5O1 ▦ only when crossing W-E.
The three tubes of the tunnel were completed in 1937, 1945 and 1957. That in the middle is the longest, at more than $1\frac{1}{2}$ miles. Remarkable as it might seem to the rational among us, it is the annual site of what the organizers choose to describe as a "fun run." About 800 athletes take part.

The tunnel connects the city of Weehawken in New Jersey with W 38th St. in Manhattan, providing an additional Hudson River crossing.

LIPSTICK BUILDING
885 3rd Ave. (53rd St.), NY 10022. Map 6N5. Not open to public.
Architect Philip Johnson has had several large commissions in the city, virtually all of them controversial, at least when first unveiled. None, however, has been so widely scorned as this office tower, with its oval floor plan and reddish-brown facing. "Lipstick Building" isn't its official name, but it has no other commonly known identity. New Yorkers dubbed it that because it looks like (a) a telescoping lipstick, or (b) the

container it came in. Johnson shares credit for the blunder (as it is widely perceived) with John Burgee. It makes the **Citicorp Center**, which it faces, look like a triumph of post-modernist design.

LITTLE ITALY
Map 4S5.
Sicilian and Neapolitan immigrants made this their urban hamlet during the same period (1880-1925) that European Jews were establishing their Lower East Side community on the other side of THE BOWERY. Bounded on the W by Lafayette St., and by Houston St. and Canal St. to the N and S, the neighborhood is shrinking, but still vigorous. The quarter was always small, for arriving Italians and their children dispersed quickly throughout the five boroughs and into the suburbs.

But this warren of narrow streets and stunted tenements became symbolic of the Old Country and retains that flavor. Gray-haired women, dressed in black, clutch string bags as they move from fish store to bakery while their menfolk play *bocce* or sip espresso in murky coffee houses. The *Festa di San Gennaro* in September booms with brass bands and sizzles with booth after booth of sausage and *calzone*. (See CALENDAR OF EVENTS and WALK 3, page 61.)

LOWER EAST SIDE
Map 4R5.
Immigrants of every race and nationality have made this shabby tenement district E of THE BOWERY and N of Canal St. their first stopover, but its identity for many decades was East European Jewish. Millions of indigent Slavs, Poles, Russians and Lithuanians poured into these mean streets, from 1870 until harsh new laws stemmed the flow in the 1920s. They lived in five-story buildings without plumbing, two or three families to an apartment, creating a population density surpassing that of Calcutta. The lucky ones were pushcart peddlers, who were at least out in the fresh air; the others labored in the sweatshops of the garment trade. Yiddish was the prevailing tongue, and at one time there were 500 synagogues.

Blacks and Hispanics now dominate, but a taste of that former era — and some remarkable shopping bargains — can be had along **Orchard St.** On Sunday, the three blocks between **Delancy St.** and **E Houston St.** are the liveliest on the Lower East Side, so jammed with shoppers, residents, and merchants that cars are banned. Discount stores are the reason, most of them selling clothing, but also luggage, fabrics, shoes, and accessories. Bargain-seekers pick their way through the blare of salsa and disco music, past signs in at least four languages, beneath clothes hung above like heraldic banners. Designer items can be found at prices 20-50 percent below retail, if you are willing to accept the inconveniences of communal changing rooms, shabby fixtures, and harried and often brusque sales people.

Do not go on Friday or Saturday, when almost everything is closed and the absence of crowds leaves the streets both less safe and less interesting.

MADISON SQUARE GARDEN

8th Ave. (33rd St.), NY 10001 ☎*465-6741. Map 5P3* ■■ =◾ ■ *Opening times vary according to events scheduled.*

The present complex is the fourth version on the third site. Only the first two were even in the vicinity of Madison Square, nor did any of them have plants or flowers in sufficient quantities to justify the "Garden" label. In all its manifestations, from 1871 to the present day, Madison Square Garden has been concerned with sports and popular entertainment. It has conventions, a circus, ice shows, hockey, basketball, horse and dog competitions, rodeo, wrestling, prizefighting, and rock concerts.

For no good reason, the architecturally imposing Penn Station was razed to street level in 1968 to permit the construction of this insipid building. Incredibly, plans were afoot to abandon this structure and erect a *fifth* version, but reason prevailed. The powers decided instead to spend $200 million on a complete makeover of the existing complex. This included the installation of a concert venue, the **Paramount**, and two new restaurants, **Play by Play** and **The Club.** Any given afternoon and evening, the facility might host a tennis tournament, a Barry Manilow concert, and a Knicks basketball game.

And now, belated regrets for destroying the old Penn Station have prompted discussions about converting the nearby 1913 General Post Office into a railroad terminal. Located on 8th Ave. from 31st to 33rd Sts., it is of the same era and colonnaded design and evidently could be transformed with relatively little difficulty, since some train tracks and platforms already run beneath the building.

MARBLE COLLEGIATE CHURCH

272 5th Ave. (29th St.), NY 10001 ☎*686-2770. Map 6P4. Open Mon-Sat 9am-6pm; Sunday for services only.*

An 1854 edifice by Samuel A. Warner, it was commissioned by a congregation of the Dutch Reformed faith, which had its roots in the earliest settlement. The official landmark designation is due as much to age as to architectural worth. Consistent with its time, both Gothic and Romanesque motifs were used in a satisfactory (if not especially striking) blend.

METROPOLITAN MUSEUM OF ART 🏛 ★

5th Ave. (82nd St.), NY 10028 ☎*570-3711* ☎*535-7710 (recorded information)* ☎*570-3949 (concerts, lectures). Map 8L4* ■■ ✗ *by guides or on rented tapes, in several languages* =◾ ■ ✹ ◄ *entrance on 5th Ave. (80th St.). Open Sun, Tue-Thurs 9.30am-5.15pm; Fri-Sat 9.30am-8.45pm. Closed Mon and some holidays (check ahead)* 💷 *children under 12 accompanied by adult. Photography without flash permitted, except at special temporary exhibitions.*

Grand in concept and numbing in scope, this is the largest single repository of art and antiquities in the Western Hemisphere. There are 18 departments and 248 galleries, with well over one million prints, paintings, sculptures, furnishings, costumes, ceramics, musical instruments, armor and reassembled sections of ancient temples and palaces.

Barely 25 percent of the collection is on view at any one time. There are, in addition, three libraries, two auditoriums, an art and book store, a gift store, a cafeteria, a restaurant with table service, and a snack shop. Concerts, films and lectures are also staged (☎ 570-3764).

It might all be intimidating, were it not for an imaginative administration determined to enhance accessibility. Huge, colorful banners billow from the 5th Ave. facade, touting the two or three special exhibitions that are always on offer. These nearly always tie in with popular enthusiasms of the moment — Chinese costumes, the treasures of Tutankhamen, Viking artifacts — the better to draw infrequent museum-goers who are unfamiliar with the permanent exhibits. Galleries are laid out in an orderly manner; attendants are gracious and often speak other languages; and there are special programs for children and ready access for older or disabled people. There is an air of authority flushed with innovation, and a desire to relate past to present. The philosophy works: yearly, more than 5 million people visit.

The building itself is of interest, an amalgamation of the architectural styles dominant at the time of each addition. Its core is the unassuming Ruskinian Gothic structure that was the first home of the museum in 1880. The only major edifice within the boundaries of Central Park, its front then faced w into the trees. This exterior is now enclosed by the **Lehman Pavilion**. The familiar 5th Ave. facade was completed in 1902, reorienting the building and dictating its future development. Best defined as being of the Beaux Arts school for its blending of Roman and Renaissance conceits, it is approached by broad steps rising from the street. Three massive arches are bracketed by four pairs of impressive columns with Corinthian capitals. Resulting niches were intended to house figures representing the four epochs of human history, but these were never commissioned. Wings reach N and S to a length of almost three blocks.

Inside, the **Great Hall** is the fulfillment of a Piranesi vision, but without the oppressive gloom that this implies. There are plants and benches, and huge sprays of cut flowers in stone urns. An information booth in the center stocks floor plans, and makes announcements of special events. The Met cannot be absorbed in one lightning tour. Sit down for a moment and determine which departments are of greatest interest.

The curatorial staff has been engaged in a massive reorganization program for nearly 20 years, in combination with a period of ambitious new construction that has added four major wings. Although this two-pronged effort is essentially complete, this is an organic museum that never stands still. Temporary and permanent exhibitions are constantly being mounted, and many other works are routinely shuffled in and out of storage. The following guide to the galleries can therefore only be a general one, because of the likelihood of frequent modification.

The **Egyptian Wing** (★) is as good a place to start as any, for it is acknowledged to be one of the major collections of its kind. Turn right from the main entrance on the first floor, following the passageway at the N end of the Great Hall. A child's innocent enthusiasm for the macabre may be stimulated by the sepulcher of Lord Chamberlain Per-nedbi that is seen first, and by the **mummies and sarcophagi** displayed in the corridors leading off to the left and right. There is a superb **jewelry collection**, as well as textiles, glass and ceramic objects of ceremonial and household use. **Gallery 31** is a long room of meticulous facsimiles of paintings found in temples and burial places. Next are artifacts of the Ptolemaic period, including numerous funerary figures, sculptures and reliefs. Papyri from the *Book of the Dead*, a compilation of medicinal formulas and religious rituals, date from around the 5thC BC.

Galleries 2-15 encompass the 1st-18th dynasties, followed by a similar number of rooms devoted to the delicately crafted reliefs, facsimiles of tomb paintings and funerary relics of the 18th-30th dynasties. These finally lead to the **Sackler Wing**. This handsome 2-story pavilion encloses (and somewhat overwhelms) the **Temple of Dendur**. A gift of the Egyptian government, it was painstakingly dismantled, pieces numbered and charted, and sent here for reassembly. Light bathes the temple through a vast bank of glass in the N wall and reflects on the water of the U-shaped pool that frames its base. Reorganization continues in adjacent galleries.

To maintain historical sequence, return to the Great Hall and cross to **Gallery 11**, where a portion of the **Greek, Cypriot and Roman collection of statuary and ceramics** is on view. Many of these pieces were contributed by the first director of the museum, Luigi Palma di Cesnola, who was responsible for their discovery and excavation. Just beyond is the **Fountain Restaurant** *(open Sun, Tues-Thurs 11.30am-3.30pm; Fri-Sat 9.30am-8pm)* and **Cafeteria** *(open Sun, Tues-Thurs 9.30am-4.30pm; Fri-Sat 9.30am-8pm)*.

Turn right, W, just before the restaurant and enter the **Michael C. Rockefeller Wing**. Opened in 1982, it houses, in 42,000 square feet (3,900sq.m) of exhibition space, superb examples of the arts of Africa, Oceania and pre-European America. The wing, and much of the art within, were donated by Nelson A. Rockefeller and named after his son, who disappeared on an anthropological expedition in 1961. There are more than 1,500 objects on display, including Papuan masks of bark cloth and cane, Olmec jade and ceramic figurines, Mayan reliefs, wood carvings of Benin and the Ivory Coast, and Eskimo (Inuit) sculptures. These sprawling rooms adjoin the **Nathan Cummings Collection**, with a narrower but comprehensive focus on pre-Columbian art and artifacts of Mexico, Mesoamerica and South America. Stone sculptures, ornamental censers, ceremonial masks and North American Indian crafts are viewed in engrossing profusion.

Continuing W through the Rockefeller Wing, the new, 2-story (and mezzanine) **Lila Acheson Wallace Wing** is encountered. It houses part of the museum's growing collection of 20thC art, defined to include Europeans and Americans born in the 19thC, but who lived into this century. The range therefore includes sedate academic painters, Post-Impressionists, Cubists, and figurative painters, as well as Abstract Expressionists. There are works by Picasso, Max Beckmann, Thomas Hart Benton, Matisse, Georgia O'Keeffe and Pollock, that include such famous paintings as Picasso's portrait of *Gertrude Stein* and Ivan Albright's *Fleeting Time Has Left Me Cold*. An entire long room houses a single environmental work of the artist Robert Rauschenberg. It is titled $\frac{1}{4}$ *mile or 2 furlongs,* and since only approximately *one* furlong is on view, perhaps there is more to come. Another gallery devotes itself to modern design in architecture and furniture, and yet another to prints and drawing. There is a rooftop sculpture garden.

Return again to the Great Hall and go down the corridor to the right of the central staircase. This leads into the section devoted to **medieval art**. After a clockwise circuit of the tapestries and ecclesiastical objects, make your way to the recently reorganized **arms and armor gallery**, which is dominated by a mounted troop of knights, and augmented by heraldic banners, crossbows and other armaments. At the far end of the vaulted hall are cases of flintlock pistols and wheelock rifles sumptuously inlaid with ivory, brass and exotic woods, as well as examples of the "guns that won the West." On the right are rooms of Japanese and Chinese warrior gear, with mounted Samurai of the Edo period and helmets decorated with exotic fish, birds and demons.

A door in the W wall leads into the enclosed garden court of the **American Wing**. Trees, 19thC statues and a reflecting pool provide a quiet resting place beneath a glass roof. At the N end is the 1824 Greek Revival facade of a former Wall St. bank. Enter the door at the right to view portions of the most extraordinary collection of **American furniture and decorative arts** in existence. Three floors of 18 period rooms and 12 galleries proceed from Colonial times (1630) into the Federal period, ending c.1825.

Installations still in progress will carry the story forward to the early 20thC. Splendid Chippendale bureaux and paintings of the **Hudson River School** are joined with comprehensive assortments of silver, pewterware, antique glass, ceramics and textiles. For a chronological view, begin on the third floor of the wing and walk down.

Afterwards, leave the garden court by the doorway at the S corner. Pass through a large **gallery of European sculpture and decorative arts**, which covers essentially the same period as the American Wing. Bear right, then left, through the **English period rooms**. Just beyond is the entrance to the **Lehman Pavilion**, where Robert Lehman's collection of early Italian and 19th and 20thC French art is displayed in modern galleries and somber period rooms, the latter reconstructed from his house on W 54th St. Among the Italian works are drawings by Leonardo da Vinci and Botticelli. Of the later period, Ingres' *Portrait of the Princess of Broglie* is characteristic of his uncanny aptitude for naturalistic reproduction. The Fauvists, an Expressionist offshoot of Post-Impressionism, are represented by Vlaminck and Derain. A quick circuit of the wing is sufficient.

Leave by the door through which you entered, noting in passing the 1880 facade of the original museum building. Turn right into the **French period rooms**, which include a reconstructed 18thC Parisian shopfront, and boudoir furnishings commissioned by Marie-Antoinette. An adjoining room has additional **European sculpture and decorative arts**. Return to the Great Hall. This is a good interval at which to break off the visit, saving the rest for another day.

Picking up where we left off, mount the central staircase at the w of the Great Hall. Remarkable riches are confronted on the second floor, and the layout does not lend itself to a programed tour. Straight ahead are the enormously popular **galleries of European paintings**. They commence with large Baroque canvases of debatable content but undeniable drama. Continuing w, a maze of smaller galleries reveals the gems of the **Dutch collection**. Rembrandt's *Aristotle Contemplating a Bust of Homer* is the work of the artist's mature years, less theatrical than some of his earlier masterpieces. The concern with light remains, but it is a subtle mist, not a blinding shaft through clouds or portal. An oddity was Rembrandt's decision to clothe Aristotle in 17thC dress. The *1660 Self Portrait* (★) is an unsparing examination of his late middle age, the face pallid and corpulent, but with dignity intact. Vermeer was also intrigued by the properties of light, but in a narrow optical sense. The flesh of his *Young Woman with a Water Jug* (★) has the luminosity of an eggshell lit from within by a candle flame. Any emotional impact is vitiated by the serenity of his subject matter and compositions, but he inspires admiration for his flawless technique.

For powerful imagery, move on to the **Spanish section** and El Greco's *View of Toledo*. This was his only landscape and one of his greatest works — a big, somber canvas, which conveys an uneasy sense of foreboding through its lowering storm clouds. The portrait of *Juan de Pareja* (★) by Velázquez was acquired in 1970, the most costly single purchase the museum had made until that time. Velázquez was perhaps unequaled in his sensitive portrayal of character, and in this painting he focuses all his skill on bringing the humanity of a friend to eternal life.

The connecting **French galleries** include fine examples of Claude and Watteau, as well as Poussin's celebrated *Rape of the Sabine Women*.

Complete your tour of the European galleries with a wander through the **English rooms**, where portraits by Reynolds and Gainsborough hang alongside Turner's visionary cityscape, *The Grand Canal*.

To the N of these rooms is an enchanting accumulation of lutes, sitars, gongs, temple bells, nose flutes, sarindas and other exotic **musical instruments**. Return to the top of the central staircase and turn left into a corridor given to **recent acquisitions** and **drawings and prints**.

This empties into the newly redesigned **André Meyer galleries**, an important collection of 19thC European art. Turn left into a room of drawings by Degas, Renoir and Manet. In the center are Degas' bronzes of dancers — his favorite subject. Only one piece of Degas sculpture was exhibited in his lifetime, yet in this room alone are 12. In the second gallery is the charming miniature oil on wood, *The Dancing Class,* and a dozen more sculptures, all by Degas. The instinctive grace of his dancers is only made more profound by the odd angularity or awkward position, or the implied sheen of sweat brought on by endless repetition of exercises. Further confirmation of his mastery can be found in the third room, which is dominated by a large **bronze figure** (1922) with a tutu of real muslin.

Bearing right, you enter a large hall filled with heroic sculptures by Rodin and Maillol. Especially arresting is Rodin's tormented study of

Adam. The rest of the Meyer galleries are devoted to paintings, a cornucopia of 19thC artistic fecundity. The transition away from both Classicism and Romanticism toward as yet unimagined frontiers is illustrated here in the manifold works of Corot and Courbet. The "Establishment" these artists competed with is also represented by the polished Neoclassicism of Ingres. Despite Courbet's own strivings toward greater realism, he is said to have been dismayed by Manet's rejection of principles of perspective. In the 21 canvases by this younger artist, you can see striking concessions toward the two-dimensionality of the picture-plane. His flat, poster-ish portraits are almost devoid of shadow and simulated depth. Manet is often classified wrongly as an Impressionist, but his real kinship lies with such Post-Impressionists as Cézanne and Van Gogh, who are both well represented here. The scope and complexity of these works — most of them mounted in a large central room that does them full justice — is nothing less than breathtaking.

Eventually, these galleries lead into the **Islamic art collection**, the highlight of which is the **Syrian Nur Ad-Din House** (1707). The wall panels of the room produced here are modeled out of gesso, with ornate floral patterns and inscriptions in Arabic. Adjacent galleries show ceremonial vessels, chess pieces and silk carpets and hangings. Beyond the halls containing **Greek and Roman art** and **Ancient Near-Eastern art,** you reach the open balcony square above the Great Hall.

Continuing N past **Far-Eastern art**, go through the special exhibition areas until you arrive at the **Astor Court**. Yet another recent addition, it is a reconstruction of a Chinese garden of the Ming dynasty (1368-1644), based on an authentic example that still exists in Soochow. It is a pleasantly tranquil spot in which to pause for a while and reflect upon all that you have experienced so far within the walls of this vast treasure house. Complete your tour by traveling two escalator flights down to the **Costume Institute**. Its biennial exhibitions have featured ancient Chinese garments, Parisian *haute couture,* and theatrical wardrobes.

Also down in the basement is the **Uris Center for Education**, created to introduce children and teenagers to the mysteries of art and history manifest in the floors above. There are frequent lectures and films intended to be shared with parents, as well as displays drawn from the larger collections.

Recorded cassette tours are available at moderate rentals, covering 21 subjects and galleries, some of them in languages other than English. There are also lectures, films and concerts ranging from discussions of painting techniques, to cinematic explorations of biblical and esthetic interrelationships, to recitals by the Juilliard Quartet. The museum takes on a festive, romantic air Friday and Saturday evenings after 5pm, when the music of a string quartet fills the Great Hall, and cocktails are served on the candlelit balcony.

MIDTOWN EAST
Map 6.

This concentration of corporate headquarters, foreign consulates, and publishing and advertising firms brings to it streams of business people and diplomats, and shoppers are inexorably drawn toward the fabled luxury emporia of 5th Ave. Coping with this influx are many of Manhattan's most exclusive hotels (**Palace**, **Waldorf-Astoria**, **Grand Hyatt**) and restaurants (**Four Seasons**, **Lutèce**, **La Côte Basque**). It's also a residential area, but only for people who needn't concern themselves with the price of a second Mercedes. Penthouses with roof terraces, gardens and even swimming pools perch above the East River, their foliage visible from the streets. Principal sights are ST PATRICK'S CATHEDRAL, the UNITED NATIONS HEADQUARTERS, GRAND CENTRAL TERMINAL, and those exemplars of the International Style in architecture, LEVER HOUSE and the SEAGRAM BUILDING.

MORRIS-JUMEL MANSION 🏛

1765 Jumel Terrace (near W 161st St.), NY 10032 ☎*923-8008. See* ORIENTATION MAP *on pages 78-9* 🖂 *✗ Open Tues-Sun 10am-4pm. Closed Mon. Subway 1 to 157th St.; B to 163rd St.-Amsterdam Ave.*

Given its age (it was built in 1765), Georgian core, and Federal overlay (1810), the mansion warrants attention for its architecture alone, start-

ing with its lordly Palladian portico. But great historical figures lived and loved and dined here, and as is only fitting, ghosts are reported to have materialized. Roger Morris was the builder. Although a friend of George Washington, he was a loyal subject of the King and left the country at the outbreak of the Revolution. Both Washington and the British general Henry Clinton made the house their headquarters during the War. After a period of service as a tavern, it was bought by French wine merchant Stephen Jumel for his wife Eliza. They renovated the house in Federal style and filled it with Empire furniture, much of which is still here.

The Jumels held lavish parties and banquets, which encouraged New York Society to overlook the rumor that Eliza was the illegitimate child of a prostitute and had pursued that profession herself. She reportedly started an affair with Aaron Burr before Stephen died in 1832, surprising only in part because the former Vice President was then in his seventies. Scheming Eliza and the brilliantly devious Burr kept house for a while after Stephen's death, but it was not a happy match and he soon moved out. Burr's room is at the top of the stairs, and there is a portrait of Eliza in her 80th year. The ghosts? A Hessian soldier and Eliza herself. Perhaps they are aided by the secret passageways.

MURRAY HILL
*Map **6**P4.*

A low-key residential quarter with indistinct boundaries, Murray Hill lacks the kind of attractions that capture the attention of developers and tourists. No doubt that suits the residents. Following the usual progression from Colonial farmland to Federalist village to elegant suburb to bypassed backwater, Murray Hill managed to avoid the usually inevitable decay. Compressed by commercial development along the central N-S avenues, it is delineated, roughly, by Park Ave. and 3rd Ave. from 33rd St. to 42nd St. Strips of 19thC row houses and carriage house mews such as **Sniffen Court** (36th St., between Lexington and 3rd Aves.) have been transformed into quietly handsome private apartments and homes. Several good hotels trade the slightly out-of-the-way location for its relative tranquility, and a number of competent restaurants have opened in recent years.

MUSEO DEL BARRIO
1230 5th Ave. (104th St.), NY 10029 ☎*831-7272. Map 8J4* ▨ *✗ Open Wed-Sun 11am-5pm. Closed Mon, Tues.*
The vitality of Hispanic culture is repeatedly validated by the changing exhibitions of photographs, paintings and crafts in this gallery of El Barrio (Spanish Harlem). Pre-Columbian figures and works by other modern Latin Americans broaden the appeal.

MUSEUM OF AMERICAN FOLK ART
2 Lincoln Square (Columbus Ave., between 65th and 66th Sts), NY 10023 ☎*977-7298. Map 7M3* ▨ *Open 11.30am-7.30pm.*
Cast out of its crumbling former digs on W 54th St., the museum was without a home for three years. Now ensconced in a glass-enclosed plaza opposite Lincoln Center, it can once again display its collections of works by unschooled but talented American craftspeople from Colonial times to the present day. There is an enchanting assortment of weather vanes, carved and painted saints, whirligigs, toys, kitchen implements, quilts, shop signs, bird decoys, and clean-lined furniture that predates the Danish Modern style by a century. Frequent temporary shows are mounted, and the popular gift store sells examples of contemporary folk art — dolls, rugs, crafts — and has an excellent book selection. Permanent although it seems, this, too, is a way station. In 1994, the museum is scheduled to move to still another facility, this one on W 53rd St., near the MUSEUM OF MODERN ART. It is well worth following.

MUSEUM OF AMERICAN ILLUSTRATION
128 E 63rd St. (Lexington Ave.), NY 10021 ☎*838-2560. Map 8M4* ▣ *Open Mon-Fri 10am-5pm; Tues 10am-8pm. Closed Sat, Sun, Aug.*
Rotating exhibitions of commercial art for books, magazines and print advertising are mounted in this museum, under the sponsorship of the Society of Illustrators. The permanent collection is augmented by theme shows and the eagerly-anticipated annual exhibition of award-winning works.

MUSEUM OF THE AMERICAN INDIAN   Presently part of the AUDUBON TERRACE complex, this has the largest collection of Native American artifacts in the United States. Part of it is to be moved downtown to the

US Custom House, the other part to the Smithsonian Institution in Washington, DC.

MUSEUM OF THE CITY OF NEW YORK ★
5th Ave. (103rd St.), NY 10029 ☎534-1672. Map 8J4 ▩ *ⅹ ✽ Open Tues-Sat 10am-5pm; Sun and holidays 1-5pm. Closed Mon.*

A museum as lively as the city it celebrates, the five floors of this Neo-Georgian building are crammed with historical dioramas, antique playthings, model ships and decorative arts. Take the elevator to the top and work down.

On the fifth floor are two rooms from the first Rockefeller mansion, done up in High Victorian manner and featuring furnishings by English designer Charles Eastlake. On the third floor are the dollhouses and tiny trams, model farms and penny banks, miniature table settings and hobby horses. On the way out, linger over the Duncan Phyfe furniture, characterized by graceful curves, restrained inlays and stylized swags and lyres. Phyfe worked in Albany, NY and New York City from c.1783 to 1854, and borrowed from Hepplewhite, Sheraton and French Empire examples to formulate his own style.

The second floor has still more period rooms, ranging from the Colonial to the Theodore Roosevelt era. Model ships and displays trace maritime development from New Amsterdam onward, and spill over to the first floor. Space is left on the main floor for an engrossing multimedia presentation that spins through 400 years of local history in barely 20 minutes, employing light, sound, and 24 synchronized projectors. Concerts and walking tours of the city are presented some Sundays during warm weather. After a visit, it may take a while to obtain a taxi, but the tawdry streets immediately to the E of the museum do not invite exploration.

MUSEUM OF HOLOGRAPHY   Located for 16 years in SoHo, this fascinating science-as-art museum ran out of funds and closed its Mercer St. doors in 1992. Its supporters are actively seeking other quarters.

MUSEUM OF MODERN ART ★
11 W 53rd St. (6th Ave.), NY 10019 ☎708-9480 (current exhibitions) ☎708-9490 (films) ☎708-9500 (other info). Map 6N4 ▧ *ⅹ ▣ Open Fri-Tues 11am-6pm; Thurs 11am-9pm. Closed Wed.*

Known with ironic affection by its acronym — MOMA — this daring and innovative museum first lobbied for the validity of modern art at a time when that belief was by no means conceded, then in later years assumed the role of arbiter. An artist represented in the collection is among the anointed, assured of at least a sliver of immortality.

It is alleged by some that the museum has retreated from the forward edge of the avant-garde, that it has grown conservative and protective of its stature. Evidence can be cited in support of that conclusion, but, given the uncertain directions of contemporary art over the last decade or two, caution is understandable. In any event, controversy is the life-blood of an institution such as MOMA.

Modern art is here defined as commencing with the Impressionists in the 1880s and, although the history of the many movements that have since evolved favors abstract and nonobjective modes, figurative options are also shown. Magic Realist Andrew Wyeth's *Christina's World,* for example, is one of the most popular canvases on view. The scope of the founders' intentions is demonstrated by the extensive film library and samples of superior design in such otherwise mundane objects as toasters and tableware.

An ambitious expansion program has been completed, involving the construction of a new West Wing that nearly doubled gallery and storage space. About 30 percent of the permanent collection can now be placed on view.

The book and gift store is to the right of the main entry hall; the admission booths and information desk are straight ahead. Beyond these, an escalator takes you to two lower levels, housing the **René d'Harnoncourt Galleries**, which display temporary exhibitions, and the **Titus Theaters**. The glass wall bordering the hall gives access to the outdoor **Abby Aldrich Rockefeller sculpture garden**, a leafy retreat of pools and fountains dominated at the w end by Rodin's majestic *Balzac* and Gaston Lachaise's equally heroic *Standing Woman.* In counterpoint at the E end are monumental metal sculptures of more recent vintage, including works by Caro, Newman and Oldenburg.

To view the permanent exhibitions inside, return to the main hall. Take the escalator to the second floor and turn left into the first room of the painting and sculpture collection. On-going evolutionary changes are altering the composition and sequence of these galleries, and individual works are frequently put out on loan, so the following sketch of the layout is subject, as always, to continual change. Approximate chronological order of the development of modern art commences with the Post-Impressionists, represented here by *The Bather* and several smaller works of Cézanne. The next three galleries exhibit the work of Gauguin, Seurat, Redon, Toulouse-Lautrec *(La Goulue at the Moulin Rouge)* and Van Gogh *(The Starry Night).* A powerful study of three bathers by Derain dominates the smaller Matisses in the fourth room.

Next are the Cubists, primarily Georges Braque and Pablo Picasso. At the far wall, detour to the left to see Monet's vast angled triptych and the only slightly smaller flat painting of his famous lily ponds. Retrace your steps and continue straight ahead, bearing right, past varied examples of Picasso's Cubist paintings and sculptures, large Léger canvases and a platform of sculptures by Brancusi. A large Chagall looks as fresh as if it were finished yesterday, however faint its Cubist elements. The Expressionists are highlighted by Wilhelm Lehmbruck's sculptures, *Kneeling Woman* and *Standing Youth.* Two rooms on, the eye must adjust to the linear geometrics and flat rectangles of 14 deceptively simple studies by Piet Mondrian. A large gallery, farther on, is devoted to Matisse; his vibrant tones invest *The Red Studio* with delightful intimacy.

After two rooms of intriguing paintings by Klee, Kandinsky and Modigliani, another large space is devoted to Picasso. These astonishingly inventive sculptures and canvases show his advance beyond Cubism, as in the celebrated *Girl Before a Mirror* and *Head of a Woman.* His wrenching antiwar mural *Guernica,* installed here for more than 40 years, has now been returned to Spain, in deference to the artist's wishes. But there is ample testimony to his genius in the works that remain.

Through the door to the right, a salon of Dadaists includes the once-shocking work of the French-born American Marcel Duchamp. Joan Miró is next, his light and witty work classified as Surrealist, but quite unlike the often dark visions of Dalí, Magritte and Pavel Tchelitchew that follow.

On the third floor, the American realists Andrew Wyeth and Edward Hopper are first on view, followed by abstractionist Stuart Davis. Bear left, then right, through two rooms of the early 1940s Abstract Expressionists, notably Newman, Gorky, Pousette-Dart, Rothko, De Kooning and Motherwell. Also displayed are works by the "action painter" Jackson Pollock, who galvanized the art world toward the end of that decade with his technique of applying paint in balletic swoops and traceries. A hiccup in the chronological layout, Room 6 contains Matisse's canvases jointly labeled *Swimming Pool;* but they are followed by more Abstract Expressionists.

The next large rooms are concerned with contemporary works that push the boundaries of even these mid-century pioneers. Among them are assemblages by Robert Rauschenberg, plaster figures by George Segal, Jasper Johns' flag painting, Warhol's and Lichtenstein's Pop icons.

The **architecture-and-design collection** is displayed on the fourth floor, featuring industrial objects and handcrafted items of the last few decades; for example, bentwood chairs, Art Nouveau glass, office equipment, architect-designed furniture, television sets and even a 1946 Pinin Farina car. (A museum store annex at 37 W 53rd St., next to the American Craft Museum, sells objects deemed of similarly superior design.)

MUSEUM OF NATURAL HISTORY   See AMERICAN MUSEUM OF NATURAL HISTORY.

MUSEUM OF TELEVISION AND RADIO
25 W 52nd St. (between 5th and 6th Aves.), NY 10019 ☎*621-6600. Map **6N4*** ▧ *✗ by appointment* ✽ *Open Tues-Sun noon-6pm; Thurs noon-8pm. Closed Mon, major holidays. Mornings reserved for groups, by appointment.*

The former **Museum of Broadcasting** moved to this impressive new 17-story building in 1991. With nearly four times more space than the old facility, there is now room to contain and display the 40,000-plus radio and television programs in the ever-growing collection. (About 3,000 new programs are added each year.) The entire inventory can be summoned via user-friendly computer terminals in the library, and they are available for transmission at 96 individual listening/viewing consoles.

Selected shows, changed daily, are presented on giant screens in four theaters, the largest with 200 seats. These programs usually illustrate a sociological, journalistic or dramaturgical point, for the curators take their responsibilities seriously. There is, for example, an arresting documentary that shows Pablo Picasso transforming a clay pot into a bird. Another records Toscanini conducting his final concert, and yet another follows John F. Kennedy on the campaign trail.

Although the emphasis is on television, with particular attention to the years prior to the introduction of tape technology around 1960, there are recorded radio broadcasts by President Warren Harding and Lord Haw-Haw, as well as a lengthy catalog of commercials. To contain the avid viewing habits of fans of *Star Trek* or *I Love Lucy,* visitors are limited to two hours a day at the consoles.

NATIONAL ACADEMY OF DESIGN

1083 5th Ave. (89th St.), NY 10024 ☎*369-4880. Map 8K4* 📷 *Open Tues noon-8pm; Wed-Sun noon-5pm.*

Founded in 1825 by a group of American artists that included Thomas Cole and Samuel Morse (who was both a skilled painter and inventor of the telegraph), the academy was patterned after the art schools of Europe. More recent members have been Frank Lloyd Wright, Robert Rauschenberg and Winslow Homer. A requirement of membership is the submission of works by each applicant, which form the 7,000-item collection. The Academy's principal interest to casual visitors lies in its frequent exhibitions of some of these paintings, drawings, prints and sculptures, which are usually figurative, rather than abstract, in technique and content.

NATIONAL MUSEUM OF THE AMERICAN INDIAN

1 Bowling Green (between State and Whitehall Sts.), NY 10006. Map 1U4.

Years were lost in agonized discussion over various proposals for disposition of the much-coveted Heye Collection of Native American art and artifacts. Largely ignored by the public and inadequately housed for decades in the MUSEUM OF THE AMERICAN INDIAN at AUDUBON TERRACE in Harlem, the fate of the one-million-item collection became a political, as well as scholarly issue.

"American" here refers to the entire Western Hemisphere, with Inuit carvings, Hopi kachina dolls, Chilean silverwork, and costumes and fetishes from many Indian tribes and empires. Finally, it was decided to divide them between Washington, DC and New York, both parts to be administered by the Smithsonian Institution. The New York portion is to go on view in 1993 in the old **United States Custom House**, near Battery Park. (See WALK 2, pages 56-7.)

NEW MUSEUM OF CONTEMPORARY ART

583 Broadway (near Houston St.), NY 10012 ☎*219-1222. Map 3S4* 📷 *Open Wed, Thurs, Sun noon-6pm; Fri-Sat noon-8.*

And they mean *NEW!* It has always been difficult for young experimental artists to find spaces in which to show the often outrageous results of their fertile creativity. Here is one to rattle even SoHo's esthetic perceptions. The artists are virtually unknown and most of their works are no more than a few years old.

THE NEWS BUILDING

220 E 42nd St. (between 2nd and 3rd Aves.), NY 10016 ☎210-2100. Map 605
☒ ⚊ *Open Mon-Fri 9am-5pm.*

This is the home of *The Daily News*. One of three remaining New York tabloids, *The News* was "saved" by British press lord, Robert Maxwell, less than a year before his suspicious death and subsequently evident insolvency. The building dates from the first wave of skyscraper fever, completed within months of ROCKEFELLER CENTER and the EMPIRE STATE and CHRYSLER BUILDINGS.

Identified by its Art Deco detailing at ground level, the building is best known for the weather instruments and **giant revolving globe** in the lobby. Children like this display (briefly), but be warned that their grasp of geography won't be strengthened overmuch. Even before the upheavals in Eastern Europe, many nations on the globe retained their old labels. Myanmar is still identified as "Burma," Bangladesh is still East Pakistan. The array of instruments on the wall display wind velocity, atmospheric pressure, temperatures, and the hour in 17 time zones.

NEW YORK AQUARIUM

Surf Ave. (W 8th St.), Coney Island, Brooklyn, NY 11224 ☎(718) 265-3474 ☒
⬛ ✳ *Open 10am-5pm.*

From 1892 until 1941, the aquarium was in Castle Clinton (see CASTLE CLINTON NATIONAL MONUMENT) in lower Manhattan. That monument was threatened by proposed highway construction, so the fish were transported to this new aquarium at CONEY ISLAND, on the southern rim of Brooklyn. It is a schizophrenic operation, part amusement center, part marine science laboratory. That does not diminish its appeal.

Predictably, popular exhibits are the sharks, stingrays, 2-ton Beluga whales, performing porpoises and sea lions, and electric eels that light up bulbs. More than 200 species are on view, including piranhas, parrotfish, and sea anemones. Some of the larger or more vulnerable creatures are flown to Florida for the winter, so the best time to go is between May and October.

NEW YORK BOTANICAL GARDEN

Southern Blvd. (200th St.), Bronx, NY 10460 ☎220-8700, 220-8777 ☒ ✗
⬛ *Grounds open Apr-Oct Tues-Sun 10am-7pm; Nov-Mar Tues-Sun 10am-5pm.*
Conservatory open Tues-Sun 10am-4pm. Museum open Mon-Thurs 9.30am-6pm;
Fri-Sat 9.30am-4pm.

Adjacent to the Bronx Zoo on its northern border (see map on page 88), these 250 acres straddle the Bronx River. Here, the river is narrow and untamed, tumbling through a deep gorge. Its course is bordered by a 40-acre preserve of virgin oak and hemlock — the stately trees that covered much of the metropolitan region before the first Europeans arrived.

Entry can be made opposite the Pelham Parkway gate of the zoo. At the first main pedestrian intersection, detour w into the **azalea glen**, then retrace the route E. After the bridge, the **Old Lorillard Snuff Mill** becomes visible on the left. The restored 1840s building is now used as a year-round restaurant. Continue E and N, pausing along the way for displays of lilac, dogwood, magnolia and rhododendron. Eventually the paths converge on the **Museum**, which mounts changing exhibitions on horticultural and ecological themes and incorporates a herbarium and botanical library. To the SW is the centerpiece of the preserve, the **Enid A. Haupt Conservatory**. A grand rotunda of leaded glass is the focus of a complex of ten connecting greenhouses. The effect, inside and out, is of an enchanted crystal palace of the Victorian era. After years of deterioration, it was in danger of demolition. Reason and philanthropy finally prevailed in this glorious rejuvenation, and the rotunda now contains topiary, desert plants and tropical flora.

Obviously the best time to go is between April and August, when the groves and gardens are ablaze with color, but special events draw visitors at Christmas and Easter. Walking is the best way to experience the gardens, but a covered tram stops at choice locations. Hayrides are scheduled periodically from April to November.

NEW YORK CITY FIRE MUSEUM

278 Spring St. (between Hudson St. and Varick St.), NY 10013 ☎691-1303. Map 3S3 ▨ ✚ *Open Tues-Sat 10am-4pm. Closed Sun, Mon.*

New York bristles with quirky and beguiling specialized museums tucked in out-of-the-way corners. They take little time to explore and are often enchanting in unexpected ways. This is one of them, and less difficult to locate than it used to be. The collection is the result of the recent merging of two smaller museums, in what was once a firehouse. A lovingly polished nickel-plated steam engine highlights the assembly of hand- and horse-drawn vehicles that date back to the 18thC, a time of great conflagrations in the city. Antique water pumpers, hose wagons, and examples of helmets and uniforms fill the rooms.

NEW-YORK HISTORICAL SOCIETY

170 Central Park W (77th St.), NY 10024 ☎873-3400. Map 7L3 ▨ *Open Sun, Tues-Fri 11am-5pm; Thurs 11am-8pm. Closed Mon.*

The name is misleading, for while the orientation is America as viewed from a New York perspective, the net is widely cast. Founded in 1804, the society moved to its present home in 1908. Although it lives in the shadow of the AMERICAN MUSEUM OF NATURAL HISTORY, just across the street, the five floors of galleries are well worth perusal. Some galleries are open only on a rotating basis, and many objects that were once on view have been withdrawn, including the horsedrawn carriages formerly displayed in the basement. This is due to a current need for financial retrenchment. Items from the **Jewish Museum's** collection were exhibited here during that institution's extensive renovation.

There are examples of folk art, period rooms, works in silver, Colonial maps and prints, early American toys and carvings, farm and household implements. The fourth floor is devoted primarily to portraits and landscapes by painters of the Hudson River School; the third floor has a collection of antique toys, far fewer in number than on display in the past, but entrancing nonetheless.

The highlight of the second floor is the **World of Tiffany** collection, with dozens of the valuable stained-glass lamps by the turn-of-the-century designer. On the walls of the entry hall are the drawings and watercolors of birds by the naturalist John James Audubon. On the first (ground) floor, paintings, maps and drawings illustrate the city's growth from the days of Dutch rule.

NEW YORK PUBLIC LIBRARY 🏛 ★

5th Ave. (42nd St.), NY 10018 ☎*790-6161. Map 604 ϰ* ▣ *Open Tues, Wed 11am-7.30pm; Thurs-Sat 10am-6pm. Closed Sun, Mon, holidays.*

The city-wide library system has more than 6 million volumes and three times as many related materials — much of it in this, the main branch. They are housed in what many regard as *the* paradigm of the Beaux Arts style that was in vogue at the beginning of the 20thC. Certainly its 5th Ave. facade is more subdued than that of the flamboyant METROPOLITAN MUSEUM OF ART. Beyond the famous pair of reclining lions (sometimes called Patience and Fortitude), long steps and a terrace lead up to the Roman portico. The majestically proportioned lobby beyond the entrance doors is impressive, but it is surpassed in grandeur by the palatial salons on the third floor.

First of these is the **McGraw Rotunda**, lined on walls and arched ceiling with carved and grooved paneling and several large murals depicting what might be described as "great moments in literature" — including Moses in a snit over his flock's bad behavior. Off the rotunda is the **Public Catalog Room**, with similarly effusive gilt and wood gone to waste framing a ceiling painting of no distinction whatever. The library is for reference, not for lending, but most of the volumes in the collection can be summoned from the stacks at the central desk here. This leads into the grandest space of all, the **Main Reading Room**. The paneling is as impressive here , and there is more of it. Computers are available to scan available books and related materials by subject and author, and microfilms of newspapers and periodicals can be reviewed on several machines.

There are frequent exhibitions of books, manuscripts, photographs and prints in exhibition halls on this and the first floor. A copy of the Declaration of Independence written by Thomas Jefferson is on view, as is a desk once owned by Charles Dickens. A library shop on the main floor sells jewelry, greeting cards, assorted *objets,* and, of course, books, including *The New York Public Library Desk Reference.* There is another, larger shop diagonally across 5th Ave. at 6 E 40th St., with a larger selection. The library has a noted telephone reference service, whose personnel can provide answers, with surprising alacrity, to questions ordinary and obscure *(* ☎ *340-0849 Mon-Fri).* Unfortunately, the line is often busy.

BRYANT PARK is behind the library, fronting 6th Ave. It has recently been rehabilitated, roofing over new underground library stacks.

NEW YORK STOCK EXCHANGE 🏛

20 Broad St. (Wall St.), NY 10004 ☎*656-3000. Map 3U4 ϰ compulsory* ▣

Open Mon-Fri 9.15am-4pm, but tickets must be obtained from the guards at the entrance by 1pm for a visit the same day.

A Neoclassical "temple" a few steps away from Wall Street houses the oldest and most powerful stock exchange in the US. On workdays with decent weather, the sidewalk out front is crowded with brokers on lunch or tobacco breaks. Their shapeless jackets are in blue, beige, green and other colors, the better to identify each other on the trading floor. After noting the elaborate sculptural scene contained by the pediment, enter at #20, next door. Guards direct visitors to elevators that carry them to a gallery overlooking the main room. A number of interactive machines and displays attempt to explain, with only moderate success, what the seemingly anarchic frenzy down there attempts to accomplish.

NEW YORK UNIVERSITY 🏛

Washington Sq., NY 10003 ☎*598-3127. Map 3R4. Open Mon-Sat 8am-9pm. Closed Sun.*

Founded in 1831, New York University is one of the largest private universities in the country, with more than 32,000 graduate and undergraduate students. Its first permanent home was a Gothic Revival pile at the NE corner of WASHINGTON SQUARE in Greenwich Village (see WALK 4 on pages 62-4). That was replaced by the present structure in 1894.

Over the last century, expansion has brought the additions of a postgraduate School of Business Administration in the FINANCIAL DISTRICT, a medical-dental complex on the EAST SIDE, a respected Institute of Fine Arts on 5th Ave., and a second campus in The Bronx. Fiscal difficulties in the 1970s forced the sale of the Bronx campus and other smaller units, but the university retains ownership of most of the buildings on the E and s sides of Washington Sq., as far over as 2nd Ave. and down to Houston St. Purple-and-white banners proclaim its presence.

In recent years, the university has enjoyed considerable success in fundraising and a markedly enhanced perception of its academic stature. The schools of law, medicine and the performing arts are ranked among the best in the nation. Distinguished teachers and graduates have included Samuel Morse, Thomas Wolfe, Jonas Salk, Joseph Heller, Albert Sabin, Lillian Hellman and former mayor Edward Koch.

NUMISMATIC SOCIETY   See AMERICAN NUMISMATIC SOCIETY.

OASES

Walking the streets of Manhattan can come to feel like a mental and physical pummeling. Tranquil retreats abound when feet and legs are ready to give out, places to sit or plan or read awhile — and they are free. Churches and libraries (see USEFUL ADDRESSES on pages 44-5) are obvious choices. Here are some others.

AT&T Building

550 Madison Ave. (55th St.)

Tables and chairs are available all around the street-level arcade, protected from rain and snow, but not the cold.

Chemcourt
277 Park Ave. (47th St.)
A bronze sculpture of a businessman hailing a taxi causes double-takes at the entrance to this lush greenhouse-atrium. There's a small art gallery, too.

Crystal Pavilion
805 3rd Ave. (50th St.)
A three-level atrium offers tables and chairs, artificial waterfalls, plants, and several shops and restaurants.

Ford Foundation
42nd St. (between 1st and 2nd Ave.)
One of the first enclosed atriums is a jungle of trees and plantings, with a pool. Open Monday to Friday 9am-5pm.

Hotel Parker Meridien
118 W 57th St. (near 6th Ave.)
To gain building code variances, the developers included a walk-through public atrium. The hotel has removed the tables and chairs it first set out, presumably to discourage loitering by homeless people, but the corridor is still a pleasant way from 56th St. to 57th St.

IBM Garden Plaza
590 Madison Ave. (56th St.)
Tall bamboo trees, chairs, a snack bar, occasional lunchtime concerts, and — scarcest of commodities — clean public rest rooms/lavatories. Open 8am-10pm.

New School for Social Research
66 W 12th St. (near 6th Ave.)
Pass through the lobby, with chairs and telephones, to the terrace and sculpture garden beyond.

Olympic Tower
645 5th Ave. (51st St.)
Another office building atrium, with a waterfall and cafés.

Paine Webber
1285 Ave. of the Americas (between 51st and 52nd Sts.)
The brokerage firm sponsors changing art exhibitions in its headquarters building. Open Monday to Friday 8am-6pm.

Park Avenue Plaza
55 E 52nd St.
Tables and chairs for playing chess and listening to frequent jazz concerts. Snack bar. Daily 8am-10pm.

Pierpont Morgan Library
Madison Ave and 36th St.
The new light-filled, glass-enclosed garden court is climate-controlled, with trees, tables and chairs. A café or snack bar is being considered. To avoid paying an entrance fee, enter through the bookstore in the building at the corner of Madison and 37th St.

Whitney Museum of American Art at Philip Morris
Park Ave. and 42nd St. (opposite Grand Central Terminal)
A surviving branch of the Whitney Museum, this is a high-ceilinged gallery with sculptures by contemporary Americans, housed in the gray

granite Philip Morris Building. Several tables and chairs are placed about, there is a coffee bar, and it's air conditioned.

World Financial Center
Battery Park City.
The splendid **Winter Garden** of the WORLD FINANCIAL CENTER is one of the city's great new urban spaces, with benches and restaurants beneath towering palm trees.

OLD MERCHANTS' HOUSE
29 E 4th St. (Broadway), NY 10543 ☎ *777-1089. Map 3R4* ▧ *Open Sun 1-4pm, other times by appointment. Closed Aug.*
No one seems to be certain, but the house is attributed to Minard Lafever, pre-eminent architect of the early 19thC. The design falls between Federal and Greek Revival, and was completed as a speculation in 1832. Merchant Seabury Tredwell bought it in 1835 and his family lived here until 1933. Since then it has been restored and preserved by the Historic Landmark Society, which recently spent more than $600,000 on structural repairs.

The original furnishings and floor coverings are still in place, and there is an intriguing secret passage.

PALEY PARK
3 E 53rd St. (5th Ave.). Map 6N4. Open Mon-Sat 8am-6pm. Closed Sun, Jan.
A chunk of valuable midtown real estate was here employed, not as a multistory garage or apartment building, but as an enclosed "pocket" park. The combination of trees, tables, chairs, snack wagon and simulated waterfall was underwritten by a former chairman of the board of the Columbia Broadcasting System and was presented as a gift to the people of New York City. It is so popular that there is often a line to get in.

PAN AM BUILDING ▥
200 Park Ave. (45th St.), NY 10017. Map 6O4 ▣ ♈ *Open 6am-2am.*
Praise has not been the Pan Am Building's lot, even before its completion in 1963. By forming a visual octagonal wall across Park Ave., it does almost nothing right. The fact that Bauhaus doyen Walter Gropius had a hand in its design is little compensation. A fatal accident in 1977 ended the function of its rooftop heliport. The parent airline company has passed into history, and the building, which is officially known as "200 Park Avenue," is now owned by Metropolitan Life. It is expected to order the removal from the crown of the giant letters spelling "PAN AM."

PIERPONT MORGAN LIBRARY ▥ ☆
29 E 36th St. (Madison Ave.), NY 10016 ☎ *685-0008. Map 6P4* ▧ ✗ *Tues and Thurs. Open Tues-Sat 10.30am-5pm; Sun 1-5pm. Closed Mon.*
One of the quiet pleasures of subdued MURRAY HILL, the library was constructed for financier J. Pierpont Morgan in 1902 by the omnipresent firm of McKim, Mead & White. The Neoclassical design reflects

Pierpont Morgan's passion for the Italian Renaissance. A less grand but unobtrusive 1928 addition was finished 15 years after his death, and a nearby 45-room mansion, purchased in 1988, has doubled the size of the facility. It contains, as would be expected, an excellent bookstore featuring fine art books and replicas of old manuscripts. In 1991, a climate-controlled glassed-roof garden court was completed, connecting the latter two buildings.

Consistent with its name, the library is primarily a repository of rare books, illuminated manuscripts, and other documents of the Middle Ages and Renaissance, but there is also a great deal more that warrants attention: stained glass, sculpture, enamel- and metal-work, and a number of somber Italian and Flemish paintings.

The **West Room**, with its carved, painted ceiling and red damask curtains, was Morgan's study. It has been kept exactly as it was during his lifetime. Particular attention should be accorded the **antique wooden ceiling**, purchased in Florence and reassembled here. The decorations, coats of arms from 16thC bookplates, were added after the installation. Over the fireplace is an 1888 portrait of Morgan, while the painting opposite the door is of his son. Leaving the West Room, visitors enter a grand **Rotunda**, its vaulted dome ceiling painted to resemble Raphael's efforts in the Vatican. Columns are of lapis lazuli, and other surfaces are covered with mosaics and marbles.

Next is the **East Room**, lined with tiered bookcases so high they require balconies and staircases. The prominent Renaissance-style fireplace is carved from Istrian marble, the Dutch tapestry hanging above it dates from the mid-1500s. Cases display ancient musical scores, autographed manuscripts and 11th and 12thC books with bejeweled bindings of exquisitely modeled silver and ivory. Other rooms and hallways are utilized for temporary exhibits of drawings or items from the library's collections.

PLANETARIUM, HAYDEN   See AMERICAN MUSEUM OF NATURAL HISTORY.

POLICE ACADEMY MUSEUM
235 E 20th St. (2nd Ave.), NY 10003 ☎*477-9753. Map 6Q5* 📷 ✱ *Open Mon-Fri 9am-3pm. Closed Sat, Sun, holidays.*

Installed on the second floor of the city's police academy, where fledgling cops trot briskly and earnestly down the halls between classes, the museum makes a forthright depiction of crime prevention and punishment in New York. Displays of the improvised weapons used by teenage street gangs are mixed with semihistorical lethal artifacts of the gangster era. Much of the material is unlabeled, and the collection is modest in scope, so don't make a special trip. It is an opportunity to eavesdrop on cop talk, however.

POMANDER WALK
W 95th St. (between West End Ave. and Broadway). Map 7K2.

It looks older, but this private mews of two-story houses wasn't built until 1922. The architect patterned it after the set of a popular play of the same name, with shuttered windows, flower boxes, brick facades and Tudor gables here and there. Theater people were the original inhabitants, among them Rosalind Russell and Humphrey Bogart in his early "tennis, anyone?" years. Woody Allen later showed it off to friends in his film, *Hannah and Her Sisters.*

PROSPECT PARK
w of Flatbush Ave., Brooklyn ▫ *Gateway from Grand Army Plaza. Subway 2,3 to Grand Army Plaza, D to Prospect Park.*

Frederick Law Olmsted and Calvert Vaux collaborated on this land-scape design (1866-74), as they had on the larger CENTRAL PARK in Man-hattan. Many think this is the better of the two, with fewer roads and a more imaginative composition of wooded glades, water, and path-ways. A small **zoo** established in 1935 along Flatbush Ave. contains elephants, zebras, monkeys and bears (☎ *965-6560, open 11am-4pm; call ahead, as restoration is underway).* A 1912 **carousel** with charm-ingly carved horses functions Friday to Sunday.

Nearby is the **Lefferts Homestead**, built in 1783 in the Dutch Colonial style, and fitted out with period furnishings (☎ *965-6560, open Wed-Sun 10am-4pm; Jan-Mar open weekends only; closed Mon, Tues).*

In gentler times, this bucolic setting adjacent to the BROOKLYN MUSEUM and BROOKLYN BOTANIC GARDEN would constitute a rare urban retreat. Sad to say, it is the victim of frequent acts of vandalism and lack of funds. The city has made a verbal commitment to overcome these problems. Until it does, go only during daylight.

QUEENSBORO BRIDGE
Map 6N5 ▫

Once it was possible to drive halfway along this bridge over the East River and turn right into an elevator that lowered to **Roosevelt Island** (formerly Welfare Island). For safety and security reasons, that service was ended in the mid-1970s, when the island became home to an ambitious new residential community called Southtown, which was an attempt to integrate all economic classes in new housing financed by both public and private funds. No cars are allowed, and travel to and from the island is now by cable car and a new subway line.

The bridge, which symbolizes the glamor of the EAST SIDE, appears in dozens of old movies.

QUEENS-MIDTOWN TUNNEL
Map 6O5 ▤

This two-tube, four-lane East River tunnel is of note only because it is likely to be the one used by arrivals from LaGuardia and JFK airports. It emerges between 36th and 37th Sts. in Manhattan.

QUEENS MUSEUM OF ART
Flushing Meadows-Corona Park, Queens, NY 10055 ☎*(718) 592-9700 or (718) 592-5555 for recorded information. See* ORIENTATION MAP *on pages 78-9* ▤ ✽ *Open Tues-Fri 10am-5pm; Sat and Sun noon-5pm. Closed Mon.*

For those enamored of maps and models, it can be worth the trek out here to see a remarkable scale model of New York City. All five boroughs, more than 835,000 buildings, and every park, bridge and roadway are replicated in minute detail. The model takes up 9335 square feet of floor space and is billed as the largest of its kind in the world. It was commissioned for the 1964 World's Fair and is displayed in a building erected for that not especially memorable event. In addition, gallery space is given to traveling art exhibitions, usually by 20thC artists and often incorporating video and mixed media. Not far away are the **Hall of Science** and the **Unisphere**, a large representation of Earth that was the symbol of the Fair.

With so many other attractions in New York, getting out here may not be worth the time for most visitors. It isn't far from *Shea Stadium,* LaGuardia Airport and Forest Hills Tennis Stadium, so a detour to the museum might fit in with a trip to those destinations. The easiest way to get there is by car, taking the Long Island Expressway (Interstate 495) w, exiting N onto the Grand Central Parkway, and following signs to the museum.

RCA BUILDING   After a change in corporate ownership, this Rockefeller Center skyscraper is now known as the GE BUILDING.

RICHMONDTOWN RESTORATION 🏛 ★

441 Clarke Ave., Staten Island, NY 10306 ☎*(718) 351-1611* 📧 *✗ required* 📽 *✦ Open Wed-Sun 1-5pm. Ferry from Battery Park. Take a taxi or S74 bus from the Staten Island Ferry terminal.*

Eventually this is to be a museum village of more than 30 buildings — restored, reconstructed, reassembled, recreated — ranging from the early Colonial period up to the 19thC. The Staten Island Historical Society has been working on this project for more than 40 years, and while progress is painstakingly slow, some rewards are evident. A dozen buildings are open to the public, among them a colorful general store and a 1696 elementary school. The grounds include a mill pond, and picnicking is encouraged.

That is just as well, since the small restaurant has now been closed. Budgetary constraints have also caused the elimination of the costumed artisans who used to give demonstrations of arts and crafts, and the only way to see the interiors of the buildings is now on guided tours. Tickets are on sale at the red-brick **Historical Museum**, not at the **Visitor's Center**.

RIVERSIDE CHURCH 🏛

490 Riverside Dr. (122nd St.), NY 10027 ☎*222-5900, ext. 265. See* ORIENTATION MAP *on pages 78-9* ◁ *Open 8am-10pm.*

Despite the 74-bell carillon and 20-ton bell at its top (both the largest of their kind anywhere in the world), the 392 feet (120m) tower of this interdenominational church looks vaguely like a Gothic 1930s office building — and is, in part. There is an **observation deck**, which affords a sweeping panorama of the Hudson River from Wall St. to the

GEORGE WASHINGTON BRIDGE *(open Mon-Sat 11am-3pm; Sun 12.30-3pm* ☎ *749-7000 for times of carillon performances).*

RIVERSIDE PARK
See ORIENTATION MAP on pages 78-9.
New Yorkers owe an eternal debt to Frederick Law Olmsted and Calvert Vaux, the 19thC landscape architects who created CENTRAL PARK, PROSPECT PARK in Brooklyn, and this sylvan strip of trees and hills bordering the Hudson River. It runs from W 72nd St. to W 125th St., banked to the E by a wall of handsome apartment houses and blemished only by the Hudson Parkway, which was built along its length in the 1930s. The **Soldiers and Sailors Monument** *(W 89th St., map 7K2)* and GENERAL GRANT NATIONAL MEMORIAL *(W 122nd St.),* are within its boundaries.

ROCKEFELLER CENTER 🏛 ★
Map 604.
John D. Rockefeller Jr. put together the grand scheme for this 22-acre compound of office towers — a "city within the city." It has an ordered integrity that is in sharp contrast to such flashy later edifices as TRUMP TOWER. The heart of the complex is between 5th and 6th Aves. and 49th and 50th Sts. Here are found the sights familiar from tourist literature, most of them completed in the 1930s.

Dominating is the GE BUILDING (the former **RCA Building**), facing E. While it cannot compare in scale or inventiveness with the contemporary CHRYSLER BUILDING, it bears a mantle of restrained elegance.

At the NW corner of its base is the Art Deco **Radio City Music Hall**, with a breathtaking vaulted interior in which rock concerts and elaborate revues are staged. To the E, directly in front of the entrance, is a sunken plaza, which is an ice-skating rink in winter and an outdoor café in summer. A gold statue of *Prometheus* floats above. At the approach of Christmas, a tree more than 70 feet (21m) high is placed behind him. Still farther E, banks of plants and flowers take up the center of a pedestrian mall that ends at 5th Ave. (See WALK 1 on page 55.)

ST BARTHOLOMEW'S CHURCH 🏛
109 E 50th St. (Park Ave.), NY 10022 ☎ *751-1616. Map 604. Open 8am-6pm. Closes 3pm during major holidays ✗ after Sun services.*
Providing a welcome antidote to the slab-sided canyon of midtown Park Ave., this pinkish pile of Byzantine-Romanesque excess features Stanford White's **triple portals** (1903), salvaged from an earlier church by James Renwick, located downtown on 24th St. This one opened in 1919, and the prominent dome was finished in 1930. The Episcopalian church has had financial problems, and directors wanted to sell part of

the property to developers. That plan ended when the Supreme Court refused to overturn the church's designation as a landmark property, which means it cannot be physically altered. Concerts take place some Sunday and Tuesday afternoons. Late at night, the vestibule serves as a shelter for homeless people.

ST MARK'S-IN-THE-BOWERY 🏛

2nd Ave. (10th St.), NY 10003 ☎*674-8112. Map* **4***R5. Open 9am-5pm.*

One of the oldest houses of worship in Manhattan, this church was built on farmland in 1799. The basic structure of the building is Federal, with a Greek Revival steeple added in 1828. The Dutch Director-General Peter Stuyvesant is buried here, in ground that he once owned. A fire in 1978 destroyed much of the roof and interior of the church, but costly restoration has returned it to its former condition. There is a long tradition here of music, poetry and dance.

ST PATRICK'S CATHEDRAL 🏛 ★

5th Ave. (51st St.), NY 10022 ☎*753-2261. Map* **6***N4* 🚶 *except by prior approval. Open 7am-8pm.*

When James Renwick submitted his drawings in 1850, the fashion for Gothic Revival was on the wane. By the time the cathedral was completed in 1888, it must have seemed dated. No matter, for the style returned to favor soon afterward, and by then St Patrick's was already in the ranks of the timeless. Echoing great cathedrals of Europe (for Renwick formulated his ideas after intense study of European examples), it is part lacy stonework, part soaring caprice, part massive pretense. Authenticity might have demanded flying buttresses, but the site would not accommodate them and they were not required structurally, for the roof was lighter than in the earlier Gothic prototypes.

The siting of the cathedral was to cause consternation in some quarters. At the time, Irish immigration had reached sufficient proportions to be threatening to the Protestant majority. The latter found it distasteful in the extreme to endure such a blatant monument to the Roman faith, especially in the midst of a neighborhood chosen by the wealthy as refuge from the masses downtown. In time, both groups came to uneasy union, in the face of succeeding waves of even less familiar creeds.

ST PAUL'S CHAPEL 🏛

Broadway (Fulton St.), NY 10002 ☎*285-0874. Map* **1***T4. Open Mon-Fri 8am-4pm; Sun 7am-3pm. Closed Sat, some holidays.*

The only existing nonresidential building in New York that predates the Revolution (1766), St Paul's holds its own against the silvery glass curtain walls of the WORLD TRADE CENTER, at least when viewed from street level. Made of Manhattan schist quarried at the site, the exterior facing is brownstone. Apart from the steeple, added in 1794, it is authentic Georgian, inside and out, although the blue and pink paint of the interior was perhaps not always so vivid. Architect Thomas McBean is believed to have been a pupil of James Gibbs, who designed the church of St Martin-in-the-Fields in London.

Fourteen chandeliers of Waterford crystal dominate the interior, and the sunburst altar screen (1787) is credited to Pierre L'Enfant, the Frenchman who later planned Washington, DC. George Washington put in frequent appearances during his first presidential term. His pew is marked. The graveyard is a shaded resting place for footsore souls still living, and there are lunchtime concerts of classical music on Mondays and Thursdays (☎ 602-0760).

SEAGRAM BUILDING 血
*375 Park Ave. (52nd St.), NY 10022. Map **6**N4.*
First came LEVER HOUSE, just across Park Ave., then the Seagram (1958). After them, the glass-and-metal box International Style went downhill, swallowed up in greed and misinterpretation of its deceptive simplicity. (For confirmation of that conclusion, simply look s to the PAN AM BUILDING.) The plaza in front of the Seagram may appear banal but, considering the almost unbelievable cost of midtown property, even this much walking space seems generous. The narrow slab looming above is the color of well-aged bourbon, consistent with the preoccupation of the client, a prominent distiller. Landmark status has been extended to the building and even to the restaurant within, **The Four Seasons** (see WHERE TO EAT). Ludwig Mies van der Rohe was the architect, Philip Johnson his assistant.

SEVENTH REGIMENT ARMORY
*643 Park Ave. (between 66th and 67th Sts.), NY 10022 ☎744-2968. Map **6**M4.*
This 1880 red-brick approximation of a fortress is the most prominent of several headquarters of military units in the city. While it retains that function, it also contains two major antique shows each year, tennis courts, occasional theatrical productions, a shelter for the homeless, and a good restaurant, **7th Regiment Mess** (☎ 744-4107). The interior, from the Park Ave. side, has wood paneling and stained glass by Tiffany.

SNUG HARBOR CULTURAL CENTER 血
914 Richmond Terrace, Staten Island, NY 10301 ☎(718) 448-2500 ▣ to grounds and most exhibitions ▨ some exhibitions and performances. Open 8am-dusk ▣ ✗ weekends. Ferry from Battery Park. Take a taxi or S1 bus from the Staten Island Ferry terminal.
Sailor's Snug Harbor, a wealthy charitable foundation providing shelter for retired merchant seamen, purchased these 80 waterfront acres in 1831. The organizers then proceeded to build, in a grand manner that might seem inconsistent with their mission. Their dedication left a complex of more than 20 contiguous buildings representative of the Greek Revival, Italianate, Victorian and Beaux Arts modes. One of the archi-

tects was Minard Lafever, as prominent in the early 19thC as Stanford White, 75 years later.

Now renamed and designated a National Historic Landmark District, Snug Harbor is still in the process of often-tentative conversion to an arts center. Should all the acquired buildings be utilized eventually for that purpose, it would be an unprecedented complex. As it is, only a few galleries are presently in use, and on a limited schedule. Fiscal concerns and public indifference appear to be frustrating the great plans of the trustees. In the meantime, the complex is a compressed lesson in 19thC architecture. Also in the grounds are the **Staten Island Botanical Gardens** *(☎ (718) 273-8200),* which contains a marsh habitat and a collection of Japanese bonsai trees, and the **Staten Island Children's Museum** *(☎ (718) 273-2060).*

SOHO ★
Map 3S4.

Whoever coined the name no doubt had the famous London quarter in mind, but the two places have little in common. This "SoHo" is a contraction of "SOuth of HOuston St." (Incidentally, that street is pro-nounced "HOWston," not "HEWston.") Barely three decades ago, SoHo was a dreary industrial district with broken concrete sidewalks piled high with boxes of refuse and pot-holed streets of worn Belgian blocks. Trucks backed into loading bays, rows of sewing and die-cut-ting machines clattered and thumped behind grimy windows, crates of fabrics and plastics were trundled about by forklifts and bowed backs. At night, everyone left.

Apart from the condition of the streets and those buildings that have thus far escaped renovation, that description no longer applies. In the early 1960s, artists of the New York School, no longer content with easel painting in conventional studios, sought ever-larger work space. The problem was cost. They discovered the lofts of what was then called "The Valley" — five- to ten-floor buildings with vast unpartitioned rooms designed for warehouses, shipping firms and labor-intensive light indus-tries. Marginal businesses were closing up, and artists moved in. This was illegal, according to zoning laws. Yet they doubled their transgression by adding living spaces to their new studios, installing bathrooms and kitchens. Hanging plants and curtains were glimpsed from the streets. In due course, other artists with similar needs — film-makers, dancers, sculptors — followed the leaders.

By 1970, the trickle became a torrent. Since the municipal authorities could no longer ignore the fact that their ordinances were being violated, they simply changed them. Bona fide artists *could* now live in the converted lofts.

SoHo went from cultural workplace to artistic community to general free-for-all in just a few years. Bars, restaurants, food and craft stores catering to artists were supplemented by branches of established uptown galleries. Stockbrokers and lawyers bought up the lofts and fitted them out with saunas, billiard tables, and luxury bathrooms. Rents skyrocketed and many artists left. Nevertheless SoHo remains a vital, passionate community, despite pretentious boutiques and eating places that charge breathtaking prices.

Saturday is the time to go, for the art-lover's ritual gallery tour and a drink at an engaging pub. Along the way, observe the **cast-iron facades** for which the district is also known. After a brief mid-19thC period during which SoHo was the fashionable center of town, hotels and shops were displaced by factory buildings. To dress them up, iron-cast motifs taken from European palaces were prefabricated in sections and assembled on the site, apparently an American innovation. Entire buildings were erected in four or five months by this method. Although they proved to be not fireproof and the technique was abandoned in the early 20thC, more than 200 examples survive. They are notable for their **gargoyles, Corinthian columns,** and **ornamentation** and **sculptural detail** taken from Venetian, Romanesque and French Second Empire examples. Most of them are within an official landmark district created by the city to ensure their preservation.

SoHo is bounded by Houston St., Canal St., Sullivan St. and Broadway. The main street is West Broadway, and the oldest house (1806) is at **107 Spring St.**

SOUTH STREET SEAPORT � ★

Museum Visitor's Center: 12 Fulton St. (between South St. and Front St.), NY 10038 ☎669-9424 for recorded information. Map 2U5 ☒ 𝒓 ⊒ ✦ ⬛ ⊏ ⪡
Museum buildings open 10am-5pm. Closed Christmas and New Year's Day.

A living museum-in-progress, the Seaport contributes mightily to the resurrection of lower Manhattan as a place to live and stroll and cherish. Beginning more than 25 years ago with a group of volunteers interested in preserving a segment of New York's maritime past, an alliance was forged with commercial interests to underwrite restoration of some of the last remaining blocks of early 19thC buildings and of a growing collection of antique sailing vessels. The largely salutary result is an expanding neighborhood of tasteful shops and restaurants that has proven to be immensely popular with both natives and visitors.

Standing just s of the Brooklyn Bridge, its appeal has at its heart seven ships of the early steam and clipper days, all docked in the East River. Their masts and spidery rigging stand in arresting contrast to the majestic backdrop of Wall St. skyscrapers. Most of them are in a seemingly endless process of renovation and ongoing maintenance, but they easily convey a sense of the romantic epoch that made the city the busiest port in the New World.

Three of the ships can be boarded by visitors. Prides of the fleet are the four-masted, metal-hulled 1911 bark *Peking* and the classic 1885 square-rigger *Wavertree.* Among the others are the 1906 lightship *Ambrose* and an 1893 fishing schooner, the *Lettie G. Howard.* Cruises of the harbor can be taken aboard replicas of the paddlewheeler *Andrew Fletcher* or the steamboat *De Witt Clinton (Apr-Nov* ☎ *406-3434)* and on the century-old schooner *Pioneer (May-Sept* ☎ *669-9400).* They vary in length from 90 minutes to 3 hours, including twilight cocktail cruises and evening music cruises.

Puppet shows and jazz and folk concerts are among the special events held during the warmer months. Underlining the maritime theme are the Wooden Boat Festival in May, the Model Ship and Boat Festival in August, and the Mayor's Cup Schooner Race in September (see CALENDAR OF EVENTS on page 49). Tall ships from other nations and states often dock here on official visits and welcome boarding parties.

Seafarers required land-based support services, and the developers have taken them into account. Restoration is nearly complete on the 11-block official national historic district adjacent to the piers. More than $5 million has been spent on quayside rows of Greek Revival, Georgian, Federal and Victorian warehouses and ships' chandleries. Venerable **Schermerhorn Row** and **Front St.** have undergone careful renovation, with much of their interior space given over to retail enterprises. A new three-story structure was opened in 1983. Dubbed the "**Fulton Market**," it is crammed with specialty food stores and sidewalk cafés. Nearby is what remains of the old Fulton Fish Market, source of most of the fresh seafood served in Manhattan's better restaurants.

The **Cannon's Walk** block of buildings opposite the Fulton Market is partly old, partly new, and contains a variety of shops, exhibition galleries, and a theater showing a slick multiscreen film about the evolution of the district, *The Seaport Experience.* Another three-story pavilion, **Pier 17**, was erected on an over-water platform N of the ships. Opened in 1985, it contains 100 shops and restaurants. A single ticket obtained at the Visitor's Center pays for admission to the several buildings constituting the museum. Strolling the district's streets is free, assuming none of the shops and cafés prove too tempting. Combination museum and cruise tickets are also available. (See also WALK 2 on pages 58-9.)

SPANISH INSTITUTE
684 Park Ave. (68th St.), NY 10021 ☎*628-0420. Map 8M4* ◙ *Open Mon-Sat 11am-6pm. Closed Sun.*
The home of the Center for American-Spanish Affairs is an architectural echo of the neighboring neo-Georgian structure, erected in 1926. Frequent lectures, recitals and art exhibits showcase Spanish writers, poets and artists. Native speakers hold classes in Spanish and Catalan.

STATEN ISLAND ZOO
613 Broadway (Forrest Ave.), Staten Island, NY 10310 ☎*(718) 442-3100* ▧ *(◙ on Wed 2-4.45pm)* ✿ *Open 10am-4.45pm. Ferry from Battery Park. Take a taxi or S-48 bus from the Staten Island Ferry terminal.*
Specialization can make otherwise modest institutions rival grander establishments blessed with better resources. Although this zoo is of principal interest to residents of Staten Island, its reptile collection rivals any in the US. There are several types of python and specimens of every known type of rattlesnake. The aquarium has sharks and piranhas, just the thing for bloodthirsty little folk. Children also have deer and goats to pet and ponies to ride. A new **Tropical Forest** exhibit enhances the property, which looks more like a college campus than a zoo. Further renovations are underway in some areas.

STATUE OF LIBERTY ★

Liberty Island, New York Harbor, NY 10004 ☎ *732-1236* ☒ ◁≪ ▇ ✱ *Open 9am-6pm. Ferry from Battery Park every 30mins 10am-4pm. Tickets sold in* CASTLE CLINTON NATIONAL MONUMENT.

A description of "Miss Liberty" is as enlightening as one of a telephone. Everyone knows what she looks like, although the first sight of her is undiminished by *déjà vu.* French sculptor Auguste Bartholdi created her out of thin, beaten copper panels, with the engineering counsel of Gustave Eiffel, a man of recognized expertise in such matters. At 151 feet (46m), the statue dwarfs that wonder of the ancient world, the Colossus of Rhodes. Extensive renovation prepared her for the 1986 centennial.

While the cost of the statue itself was underwritten by French contributions, the American public was slow to come up with the requisite matching funds to build the pedestal. It took nearly 20 years from its first conception to the unveiling, in 1885. The statue weighs 225 tons, each eye is 2 feet 6 inches (75cm) wide, and the tip of the upraised torch is 395 feet (120m) above sea level.

Inside, an elevator carries visitors halfway up, and 168 steps lead to the perforated crown. This gives a remarkable view of the bay, from the VERRAZANO NARROWS BRIDGE to the spires of Manhattan. Visitors on ferries leaving after 2pm for the Statue of Liberty may not be able to get up to the crown due to long lines. Waits can be as long as 2-3 hours.

See illustration on page 281.

STUDIO MUSEUM IN HARLEM

144 W 125th St., (near Lenox Ave.), NY 10027 ☎ *864-4500. See* ORIENTATION MAP *on pages 78-9* ☒ *Open Wed-Fri 10am-5; Sat-Sun 1-6pm. Closed Mon, Tues.*
One of the most important cultural institutions in Harlem, especially since opening in these expanded and rehabilitated quarters, the museum concerns itself with the work of African-American artists. Most of the works on display are contemporary, some polemical in nature, some not. Every technique and medium can be seen, along with insights into the African-American experience that larger mainstream museums rarely pursue.

TEMPLE EMANU-EL

5th Ave. (65th St.), NY 10021 ☎ *744-1400. Map* **8M4** ✗ *by appointment. Open 10am-5pm; services Mon-Thurs 5.30pm, Fri 5.15pm, Sat 10.30am. For services, enter by 5th Ave. door; at other times, by E 65th St. door.*
The largest Reform Jewish synagogue in North America, it can accommodate 2,500 worshipers. Limestone is the primary material, buttressed by steel. Its size is the principal attraction for sightseers, given the ambiguity of its half-Turkish, half-Italianate architecture.

THEATER DISTRICT

Map **5** *O3.*
Depending upon context, Broadway is either the city's longest avenue or a synonym for the theatrical district through which it passes on its

diagonal slash through midtown. And **Times Square** is essentially the intersection of that famous street and 7th Ave.

Within the area bounded by 40th St., 55th St., 6th Ave. and 8th Ave. are many large movie houses and most of the major legitimate theaters. The huge electrified signs and marquees that gave Times Square the sobriquet "Great White Way" are still there, although they now advertise Japanese cameras and electronic gadgets more than coming attractions. Crowds of gawkers, New Jersey teenagers, matinee ladies from the suburbs, French sailors, winos, hustlers, and tourists from everywhere fill the streets. On New Year's Eve, they are wall-to-wall, more than 100,000 strong (but watch it on television).

Despite repeated efforts to clean it up, 42nd St. between 7th and 8th Aves. remains a sludge of pornographic movie houses, prostitutes, addicts and troublemakers. Avoid it, and the northerly stretch of 8th Ave. it joins, but don't be deterred from seeing a show on the streets nearby. Restaurants in the area cater to every taste and budget. Few are more than middling-good, most are noisy, but they specialize in pre- and post-show meals. A number of new hotels have sprung up in and around Times Square in recent years, including the **Embassy Suites**, **Paramount**, **Ramada Renaissance**, **Holiday Inn Crowne Plaza** and **Macklowe**.

THEODORE ROOSEVELT BIRTHPLACE

28 E 20th St. (5th Ave.), NY 10003 ☎*260-1616. Map* **6Q4** ▨ ✗ *Open Wed-Sun 9am-5pm. Closed Mon, Tues.*

The 26th President (1901-9) was born in 1858 and lived in a house at this site until 1873. The Roosevelts were a large and wealthy family even then, and this four-story brownstone rowhouse, a replica built to the original specifications, reflects that prosperity. In the five period rooms open to the public, careful attention has been paid to authenticity. The parlor is agleam with crystal chandeliers and gilt-framed mirrors. Plump horsehair sofas and chairs are arranged in inviting groups, and fringed satin curtains frame the tall windows. The result is a faithful impression of elegant solidity consistent with the time and social class of the original occupants.

Trophies reflect Roosevelt's roles of rancher, big-game hunter, explorer and soldier. Tiger and bear skins cover the floor of one room, and there are branding irons, a stuffed lion, uniforms and cavalry bugles. Yet this complex man — a progressive Republican at home, an imperialist abroad — was above all a dedicated public servant. One glass case after another, filled with campaign buttons, public documents, family records and letters, and newspaper cartoons, attests to the energy he applied to that calling. (See also GRAMERCY PARK.)

TRIBECA

*Map **1T4**.*

When the artists who resurrected SOHO were forced out by landlords and speculators who saw the profits to be realized in sales to non-artists with regular incomes, many simply moved a few blocks s and w. They called their new homestead TriBeCa, for "TRIangle BElow CAnal

St." Inevitably, the SoHo phenomenon asserted itself once again, with bars, restaurants and funky nightclubs. It has some successful art galleries, too, but doesn't yet challenge SoHo's suzerainty or numbers in that regard. Down here, where streets have names instead of numbers and the straightforward grid of uptown does not apply, the approximate boundaries are West St. to Church St. and Barclay St. to Canal St.

TRINITY CHURCH 🏛

*Broadway (Wall St.), NY 10006 ☎285-0872. Map **3U4** ✗ Open 7am-6pm ▣ Museum open Mon-Fri 9-11.45am, 1-3.45pm; Sat 10am-3.45pm; Sun 1-3.45pm.*

The first Trinity Church was erected here in 1698, entirely of wood. That burned down in 1776, in the first of the two great fires that decimated old New York. The second version was razed in 1839, and the present Gothic Revival manifestation (by Richard Upjohn) went up in 1846. The tower contains ten bells, three of them dating from 1797. Decades of urban grime turned the red sandstone so black it nearly shone. Now it has been thoroughly cleaned, which some people complain has removed its distinctiveness. Over the years, additions have included a chapel (1913) and bronze entry doors (1894) modeled on those of the Baptistry in Florence. A small museum displays photographs and artifacts relating to the history of the church. Pause in the graveyard (under renovation) for a glance at the memorials to statesman Alexander Hamilton and steamboat inventor Robert Fulton. Noon concerts of classical music are held on most Mondays and Thursdays.

TRUMP TOWER

*725 5th Ave. (56th St.) ☎832-2000. Map **6N4** ▣ ▣ ▣ Open Mon-Sat 8am-10pm. Closed Sun.*

Only one of many monuments built by, and dedicated to, New York's most visible multimillionaire, this office-residence-store tower characteristically falls on the glittery side of luxe. Donald Trump's empire is trembling at the edge of the fiscal precipice, as has been tirelessly (and tiresomely) documented. Even now, however, no one accuses him of restraint or reclusiveness.

His sense of showmanship, revealed in this flossy structure, begins with exterior terraced stepbacks from the third through to the eighth floors, each planted with trees and ivy. Inside, more real trees line the entrance hall, which leads to an atrium aglint with brass and polished marble and a three-story waterfall cascading into a sunken courtyard. There is a bistro-style café down below, and a restaurant on the fifth floor. On the intervening floors there are representatives of such pricey shops as Cartier, Blantre, Charles Jourdan, Abercrombie & Fitch and, in a recent expression of confidence in The Donald's ultimate recovery, the Galeries Lafayette.

TURTLE BAY

*Map **6O5**.*

Diplomats, writers and assorted celebrities make their homes in this neighborhood bordering the East River at midtown. Its best-known occupant is the **United Nations**, built on land donated by John D. Rockefeller Jr. The arrival of that international body helped rejuvenate an area struggling back from decline. Around World War I, it was home to stockyards, abattoirs and tenements crowded with immigrants. The development of the Turtle Bay Gardens residential complex, now an official landmark, began the ascent back to the respectability it enjoyed in the post-Revolution period. The district, bounded by 3rd Ave. and 53rd and 43rd Sts., contains several excellent hotels and restaurants, including the **UN Plaza** and the celebrated **Lutèce** (see WHERE TO EAT).

UKRAINIAN MUSEUM
203 2nd Ave. (12th St.), NY 10003 ☎*228-0110. Map 4R5* 🚇 *Open Wed-Sun 1-5pm. Closed Mon, Tues.*
Embroidery is the specialty — on garments, textiles and ritual panels — but the intricately decorated Easter eggs are equally entrancing. There are two galleries, also featuring folk carvings and metalwork.

UNION SQUARE
Map 6Q4.
In the 1930s, the 3.6-acre park was a vigorous if shabby version of Speakers' Corner in London's Hyde Park. Anarchists, trade unionists, radicals and simple eccentrics mounted soapboxes and endured hecklers. Its decline accelerated after World War II, and it eventually became the habitat of drug peddlers and prostitutes. An increased police presence and a major beautification project completed in 1985 encouraged families and office workers to return there, to lunch and play and pass time. New restaurants and shops have opened around the perimeter. A farmer's market is held three times a week — usually Wednesday, Saturday and Sunday. The statues of the Marquis de Lafayette and George Washington on horseback have been joined by one of Mahatma Gandhi.

UNITED NATIONS HEADQUARTERS
1st Ave. (45th St.), NY 10017 ☎*754-1234. Map 605* 🅾 *✗* 🚇 🚺 *Open Mon-Fri 9am-5pm; Sat, Sun 9.15am-5pm; last tour at 4.45pm.*
John D. Rockefeller Jr. donated the East River site, and the first three buildings were ready for occupation in 1952. Despite the presence of a number of significant works of art by Marc Chagall, Henry Moore and Barbara Hepworth, the overall visual effect of the complex is somewhat vapid, in the manner of quasi-governmental edifices. At last count, there were 175 member countries, their flags displayed in ranks along bordering 1st Ave., which is called United Nations Plaza for the six-block frontage of the property.

Most offices and rooms are closed to the public, but are of little general interest. The library is open to scholars and journalists. One-hour tours with multilingual guides leave about every 15 minutes from the Main Lobby of the **General Assembly Building**. That is the low structure with the concave roofline to the N of the simple slab of the **Secretariat**

Building. The latter is probably the more familiar from photographs. Most tours are conducted in English, French, German, Japanese, or Spanish, but other languages are available. Highlights are more often the artworks bequeathed by member nations, rather than the assembly halls of the Security and Trusteeship Councils. Near the Economic and Social Council chamber, for example, are eight joined pieces of ivory meticulously carved by Chinese artisans into a landscape of bridges, trees and farmers; a replica of a Thai royal barge; a Belgian tapestry said to be the second-largest in the world.

Tickets to sessions of the General Assembly, the Security Council and certain other meetings can be obtained at the Information Desk shortly beforehand. *(Admission is free, but on a first-come basis; starting times are usually 10.30am and 3pm.)* The opening of the General Assembly, usually Monday of the third week in September, is the most intriguing time to go.

Outsiders can lunch at the Delegates' Dining Room on the top floor of the **Conference Building**, which sits astride the FDR Drive at the edge of the river. They are seated in order of arrival; no reservations are accepted *(lunch only, Mon-Fri)*. A coffee shop in the below ground level public concourse is open daily *(9.30am-5pm)*. Nearby shops sell souvenirs, books, UN postage stamps, and — best of all — handicrafts of many nations.

UPPER WEST SIDE
Map 7J2.

Of all the recently resurgent neighborhoods — SOHO, TRIBECA, CHELSEA, **Park Slope** in Brooklyn — the Upper West Side most resists easy classification. It is too large, for one thing — from Central Park W to the Hudson River, and from 59th St. to as far N as 120th St., according to some definitions. Secondly, it lacks the handy ethnic, social or cultural identity of other districts. Well-to-do refugees from the more fashionable EAST SIDE have long lived here, in such still desirable apartment houses as the gabled DAKOTA APARTMENTS. But they understandably chose the narrow strips along CENTRAL PARK and Riverside Drive, and the blocks in the middle were allowed to fester.

Many people mark the checkered renaissance of the Upper West Side from the completion of LINCOLN CENTER (1966), and this event was no doubt influential. Another factor was the escalating rents of Greenwich Village, which drove out writers and other professionals associated with publishing and communications. The newcomers spruced up their apartments, their buildings, even whole blocks. They opened gourmet food stores and bookstores and brought new life to those already there. Pubs of sufficient atmosphere attracted customers whose conversation was of royalty contracts and writer's block. Dim, woody bistros featuring allegedly Provençal cuisine proliferated at such a rate that natives used to refer to one stretch of Columbus Ave. as "Quiche Alley." Ratification of the area's new-found panache was the arrival of Eastsiders, who not long ago were insisting that only the imminent demise of a close relative would cause them to cross Central Park.

Diversity continues, with smart boutiques beside seedy but colorful *bodegas,* working-men's bars adjoining glittery singles' hangouts, upper-crust Bohemians jostling with welfare mothers in corner delis. Important sights and institutions include the AMERICAN MUSEUM OF NATURAL HISTORY, the NEW-YORK HISTORICAL SOCIETY, the CATHEDRAL CHURCH OF ST JOHN THE DIVINE, COLUMBIA UNIVERSITY, GENERAL GRANT NATIONAL MEMORIAL and the city's grandest boulevard, Riverside Drive. To food-crazed New Yorkers, however, the single destination that requires repeated ritualistic pilgrimages is that delicatessen without peer, **Zabar's** (see SHOPPING).

VAN CORTLANDT MANSION AND MUSEUM 血

Van Cortlandt Park (242nd St. and Broadway), Bronx, NY 10471 ☎543-3344
💺 ✗ *Open Tues-Fri 11am-3pm; Sun noon-5pm. Closed Mon, Sat. Subway 1 to 242nd St.-Van Cortlandt Park.*

George Washington spent a lot of time in and around New York, usually with British troops hot on his heels. This country house, with its deceptively modest fieldstone exterior, served as one of his headquarters, as did the MORRIS-JUMEL MANSION in Manhattan. Jacobus Van Cortlandt, destined to become a mayor of the city, bought the land in 1694 and made it a wheat farm and mill. His son built the existing mansion in 1748. The building has elements of the Dutch Colonial style, but is essentially Georgian. Note the carved faces in the window keystones.

Like most of the city's historic houses, it remains in a preserved rural setting, although the nearby meadows are now playing fields. Nine rooms are open to the public, including a cellar kitchen with a Dutch oven, and a parlor with a spinet and excellent Chippendale pieces. On display are Delftware and English china, crewelwork, cooking implements, a dollhouse and unusual cupboard bed. It has recently been renovated.

VERRAZANO NARROWS BRIDGE

💺 *only when crossing w-E.*

When opened in 1964, it became the longest suspension bridge in the world. England's Humber Bridge surpassed it in 1981. Two decks and 12 lanes link Staten Island and points w with the Belt Parkway in Brooklyn. Giovanni da Verrazano was an Italian explorer in French employment, believed to have been the first European to sail into the bay. The New York Marathon starts at the w end in November.

VILLARD HOUSES (Palace Hotel) 血

451 Madison Ave. (51st St.), NY 10022. Map 6N4.

This U-shaped Italian Renaissance palace, commissioned by German-born financier Henry Villard, was a departure for the firm of McKim, Mead and White. As the most popular architects of the late 19thC, they had dabbled in most revivalist styles except this one. In effect, these are six connected brownstone houses unified by a Roman esthetic.

After various changes of owner, including the New York Catholic diocese and the Random House publishing firm, they were purchased by Harry Helmsley. He was prevailed upon to restore, rather than raze them and erect his **Palace Hotel** to the E. The houses were incorporated into the overall design and became part of the hotel. The cost was substantial, but the result is a triumph of enlightened development (for an entrepreneur who could use all the plaudits he and his wife could gather).

WASHINGTON SQUARE 血

Map 3R4.

Now it is the heart of GREENWICH VILLAGE — playground, meeting place, open-air venue for street musicians, de facto campus of NEW YORK UNIVERSITY. Over the centuries, it has been put to many other uses, including hunting preserve, potter's field, public execution place and military parade ground. Brick row houses of the 1830s survive along the N side, E of 5th Ave. Stanford White's **Washington Arch** (1892) marks the S end of 5th Ave., while Philip Johnson's **Bobst Library** dominates the SE corner. (See WALK 4, page 63.)

WAVE HILL CENTER FOR ENVIRONMENTAL STUDIES

675 W 249th St. (Independence Ave.), Bronx 10071 ☎549-3200 ▨ Sat and Sun ▣ weekdays. Open 10am-4.30pm; longer in summer, so check ahead.

A distinguished estate with sweeping views of the Hudson River and the craggy cliffs called the Palisades, Wave Hill has been home to a British UN ambassador as well as Mark Twain and Theodore Roosevelt. Its 28 acres were bequeathed to the city of New York for use as an environmental study center. Its many nature trails and gardens are open to the public.

Concerts, art exhibitions and other cultural programs were once regular parts of the center's offerings, but they have been eliminated due to funding difficulties. What remains is more than enough to justify a visit, which might be co-ordinated with one to nearby VAN CORTLANDT MANSION.

WHITNEY MUSEUM OF AMERICAN ART 血 ★

Madison Ave. (75th St.), NY 10021 ☎570-3676 (general information) ☎570-0637 (film information). Map 8M4 ▨ ▣ Open Wed, Fri-Sun 11am-6pm; Thurs 1-8pm. Closed Mon, Tues, holidays.

The city's foremost repository of solely American modern art is a perpetual whirlwind of controversy, lately revolving around its new director and rancorous debate about his leadership and intentions for the future. Depending upon whose interests are promoted — or ignored — the show called the Whitney Biennial is predictably cited as presumptuous, bland, stunning, inept and seminal. That ambitious survey of art by currently active painters and sculptors rarely fails to outrage or dismay the creative community, which many observers take as evidence that the museum is doing something right. As befits its basic premise, the exhibition has ranged traditionally from unheralded talents to such luminaries as James Rosenquist and Wayne Thiebaud, the work sweeping from the arrestingly experimental to polyresin sculpture so lifelike it all but breathes. There are, in addition, avant-garde films, slide and video presentations of "site works" by conceptual artists, and dance programs and events that endeavor to push conventions beyond their limits. The Biennial is normally held from late January to mid-April.

At other times, works of momentarily trendy artists are given one-person shows, and there are group exhibitions marshalled around often amorphous themes. They are supplemented by traveling exhibits organized by other museums. Virtually every major American talent since 1900 is represented in the permanent collection, examples of which are rotated into view as the limited space allows. Among these are pieces by Willem de Kooning, Louise Nevelson, David Smith, Andy Warhol, Hans Hofmann, Stuart Davis, Edward Hopper, George Bellows and Reginald Marsh. Some 50 Alexander Calder mobiles and stabiles are positioned around the courtyard and can be seen through the tall plate glass windows of the basement floor.

The strength of the Whitney lies in its refusal to settle back and wait for artists to establish themselves. The museum has always taken chances. In the process, curious choices are made, but the curatorial nerve they demonstrate is refreshing.

All this came about through the energy and commitment of Gertrude Vanderbilt Whitney, a sculptor who happened to be rich. She began by expanding her studio in GREENWICH VILLAGE into exhibition space and purchasing the work of unacknowledged young artists. Periodic moves to larger premises led from 8th St. to 54th St. to the present location. As is often true of New York museums, the Whitney building (1966) is as provocative as the creations it houses. Marcel Breuer met the requirements of his clients with the sort of unconventional solution for which he was noted.

The building is sheer on three sides, but the facade rises in three cantilevered tiers from the moated patio below street level, the top floor looming over the sidewalk and the suspended bridge connecting sidewalk with lobby. The granite sheathing is pierced by asymmetrically placed trapezoidal windows. Interior walls are, in part, raw concrete, bearing the impressions of the grains of the forming planks. A planned addition to the building is currently in limbo, a victim of internal and external disagreements and the museum's presumably temporary financial difficulties.

A small airy cafeteria edged with potted trees serves lunch, snacks and cocktails. The Whitney's outreach branches at 33 Maiden Lane and in the EQUITABLE CENTER on 7th Ave. have now been closed due to withdrawal of corporate sponsorship, but the one housed in the **Philip Morris Building**, opposite Grand Central Terminal (42nd St. and Park Ave.), remains open.

WOOLWORTH BUILDING 🏛

233 Broadway (Barclay St.), NY 10007. Map 1T4 🔲 *Open Mon-Fri 9am-5pm. Closed Sat, Sun.*

Although best known as the consulting architect for the GEORGE WASH-INGTON BRIDGE, Cass Gilbert was a favorite of tycoons and Federal bureaucrats, largely on account of his unabashed enthusiasm for the Neoclassicism in vogue during the 50 years bracketing the turn of the century. His 1907 Beaux Arts **US Customs House** (next to BOWLING GREEN) bows only to the METROPOLITAN MUSEUM OF ART in effusive grandeur. It is said that he drew inspiration for that design from the Paris Opera House, and there is little question that the British Houses of Parliament played a role in his Woolworth commission. Replete with Gothic traceries and terracotta gargoyles, a blend of modern technology and stylistic nostalgia that so often fails, this "Cathedral of Commerce" is one of the most successful of the first generation of skyscrapers.

From its completion in 1913 until the opening of the CHRYSLER BUILDING in 1930, Woolworth's monument to himself and his empire of nickel-and-dime stores was the tallest in the world. The observation floor has long been closed to the public, but you can step into the lobby to admire the terracotta and marble walls, bronze ornamentation, and vaulted ceiling. Two of the statues found there are of Gilbert and Woolworth, up to the left, the latter shown counting coins.

WORLD FINANCIAL CENTER 🏛

Battery Park City (West St., between Vesey and Liberty Sts.), NY 10048 ☎*945-0505. Map 1U4* 🔲 ⚏ ⚐ *Open 7am-1am.*

An ambitious cluster of buildings that contributes mightily to the resurgence of lower Manhattan as a place to live and play as well as work, this new complex is the centerpiece of the multi-use BATTERY PARK landfill development. It stands opposite the WORLD TRADE CENTER, at the cusp of the Hudson. Included in its beguilements are a marina for those who can afford such extravagances, an unobstructed vista of the STATUE OF LIBERTY and ELLIS ISLAND, 50 upmarket shops, and, at last count, 12 restaurants, including the already celebrated **Hudson River Club** *(* ☎ *786-1500).*

All these cluster around the fabulous **Winter Garden**, a stunning urban space rivaling GRAND CENTRAL TERMINAL and ROCKEFELLER CENTER. Under its vaulted glass-and-steel roof is a grove of 16 palm trees, each at least 60 feet high, yet dwarfed by the soaring atrium. Cafés are gathered around them, for a cappuccino or a full meal, and a gleaming marble staircase rises at the E end. Music, art exhibits, and other entertainments are frequently staged. The Garden is especially dramatic at sunset, as it is oriented W, looking toward the New Jersey shore and the Lady in the Harbor.

WORLD TRADE CENTER 🏛

Church St. (Liberty St.), NY 10007 ☎*435-7377. Map 1U4* ⚓ 🔳 ⚔ ⚏ ⚐ ✦
Observation decks open Oct-May 9.30am-9.30pm; June-Sept 9.30am-11.30pm.

Long before their completion in 1974, the twin towers of the World Trade Center encountered censure, on both esthetic and environmental grounds. They were said to be visually banal, to have displaced a thriving market district of little charm but much vitality, to have thrown the lower Manhattan skyline out of balance, and to have placed unnecessary strain on public transport and services.

Those complaints are now irrelevant. Rentable space was leased, shops and restaurants were installed, and there is not a more stunning vista in the urban world. At 1,350 feet (411m) they are eight stories taller than the EMPIRE STATE BUILDING, but were surmounted within months by the Sears Building in Chicago.

The **observation decks** are in 2 World Trade Center, and nearly 2 million visitors a year take the quarter-mile trip to the summit. There is an **enclosed deck** on the 107th floor, and an open **rooftop promenade** on the 110th. The latter is not for the vertiginous, nor is it open in blustery or otherwise inclement weather. On a clear day, you can see for 75-100 miles. Most of the 40 shops and 22 restaurants are at ground level or below, but the **Windows on the World** restaurant in 1 World Trade Center takes advantage of the views from the 107th floor.

The **Vista International Hotel** between the towers opened in early 1981, the first important downtown hotel in more than 100 years.

Free outdoor performances of theater, dance and music are frequently staged at noon in summer in the Tobin Plaza at the base of the towers. In cold weather, they are moved inside to the mezzanine and lobbies *(for information ☎435-4170)*.

YESHIVA UNIVERSITY
187th St. (Amsterdam Ave.), NY 10033 ☎960-5400. See ORIENTATION MAP on pages 78-9. Subway 1 to 181 or 191 Sts.

This is both the largest and the oldest Jewish university in the Western Hemisphere, and it first began in 1886 as a seminary called Yeshiva Eitz Chaim. Now a fully-fledged university with more than 7,000 students engaged in both undergraduate and postgraduate studies, it still maintains reverence for its origins while drawing wide respect for its courses in medicine and the mathematical sciences. The main building is a Moorish-Byzantine extravaganza of tiles, cupolas, minarets, domes and arches, completed in 1928.

Yeshiva University Museum
Yeshiva University Library, 2520 Amsterdam Ave., NY 10033 ☎960-5390 ▨ Open Tues-Thurs 11am-5pm; Sun noon-6pm. Closed Mon, Fri, Sat.

A rich collection focuses on the Jewish experience, through photography, religious objects, paintings, and scale models of ten famous synagogues of the ancient world.

YORKVILLE
Map 8L5.

Germans were among the earliest large 19thC immigrant groups, and many settled in this Upper East Side district centering on 86th St. They were speedily assimilated, and had largely dispersed by the 1930s.

Traces of their occupation remain, with a *bierstube* or two, several bakery-coffee houses, and some dark-paneled restaurants specializing in *wienerschnitzel* and *sauerbraten*. Prodigals return for the **Steuben Day** parade in mid-September.

If I live in New York, it is because I choose to live there.
It is the city of total intensity, the city of the moment.
(Diana Vreeland)

Where to stay

Making your choice

An unprecedented surge in hotel construction has added more than 20 new hotels to the already crowded inventory. Many are in areas, such as **Chinatown** and the **Financial District**, where few or none previously existed. **Times Square** alone attracted five in the last four years, in addition to the huge **Marriott Marquis** and several others already in place. Many are large, but a parallel trend is toward smaller, luxury hotels operated in the European manner, such as **The Mark, Royalton**, and **Parc Fifty One**.

The greater number of these thousands of new rooms are in the deluxe (▥ or ▦) category, however, and there's the rub. New York already has the highest room rates in the nation, but with occupancy levels running at 72 percent or better, even during the recent recession, there is little incentive to lower prices. The budget accommodation that does exist is usually mean and soulless.

BUDGET ACCOMMODATION
Exceptions are a few new enterprises, including **Journey's End** and **Chatwal Inn**, that provide entirely acceptable rooms with basic comforts at what are, for New York, surprisingly reasonable rates. Little is available that might be compared in cost and coziness to family-run Italian *pensioni*. Efforts are being made to rectify this situation. At the delightfully idiosyncratic end of the spectrum are the **Box Tree** and the **Inn New York City**, in-town inns for people who are weary of the chain hotel norm. For other possibilities, see BED AND BREAKFAST at the end of this section.

Otherwise, the best that can be expected in the inexpensive and lower mid-priced price categories is a clean room with minimal amenities: no more than a private shower, air conditioning, and a TV set. Some of the better hotels in this group (in price bands ▥ and ▦) are listed under FURTHER RECOMMENDATIONS on page 184.

LUXURY ACCOMMODATION
In the luxury category, full baths, ankle-deep carpets, and meticulous housekeeping are the rule, and such additional touches as refrigerators, fresh-cut flowers, terry robes, and hairdryers are common. Always looking for ways to distinguish their properties, managers of these hotels started introducing complimentary limousines, concierges, and

afternoon tea a decade or so back. Now, such extras are almost routine, and the search is on for new ones.

Fitness centers are increasingly available, too, within the hotel or at nearby clubs. They can be tiny rooms with a few barbells and an exercycle up to multi-floor extravaganzas with river views and rows of every conditioning device yet invented.

While 24-hour room service (euphemistically, "private dining") is widely available at this level, canny travelers tend to avoid using it. Breakfast, for example, can easily cost four times what it does at a coffee shop around the corner. The same *caveat* applies to snacks or bottles of liquor or wine purchased in the hotel, or taken from the minibar, rather than from an independent shop.

LOCATION

Whatever their classification, a majority of the worthiest choices are found in **midtown Manhattan**, in an area bounded by 3rd Ave. and 7th Ave. from 38th St. to 60th St. There is a scattering through the **Upper East Side**, almost a dozen on and around **Times Square** and four or five near each **airport**.

Rates are moderated by location, season, and duration of stay. To make up for the absence of business travelers on weekends, for example, hotels devise package plans to entice suburbanites and tourists with such extras as theater tickets or brunches, and up to 40 percent off standard room rates. Availability of discounts fluctuates with occupancy levels, obviously, and finding a room at any price can be a chore between April and October, especially on short notice. On those occasions, it is wise to inquire at hotels outside the immediate midtown area, particularly those in the **Gramercy Park** and **Murray Hill** districts. Ideally, reservations should be made at least a month in advance.

Children under 16 may often stay in their parents' room at little or no extra charge; ask when reserving. Several hotels have swimming pools and other recreational facilities to keep teenagers occupied, and lists of baby-sitters are customarily available. Dogs and other pets are usually prohibited or discouraged. Garage parking is costly, and most levy an in-and-out charge when cars are used.

Sales and occupancy taxes add nearly 21 percent to room bills, including an annoying $2 tacked on to the inexcusably high state and city levies. Tipping is expected, need it be said, but is not especially complicated. Give the bellman about $1 per bag, and something extra if they are heavy, or he must take them a long way. A doorman expects something for merely opening a car door, and about $1 if he devotes some time to hailing a taxi. Add 15 percent to the bill for room service waiters unless a service charge is added, as it often is. Chambermaids are accustomed to receiving about $1 per night for routine cleaning.

Unless stated otherwise, all the hotels listed below have elevators, air conditioning, private baths, room TV and telephone, and accept American Express, Diners Club and other major charge/credit cards. Most hotel TV sets are linked to cable systems with a multitude of channels, some of them in Spanish, Italian, and other languages. Many also offer recent

HOTELS CLASSIFIED BY AREA

LOWER MANHATTAN (BELOW 14TH ST.)
New York Vista ▥
    to ▥
Marriott Financial Center ▥
Seaport Suites ▥
    to ▥

GRAMERCY PARK/MURRAY HILL (E 14TH ST.–E 42ND ST.)
Doral Court ▥ ♣
Doral Park Avenue ▥
Doral Tuscany ▥
Journey's End ▱ ▰
Gramercy Park ▥
Morgan's ▥
Sheraton Park Avenue ▥

LOWER WEST SIDE/GARMENT CENTER (W 14TH ST.–W 42ND ST.)
Ramada Pennsylvania ▥

MIDTOWN EAST (E 42ND ST.– E 59TH ST.)
Beekman Tower ▥
Beverly ▱ ♣
Box Tree ▥
    to ▥
Drake ▥
Fitzpatrick Manhattan ▥
Grand Hyatt ▥ ▦
Inter-Continental ▥
Leow's New York
    ▥ to ▥
Lexington ▥
Marriott East Side ▥
Middletowne ▱ ♣
New York Helmsley ▥
New York Helmsley Palace
    ▥ ▦ ▥
Omni Berkshire
    Place ▥
Peninsula ▥ ▦
Plaza ▥ ▦
Roger Smith
    ▥ to ▥
St Regis ▥ ▦
Tudor ▥
UN Plaza-Park Hyatt ▥ ▦
Waldorf Astoria
    ▥ to ▥ ▦

MIDTOWN WEST (W 42ND ST.– W 59TH ST.)
Algonquin ▥
Chatwal Inn ▱ ♣
Dorset ▥
Embassy Suites ▥ to ▥
Essex House ▥
Holiday Inn Crowne
    Plaza ▥
Howard Johnson's ▥ ♣
Macklowe ▥
Marriott Marquis ▥
Milford Plaza ▱
New York Hilton ▥
Novotel ▥ to ▥
Paramount ▥
Parc Fifty One ▥ ▦
Parker Meridien ▥ to ▥ ▦
Park Lane ▥ ▦
Ramada Inn ▥
Ramada Renaissance ▥ to ▥
Ritz-Carlton ▥
Royalton ▥ to ▥
St Moritz ▥
Salisbury ▱ ♣
Sheraton Manhattan ▥
Sheraton New York ▥
Warwick ▥ to ▥
Wyndham ▱ to ▥ ♣

UPPER EAST SIDE (E 60TH ST.– E 95TH ST.)
Barbizon ▥
Carlyle ▥ ▦
Lowell,The ▥
Mark, The ▥ to ▥ ▦
Mayfair Baglioni ▥ ▦
Pierre ▥ ▦
Plaza Athénée ▥ ▦
Regency ▥ ▦
Stanhope ▥ ▦
Wales ▱ ♣
Westbury ▥ ▦

UPPER WEST SIDE (W 60TH ST.– W 96TH ST.)
Broadway American ▱
Empire ▥ to ▥ ♣
Mayflower ▥
Inn New York City ▥

movies on a pay-per-view basis. A 1989 state law allowed hotels to install stocked minibars in their guestrooms. Nearly all have facilities for persons using wheelchairs, at least in terms of access. Many have special rooms with wider doors and modified bathrooms. Inquire when reserving. Similarly, all but the smallest hotels have conference rooms for at least small groups, and most can supply audiovisual and related equipment. Nonsmoking rooms and floors are increasingly available.

The "800" numbers noted in the entries below are for reservations only. Since their operators often are not located in the hotels or even in the state, don't expect them to be able to answer any but the most obvious questions. No matter what rate he or she quotes initially, always ask if there are less expensive rooms to be had. Frequently, the answer is "yes", and for exactly the same type of accommodation. Discounts are routinely given to callers who are more than 62 years old or who work for identifiable companies. The telephone area code for Manhattan is **212**.

New York's hotels A to Z

ALGONQUIN
59 W 44th St. (near 5th Ave.), NY 10036
☎840-6800 or 800-548-0345 ☒944-1419. Map **604** ▥▢ 165 rms ▣ ▱ ☙
▰ ♫
Location: Near Grand Central Terminal. Back in the Twenties and Thirties, the storied writers and humorists Dorothy Parker, George Kaufman, Robert Benchley and others traded japes and aphorisms around the Algonquin's famous Round Table. That is history. But this turn-of-the-century hotel is still the clubby choice of many literary and theater folk. The lobby, tidied up and less crowded than it used to be with sofas, wing chairs and ill-matched tables, still has the feel of a well-used country inn. Afternoon tea and cocktails can be taken there. A bell on each table summons the waiter. Extensive redecoration and renovation has upgraded many of the once-dowdy rooms, and added security safes and remote-control TV. The *New York Times* is delivered daily. Caution: while an evening at the **Oak Room** cabaret is a treat, dining at the hotel is not.

BARBIZON ♣
140 E 63rd St. (Lexington Ave.), NY 10021
☎838-5700 or 800-223-1020 ☒753-0360. Map **8M4** ▥▢ 342 rms ▱ ▣ ▱
◖ *from some rooms* ☙
Location: At center of the Upper East Side. The Gothic and Romanesque architecture speaks of an era when the Barbizon was a sanctuary for young ladies of gentle breeding. Men were allowed only in the lobby, to which residents were summoned when their escorts arrived. That was the time after chaperones and before the sexual revolution, which proved fatal to such enterprises. Now, following protracted renovations undertaken by consecutive owners, the Barbizon is a first-class hotel open to all. A certain gentility still reigns, despite ownership by the same people who run the relentlessly hip MORGAN'S and PARAMOUNT hotels. Standard rooms are small, but with their creamy color schemes and uncluttered furnishings, they manage not to feel cramped. Even in their costlier configurations, they represent a substantial savings over the better-known luxury hostelries in the vicinity. Some suites have terraces and kitchenettes, and a number of rooms have good views.

BEEKMAN TOWER
3 Mitchell Place (corner of 1st Ave. and 49th), NY 10017 ☎355-7300 or

800-637-8483 [Fx]*753-9366. Map 605* ▥
170 rms and suites ♈ ☰ ▣ ◄ *from
some rooms* ♈ ♪ ☞ ▣ *refrigerator.*
*Location: Immediately N of the United
Nations.* Flagship of a local chain of
nine suite hotels, this 1928 Art Deco
structure has been the beneficiary of a
recent top-to-bottom renovation. The
tranquil lobby is expertly done in trappings of the original period, and the
new **Zephyr Grill**, with similar detailing, is a decided improvement over its
predecessors. On the 26th floor is the
Top of the Tower cocktail lounge,
which takes full advantage of the excellent views and has background piano
music Tuesday to Saturday to enhance
the mood. While the claim of "all suites"
is a slight exaggeration, since much of
the accommodation is in one-room studios with sitting areas, all are equipped
with kitchenettes and some have terraces. Also on the premises is a complete fitness center.

Standard rates are admittedly at the
high end, but special weekend, extended stay, and summer discounts
bring them down to moderate levels. In
addition, most of the suites have sofas
that can be converted into beds, saving
the additional charges most hotels
charge for roll-away cots for children.
For a list of the other hotels in the group,
see MANHATTAN EAST SUITE HOTELS on page
185.

THE BOX TREE 🏨
250 E 49th St. (3rd Ave.), NY 10017
☎*758-8320. Map 604* ▥ *to* ▥ *13 rms
and suites* ▣ ☰ ♈
*Location: On residential block a short
walk from 5th Ave. shops.* There is no
hotel remotely comparable to The Box
Tree within the city limits. Known primarily for its restaurant, these adjoining
brownstones (and a third yet to be remodeled) also contain lodgings
wrapped in an over-the-top voluptu-
ousness that few people unrelated to
the Bourbons could imagine. It starts off
gently enough, in an anteroom with
emerald walls, waxed brick floor, and a
leather sedan chair beside a fireplace
flanked by two 18thC porcelain Pans.

But beyond the service bar, an ornately
carved altar from a French church, is a
glorious staircase that looks at first to
have been carved out of alabaster. It
flows down and around in an sinuous
Art Nouveau cascade. All the bedrooms
are as singular in their trappings, some
of them formal suites, some double
rooms with sitting areas. A favorite of all
who see it is the one named for King
Boris III of Bulgaria (the owner's homeland), its mirrored walls and gilt and silk
as regal as a Versailles salon. Louis XVI
might have swept in here to elude Marie
Antoinette. Other rooms boast fine mar-
quetry screens, ancestral portraits,
sumptuously detailed European antiques and Oriental carpets. All have
gas-burning fireplaces. Bathrooms, although small, are lavished with lapis
lazuli and pink marble. A fax machine
is available to workaholics, but this is a
place meant for the ultimate intimate
weekend. And while the outlay for all
this sounds steep at first blush, it might
help to know that room rates include
continental breakfast *and* a $100 credit
toward dinner in either of the two restaurants.

CARLYLE 🏨
35 E 76th St. (Madison Ave.), NY 10021
☎*744-1600 or 800-227-5737* [Fx]*717-
4682. Map 8L4* ▥ *500 rms* ▣ ♈ ☰
▣ ♈ ♪
*Location: Upper East Side, one block
from the Whitney Museum.* Many hotels
pretend to offer continental standards
of hospitality, but here the grand tradi-
tions of Europe really are emulated.
Over-sized rooms pamper with bathroom phones and custom toiletries. All
have dedicated fax lines, VCR, stereo
and CD players, and most have serving
pantries and well-stocked refrigerators.
There is 24-hour room service, and the
cashier exchanges foreign currency
until midnight. Pets are permitted at an
extra charge, and dog walkers are on
hand. Afternoon tea is an event, as is an
hour spent with stylish singer-pianist
Bobby Short or the jazz musicians and
vocalists who often appear in his stead
in the **Café Carlyle**. **Bemelmans' Bar**

is the clubby home of murals by the famous author and illustrator of the Madeline books. It is scotch-and-soda country, with piano music from 5.30pm. Limousines stand ready to shuttle guests to midtown shops and theaters. A new health club has now opened, about the only thing the Carlyle didn't already have to undergird its near-flawless reputation.

DORAL COURT ♣

130 E 39th St. (Lexington Ave.), NY 10016 ☎*685-1100 or 800-624-0607* 🖷*889-0287. Map 604* 🔲 *to* 🔲 *248 rms* ▤ ⌂ ♉ ▣ *refrigerators.*

Location: Near Grand Central Terminal and the United Nations. One of a trio of ingratiating Doral hotels in upper Murray Hill, a recent overhaul qualifies this as a new entry. To the bare-bones amenities of others in its class are added remote-control TV and VCRs, bathrobes, refrigerators, and, on request, in-room exercycles. King-sized beds, commodious dimensions, and a soothing Sister Parish-style decor are the norm. Downstairs, the **Courtyard Café** is favored by neighborhood executives, who use it for every animated meal of the day. Rates are at the low end of the expensive range, and are cut by 40 percent on weekends, when free parking is included. A fully equipped fitness center on nearby Park Ave. is available to guests of the three Doral hotels in the immediate vicinity.

DORAL PARK AVENUE

70 Park Ave. (38th St.), NY 10016 ☎*687-7050 or 800-847-4135* 🖷*808-9029. Map 604* 🔲 *220 rms* ▤ ⌂ ♉ ♉ ▣ *refrigerator.*

Location: Near Grand Central Terminal. Murray Hill doesn't have the gloss and hum of the midtown core, but that is its virtue. This serene stopping-place, small by Big Apple standards, makes the most of its setting. Reasonable needs are skillfully met, without fuss or show, although the restaurant and room service close down early. Bedrooms have refrigerators and computer ports; some have serving pantries.

There are two restaurants and a sidewalk café in summer, and most central office buildings and tourist sights are within walking distance. The **Saturnia** restaurant specializes in tasty "healthy" food. Guests can use a nearby health club.

DORAL TUSCANY

120 E 39th St. (near Park Ave.), NY 10016 ☎*686-1600 or 800-223-6725* 🖷*779-7822. Map 604* 🔲 *143 rms* ▤ ▤ ♉ ⌂

Location: Near Grand Central Terminal and United Nations. This, the third of the trio of admirable Murray Hill Dorals, charms in many small details — at the entrance, a large thermometer-barometer; on the desk, an arrangement of flowers; in the bedroom, a serving pantry with a refrigerator stocked with soft drinks; in the bathroom, a telephone and a 3-nozzle massaging showerhead; outside the window, another thermometer. Even exercycles are available, on request. It is quieter by many decibels than its larger midtown cousins, yet is only a few blocks farther from the action. **Time and Again** is as good a restaurant as can be found in the immediate neighborhood. The staff treats guests with an avuncularity that is at once amusing and reassuring. Conventioneers and tour groups are never in evidence, and the hotel is less likely to be booked up on short notice. The chain makes its Park Ave. health club available to guests.

DORSET

30 W 54th St. (near 6th Ave.), NY 10019 ☎*247-7300 or 800-227-2348* 🖷*581-0153. Map 6N4* 🔲 *400 rms* ▤ *nearby* ▤ ⌂ ♉

Location: Near Rockefeller Center and Museum of Modern Art. The fact that more than half its rooms are under permanent lease is testimony to the desirability of this underpublicized hostelry. The paneled lobby is a welcoming retreat from the midtown bustle, the front desk staff amiable. Personalities from the nearby television network headquarters often lunch at the streetside bar-café. There is no charge for children under 14 sharing their parents' room. The Dorset is said to be up for sale, so its future is uncertain.

DRAKE SWISSÔTEL

440 Park Ave. (56th St.), NY 10022 ☎*421-0900 or 800-372-5369* ✉*371-4190. Map 6N4* ▥ *to* ▥ *622 rms* ▣ ⇶ Ⴤ ♪ ▣ *refrigerator.*

Location: Midtown East. It can confidently be observed that the Swiss know how to run hotels. Their takeover here has brought renewed luxury and crispness of operation to a once-faltering establishment. The **Restaurant Lafayette**, for example, is one of the city's best, in or outside of hotels. Fine wines are served by the glass in the plush bar, to the tunes of the nightly pianist. Upstairs, the spacious rooms leading off the twisting halls reveal such touches as hideaway refrigerators, AM-FM radios, and first-run movies. A same-day laundry service is available. The prime East Side venue is a bonus, and things have improved even more with completion of a $52 million renovation. New high-speed elevators were installed. Free morning transport to the FINANCIAL DISTRICT is available.

EMPIRE ♣

44 W 63rd St. (Broadway), NY 10023 ☎*265-7400 or 800-545-7400* ✉*765-4913. Map 7M3* ▥ *to* ▥ *400 rms* Ⴤ ⇶ Ⴤ ▣ *minibar* ⚡

Location: Opposite entrance to Lincoln Center. New ownership has brought this once-shabby hotel back from the edge of oblivion. More than mere painting and plastering has been going on. The lobby is downright grand, with its 1710 French tapestry and 1890 Oriental carpet; a large space on the mezzanine floor has been transformed into what looks like an exclusive gentlemen's club, complete with billiard table. In the bedrooms are stereo tuners, CD players, VCRs, and audio tape decks. Guests can order room service or checkout on a special channel on the remote-control TV, and messages are conveyed via electronic voice mail. Use of the adjacent health club is free — another rarity in New York — and private offices are available, with computers, printers, copiers and fax machines on hand. Culture-seekers are just across the street from all that Lincoln Center offers, and Carnegie Hall and Broadway theaters are in walking distance. While the Empire is no longer in the budget category, as some sources continue to insist, its tariffs are certainly reasonable considering all that it provides. The only serious caveat is that some rooms and/or baths are of cramped or odd dimensions, the legacy of a building erected between the wars. If assigned one, simply ask for another. Plans are afoot to create a jazz club on the Broadway side; a pre-concert crowd fills the existing street-level restaurant.

ESSEX HOUSE 🏨

160 Central Park S (near 6th Ave.), NY 10019 ☎*247-0300 or 800-645-5687* ✉*315-1839. Map 6N4* ▥ *591 rms* ▣ ♥ ⌖ ⇶ Ⴤ ▣ *minibar* ⚡

Location: On Central Park, near Lincoln Center and shopping areas. The Essex House long aspired to rank with the cream of Manhattan hotels, but it fell short, even after its purchase by a subsidiary of Japan Airlines in 1985. Now, however, a two-year closing and remarkable expenditures of funds and dedication have thrust it decisively to the front ranks. About all that remains of the old hotel are Art Deco details of the exterior and lobby. Bedrooms are fewer and larger, the plumbing, airconditioning and heating systems have been replaced. The service staff has been trained to razor-edge alertness, many of them learning guests' names by some computerized magic. Little expense has been spared on the bountifully equipped fitness center, which amounts to a full-fledged spa. Personal trainers, aerobics classes, massages, and herbal wraps complement the array of weight machines and exercycles. Both the luxurious 14-table **Les Célébrités** restaurant and casual **Café Botánica** have gathered plaudits from reviewers and devoted gourmands. The former is decorated with paintings by such personages as Peggy Lee, Gene Hackman, James Dean, Tennessee Williams and other famous hobbyists, explaining the name. An accomplished pan-Pacific cuisine compensates for their sometimes shaky efforts.

FITZPATRICK MANHATTAN

687 Lexington Ave. (between 56th and 57th Sts.), NY 10022 ☎ *355-0100 or 800-367-7701* ⊠ *308-5166. Map 6N4* ▥ *92 rms* ✛ *nearby* ⊐ ⬛ ⏀

Location: Steps to 57th St. shopping. The first North American venture of an Irish hotelier is this resuscitated oldster built in 1926 and abandoned for most of the last decade. A top-hatted bellman bows guests into a bright blue and (of course) emerald green lobby. Off to the right are the bar and **Fitzer's** restaurant, where the featured dish, naturally, is Irish lamb stew. The configurations of the rooms and suites in the upper 16 floors are largely unchanged from the years as the Dover Hotel. They are of good size, the bathrooms newly fitted out with black marble and white tiles. Every tub is a whirlpool bath, no less standard equipment than is the trouser press. Visitors who have been distressed by overheating and hypercooling in other US hotels appreciate the individual controls provided. Computer and fax hookup, too. Suites have wet bars and two-line phones.

GRAND HYATT ▥

42nd St. and Park Ave., NY 10017 ☎ *883-1234 or 800-228-9000* ⊠ *697-3772. Map 604* ▥ *1,407 rms* ⬛ ✛ ⬠ ⊐ ⏀ ⏀ ♫

Location: Next to Grand Central Terminal. A leader in the 1980s hotel boom, this addition to the Hyatt holdings takes a share of the credit for the continuing rehabilitation of E 42nd St. Sleek and showy as it unarguably is, it is downright sedate by the standards of others in the chain. Original owner Donald Trump even resisted putting his name on it. There is drama in abundance in its exuberant architecture,

nevertheless. The 4-story atrium is horizontal rather than vertical, the rule in other Hyatts, with one side knuckling out over 42nd Street. There is a reflecting pool with tiered waterfall beneath a vast spidery tubular sculpture, rows of greenery, great columns cloaked in brass and steel. A duo plays cocktail music for the bustling crowd. All rooms have color and cable TV, there is a health club with sauna, squash and tennis, and **Trumpet's** was among the vanguard of hotel restaurants that actually tried to measure up to their prices. Room rates on the costlier **Regency Club** executive floors cover such extras as continental breakfast and terry robes.

HOLIDAY INN CROWNE PLAZA

1605 Broadway (49th St.), NY 10019 ☎ *977-4000 or 800-465-4329* ⊠ *333-7393. Map 503* ▥ *770 rms* ⬛ ⊐ ✛ ⬠ ⏀ ⏀ ⬛ *minibar* ⬠

Location: Times Square theater district. Place this gaudy newcomer in the jukebox subspecies of Post-Modernist architecture. The designer giddily admits he wanted the pink-and-burgundy exterior to look like a Wurlitzer, complete with huge bands of multicolored lights racing around the sides. Certainly no one can claim it is an intrusion on its Times Square neighborhood. Opened in December 1989, it was expected to appeal to businesspeople and a substantial proportion of foreign tourists, for whom it no doubt confirms everything they ever believed about the United States. Among its attractions are the largest indoor pool of any Manhattan hotel, 24-hour room service, and three restaurants, two of which, **Samplings** and the **Broadway Grill**, quickly drew good reviews. The executive floors have a private concierge.

INN NEW YORK CITY ♣

266 W 71st St. (between Amsterdam and West End Aves.), NY 10023 ☎ *580-1900. Map 7M2* ▥ *4 suites* ⬠ ⬛ *refrigerator Location: Walking distance from Lincoln Center and Museum of Natural History.* There is no sign out front, and not because they're trying to be chic.

With only four apartment suites and a loyal and growing clientele that reserves all of them far in advance, there is no point in encouraging passersby to drop in, even for a look. But what an eyeful they would get! Four floors of a brownstone on a quiet side street have been painstakingly remodeled and furnished by their energetic on-premises hosts. All are equipped as completely as any home, including cable TV, telephone answering machine, stereo, intercom, clothes washer and dryer and kitchens with pots, crockery, and stocked refrigerator (yes, that's a quiche in there with the wine and soft drinks). A self-serve breakfast is laid out, including, but not limited to, bagels, muffins, freshly ground coffee, tea, juice, milk. Apart from those commonalities, none of the four apartments look like any of the others. The "Spa" suite, for one, has a whirlpool bath that could accommodate three or four friends with room to spare. In the "Parlor" suite is a piano, a working fireplace, a terrace, a stained glass ceiling and a dining table already set with china, glasses and silverware. Fax and copy machines are available for a fee. They impose a two-night minimum stay, as a rule, but might allow a single night for a small surcharge.

INTER-CONTINENTAL
111 E 48th St. (Lexington Ave.), NY 10017 ☎755-5900 or 800-332-4246 ⊠644-0079. Map 604 ▥ 692 rms ▣ ▦ ▨ ▼ ▰ ▤ minibar.
Location: Near Grand Central Terminal and United Nations. A courtly European flavor persists here, announced by the lobby trademark, a large aviary with live birds. The spacious public areas and halls suggest bedrooms of larger dimensions than they usually prove to be, but thick walls and double windows keep them quiet. TV, AM-FM radio, free in-room movies, and 24-hour room service remove the need to brave the streets for food and diversion. A fully appointed health club was inaugurated in 1990, with treadmills, weight-lifting and stair-climbing machines. They've even installed TV

sets at eye-level in front of the Lifecycles. Sauna, steam, and massage are available. In the same healthy spirit, floors have been set aside for nonsmokers. The Theater District is only a few blocks w, and several celebrated restaurants are even closer. Within the building is the oldest pharmacy in New York, **Caswell Massey**, featuring soaps and hairbrushes that have their origins in Colonial times. Several enticing weekend packages are available.

JOURNEY'S END ▰
3 E 40th St. (near 5th Ave.), NY 10016 ☎447-1500 or 800-668-4200 ⊠213-0972. Map 604 ▥ 189 rms ▣
Location: Around corner from New York Public Library. The growing Canadian economy chain has made this welcome addition to Manhattan lodging possibilities. Frills are few, but public and private rooms in the 30-story sliver of a building are crisp, clean, uncluttered. Most rooms have queen-sized beds. Complimentary coffee and copies of *USA Today* are available in the lobby. Arrangements can be made for use of a nearby health club. No room service. Weekend discounts push costs down into the inexpensive category.

LEOW'S NEW YORK
569 Lexington Ave. (51st St.), NY 10022 ☎752-7000 or 800-223-0888 ⊠758-6311. Map 6N4 ▥ to ▥ 729 rms ▣ ▦ ▼ ▰ ▨ ▼ ▤ refrigerator.
Location: Near midtown shopping and United Nations. All the usual comforts are to be found in this large, international-breed hotel, the re-named **Summit**. Once inside, you might be in any of its counterparts in Lisbon, London or Rio, but $26 million has just been spent to nudge it higher in the perceptions of international travelers. Refrigerators, bathroom telephones, in-room movies and radios are standard. The well-equipped fitness center is welcome. For additional indulgences, ask for a room on the executive floor, but expect a surcharge. One weekend package includes theater tickets, dinner, free parking and unlimited use of

the health club; another, of the "no-frills" variety, squeezes costs down to the moderate level.

THE LOWELL

28 E 63rd St. (near Madison Ave.), NY 10021 ☎*838-1400* ⊠*319-4230. Map 8M4* ▥ *60 rms* ⊟ ☒ ☒ ▣ *refrigerator. Location: Residential street near Central Park Zoo.* The first thing you notice about The Lowell is its rose-and-cream-tiled Art Deco exterior, a mild visual shock on this sedate block. Erected as a residential hotel in the late 1920s, it had gone through several ownerships and marked decline until its recent facelift. There is much to distinguish it now from its midtown rivals. In a city of sealed glass and steam heat, all of the casement windows open, and 34 of the units have woodburning fireplaces. There are real books on the shelves, and live plants, cut flowers, twice-daily maid service and two bathrobes in every bathroom. None of the rooms is exactly alike, although a crisp contemporary look sets the tone. The charming **Pembrooke Room** is hidden away on the second floor, serving breakfast, lunch and afternoon tea. Management promotes highly personal attention and is discreet almost to a fault about its more celebrated clients — one reason they keep coming back.

MACKLOWE

145 W 44th St. (between Broadway and Ave. of the Americas), NY 10036 ☎*768-4400 or 800-62255693* ⊠*768-0847. Map 503* ▥ *638 rms* ☒ ⊟ ▣ ☒ ☜ ▣ *minibar.*

Location: In the Times Square theater district. Expanses of veined black marble and wall-sized paintings contribute to one of the most stunning interiors in New York. The dramatic lobby runs all the way from 44th to the next block, and is invariably a-stir and a-glimmer with handsome people from the high-profile industries that routinely use the Macklowe for its conferences and media presentations. The on-premises presence of the restored 1902 **Hudson Theatre** underlines this

showbiz pizazz, as does the **Charlotte** restaurant, which traffics in such trendibles as squid ink fettucini with salmon caviar. After all that, the size of the bedrooms — smallish — may disappoint, but they aren't short on the electronics now deemed essential to the international business traveler. Voice mail in four languages is one; dual-line phones with modem hook-up, another, as well as an interactive TV service, MackTel, that allows guests to order airline and theater tickets and make restaurant reservations without leaving the room. Oh, and one old-fashioned comfort — windows that open. The fitness center is fully equipped, with weights, exercycles, rowing machines, steam rooms and, for a fee, personal trainers.

THE MARK ▥

Madison Ave. and E 77th St., NY 10021 ☎*744-4300 or 800-843-6275* ⊠*744-2749. Map 8L4* ▥ *180 rms* ⊟ ▣ ☒ ☒ ▣ *minibar.*

Location: Upper East Side, among art galleries, near Metropolitan Museum of Art. Madonna slept here. Since it can be assumed that she can stay where she wants, the relatively new Mark obviously has something going for it. After all, the **Carlyle**, dowager empress of Manhattan hostelries, is just across the street. Two-thirds of these units are suites, and those on the top three floors — 14 to 16 — garner the raves. Details include meticulously crafted moldings, custom-designed fabrics, marble bathrooms, and Italianate furnishings. King-sized beds and coffee-makers are the norm. All rooms have VCRs, dual-line phones, and fax ports. Many suites have wet bars or terraces, many have serving pantries, and all have VCRs. (More than 200 video cassettes are available for rent.) There is no health club, but guests have access to one nearby, at a too-high price. Many good restaurants are within a few blocks, but the one downstairs, **Mark's**, is more than satisfactory.

MARRIOTT EAST SIDE

525 Lexington Ave. (near 49th St.), NY 10017 ☎*755-4000 or 800-228-9290*

751-3440. Map 604 ▥ 677 rms ▣
⥑ ✿ ♈ ⋔ ▣ minibar.

*Location: Midtown East, near Grand
Central Terminal and United Nations.*
Another of the fairly anonymous hotels
that line Lexington Ave. near Grand
Central, this, the former Halloran
House, might perk up under new Marriott ownership. Or not. So far, the only
significant changes are in prices —
higher, of course. The six "concierge"
floors have a private lounge and honor
bar. **Biff's Place**, the once-popular bar
named for the previous owner, is closed.

MARRIOTT FINANCIAL CENTER

85 West St. (Albany St.), NY 10006 ☎*385-
4900 or 800-228-9290* ▣*227-8136. Map
1U4* ▥ *511 rms* ⥊ ≈ ♈ ⥑ ♈ ⥇ ▣
minibar.

*Location: Near the World Trade Center
and Stock Exchange.* Only the second
major hotel erected in the Financial District in this century (see the NEW YORK
VISTA below), this addition to the pervasive chain does its job well, if without
particular distinction. Within walking
distance are the **World Financial Center, South Street Seaport, Wall
Street**, and the ferries to the **Statue of
Liberty** and **Ellis Island**. The fitness
center has the requisite instruments of
exertion as well as the relatively rare
luxury of an indoor swimming pool.
Rates are deeply discounted on weekends in this mostly Monday to Friday, 9
to 5 neighborhood.

MARRIOTT MARQUIS

1535 Broadway (45th St.), NY 10036
☎*398-1900 or 800-228-9290* ▣*980-
6175. Map 503* ▥ *1,874 rms* ♈ ⥑ ▣
♈ ▣ ⋔ ⥇ ⌑

*Location: On Times Square, near
theaters.* Big. Garish. With a revolving
restaurant more appropriate to Los
Angeles or Houston, and halls and lobbies awash at all hours with frolicking
conventioneers. Don't expect to meet
anyone but other tourists. It is mentioned here mainly because of its convenient location, and also because it is
too large to ignore (hard as the majority
of New Yorkers may try).

MAYFAIR BAGLIONI ▨

610 Park Ave. (65th St.), NY 10021 ☎*288-
0800 or 800-223-0542* ▣*737-0538. Map
6M4* ▥ *199 rms* ♈ ⥑ ▣ ♈ ▣
refrigerator.

*Location: Upper East Side, in art and
antiques country.* The former Mayfair
Regent has earned a respect bordering
on the reverential, and that hasn't varied
with the recent change in name and
ownership. This is largely due to the
flair and care of a management that
learned its trade at such establishments
as London's Connaught and Venice's
Gritti Palace. Its success in replicating
the atmosphere of such exalted ca-
ravanserais can be seen in the number
of privileged Europeans, many of them
in the fashion field, who make this their
home in New York. They gather for
high tea and cocktails in the vaulted
lobby lounge, a fantasy of arabesque
flourishes that might have been the creation of a markedly secular caliph. The
presence on the premises of the re-
doubtable **Le Cirque** restaurant (see
RESTAURANTS) lends even more stature. A
majority of the accommodation is in
suites, understated but sumptuously
appointed. Ceilings are high, feet sink
in plush carpets, wood and metal surfaces glow, colors soothe in dove gray
and peach and beige. Some suites even
have working fireplaces, a warming
thought on a blustery January night.
Telephones have several lines, and buttons for conference calls, speaker-
phone and computer and fax
capability. (Portable cellular phones are
also available for rent by the day.) Bathrooms are supplied with hairdryers,
scales, towels that wrap twice around
the body and oversized terrycloth robes
that actually fit adults taller than jockeys. Guests confronted with a rainy
day will find an umbrella hanging in the
closet or in a stand by the door. Newspapers in choices of several languages
are hung on the door each morning.
The Fitness Centre has all the requisite
devices to tone and test the body, a
practice putting green, and good views.
When price is not a factor, this beauty
has few equals.

MAYFLOWER ♣

Central Park W (61st St.), NY 10023
☎265-0060 or 800-223-4164 (US and
Canada) or 0-800-891-256 (UK)
📠4972657 📠265-5098. Map **5N3** ▥
577 rms ▣ ═╪

*Location: Near Lincoln Center and
Carnegie Hall.* The refurbished Empire
Hotel, a short walk away, is giving the
Mayflower its first serious Upper West
Side competition in living memory. Yet
it remains the sort of dowager that applies rouge and powder in lieu of serious reconstruction. The maladroit
contractor who wallpapered the dated
bathrooms, for example, must have
been hired for his low prices rather than
his skill. Still, the Mayflower remains a
reliable choice. The parkside
Conservatory Café looks across to
Central Park, and its busy bar attracts
even neighborhood New Yorkers.
Suites with pantries cost no more than
a standard double at many of the fancier
crosstown hotels. That makes for a loyal
client roster of musicians, movie-
makers, and executives who don't want
to sacrifice convenience or comfort to
the dictates of their budget-keepers.
They get spacious rooms with traditional furnishings, many with park
views. Guests have access to a health
club on 57th St.

MIDDLETOWNE ♣

*148 E 48th St. (near Lexington Ave.), NY
10017* ☎755-3000 or 800-321-2323
📠832-0291. Map **604** ▥ 192 rms ➡
▣ ✿ ▤ refrigerator.

*Location: Midtown East, near Grand
Central Terminal.* Visitors staying for a
week or more sometimes wish they
could exchange costly full hotel services for more homelike quarters. They
can do that here, trading room service
waiters and elaborate lobbies for comfortable rooms equipped with full kitchens, including stoves, refrigerators
and, if desired, silverware and crockery.
Some suites have fireplaces and/or terraces. Rates might be negotiable for
longer stays. There is neither bar nor
restaurant, but both are abundant in this
neighborhood.

MORGAN'S

*237 Madison Ave. (near 37th St.), NY
10016* ☎686-0300 or 800-334-3408
📠779-8352. Map **6P4** ▥ 154 rms ▣
✿ ═╪ ☿ ▤ refrigerator.

*Location: Busy avenue near Morgan
Library and the Empire State Building.*
Call it a "boutique hotel." The owners
do. Two of the original principals were
responsible for the Studio 54 and the
Palladium mega-discos. It is zippy,
youthful, and trendy enough for Mick
Jagger, Billy Joel and executives of the
fashion and design industries. To highlight this in-the-know status, there is no
identifying sign outside and never will
be. Guests are whisked into rooms of
almost Oriental simplicity decked in
chic black, white and gray tones. Built-
in storage walls are of gray-stained
bird's-eye maple, the low beds covered
with pinstriped duvets. There are refrigerators, and this was one of the first
hotels in the city with stereo cassette
decks as well as VCRs in its rooms. (The
front desk can provide videocassettes
from its library.) A fresh-faced staff provides twice-daily housekeeping and 24-
hour room service. The duplex penthouse
suite has a dramatic view of the Empire
State Building.

NEW YORK HELMSLEY

212 E 42nd St. (3rd Ave.), NY 10017
☎490-8900 or 800-221-4982 📠986-
4792. Map **605** ▥ 800 rms ▣ ✿ ═╪
✿ ☿ ♪

*Location: Near Grand Central Ter-
minal and United Nations.* One of the
chain assembled by Harry Helmsley
and long ruled with an iron hand by his
wife, Leona, this one doesn't seem to
have suffered as a result of their considerable legal difficulties. Geared to
the expense account crowd and the
corollary assumption that traveling executives have little time for ceremony,
it is forthright rather than frisky. Multilingual stenographers are available.
Breakfast trays arrive with a copy of the
Wall Street Journal. Rooms are crisply
conservative. When business people go
home for the weekend, sharply discounted rates bring in suburbanites for

museum-hopping and the Broadway shows.

NEW YORK HELMSLEY PALACE 🏨 🏛

455 Madison Ave. (50th St.), NY 10022
☎*888-7000 or 800-221-4982*
🗟*303-6000. Map 6N4* 🎞 *773 rms* 🖃
� 🍴 ♈ ♪ 🖃 *refrigerator.*

Location: Midtown, near shopping.
Preservation of worthwhile buildings has a checkered history in New York. More often than not, commerce has triumphed over heritage. Not so in the case of the Palace. Bent upon erecting a princely flagship for his real estate empire, Harry Helmsley was persuaded not only to spare the proud Villard Houses from demolition, but to restore them to their 1886 opulence. The Franco-Italianate interiors were lovingly scrubbed and mended, revealing marble inlays, Tiffany glass, frescoes, rich paneling, gold-leaf ceilings, and intricately carved wood friezes. His efforts were rewarded by a fat dossier of enthusiastic press notices. In the adjoining modern tower, guest rooms are spacious and continue the theme with huge Baroque headboards, soft velvets, and tasteful Louis XV reproductions. Despite the recent hotly publicized legal and financial problems of Helmsley and his wife Leona, standards haven't noticeably faltered. The concierge, for example, can arrange for translators in nearly 40 languages. Guests have access to a health club and pool. There aren't many hotels in town that can match this experience.

NEW YORK HILTON

1335 6th Ave. (53rd St.), NY 10019
☎*586-7000 or 800-445-8967* 🗟*315-1374. Map 6N4* 🎞 *to* 🎞 *2,131 rms* 🖃
� ♈ ☞ ♈ 🖪 ♪

Location: Midtown, at Rockefeller Center. Big, brassy and bustling, this vertical town within the city makes it unnecessary to brave the weather. Everything is here, from shops to secretarial services to a week's worth of bars and restaurants and live entertainment. Of the many types of room, only the claustrophobic singles are to be avoided. Comforting features include closed-circuit movies and heated bathroom floors. Half-day rates are available for lie-downs and wash-ups between shopping excursions and theater matinees. The separate **Towers** floors are less trampled by the humanity that engulfs the rest of the building.

NEW YORK VISTA

3 World Trade Center, NY 10048
☎*938-1990 or 800-258-2505*
🗟*321-2237. Map 1U4* 🎞 *to* 🎞 *821 rms* 🖃 � ⇌ ♈ ☝ 🖳

Location: At base of World Trade Center. Apart from filling a glaring need (since 1836 no one had built a major hotel in lower Manhattan), the Vista has enhanced a neighborhood. Its three restaurants are cuts above most of the Financial District competition, and add such weekend features as dancing and specialized food festivals. Rooms are conventionally comfortable, with such amenities as alarm clocks, AM-FM radios and closed-circuit movies. "Vista Club" rooms on the 20th and 21st floors enjoy complimentary breakfasts in morning newspapers, a private lounge with free drinks and *hors d'oeuvres,* and a special concierge and check-in. All guests have access to the jogging track, racquetball courts, sauna and swimming pool on the top floor. Upper floors still have good views of the harbor, despite the construction of Battery Park City between the hotel and the river. Weekend packages include champagne reception, buffet lunch, and free use of the fitness center. Still, the rates may seem a little higher than can be fully justified.

NOVOTEL

226 W 52nd St. (Broadway), NY 10019
☎*315-0100 or 800-221-3158* 🗟*765-5369. Map 5N3* 🎞 *to* 🎞 *470 rms* 🖃
� ♈ ♪

Location: Midtown theater district. Proof positive that American hotel designers do not own exclusive rights to bad taste, this European-owned tower assaults the eye with its orange-and-green exterior, built above an existing

4-story commercial building of grim aspect. The riotously gaudy lobby is on the 7th floor. None of this is meant to suggest that the Novotel is not comfortable, for the usual services and facilities of its class are at hand, and it is quieter and less expensive than might be expected. Nonsmoking rooms are available. Breakfast is included. Visitors intent upon a week of theater-going are within a few blocks of all the major houses.

OMNI BERKSHIRE PLACE

21 E 52nd St. (Madison Ave.), NY 10022 ☎753-5800 or 800-843-6664 355-7646. Map 6N4 420 rms

Location: Near Rockefeller Center, St Patrick's Cathedral. During the week, it is essentially a posh executive stopover; on the weekends, suburban couples escaping the kids find themselves treated to breakfast in bed, chocolates and wine at their bedside and bowls of fresh flowers, all at about 30 percent less than the price of the same rooms Monday to Thursday. Harmonious tints of green, peach and beige accompany tasteful seating arrangements and decorative accessories. The handsome lobby soothes with print fabrics, potted palms and ivy, amidst which you can take an above-par afternoon tea. Added to these allurements are the best 5th Ave. shops, just outside the door.

PARAMOUNT

235 W 46th St. (8th Ave.), NY 10036 ☎764-5500 or 800-225-7474 354-5237. Map 503 610 rms

Location: Center of the theater district. European designer Philippe Starck was commissioned to overhaul the dowdy old Century Paramount. He didn't hold back, and the result was a blizzard of feverish media notices that has yet to cool down. It is apparent upon entering that he did not take into account the tastes of the American heartland, not with all that gray marble and loopy furniture with no real antecedents. To the

right is an outpost of the gourmet deli, **Dean & Deluca**; to the left, **The Whiskey**, an essential stop for fashionable nightbirds. A supper club is planned. The bedrooms are small, but too amusingly off-the-wall to feel constricted. Sinks are conical stainless steel, remote TV and VCR are housed in a column that projects worm-like lights on the ceiling at a twist of a button, bedsteads are big gilt picture frames, some with enlargements of Renaissance paintings. More than 500 titles are available from the hotel video library. The international clientele is mostly young, denimed and bright-eyed. Many are in the fashion and entertainment trades, and they have access to a well-equipped business center. Pagers and cellular telephones are available for rent. They are also only steps away from several major theaters, on one of the district's better blocks. In an affectation observed by other hotels in the owners' growing empire, there is no identifying sign outside. Look for the row of lollipop-shaped trees. Late night sojourns on gritty 8th Ave. are to be avoided.

PARC FIFTY ONE

152 W 51st St. (7th Ave.), NY 10019 ☎765-1900 or 800-338-1338 541-6604. Map 5N3 178 rms

Location: Opposite Equitable Center, walking distance from theaters. The Parc Fifty One has been slow to imprint itself on the New York consciousness. It will, it will. For one thing, it is the only true luxury hotel in its central midtown neighborhood. For another, it is intimate and discreet, no doubt reasons it has been discovered by people who seek those qualities — Carol Burnett, John Cleese, Jane Fonda, and Julio Iglesias, among them. Personalized, anticipatory service prevails, from the front desk to 24-hour room waiters to the off-lobby lounge, but the staff never crosses the line into undue chumminess. The gadgets and goodies that have endeared themselves to travelers who can afford this level of cosseting are, naturally, in place. Press a button on the wall of your suite, and a television set descends from its hiding place in a mirrored cube. All rooms have two multiline telephones with fax hookups, and in their bathrooms are hairdryers, robes, and another TV to catch the morning news. Courtesy limos leave each morning for Wall Street. And when the Sunday *New York Times* is delivered, it comes with white gloves so the ink won't smear on the guest's hands. Now we couldn't have that, could we?

PARKER MERIDIEN

118 W 57th St. (6th Ave.), NY 10019
☎245-5000 *or* 800-543-4300 ⊠708-7477. *Map* 6N4 ▥ *to* ▥ *700 rms* ▣
≋ ▽ ⌖ ⅋ ⋔ ▤ *minibar.*

Location: Near Central Park, Rockefeller Center and Carnegie Hall. Air France is the parent company, and the Gallic touch is evident, although hardly as pervasive as its advertisements insist. Aubusson tapestries adorn the walls, a multilingual concierge attends to arrangements for theater tickets and limousines, and the bars and restaurants smack, just barely, of the Champs-Élysées. The jogging track, the squash and racquetball courts, and the whirlpool and sauna cater to the fitness mania of the contemporary international businessperson. Instructors are available. The until-now unremarkable bedrooms are in the process of being redecorated, but breakfast includes authentic croissants and is usually accompanied by a copy of the *International Herald Tribune,* published in Paris. The atrium/hallway that runs from 56th to 57th St. is not as inviting as it once was, since the chairs and tables were removed, but it is still a pleasant shortcut on the way to Carnegie Hall.

PARK LANE 🏨

36 Central Park S (near 5th Ave.), NY 10019 ☎371-4000 *or* 800-221-4982 ⊠319-9065. *Map* 6N4 ▥ *to* ▥ *640 rms* ▣ ⥱ ⋘ *from some rooms* ▽ ✍ ▤ *refrigerator.*

Location: Across from Central Park, near shops and Lincoln Center. Much used to be made of the fact that Harry

and Leona Helmsley, owners of half a dozen New York hotels, chose to live in this one. The in-house management sets high standards, for although this modern high-rise cannot achieve the grace of the older luxury hotels, it certainly tries. Lavish applications of brocade and suede dress the corridors and public rooms. There is a concierge to secure theater tickets and limousines. Health club privileges are available to guests. The higher the room on the park side of the hotel, the better the views.

PENINSULA 🏨

700 5th Ave. (55th St.), NY 10022
☎247-2200 *or* 800-223-5652 ⊠903-3949. *Map* 6N4 ▥ *251 rms* ▣ ⥱ ⋚
⋘ ≋ ▽ ▽ ⌖ ▤ *minibar.*

Location: In heart of 5th Ave. shopping, near Museum of Modern Art. The jinx on this property has been lifted. Built in 1905 as a twin to the St. Regis, it was one of the luxury addresses of that day, and is again. After decades of deterioration, it was bought by a Swiss entrepreneur with more money than taste, and suffered eight tenant-less years before he gave up. Resurrected as Maxim's de Paris, the paint was barely dry before it was sold to the Hong Kong Peninsula group. Now a stable enterprise, it vies for ranking among the top ten hotels in the city, no small feat. What might be the most photographed lobby in the city has a grand staircase sweeping down in the glow of a glittering chandelier beneath a spectacular coffered ceiling. There are antiques everywhere, including the guestrooms, along with Art Nouveau flourishes, marble, and plush carpeting. The rooftop fitness facility takes up three levels, with sauna, whirlpool, weights and aerobic rooms and an indoor swimming pool. Cocktails and a delightful high tea are served in the resplendent **Gotham Lounge**, steps up from the lobby. On the 23rd floor is the **Pen-Top Bar & Terrace** with casual outdoor dining in good weather. And while the New American menu of **Adrienne's** restaurant has yet to fire much enthusiasm, partly due to frequent changes of chef, the setting can't be faulted. At least 20 languages are spoken by the staff. The front desk offers competitive foreign exchange rates.

PIERRE 🏨

2 E 61st St. (5th Ave.), NY 10021 ☎*838-8000 or 800-332-3442 (US) or 800-268-6282 (Canada)* ⊠*940-8109. Map 6N4* ▥ *206 rms* ▣ ➪ ◱ ✕ ◈ ✿

Location: Across from Central Park, near museums and shops. Monarchs and presidents select the Pierre, the New York outpost of the distinguished Four Seasons chain. Outside, a red-and-white Maple Leaf flag flutters beside the Stars and Stripes, emblematic of the Canadian ownership. Stretch limousines line the curb and studiedly inconspicuous men often stand about whispering into micro-transmitters. There isn't a safer address in town. The 5th Ave. lobby was restored in time to celebrate the 60th anniversary in 1992, and other rooms were brightened. They needed it. In the bedchambers, marble baths and floral-painted basins are happy touches, as are magnifying shaving mirrors, electrically operated window drapes, terry robes, and safes for valuables. Chambermaids stop by twice daily, same-day laundry service is available, and skirts and trousers can be ironed in an hour. The staff members make notes of preferences in flowers and other idiosyncracies and try to remember names. Barely half the total rooms and suites are available to temporary visitors, but they are given no hint of second-class status. Reserve as far ahead as possible. Incidentally, even the Pierre has substantial discounts on weekends.

PLAZA 🏨

5th Ave. and 59th St., NY 10019 ☎*546-5495 or 800-759-3000* ⊠*759-3167. Map 6N4* ▥ *815 rms* ▣ ➪ ◈ ✕ ♫

Location: Corner of 5th Ave. and Central Park. Klieg lights and cameras are a frequent presence around the famous exterior, for the Plaza continues to serve as Hollywood shorthand for Manhattan glamor. Although a hair too populist to stand among the most elite hostelries, the Plaza remains a living symbol of between-the-wars opulence. Indeed, it has been declared a National Historic Landmark. In honor of that, owner Donald Trump continues to scour away flaws, and he has, unusually, resisted putting his name on it. Walls are thick, ceilings high, and floors carpeted, making for unusually quiet bedrooms and suites. In the public areas, brass window- and door-frames gleam, and statuary and capitals sparkle. Afternoon tea and Sunday brunch in the central **Palm Court** evoke the Gatsby-Fitzgerald era, complete with Viennese strings, and the atmospheric **Oak Bar** is so popular that it requires a maître d' to control the crowds. The cuisine of the handsome **Edwardian Room** has been successfully upgraded, currently following a contemporary American path. There is 24-hour room service, and many rooms overlook Central Park. The best of 5th Ave. shopping is directly outside.

PLAZA ATHÉNÉE 🏨

37 E 64th St. (near Madison Ave.), NY 10021 ☎*734-9100 or 800-447-8800* ⊠*772-0958. Map 6M4* ▥ *160 rms* ➹ ➪ ➪ ◱ ✕ ▤ *refrigerator.*

Location: Upper East Side, near bistros, shopping and Central Park. Literally no expense was spared to transform what was the lackluster Hotel Alrae into a paragon of the Continental standard of superb innkeeping. The aged, tiered structure was stripped to the shell and rebuilt, from plumbing and wiring to the lavish use of Brazilian mahogany in the public rooms, and padded silk wall-coverings in the spacious suites. The overhaul cost $50 million, and operating expenses are as dazzling a testament to intent — the monthly florist bill is said to exceed $100,000. Now it matches up favorably with such paragons as the **Carlyle** and **Mayfair Regent**. Only the sourest curmudgeon could find serious fault, apart from the smallish rooms. Consider this roster of amenities, by no means complete: newspaper at the door each morning;

every message delivered by phone, at the desk *and* to the guest's room; room safes; bathroom scales; bathrobes; 24-hour room service, afternoon tea in the lounge, superb dining in the glamorous *fin de siècle* setting of **Le Regence**. And, guests have access to tennis and a health club.

RAMADA PENNSYLVANIA

7th Ave. (33rd St.), NY 10001 ☎*736-5000 or 800-223-8585* ⊡*502-8712. Map* **5P3** ▥ *1,700 rms* ➥ ⇶ ♈

Location: Across the street from Penn Station. Large, anonymous, unremarkable, this giant spent a reported $6 million for renovations in anticipation of the 1922 Democratic National Convention, which took place in MADISON SQUARE GARDEN, across the street. Another few million might have made a real difference. Look upon it as an alternative to more desirable stops, perhaps when they are full or when business or pleasure require ready access to The Garden, Penn Station, or the GARMENT CENTER. Tariffs are moderate, by local standards, and the rooms are comfortable enough. For not too much more money, there are better rooms and suites on the "Concierge Floor," which has a private lounge.

RAMADA RENAISSANCE ▥

2 Times Square (47th St.), NY 10036 ☎*765-7676* ⊡*765-1962. Map* **503** ▥ *305 rms* ♈ ⇶ ♈ ▣ *minibar.*

Location: Overlooking Times Square. Those who think of this merely as that chain of roadside motels it once was need to revise that image, at least for this flashy newcomer. The directors are making a courageous roll of the dice, both in banking on the continued improvement of seedy Times Square and in launching a luxury hotel in the teeth of heavy competition. Three other ambitious new hotels have opened nearby in the last few years, and the monster MARRIOTT MARQUIS is only a block away. Nevertheless, they've tinkered with the odds. Convinced that the only way to distinguish themselves from the others is in service, they have assigned a butler

to every floor. A kind of super concierge, he (or, possibly, she) supervises the housekeeping staff, arranges limousines and theater tickets, has shirts pressed, brings umbrellas and coffee, makes wakeup calls, unpacks luggage — just about anything legal. All the inanimate comforts and conveniences are on hand, of course, including two-line speakerphones with "call waiting," VCR, fax, hairdryer and cotton robes. Rooms are of average size, but with big, deep furniture and quilts on the beds. The restaurant is introduced by a waterfall, and has banks of windows with an unobstructed panorama of The Great White Way. A seat there on New Year's Eve? Last price quoted: $1,000. In five years, that might look like a bargain.

REGENCY ▥

540 Park Ave. (61st St.), NY 10021 ☎*759-4100 or 800-223-0888* ⊡*826-5674. Map* **6N4** ▥ *400 rms* ▣ ♈ ≈ ⇶ ▱ ♈ ♨ ♈ ▣ *refrigerator.*

Location: Upper East Side, amidst exclusive shops and galleries. Cherished by New York's power elite and their compatriots from across both oceans, the Regency is the ideal place for those compulsive capitalists who roll out of bed and hit the floor running. The downstairs **540 Park** restaurant is *the* place to conduct pre-office morning meetings. Waiters make photocopies betwixt serving eggs and pouring coffee. Guests can keep in fighting trim in the lower lobby fitness center, which is equipped with stationary bicycles, rowing and skiing machines, jogging treadmill, Nautilus machines, whirlpool and sauna. Even on-the-go entrepreneurs expect their comforts — and they certainly get them. A small person could almost take up residence in one of the 400 bathrooms. Apart from the customary fixtures, each bathroom has a powerful hairdryer, a refrigerator, a telephone, a set of scales, bathrobes, and, in most, a TV set. The spacious bedrooms have large-screen TV with remote controls, and are furnished in a style that might be called Corporate Louis XVI. Afternoon tea is served in the bar-lounge, and a 24-hour limousine office arranges suitable transport. Reserve rooms or suites well ahead.

RITZ-CARLTON

112 Central Park S (near 6th Ave.), NY 10019 ☎757-1900 or 800-241-3333 ⌧971534 ⌧757-9620. Map **6N4** ▥ 228 rms ▣ ▭ ▱ ◁ ▨ ♈

Location: On Central Park, near Lincoln Center. A drumbeat of gushing press notices attended the opening of New York's Ritz-Carlton, another in the burgeoning chain that now has 27 entries in five countries. Expectations proved too grand, and the hotel soon plunged into bankruptcy. Now it has re-emerged, equal at last to the original hyperbole. The location was always excellent, and such celebrities as Warren Beatty no doubt continue to appreciate the quiet of a hotel free of conventioneers and package groups. In the suites he and his chums inhabit, there are chintz and Chinoiserie, antique pine and carved mahogany. Any upper-crust Briton will feel at home. That country manor look is expected by the habitués of the chain, as are such details as the temperature gauge on the shower. Reserve one of the rooms overlooking Central Park, preferably on the club levels from the 12th floor up, if the expense can be disregarded. Up there, a special lounge provides complimentary breakfasts, midday snacks, afternoon tea, cocktails and hors d'oeuvres. A newspaper is outside every door each morning, and a free limo carries guests to Wall Street. Service is solicitous and proper, and the first-floor **Jockey Club** restaurant is a soothing place for power lunches. The biggest single attraction, though, may be Norman, who mans the bottles in the woody lounge. A classic New York bartender, he keeps up a nightly barrage of jokes and patter in pure Brooklynese. Fortunately, he also knows when to leave patrons alone.

ROGER SMITH

501 Lexington Ave. (47th St.), NY 10017 ☎755-1400 or 800-445-0277 ⌧319-9130. Map **604** ▥ to ▥ 183 rms ▭ ▣ ♈ ▣ refrigerator.

Location: Slightly N of Grand Central Terminal and the United Nations. Possessed of far more personality than its competitors along this Lexington Avenue strip, the evolving Roger Smith announces its presence with two semi-abstract bronze female nude sculptures beside the entrance. They are the work of the artist owner, who also painted the murals in the bar and dining room. Once the temporary resting place of weary Willie Lomans and the employees of parsimonious airlines, ongoing rehabilitation is lifting the Roger Smith to a more desirable plateau. Whether you agree depends in large measure upon which room you draw. Upgrading proceeds at an unhurried pace, and many rooms remain their old-fashioned selves — large and pleasant enough, but nothing special. By the time these words appear in print, more will have been made over in the crisp contemporary style of the already finished 9th floor. Floors three and 14 are scheduled to be next. Play it safe, though, and ask to see the room first. New or old, each has a coffee maker, a nice touch, along with a refrigerator, remote-controlled cable TV, VCR, and the morning newspaper outside the door. Prices include continental breakfast, an unusual practice in New York that effectively lowers the room rate. The new restaurant has yet to establish a reputation, but a Swiss chef with impressive credentials has taken over the kitchen.

ROYALTON

44 W 44th St. (between 5th and 6th Aves.), NY 10036 ☎869-4400 or 800-635-9013 ⌧869-8965. Map **604** ▥ to ▥ 205 rms ▭ ♈ ▣ minibar.

Location: Between the theater district and Grand Central Station. Ian Schrager, who muscled into the social pages with two of the biggest discos in town, Studio 54 and The Palladium, has moved on to hotels — **Morgan's**, the **Paramount**, the **Barbizon**, and this one, hippest of the hip. The ubiquitous French designer Philippe Starck assembled this *nouvelle-vague* eye-filler, which surpasses even his knockout Paramount transfiguration. His lobby is a shiny blue-black mine tunnel running from 43rd to 44th Sts., its couches and chairs wrapped in bone-white cotton. At one end is the arresting eatery, **44**, which successfully plays the culinary field. Mr. Starck got a little carried away with the restrooms, as is his wont, but the bedrooms are more amusingly provocative than perplexing. Sinks are conical, of stainless steel, planted in glass counters, the bathroom walls of greenish granite; sleeping areas are caves with burnished surfaces with arty illumination that doesn't particularly encourage reading. The clientele is Euro-ritzy, in pelts and denim, a few steps up the economic scale from the otherwise similar Paramount crowd. That's to be expected, since the tariffs are twice as high.

ST MORITZ

50 Central Park S (6th Ave.), NY 10019 ☎755-5800 or 800-221-4774 🖻751-2952. Map **6N4** ▯▯ to ▯▯ *680 rms* 🖳 ⇌ 🖾 🍴 ⟨⟨ ⨖

Location: Overlooking Central park, near theaters and shopping. Decades of advertisements in *The New Yorker* magazine proclaimed it the "Biggest Little Hotel" in town, but most citizens know it for its sidewalk café. Rooms are compact, but those high in front seem larger by virtue of the expansive views of the park. The entry to the street-level **Rumplemayers** restaurant is, improbably, lined with stuffed animals; ice cream concoctions are the big item, but all meals are served. Since an Australian entrepreneur has spent a reported $180 million to purchase it, perhaps there will soon be noticeable improvements in service and housekeeping.

ST REGIS 🏨

2 E 55th St. (5th Ave.), NY 10022 ☎753-4500 or 800-759-7550 🖾148368 🖻787-0447. Map **6N4** ▯▯ *362 rms* 🖳 ⇌ 🖾 ⨖ ⩊ ⥠ 🖃 *refrigerator* 🛗

Location: Midtown, near Rockefeller Center. Unlike most of its contempo-

raries of the turn of the century — decayed, demolished or converted to other uses — the 1904 St Regis prevailed. Even back then, it cost financier John Jacob Astor nearly $6 million to build and furnish what was to be the tallest hotel in the city. In opulent detail, it rivaled the **Waldorf-Astoria**, its principal competitor for the carriage trade. Astor went down with the *Titanic* in 1912. Exactly 80 years later, his grand-luxe hotel polished off a bow-to-stern renovation said to cost $100 million. That undertaking used up 2,500 sheets of 22k gold leaf, 30,500 square yards of carpeting, and 140,000 square feet of Italian marble. They added 600 crystal chandeliers by Waterford, silverware and china by Tiffany, a complete fitness center. The famous buffed brass doorman's booth was retained, as were the intricately carved moldings, and the marvelous Maxfield Parrish mural in the **King Cole Bar**. Every floor has its own British-trained butler on 24-hour duty. In the enlarged bedchambers, furnishings are Louis XV and XVI reproductions, but the hi-tech telephones are programed in six languages to control lights, room temperatures, TV and radio. The new **Lespinasse** restaurant drew instant raves and the executive center enjoys every plausible amenity, including word processing, multilingual secretaries, and Dow Jones and Reuters stock quotations. It will come as no surprise that all this comes with the highest room rates in New York. And don't bother asking about corporate discounts.

SEAPORT SUITES

129 Front St. (near Wall St.), NY 10005 ☎742-0003 or 800-427-0788 🖻742-0124. Map **2U5** ⇌ ▯▯ to ▯▯ *49 rms and suites* 🖃 *refrigerator.*

Location: A stone's throw s of South Street Seaport. A somewhat confused identity conceals one of the better lodging deals in lower Manhattan. While some of its advertising and signs call it an "apartment hotel," which suggests permanent guests, it is, in fact, a hotel accepting guests on a nightly basis. All of the accommodation, from "studios" to one-bedroom suites, has kitchenettes equipped with microwave ovens, coffeemakers, dishwashers, fridges, and minimal silverware and crockery. That makes it a desirable alternative to more conventional hotels, especially for businesspeople in town for several days or more and for families on vacation. Furnishings are spare, but comfortable enough, with some reclining chairs and sofabeds and choices of twin to king-sized beds. Room safes are provided, as are voice mail and intercoms with TV monitors. Tariffs might seem high at first glance, but discounts are available for extended stays and weekends, and prices are per suite and can be shared by up to four people. Continental breakfast is available. Most of the rooms on the 8th floor have skylights.

SHERATON MANHATTAN

790 7th Ave. (near 51st St.), NY 10019 ☎581-3300 or 800-325-3535 ⨳541-9219. Map **5N3** ▥ 656 rms ▣ ⥤ ✔ ✆ ⨾

Location: N edge of Times Sq. Theater District. The ITT Sheraton Corporation has spent $190 million to revamp this and its larger sibling, the Sheraton New York, across the street. Before, as the City Squire, it was no more than a vertical motel, and not one designed to add luster to the family name. Maintenance was lacking and the staff sullen. The rooms are still small, but at least cosmetically more attractive, and there is a swimming pool. Its situation is central.

SHERATON NEW YORK

811 7th Ave. (52nd St.), NY 10019 ☎581-1000 or 800-325-3535 ⨳262-4410. Map **5N3** ▥ 1,842 rms ▣ ⥤ ✆ ✆ ▣ *minibar.*

Location: Near Rockefeller Center and Theater District. When it opened as the Americana, the jibe was that it was "a little far from the beach," implying its style was more appropriate to Miami than New York. This was not unfair, but things improved somewhat under the Sheraton Centre name. Now, as the Sheraton New York, it has stepped up to an even higher level. Tranquility still cannot be claimed an asset in a place so large, and service can be variable. Yet the rooms are more comfortable than ever, and every midtown tourist attraction is within walking distance. Major upgrading was first given to the luxury section known as the **Sheraton Towers**, which has a separate reception area on the 46th floor with its own express elevator and lobby bar-restaurant. The rooms are not usually larger than those below, but come with extra touches — electric blankets and shoepolishers, nightly turndown service, bathrobes, and complimentary continental breakfasts.

Now, a major renovation effort has been extended to the remaining rooms, and, astonishing but true, the Sheraton chain has announced new, *lower* rates! That's a first.

SHERATON PARK AVENUE

45 Park Ave. (37th St.), NY 10016 ☎685-7676 or 800-325-3535 ⨳889-3193. Map **6P4** ▥ 150 rms ▣ ⥤ ⌂ ✔ ✆ ♪

Location: Murray Hill, s of Grand Central Terminal. A substantial remove from its uptown Sheraton cousins, in both quality and situation, this reminds many travelers of their favorite London hideaway. The oak-lined lobby and its library set the cultivated tone. Fireplaces in some rooms and the prevailing calm of corridors and public spaces buttress that impression. Previously this winning ambience came at a price somewhat lower than those hotels closer to midtown. Recent renovations have changed all that, but it remains a pleasant stop. Extras include a multilingual concierge, free shoeshines, TV speakers in bathrooms, and nonsmoking floors. Guests have access to a health club and the jazz lounge downstairs has many loyal patrons. Some suites have serving pantries. Just don't expect a bargain.

STANHOPE ⌂

995 5th Ave. (81st St.), NY 10028 ☎288-5800 or 800-828-1123 ⨳517-

0088. Map 8L4 ▥ *141 rms* ⇍ *from upper floors* ♈ ☎ ⊚ ▣ ⇥ ▱ ▣ *minibar.*

Location: Opposite Metropolitan Museum of Art. What was once a comfortably unremarkable stopping place has been transformed, with little regard for cost, into a hostelry of unabashed luxury. Scores of rooms were sacrificed, their walls torn down to shape far more spacious bedrooms and suites, many with views of Central Park. Baccarat crystal chandeliers, 18thC lobby furniture and hand-loomed carpeting are merely partial evidence. Room furnishings are several notches above even this rarefied norm: European fabrics and designs are used with *élan,* and real plants and fresh flowers are set around to provide warmth. Telephones have two lines, there are CD and cassette players and private safes. No lamps bolted to tables here, nor the blizzards of promotional announcements that often clutter hotel desks and TV sets. Tariffs, of course, are among the highest in Manhattan, but clients in a position to pay them are accorded such niceties as twice-daily maid visits, 24-hour room and valet service, and complimentary transport to midtown, in Mercedes Benz limousines. The restaurant operation has earned the admiration of local food critics, especially for brunch, as have tea in the salon, and people-watching from the summer sidewalk café.

TUDOR

304 E 42nd St. (2nd Ave.), NY 10017 ☎*986-8800 or 800-879-8836* ▣*986-1758. Map 605* ▥ *317 rms* ♈ ⇥ ♈ ⇏ ▣ *minibar* ▱

Location: Around the corner from the United Nations. Erected in 1931, the Tudor's fortunes waxed and waned until it degenerated into a warehouse for backpackers and economy tour groups. By then, it had all the warmth and charm of an empty meat locker. So, new owners closed it down for more than two years to affect a complete overhaul, stripping down to bare brick and concrete. Now the Tudor is desir-

able again, an excellent choice for businesspeople who plan quick in-and-out visits to the city. Grand Central Terminal is only three streets E, as are the coaches shuttling between there and the three major airports. The hotel has north and south towers. Rooms in the former are small, but with no skimping on the gadgets and comforts, including trouser presses, bathroom speakers for TV sound and two-line phones with dataports. Those in the south tower are larger and quieter, and some enjoy terraces, wet bars, and/or Jacuzzis. The restaurant is a British-style carvery, and high tea is served in the afternoon.

UN PLAZA-PARK HYATT ☎

1 United Nations Plaza (44th St.), NY 10017 ☎*355-3400* ▣*702-5051. Map 605* ▥ *427 rms* ⇥ ⇏ ≋ ⚲ ♈ ♦ ▣ *minibar.*

Location: Opposite United Nations Headquarters. This may be the least appreciated of the contemporary hotels — unfairly so, since it offers more than most with similar prices. Its glassy, angular "International Style" of architecture is appropriate to its ownership by the eponymous world organization. Guest rooms begin on the 28th floor, so the views over the East River or w into midtown are arresting. They can also be enjoyed from the huge indoor swimming pool and the rather small but fully-equipped exercise room, with its stairclimbers, lifecycles, treadmill, rowing and weight machines. Massages are available and the locker rooms have saunas. On the 39th floor is a tennis court, the only such facility in a Manhattan hotel *(open 7am-11pm).* Personal trainers and swimming and tennis lessons are available. Felicitous extras include baskets of fruit on arrival, safes, in-room fax service and dual-line phones, 24-hour room service, overnight shoeshines, and courtesy shuttle van to Wall St., the World Trade Center and the garment district. The **Ambassador Grill** *(* ☎ *702-5014)* is a spangled space with serviceable and sometimes notable food, including separate spa menus, a Japanese breakfast that is presumably authentic, and a pasta buffet lunch in the lounge. High tea is served to harp music in the pretty **Wysteria Room**. Members of the staff speak an estimated 27 languages.

WALDORF-ASTORIA 🏨
301 Park Ave. (49th St.), NY 10022 ☎*872-4534 or 800-445-8667* ⚏*758-9209. Map* **604** ▥ *to* ▥ *1,410 rms* ▣ ═ ♈ 🍴 ♈ ▣ *minibar.*
Location: Midtown East, near Grand Central Terminal. The original Waldorf, a name long synonymous with luxury, gave way to the Empire State Building. This replacement threw open its doors in 1931, its public rooms a paean to the Art Deco fashion of that period. A costly facelift has restored the classic lobby and anterooms to their former glory. All the amenities that might be expected are here, and the rooms and suites of the **Towers** section are superior or equal to anything of their like in the city. In effect a hotel within the hotel, **The Towers**, with its own reception desk and concierge *(entrance on 50th St.)*, has completed its own $30 million renovation. That has included refinished hardwood floors, original oil paintings, and period European furnishings. The lower floors of the main building are crowded with a remarkable variety of shops, bars and restaurants, among them the famous **Peacock Alley**, a kind of indoor sidewalk café. There are several top restaurants within walking distance of the hotel, although every meal for a week could be taken within the hotel itself.

WARWICK
65 W 54th St. (6th Ave.), NY 10019 ☎*247-2700 or 800-223-4099* ⚏*957-8915. Map* **6N4** ▥ *419 rms* ▣ ═ 🍴 ▣ *refrigerator.*
Location: Midtown, near TV network headquarters and Museum of Modern Art. Overshadowed by the mammoth **Hilton** across the street, this medium-sized hotel has the same proximity to the major television headquarters and Broadway theaters but at lower tariffs. The middle-level executives who con-

stitute much of the custom are kept in mind, with two-line telephones and voice mail. Many bedrooms are larger than the New York norm, and some have refrigerators. Seniors receive 25 percent discounts off standard rates, and weekend discounts are deep. Be sure, however, to make a specific request for the lower rates. That said, the Warwick ranks with most midtown stopovers in its price category, and is superior to most.

WESTBURY 🏨
15 E 69th St. (Madison Ave.), NY 10021 ☎*535-2000 or 800-225-5843* ⚏*772-0958. Map 8M4* ▥ *237 rms* ▤ ▣ ═ ▣ ♈ 🍴
Location: Upper East Side, amidst boutiques and art galleries. The huge Trust House Forte chain does not always impress in Europe, but its exceptional Forte Exclusive subdivision harbors only hostelries of the very highest order — Paris' Plaza Athénée and Madrid's Ritz among them. The Westbury adheres to those exalted standards. Converted from a 1920s apartment house, this fashionable and luxurious retreat endeavors to retain a residential quality — that is, if one normally lives with crystal chandeliers, 17thC tapestries, and lavish displays of dewy-fresh flowers. Lobbies often give an inaccurate foretaste of the rooms upstairs. Not here. This one features marble and Oriental carpets, and the bedrooms carry through on that promise. They, too, have glowing semi-antique rugs and do not stint in space or detail, although some baths are on the dainty side. Even the smallest single rooms are cozy, not cramped, and are equipped with remote-control TV, stereo, personal safe, clock radios, two-line speakerphones, and useful work desks. Most have connections for computer modems and fax machines, and cellular telephones can be rented at the front desk. A health club with sauna, whirlpool, stairmaster, treadmill, exercycle, and weights machines has just been installed. The revamped **Polo** restaurant is excellent, and the lounge has

a piano player during cocktail hour. In a city of superb hotels, the Westbury has few peers.

WYNDHAM ♣

42 W 58th St. (near 5th Ave.), NY 10019
☎753-3500. Map 6N4 ▯ to ▥
202 rms ▣ ➡ ⌂ ⚐

Location: Near corner of Central Park and 5th Ave. To one of the most desirable locations in town is added the buffed patina of a Cotswolds inn. The owner-managers live on the premises. Many of their guests are theater folk settling in for long runs on Broadway. These rooms weren't designed by computer imaging. Fitted with one-of-a-kind pieces and near-antiques, they have the look of the loving care of a genteel remittance man with nothing else to distract him. (If only some of the old-shoe charm had rubbed off on the gruff gents at the front desk.) There is a reasonable bar and the restaurant is good enough; there is no room service, though. At these low prices, reservations must be made 4 to 6 weeks in advance.

Further recommendations

The hotels listed above are a personal selection of some of New York's finest hotels across the spectrum of price and location. If you have difficulty in finding a room in one of these, there is no shortage of alternatives. The following is a short selection of hotels that, while perhaps not outstanding, are seen as being reliable.

BEVERLY ♣

125 E 50th St. (Lexington Ave.), NY 10022
☎753-2700 or 800-223-0945. Map 6O4
▥ ▣ ➡ ⚐

Located in Midtown East, near Grand Central Terminal. Reasonable prices and fair-sized rooms.

BROADWAY AMERICAN ♣

2178 Broadway (77th St.), NY 10024
☎787-9521 or 800-446-4556.
Map 7L2 ▥

The 1919 apartment building has seen worse days. Primping has elevated it to economy status for transients as well as the mostly elderly permanent residents. Within walking distance of LINCOLN CENTER. Some rooms share baths. Adequate, no more.

CHATWAL INN ♣

132 W 45th St. (near Ave. of the Americas), NY 10036 ☎921-7600 or 800-826-4667. Map 6O4 ▥

A good theater district location and modest rates (which include continental breakfast) make this one of the most desirable economy hotels in midtown.

EMBASSY SUITES ♣

1568 Broadway (47th St.), NY 10036
☎719-1600 or 800-362-2779
📠921-5212. Map 5O3 ▥ to ▥ ➡ ⚐

Suites for the price of a double, free breakfasts, a supervised play center to enable kids and parents to get away from each other — this new entry has a great deal to commend it. Its only significant liability is the tawdry Times Square location.

GRAMERCY PARK

2 Lexington Ave. (21st St.), NY 10010
☎475-4320 or 800-221-4083
📠505-0535. Map 6Q4 ▥ to ▥ ➡ ⌂

Near Gramercy Park, away from the main traffic arteries. Popular with budget-minded Europeans, this peaceful hotel has a relatively quiet situation, plus access to an attractive private park nearby.

HOWARD JOHNSON'S ♣

851 8th Ave. (near 52nd St.), NY 10019
☎581-4100 or 800-223-0888
📠974-7502. Map 5N3 ▥ ▣ ➡

Shares the virtues and the liabilities of

other midtown west motels. Ready access by car, yet within walking distance from the major theaters. Tariffs are moderate.

LEXINGTON
48th St. and Lexington Ave., NY 10017
☎*755-4400 or 800-223-0888*
📠*751-4091. Map 604* 🔲 to 🔲 🖾 ⇶
Near GRAND CENTRAL TERMINAL and the UNITED NATIONS. One of the more pleasing stops along this noisy commercial strip. Most of the bedrooms are not large, but there are attractive weekend and seasonal discounts. **J. Sung Dynasty** on the main floor is one of the finest Chinese restaurants in the midtown area.

MILFORD PLAZA
270 W 45th St. (8th Ave.), NY 10036
☎*869-3600 or 800-221-2690*
📠*944-8357. Map 503* 🔲 ⬅ ⇶
Located on a tacky stretch of 8th Ave., with mostly small rooms, but the rates are reasonable, and the location is convenient for theaters.

RAMADA INN
790 8th Ave. (near 49th St.), NY 10019
☎*581-7000 or 800-223-0888*
📠*974-0291. Map 503* 🔲 🖾 ⇶ 🛥
Midtown theater district. Relatively modest family rates, swimming pool. Good value.

SALISBURY ♣
123 W 57th St. (between 6th and 7th Aves.), NY 10019 ☎*246-1300 or 800-223-0680. Map 5N3* 🔲 🖾 ⇶ 🏠 🥙
Across from Carnegie Hall. Many refurbished rooms with big new beds, some with serving pantries. One of the best buys in midtown.

WALES ♣
1295 Madison Ave. (92nd St.), NY 10028
☎*876-6000 or 800-223-088*
📠*860-7000. Map 8K4* 🔲
In Upper East Side, near Guggenheim Museum. Many rooms and suites have an airy Edwardian flair. Well positioned for Madison Ave. shops. Ask to see the room first.

MANHATTAN EAST SUITE HOTELS
Business people and families willing to forgo some minor services can obtain studios or one- to three-bedroom suites at the price of standard doubles in a glossier hotel. All have refrigerators, most have kitchens, some have terraces. Prices are per suite, not per person, so children can be accommodated on convertible sofas without extra cost. Since all suites have kitchenettes, further economies are possible with meals and snacks.

From outside New York State, reservations can be made for any of the following Manhattan East hotels at ☎1-800-637-8483. Local numbers are given below. The following are moderately expensive, but potential savings, as noted, can be substantial. Seasonal and weekend discounts and special long-stay rates are available.

Southgate Tower   31st St. and 7th Ave.   ☎563-1800, map **5P3**, health club and restaurant
Dumont Plaza   34th St. and Lexington Ave.   ☎481-7600, map **6P4**
Shelburne Murray Hill   37th St. and Lexington Ave ☎689-5200., map **6P4**
Eastgate Tower   222 E 39th St. (near 2nd Ave.)   ☎687-8000, map **6O5**, bar, garage, café
Beekman Tower   49th St. and 1st Ave.   ☎355-7300, map **6O5**, rooftop bar, restaurant, garage (see also the expanded entry above)
Plaza Fifty   50th St. and 3rd Ave.   ☎751-5710, map **6O4**

Lyden House   320 E 53rd St. (near 2nd Ave.) ☎888-6070, map **6**N5, garage
Lyden Gardens   215 E 64th St. (near 3rd Ave.) ☎355-1230, map **6**M5
Surrey   76th St. and Madison Ave. ☎288-3700, map **8**L4

BED AND BREAKFAST

The impersonality and often breathtaking expense of a stay in New York have inspired efforts to get around those twin liabilities. One answer is the bed-and-breakfast movement. Although it isn't comparable to those of the British model (or the usual American version, for that matter), the attempt is laudable. The agencies named below are essentially referral services, matching up clients with hosts. They represent hundreds of lodgings.

The variety is considerable, from SoHo lofts to East Side townhouses to spare rooms in high-rise apartments. In some, the owners are present, to provide welcome, advice, and breakfast. In others, they are not, but leave stocked refrigerators and numbers where they can be reached. With that diversity, and the frequent modifications of rosters, quality is unpredictable. Maid service, for example, is rarely provided, meaning you must make your own bed and tidy up. But prices are as much as 60 percent less than standard hotel rates, and the opportunity to live as New Yorkers is appealing to those who don't require conventional hotel services.

An advance deposit must be paid, usually equal to at least half of the first night's fee. Some, not all, agencies accept charge/credit cards. A minimum stay is required, usually at least two nights. Several days' or weeks' notice of cancellation is required for refund of deposits. Be clear about requirements when making reservations. Hosts often do not allow smoking, or young children. This is a volatile field, and no guarantees can be made about accommodation, or even the continued existence of the referral services listed below:

Aaah! Bed & Breakfast #1   P.O. Box 200, NY 10108 ☎246-4000 or 800-776-4001
Abode Bed and Breakfast   P.O.Box 20022, NY 10028 ☎472-2000
Bed and Breakfast Network of New York   134 W 32nd St., Suite 602, NY 10001 ☎645-8134, map **6**P4
New World Bed & Breakfast   150 5th Ave., Suite 711, NY 10011 ☎675-5600 or ☎800-443-3800, map **6**Q4
Urban Ventures   306 W 38th St., NY 10018 ☎594-5650, map **5**P3

Eating and drinking

Dining out in New York

In New York, eating is a basic need elevated to an event, a debating issue, an investment opportunity, a conversation topic, even a reason for existence. There are an estimated 28,000 eating places in the five boroughs, more than half of them in Manhattan alone.

Ask Americans who have spent time away from home what they most missed and it will likely be that mythic two-inch-thick slab of steak seared a charred mahogany outside, rosy-pink within, captured juices flowing at the stroke of the knife. Seafood is nearly as popular, and the ultimate fantasy dish might well be lobster and beef, unfortunately described on the menus of indifferent eateries as "surf and turf." If anything can be accurately labeled as American food, this is it: beef and seafood, simply prepared, in daunting portions. These twin yearnings are easily satisfied in New York, at tariffs that range from the almost reasonable to the heartstopping.

But this type of cooking is essentially straightforward, and less pedestrian sensations must be sought elsewhere. In this city of immigrants, that has never been a problem. Exponents of every major cuisine fostered on the inhabited continents compete for attention. The classic modes are purveyed in abundance: French, inevitably, with admirable representations of the *nouvelle* and *haute* cuisines, but also Russian, Czech, Polish, Swiss, German and Hungarian; Chinese, of course, in most of its variations, but also Korean, Indian, Japanese, Thai, Filipino, Indonesian and Pakistani; Italian, in all its manifestations, but also Greek, Portuguese, Spanish and Armenian; Mexican, but also Brazilian, Cuban and West Indian. In all, more than 30 national gastronomies are represented, supplemented by such hybrids and subspecies as Kosher Chinese, Soul, Puerto Rican, Polynesian, Jewish and Cuban Cantonese. And there is the catch-all "continental" category, harboring all manner of predilections, but usually with a Gallic rallying point.

Over the last decade, the unflagging quest to sample the latest undiscovered variation on the act of eating escalated to fevered proportions. "New American" cooking, borrowing the techniques and affectations of the *nouvelle* vanguardists, has been applied to all manner of formerly distinctive regional styles, especially Creole-Cajun and Tex-Mex (the latter rechristened "New Southwestern"). Celebrity chefs from California, who made their reputations by applying Asian and French procedures to devoutly domestic ingredients, brought their acts to the Big Apple.

Suddenly, every neighborhood that aspired to chic had restaurants grilling exotic fish over hot coals of mesquite (wood from an otherwise worthless tree that Texans were happy to sell by the carload to gullible Yankees). Baby vegetables, Louisiana blackened redfish, and designer pizzas topped with such oddments as asparagus and avocado became stupefying clichés. The price to pull a chair up to one of these experimental tables was, in most cases, staggering.

An inevitable reaction has set in. After the excesses of the 1980s, reassessment was overdue, even if a recession hadn't intervened to make it obligatory. "The Day the Eating Stopped," overstated an editorial in the *Times,* describing the new reluctance of the dining public to pay huge sums for arrogant service and gimmicky food in portions fit only for Lilliputians. Bistros and trattorias are back, along with peculiarly American variations on those proven institutions, and they boast lower tariffs and sensible surroundings. Flavor sells, not effete presentations too precious to disturb. Dogma is out, with Maryland crab cakes listed next to *risotto ai porcini* and ratatouille as common as chicken pot pie.

One result is a kind of fusion cuisine that ignores the shudders of traditionalists who rail about "authenticity." Many chefs are also striving to reduce fats and oils from their recipes, and vegetarian dishes are now widely available. Splashy neon grazing places, with the size and noise level of railroad terminals, have nearly disappeared. Revolution has slowed to evolution, and the dining scene is the better for it. New York in the 1990s can boast the widest selection of good to superior restaurants in its history.

Happily for the gourmand, ethnic groups cling more tenaciously to their food preferences than to their creeds and icons. New York still accepts tens of thousands of immigrants every year, and one of the first things newcomers think to do is to open a restaurant. Cuisines that were poorly represented now enjoy adept portrayals. True, they have to adapt local ingredients to the recipes of their former homelands, or develop their own sources.

Availability and quality of produce, along with dietetic need, have always influenced culinary invention, and it is best to approach the restaurants of New York with an understanding of the many styles of cooking. Chunks of Maine lobster and Long Island littleneck clams may be substituted for the cuttlefish and sheep innards in the *paella* of Valencia, but it will be no less tasty for that. American caviar does not yet match the vaunted Caspian standard, but it is half the price, and vastly superior to the inky lumpfish roe masquerading in the supermarkets. A few transplanted chef-proprietors still air-freight Dover sole and Brittany turbot, out of chauvinistic myopia or simple snobbery, but their scallops and bass will have been harvested within 100 miles. And while Americans don't share the French interest in larks and pigeons, the local quail, duckling, and duck *foie gras* are unsurpassed.

These efforts to duplicate the fare once set before them by parents and mentors inevitably attract audiences from the larger community. Although restaurants of French, Italian, and Chinese cuisine dominate every listing of the city's top-drawer establishments, no matter how immutably classic they pretend to be, they too continue to change and diversify. Sauces are more often suffused with herbs and essences than with thickeners, vegetables are lifted from the pot while their flavor remains, ingredients retain their separate identities. Even the once stodgy Cantonese, Neapolitan, and Provençal kitchens have aired out moldering recipe books and applied new techniques.

None of this is to assert that every meal is sublime. As everywhere else, even Paris and Rome, mediocrity and ineptitude prevail. Bringing together the elements that comprise an agreeable dining experience proves elusive. Several of the prettiest restaurants feature grumpy personnel and indifferent, if rarely appalling, food. On the other hand, above-average viands are often set before customers in garish or dreary quarters so cramped it is difficult to raise a fork.

The selection that follows is but a wisp of a hint of the available choices. As far as possible, it reflects a consensus of the best restaurants in the city. Although the price range is skewed toward the higher end, every attention has been given to selecting restaurants offering reasonable value for money. In that spirit, for this edition we have once again dropped a number of good but prohibitively expensive restaurants in favor of cheaper eateries. That is a small sacrifice, for chefs in New York are doing wondrous things with humbler ingredients and less complicated techniques.

The listings include a number of newer restaurants that appear to have sufficient strength to beat the odds against survival in a very tough business. The usual caveats still apply: even the hardiest performers stumble, through changes in management, departures of key personnel, or simple off days. Loyalists will continue to exchange blows over the relative virtues of **Spark's** and **The Palm**, **Le Bernardin** and **Le Cirque**, all recommended here. No amount of arbitration will resolve the disputes, and anyway, they're fun.

WHAT TO EXPECT
In the luxury category — achieved or pretended — four discernible strata of staff are usually present, although this is breaking down, too. The *maître* (or *maîtresse*) *d'hôtel* greets customers in calibrated degrees of warmth or *hauteur* at the entrance to the dining area. He (or she) checks reservations, assigns seating, and often escorts guests to their tables. The captain then takes over. Assigned responsibility for a specific section of the room, he brings menus, advises on unlisted specials, points out specialties of the house. He might never return, concentrating on directing his minions. Or he might take orders for cocktails and meals, supervise or perform tableside preparations, even pour water and fill wine glasses.

Waiters are the workhorses, identified by less formal attire. Depending upon the organizational structure, they may absorb some or all of the captain's duties, as well as bringing food, drinks, and wine. The busboy, usually younger and in still another costume, clears dishes, replenishes bread baskets and empties ashtrays. One other post has virtually disappeared — that of the *sommelier* or wine steward.

New York waiters — and New Yorkers in general — have an undeserved reputation for churlishness. Service can be lackadaisical, and individuals are sometimes sullen or patronizing, but in roughly the same proportion as in any large city. More often, complaints are of benign ineptitude, for there is a shortage of formally trained employees. The slack is taken up by recent arrivals to the city, by immigrants, students, and the legions of young actors, dancers and artists drawn here every year. Their spriteliness frequently compensates for their lack of experience, especially in those places in which food is less than the main event.

Foolish or irritating practices persist, but appear to be fading. Waiters used to be instructed to say, "Hi! I'm Lance [or whoever] and I'll be your server tonight." They then recited long rosters of unlisted starters and main courses, complete with descriptions of their preparations (a taxing exercise in memory retention for both sides of the transaction). Now, lists of daily specials have been shortened or are mentioned in typewritten addenda to the regular menu.

"Auctioning" is also less widespread. That's when "Lance" arrives at the table with four plates and asks, "Who gets the chicken?" (his memory bank apparently full to bursting with his prior recitation). Finally, another irritating practice is less common than it was — when Lance swooped by and inquired, at the precise moment a patron had forked a piece of meat into his mouth, "Is everything all right?" Helpless nodding was the only possible response.

Advance reservations are essential for restaurants of the upper tiers. Some ask for a telephone number so that reservations can be confirmed on the day of the anticipated meal, or ask that the patron call back by a certain hour. Despite such precautions, so many customers make reservations they do not honor that restaurants are forced to overbook. Often this results in knots of people waiting at the door or in the bar, their appointed times ticking away. The imperious manner of some hosts is clearly a defense against the angry remonstrances of clients left waiting for their tables. Another annoyance is the effort of restaurateurs to impose two complete sittings of customers in a lunch hour that comfortably accommodates only one. The attempt to serve as many "covers" (meals) as possible is understandable, given the overhead costs of a business in the city, but this can ultimately be a disadvantage to the restaurant. Indeed, many restaurants thought to be impervious to customer disgruntlement have closed or are struggling.

There are other lapses. Year-round availability of usually seasonal commodities can delight, as with oysters in non-"R" months, and fresh fruit in February. But this convenience is expensive. Winter tomatoes can be as hard as croquet balls, and April apples too often taste like potatoes. Travelers accustomed to spicy-hot seasonings may be disappointed by the mildness of Indian and Mexican dishes. Insistence on authentically fiery food usually produces results.

COCKTAILS, WINES AND OTHER DRINKS
Liquor consumption by Americans is at a three-decade low, with the hard-drinking business lunch nearly a thing of the past. The custom of

a pre-dinner cocktail or two persists, however. If trying one for the first time, be forewarned that they are large and potent. The best-known is the Martini, which is two to three ounces of gin or vodka with a splash of dry vermouth, usually served with a twist of lemon peel or a couple of olives, and with or without ice ("on the rocks" or "straight up"). Some people still order a Manhattan, perhaps out of nostalgia. It is a sweetish mix of rye whiskey with red vermouth, swirled with bitters and topped with a cherry.

Combinations and variations are endless. Even at a conservative count, there are no fewer than 1,000 recognized cocktails and related concoctions. Some are favored for particular meals or foods — the Bloody Mary for brunch, and the Margarita before Mexican or Latin meals. A glass of white wine, perhaps with a dash of cassis (kir) or soda water (spritzer), or mineral water with lime is often preferred to the harder liquors, especially at lunch, and dark-hued bourbon and Scotch have suffered steep declines in sales. The practices of smoking cigarettes and drinking cocktails throughout a meal are still seen, but are regarded as gauche, at least in more sophisticated places. (A city ordinance now requires restaurants seating more than fifty diners to provide sections for non-smokers, and some have banned smoking altogether). Although still wines are appropriate for most cuisines, beer is thought satisfactory for Middle-European, Chinese, Mexican and Indian meals.

New Yorkers were long reluctant to embrace the wines of California. This attitude was part pretension and part pragmatism. Seaports tend to face across the water rather than inland, and European bottlings were substantially cheaper than the Cabernets and Zinfandels of the West. Currency fluctuations changed that, and now more than 70 percent of all wines drunk in the US are from California. This is not deprivation. Blind tastings in Paris and elsewhere have proved that the wines of the Gironde and Napa valleys bear separate but equal virtues. Labels to look for are Robert Mondavi, Sterling, Cakebread Cellars, Rutherford Hill, Kendall-Jackson, Duckhorn, Silver Oak Cellars, Grgich Hills, Sonoma-Cutrer, Jordan Vineyard and Frog's Leap, among many others. Popular-priced wines are blends of several varieties of grapes and typically carry names suggestive of type — "Chablis," "Burgundy," "Chianti" — or such fanciful appellations as "Emerald Dry" or "Rhine Garten." The better pressings are comprised primarily of a single varietal grape, and bear that name, without adornment. Some are familiar to European wine buffs, others are native strains or hybrids. Among the prominent reds are Cabernet Sauvignon, Petite Sirah, Pinot Noir and Zinfandel; favored whites are Chardonnay, Chenin Blanc, Johannisberg Riesling and Sauvignon Blanc. Weather is a factor in California wines, but its influence is less pronounced than in Europe.

New York State is a distant second in production, accounting for only 10 percent of domestic consumption. Its Finger Lakes and Hudson Valley vineyards are best known for sparkling wines, but a number of vintners create worthy blends of offbeat varietals, and wineries recently established on eastern Long Island are doing well. Look for Bridgehampton, Clinton, Benmarl, and Bully Hill.

Beers are served at glacial temperatures, and imported brands are sold everywhere, in greatest profusion at pub-style restaurants. Brewed decaffeinated coffee is widely available. Tap water is excellent.

BUDGET STRATEGIES

Since dinner for two at a top restaurant can easily match the tariff for a night in a good hotel, funds set aside for a New York vacation or business trip can evaporate at an alarming rate. However, there are ways to economize. Consider taking the "splurge" meal at lunch, rather than at dinner, when prices are as much as 40 percent higher. Same room, same waiters, same food. Luncheon menus are merely a little shorter. Take advantage of the increasing availability of wine by the glass, as they are often from respectable bottles, and there is less waste.

In the eternal effort to make maximum use of their staff and facilities, many restaurants offer pre- or post-theater menus. They usually require that patrons order before 7pm or after 10.30pm, and choices are obviously somewhat limited—but discounts can be as large as at lunchtime. Weekend brunch is another way to sample the wares of a restaurant that otherwise seems out of reach. Seek out those places with fixed-price *(prix fixe)* meals, now becoming the rule at high-class eateries. Although the price per person does not include drinks, tips, taxes, or (sometimes) dessert, the check is less likely to be a shock. Scrutinize that check carefully. Deliberate overcharging is rare, but lapses in addition aren't, and some owners now add a service charge, in the European manner. Don't tip twice.

Families and large groups can eat very well in ethnic restaurants, at a fraction of the cost of a meal at one of the temples of cuisine. Chinatown, Little Italy, Chelsea, and Greenwich Village are filled with inexpensive Italian *trattorias,* Spanish *restaurantes,* Japanese noodle stores, Kosher delicatessens, and pizza parlors. Low-priced Chinese restaurants are everywhere, and many old-style taverns have counters laden with simple but abundant meats, sausages and vegetables. And, if you must, there are branches of all the major franchized fast-food stores.

Luxury restaurants such as **Le Cirque** and **Le Bernardin** usually close for two to four weeks in July or August. The specific dates and length of the summer vacation vary from year to year, and daily opening hours are constantly altered, so we do not provide information on these points in the recommendations below. It is always a good idea to check ahead, which is hardly an extra effort, since advance lunch and dinner reservations are a way of life in New York.

In the following pages, the ⌂ symbol following a restaurant's name identifies it as a luxury establishment, and the ♣ symbol indicates that in our opinion it provides particularly good value in its class. Symbols and price categories are explained in HOW TO USE THIS BOOK on page 7.

RESTAURANTS CLASSIFIED BY AREA

LOWER MANHATTAN (BELOW CANAL ST.)
Bridge Café, The 🔲 to 🔲 🍵 ♣
Golden Unicorn 🔲 to 🔲 ♣
Hudson River Club 🔲
Montrachet 🔲 to 🔲
Nice 🔲 ♣
Odeon 🔲
Thailand 🔲 ♣
Tribeca Grill 🔲
Windows On The World 🔲 to 🔲
SOHO/GREENWICH VILLAGE (CANAL ST. — 14TH ST.)
L'Ecole 🔲
Gotham Bar and Grill 🔲 to 🔲
Greene Street Café 🔲
Jane Street Seafood Café 🔲
Jour et Nuit 🔲 to 🔲
K-Paul's 🔲
Mulino, Il 🔲
Sabor 🔲 ♣
CHELSEA/GARMENT DISTRICT (W 14TH ST. — W 40TH ST.)
Ballroom, The 🔲
Lola 🔲 ♣
Woo Chon 🔲 to 🔲 ♣
GRAMERCY PARK/MURRAY HILL (E 14TH ST. — E 42ND ST.)
Park Bistro 🔲 to 🔲
Union Square Café 🔲 to 🔲 ♣
MIDTOWN EAST (E 42ND ST. — E 59TH ST.)
Akbar 🔲 ♣
Chin Chin 🔲 to 🔲
Dawat 🔲 to 🔲 ♣
Four Seasons 🔲 ⌂
Hatsuhana 🔲
Lutèce 🔲 ⌂
Oyster Bar and Restaurant 🔲
Palm, The 🔲
Russian Tea Room, The 🔲
Quilted Giraffe, The 🔲 ⌂
Rosa Mexicano 🔲
Solera 🔲 to 🔲
Sparks 🔲
Take-Sushi 🔲
21 Club 🔲
Wylie's 🔲
Zarela 🔲 ♣

MIDTOWN WEST (W 42ND ST. — W 59TH ST.)
Aquavit 🔲 to 🔲
Bernardin, Le 🔲 ⌂
Broadway Grill 🔲
Cabana Carioca 🔲 🍵 ♣
Carnegie Delicatessen 🔲 🍵 ♣
Côte Basque, La 🔲 ⌂
China Grill 🔲
Cité 🔲 to 🔲
Eldorado Petit 🔲
Palio 🔲 to 🔲 ⌂
Petrossian 🔲
Reserve, La 🔲 ⌂
Russian Tea Room, The 🔲
Sam's 🔲 to 🔲
Sea Grill, The 🔲
Un Deux Trois 🔲 ♣
Zen Palate 🔲 ♣
UPPER EAST SIDE (E 60TH ST. — E 96TH ST.)
Arcadia 🔲
Arizona 206 and Café 🔲 to 🔲
Aureole 🔲 ⌂
Café Crocodile 🔲
Cirque, Le 🔲 ⌂
Contrapunto 🔲 ♣
Elaine's 🔲
JoJo 🔲 ♣
Mimosa 🔲 ♣
Mortimer's 🔲
Relais, Le 🔲
Pamir 🔲 to 🔲 ♣
UPPER WEST SIDE (W 60TH ST. — W 96TH ST.)
Alcala 🔲
Amsterdam's 🔲 to 🔲 ♣
Café des Artistes 🔲 to 🔲
Café Luxembourg 🔲
Fishin Eddie 🔲 ♣
Ginger Man, The 🔲 ♣
Isabella's 🔲 ♣
Kasbah, La 🔲 to 🔲 ♣
Shark Bar 🔲 ♣
Shun Lee 🔲 to 🔲
Tavern On The Green 🔲
Vince & Eddie's 🔲 ♣
BROOKLYN
Gage and Tollner 🔲
River Café 🔲 to 🔲 ⌂

New York's restaurants A to Z

AKBAR ♣ *Indian*

475 Park Ave. (57th St.), NY 10022
☎*838-1717. Map 6N4* ▥ ▢ ▰▰ ⊞ ⊡
▣ ▨ *Closed Sat lunch; Sun lunch.*

Considering its high-rent situation, Akbar's use of space is uncommonly generous. The same can be said of the prices, especially for the so-called business lunch, offered instead of the midday buffet that is standard at other Indian restaurants. Northern *mughlai* cooking is said to be more refined than its Southern Indian counterpart. Intense combinations of flavors shine through the mild to torrid seasonings — cumin, ginger, cilantro, saffron, mint, and other curry spices in exquisite balance. Crimson tandoori chicken, fish tikka, *biriyani* (chicken and basmati rice), prawn kabob, and fiery lamb vindaloo are all satisfying, and there are several vegetarian dishes of note. Service is glum or bored, but attentive; recorded sitar music plinks unobtrusively away. Most men wear jacket and tie, but these are not required. A second branch *(256 E 49th St.* ☎ *755-9100, map 6 O4)* is within easy walking distance.

ALCALA *Spanish*

349 Amsterdam Ave. (near 76th St.), NY 10023 ☎*769-9600. Map 7L3* ▥▢ ▰▰
⊞ ▣ ▨ *Open daily for dinner.*

The brief fad for Spanish *tapas* was barely a tremor on this side of the Atlantic, submerged beneath the pan-global gastronomic earthquakes of the 1980s. Americans who never got around to these tasty bar snacks don't know what they're missing. They can find out here. Once inside, you could be in Madrid, the long bar lined with platters of fresh anchovies, delicately fried squid, mussels, marinated olives, seafood salad, and whatever else the kitchen has chosen to prepare that day. The room is cleaner and airier than the *tascas* of the country of origin, not filled with smoke and refuse. Authentic tiles line both floors and walls.

The bar and the proper dining room don't fill up until after 9pm, true to

Spanish practice. It's easy enough to fill up on *tapas:* there are 20 or 25 on view or available to order — just keep pointing and eating. If a full dinner is desired, the roast sucking pig is one of the best choices, the paella less impressive.

AMSTERDAM'S ♣ *American*

428 Amsterdam Ave. (near 81st St.), NY 10024 ☎*874-1377. Map 7L3* ▥ *to* ▥
▱ ▢ ▰▰ ⊞ ▣ ▣ ▨ *Open daily.*

Its reputation as a singles bar overshadows Amsterdam's desirability as a rendezvous for Westsiders who know a dining bargain when they eat one. The reason for the primary identity is evident any evening after 6pm, when the bar at front is elbow-to-elbow with good-looking people waiting for a table and, with luck, a stranger of the appropriate gender with whom to share it. Star attractions, however, are the racks of chicken and duck on rotating spits in the open kitchen. They send off maddeningly appetizing aromas and come to the table with three-green salads and side orders of super French fries. Simple and tasty, they are, and at prices that make Manhattan seem downright affordable. There is another, similar branch downtown *(454 Broadway* ☎*925-6166, map 3 S4).*

AQUAVIT △ *Scandinavian*

13 W 54th St. (between 5th and 6th Ave.), NY 10019 ☎*307-7311. Map 6N4* ▥ *to*
▥ ▢ ▰▰ ⊻ ⊞ ▣ ▨ *Closed Sat lunch; Sun.*

This bright and saucy place has filled a vacancy as the only authentic Scandinavian in Manhattan. Behind the MUSEUM OF MODERN ART and below an imposing Beaux Arts building, once owned by Nelson Rockefeller, which now houses a private bank, its entry floor is blond wood. A long bar faces tables at a leather banquette, and at the rear is a glass panel with a view of treetops. They prove to be the potted greenery of the formal dining room one level below. Aquavit, the Scandinavian firewater, is served ice-cold, poured to the brim of stemmed glasses. The usual chaser is beer, and both Danish and New York brews are on draft. At lunchtime only, those intricate open-faced sandwiches (*smørrebrød*)are available, evoking fond memories of Copenhagen's Tivoli. Snacks and light meals include gravlax with mustard sauce and dill, a *smörgåsbord* plate of herring, bleak roe, liver pâté and *vasterbotten* cheese, and salmon terrine. All are delectable. Downstairs, complete dinners might include monkfish with saffron, snow grouse or loin of venison. The menu is changed frequently. Fixed price lunches in the upstairs café are a relative bargain for this level of quality. This welcome newcomer has beaten the frightening odds faced by all New York restaurateurs.

ARCADIA *American*

21 E 62nd St. (between Madison Ave. and 5th Ave.), NY 10021 ☎223-2900. Map 6N4 ▥ ▭ ▰ ▱ ▱ ▱ *Closed Sun.*

Anne Rosensweig ascended rapidly into the pantheon of celebrity chefs at this, her compact and innovative Upper East Side showcase. Much in demand as a consultant, she isn't always on the premises, but her kitchen staff performs well in her absence. The menu is avowedly New American, with the customary borrowings from other continents — such delectables as crab cakes lying on a fricassée of corn, tomatoes, and *favas*, and pasta with mint-cured salmon, dill, and Jerusalem artichokes. At lunch, her trademark lobster club sandwich is a witty send-up of country-club banality, and immensely satisfying, to boot. In warm weather, the front opens, to allow two sidewalk tables. The relatively larger room in back is ringed with paintings in the manner of Thomas Hart Benton, the quintessential middle American muralist. A semicircular booth in the corner frequently encloses famous faces. Everyone else pretends they don't notice. Service is crisp and no longer as forgetful as it once was. Those customers who have grown accustomed to nonsmoking sections in restaurants

should know that this one, with only 40 seats, is too small to have one. The food is so good that such minor carps hardly seem to matter.

ARIZONA 206 AND CAFE *Southwestern*

206 E 60th St. (near 3rd Ave.), NY 10022 ☎838-0440. Map 6N5 ▱ *(Café) to* ▥ *(restaurant)* ▱ ▱ ▱ ▱ *Open daily.*

When it arrived on the scene, the then-exotic Arizona 206 single-handedly created the lust for New Southwestern victuals. That fad dissipated some time ago, and the inevitable copycats never did manage to duplicate the panache of this, the champ. The handsome main rooms are straight out of picture-book Santa Fe. They are also crowded and full of hard-surfaced stucco, which explains the high noise level. That's small sacrifice for its lessons in this great regional cuisine, one that fires the palate without (necessarily) scorching the gullet. Essential ingredients of this cooking — cactus pears, poblano chilies, and such — are foreign to the shores of the Hudson, which partly explains the high prices in the main rooms. So, in a trend gaining favor throughout the city, a no-frills annex has been attached, offering fewer, less complex dishes at sharply lower tariffs. Not a jot of taste is lost. For proof, try the black bean soup — not nearly as humble as it sounds. Both sections are open daily for lunch and dinner. Bloomingdale's is just a traffic light away.

AUREOLE ⌂ *American*

34 E 61st St. (near Madison Ave.), NY 10021 ☎319-1660. Map 6N4 ▥ ▰ ▱ ▱ ▱ ▱ *Closed Sat lunch; Sun.*

No restaurant opening was more eagerly anticipated than this. Charles Palmer made his bones at the **River Café** in Brooklyn, and when he set out on his own across the East River, his route was eagerly charted by food groupies. He didn't disappoint them. There is the space — two stories of a townhouse on the classy East Side. The downstairs looks out on a garden; upstairs is an airy, more private loft. Conservative and understated, the dining rooms are outfitted with banquettes, mostly in muted tones, and there are wall reliefs of assorted animals — deer, swans, geese. Huge baskets of flowers provide the color. Service is amiable, and not the least pompous.

And, there is the food — self-described as "progressive American," and hitting all the right notes. Appearing one night were yellowfin tuna *carpaccio* on a medley of mushrooms, partridge dumplings, sole wrapped in crisp-cooked potato and garnished with baby clams and fresh-snipped thyme twigs. Desserts, to use the word of the astonished lady at the next table, are "killers." The daunting chocolate plate, for one, has a dollop of chocolate mousse, a glob of chocolate Bavarian, rolled wands of striated white and dark chocolate, and a chocolate basket with a chocolate lid. No chocolate freak can resist it. Palmer has leapt into the front rank of New York chefs without even getting his feet wet.

THE BALLROOM *Spanish*
253 W 28th St. (off 8th Ave.), NY 10001
☎244-3005. Map 5P3 ▥ ▭ ■▪ ▤ ☙
♫ ❦ (sometimes). Closed Sun eve; Mon.

Spanish cuisine has received short shrift in the city. It deserved better than the pallid *paellas* and limp *gazpachos* that New Yorkers came to accept as representative, and it got it when chef Felipe Rojas-Lombardi emerged as a force on the local culinary scene. He started with a fresh look at *tapas* — the tasty snacks Spaniards take before, after, or in lieu of meals. They are laid out along the handsome bar: platters of marinated sliced sow ears, chunks of rabbit, fist-sized quail, scallop *seviche,* fried squid rings. The display changes by night and season. Venturesome young customers snaffle up these goodies as they absorb the live flamenco guitar. Two or three *tapas* constitute a light meal, but the full dinner is not to be shunned. There is also a cabaret in a separate room, so once settled in, there's hardly a reason to leave, unless it be the highish prices. Founder Rojas-Lombardi died in 1991, but his creation continues to satisfy.

LE BERNARDIN ⌂ *French Seafood*
155 W 51st St. (near 7th Ave.), NY 10001
☎489-1515. Map 5N3 ▥ ■▪ ➤ ▣ ☙
☙ Closed Sun.

The grandfather of the chef-proprietor was a fisherman, and his father was a fisherman who also ran a bistro. So it is in the natural order of things that Gilbert Le Coze chose to open a seafood restaurant. His first gained two stars from Michelin. This one, in the new Equitable Building, was an instant success, and so demanding that he closed the one in France. In the eyes of many New Yorkers, including the author, his creation is at the very apex of the local gastronomical pyramid. A meal at Le Bernardin is honeyed mellifluence, from entrance to satisfied departure. That assessment assumes, to be sure, that the patron is not a fish-hater. Mr Le Coze allows only a single meat entrée to sully the purity of his oceanic fare. He has had to make a few concessions to the relative naiveté of Americans as regards the exotic creatures that form part of his repertoire. The "sea squab" turns out to be blowfish, hardly a staple table item this side of the briny. But such subterfuge is infrequent, and he introduced sea urchin, skate and tuna *carpaccio* to his eager (and monied) acolytes, along with supernal preparations of grouper, scallops, halibut, and red snapper, among many. The room is large and warmly furnished, its soaring ceilings sheathed in glowing wood, and the walls hung with innocuous paintinngs of fishermen, and still lifes. The staff is friendly (when encouraged to be) and helpful. Their pride in working here is evident, and many graduated from such estimable places as **Lutèce** and **Le Cirque**. Their boss, one says, "can tell at a glance whether a cod has been out of the water 6 hours or 24." A thoughtful touch is a menu that is printed in large, readable type, without hyperbole, and in English.

It will be no surprise that such munificence comes at a price. Save a little by ordering wine by the glass — there are two reds and two whites available daily, evenly divided between French and

California vintages. And avoid those few dishes with supplementary charges over and above the *prix fixe*. But if at all possible, do not miss what may be the dining experience of a lifetime.

THE BRIDGE CAFÉ 🍽 ♣ *Eclectic American*

279 Water St. (Dover St.), NY 10038
☎227-3344. Map 2T5 ▢ to ▢ ▢ ☡
AE ● ● VISA *Closed Sat lunch. No reservations.*

Wavy floors, a stamped tin ceiling painted brown, and a well-used bar-counter attest to the age of this venerable seamen's watering hole. It is believed that the core structure went up in 1801, and although there have inevitably been remodelings, it looks much as it must have a century ago. An imaginative menu at fair tariffs brings a loyal clientele of politicians from the nearby Civic Center, and aware New Yorkers from the lower Manhattan and Brooklyn communities. Everything is at its freshest—fish, vegetables, fowl. The blackboard of the day's fare changes daily, according to market availability. Among the seasonal staples, chili, calamari, tortellini and omelets are dependable. Wines are priced at just above retail, and several imported beers are on tap. Irish coffee with real whipped cream is sufficient reason to stop by after a chilly day at the nearby SOUTH STREET SEAPORT, as is Sunday brunch.

BROADWAY GRILL ♣ *Eclectic American*

1605 Broadway (48th St.), NY 10019
☎315-6161. Map 503 ▢ AE ● ● VISA
Open daily.

David Leiderman knows a trend when he spies it on the horizon. He is the David of the *David's Cookies* chain, after all, which spawned imitators across the country. So when reaction to confiscatory restaurant prices started to set in, he opened this dining room in the flashy new **Holiday Inn Crowne Plaza**. Another good restaurant on the cheesy TIMES SQUARE dining scene is to be cherished, especially when the cost of a meal for two can be held to no more the price of two theater tickets. He

keeps things uncomplicated — grilled poultry and fish, sausages, pizzas, pastas — and watches his overhead — no monster lobsters, no triple-thick veal chops. And since he started out as a baker, expect boggling desserts. "Death by Chocolate," anyone?

CABANA CARIOCA ♣ *Brazilian*

123 W 45th St. (near 6th Ave.), NY 10036
☎581-8088. Map 604 ▢ ▢ ➽ ☡ ●
● VISA *Open daily.*

When the tariffs of the city's best-known restaurants seem dizzying, consider the ethnic restaurants. This one is on a midtown block handy to the Broadway theaters. Brazilian food has not caught the attention of the larger populace, so a full dinner for two here is still very reasonable. Inside, the place looks as if it were once a hut on the banks of the Amazon River, blaring with bright colors and gaudy folk paintings. The tropical drinks (try an inhibition-loosening *caipirinha)* are a fitting way to contemplate the joyously raucous scene. No one need remain an outsider for long. The luncheon buffets are an uncommon bargain, but if the national dish, *feijoada,* is on hand, don't hesitate. A boggling portion of the black stew of beef, pork, and sausage is easily enough to share between 2-3 people. Or, take the safer route of shrimp *paulista.* The best soup is *caldo verde.* Desserts are the bland Latin norm.

CAFÉ CROCODILE 🍽 *Mediterranean*

354 E 74th St. (bet. 1st and 2nd Aves.), NY 10044 ☎249-6619. Map 8M5 ▢ 🍽 ▢
➽ AE *Closed Sun.*

Emblematic of the downsizing of the sobered 1990s, this well-used bistro is in a basement, with bare wood floors, close tables, and no decor worth remarking upon (except for framed mirrors intended to make it look bigger). That doesn't keep it from filling up every night with value-seekers enamored of the all-points-Mediterranean cuisine. That rubric spreads its wings over Tuscany and Morocco, and from the pillars of Hercules to the Aegean. What comes out of the kitchen of the

Egyptian chef is as variable and unpredictable as it probably sounds — a watery couscous one night, an exceptional seafood sausage the next, a pallid paella, a memorable pasta. With realistically lowered expectations, however, the odds for a decent meal at a decent price are good.

CAFÉ DES ARTISTES *International*

1 W 67th St. (Central Park W), NY 10023 ☎877-3500. Map **7M3** ▥▢ to ▥▢ ▭ ■■ ▥ ▣ ▣ ▥ *Open daily.*

George Lang transformed this long dreary dining room into the most lushly romantic bistro on the West Side. Praise for the rejuvenation lies more with the menu than the decor, if only because the decor needed less effort — with touch-ups, a nostalgic 1920s glow was wrested from the former dowdiness. Murals by Howard Chandler Christy, featuring chastely voluptuous nudes, are set off by banks of plants and ornate mirrors. Vaguely familiar faces lean over hurricane lamps and snowy napery. The already ambitious card is supplemented by several daily specials in all categories. Among recent memorable offerings are a grilled swordfish *paillard* with mustard sauce, roast duck with brandied pear *compôte, pot au feu,* and *cassoulet.* The very popular weekend brunch has featured curried seafood stew, and a meal-in-itself pâté and *charcuterie* platter. Setting and value keep this satisfying retreat among those consistently favored by New Yorkers, year after year. One could wish for a trace more warmth from the service staff, but there is little else to fault. Men must wear jackets after 5pm. Reservations are essential.

CAFÉ LUXEMBOURG *International*

200 W 70th St. (near Amsterdam Ave.), NY 10023 ☎873-7411. Map **7M2** ▥▢ ▭ ■■ ▥ ▣ ▣ ▥ *Closed Mon-Sat lunch.*

This, the younger offshoot of TriBeCa's **Odeon**, replicates the blend of funk and professionalism that made that estimable *boîte* a solid success for so many years. It serves a community with a happily confused identity of high-

minded art, New Wave frivolity, traditional Bohemianism and simple urban striving. The Deco-Moderne setting of marble and mirrors, jazzy window treatments and colorful tiles is filled from late afternoon to early morning with an ecumenical spectrum of social types: elderly neighborhood couples, flamboyant singles, young executives and conceptual artists. They come for food that observes fashion and stimulates the appropriate senses, but doesn't demand the reverence of those places that imagine a *sole meunière* to be the equivalent of a Bach sonata. (Conversely, some members of the staff could use booster shots in humility.) The nightly pre-curtain dinner costs approximately half the price of a meal ordered after 6.30, which is no small matter, given the high prices.

CARNEGIE DELICATESSEN ☕ ♥*Jewish*

854 7th Ave. (55th St.), NY 10019 ☎757-2245. Map **5N3** ▥▢ *No cards. Open daily.*

The co-owner of this prototypical Jewish "deli" was a minor media star, abetted by Woody Allen, who chose the Carnegie as a set for one of his films. That fact is duly noted on the menu. The waiters are, by turns, rude, chatty and amusingly cynical. Eating (it can't be called dining) at the Carnegie means sitting elbow to elbow at tables crammed together in rows, with requisite bowls of free pickles placed at intervals among them. Matzo ball soup and cheesecake are winners. Be forewarned: when they describe their sandwiches as "gargantuan," it is not hyperbole. A construction of turkey and beef brisket is 6 inches high, with nearly a pound of each meat inside. It could satisfy a family of four. There is often a line out onto the sidewalk, but it moves quickly. Closed only from 4-6.30am.

CHINA GRILL *California Chinese*

60 W 53rd St. (near 6th Ave.), NY 10019 ☎333-7788. Map **6N4** ▥▢ ▭ ▥ ▣ ▣ ▥ *Closed Sat and Sun lunch.*

Much of the first floor of CBS headquarters, which is tagged "Black Rock" for its dark granite facing, is set aside for a restaurant. The first four attempts failed, but this one succeeded. The cavernous block-to-block space has no carpets or drapes to absorb sound, and the buzz of 400 diners soon builds to a roar, helped by a stereo system thumping out rock music. The type of Californian cuisine often called "Chinois" is served in this arena of manufactured chic, the marriage of Eastern and Western ingredients and techniques symbolized by the open kitchen in the corridor between the two dining rooms. On one side, Asians cook with huge woks, on the other, Occidentals use skillets. What they produce can be stunning. No one believes the "crispy spinach," the leaves of the humble vegetable flash-fried in peanut and sesame oil to the texture of ancient paper. Nubbins of warmed raw tuna arrive in lightest tempura batter, a feat comparable to sautéing ice cream. "Confucius Chicken Salad" comes in a much larger helping, a fitting prelude to the tasty "Grilled Dry Aged Szechuan Beef," tossed in scented oil and cilantro. Since all dishes are served Chinese-style (to share), two people can ease the bite of the bill by ordering only one appetizer, one main course and one dessert. Advance reservations are nearly always necessary, especially for dinner, when the thin and rich nightbirds flock to this fashionable aviary.

CHIN CHIN *Chinese*

216 E 49th St. (bet. 2nd and 3rd Aves.), NY 10017 ☎*888-4555. Map 605* ▥ *to* ▥ ⌧ ■ 💳 ◉ 📀 💶 *Closed Sat lunch; Sun lunch.*

With the low arched ceiling, cream walls and polished wood wainscoting, the main room suggests the first class lounge of a Kowloon ferry. The effect is heightened by rows of sepia photographs of several generations of the extended family of Wally and Jimmy Chin, the owners. They do duck well, especially in the famous Peking and meaty tea-smoked versions. For adventurous to timid eaters, the menu zips from shredded jellyfish and "thousand-year-old" eggs with pickled shallots to spring rolls and barbecued spare ribs. All are

in monster portions, cunningly presented, and appetizers aren't really necessary. Seasonal crab dishes are typically superior. The author and Chinese food expert Kurt Vonnegut, Jr. is a regular and Katherine Hepburn has been rumored to have been sighted fleetingly on the premises. Reservations are essential, for even Tuesday evenings, which are quiet in most places, are packed. It gets loud, so plan an intimate dinner elsewhere.

LE CIRQUE ⌂ *French/Italian*

58 E 65th St. (near Madison Ave.), NY 10021 ☎*794-9292. Map 6M4* ▥ ⌧ ■ ⌐ 💳 ◉ *Closed Sun; three weeks in July.*

Some of the ladies who lunch here are principally concerned with staying below their normal weight and with which $5,000 designer dress to wear for the next benefit for the homeless. Others are key players in the mightiest circles of finance, politics and Hollywood. A few may even go for the food, which is excellent. It does not, however, distract from the mutual ogling and exchanges of insider gossip that charge the atmosphere. After all, their companions often include such folk as Nancy and Ronald Reagan, Sylvester Stallone, assorted Vanderbilts, and, of course, Woody Allen. The arena is a lovely, flower-bedecked room ringed by banquettes, the tables scant inches apart (the better to eavesdrop). Mere mortals can attend, providing they dress well and have made reservations 2 weeks ahead and confirmed them the day before. They cannot expect the best tables, reserved for the regulars, but they will not be placed too far from the action, and they are not subjected to the *hauteur* of other places of similar pretense but less achievement. Rarely are restaurants of this exalted order so unintimidating. Sirio Maccioni orchestrates. He is one of those personages known by his first name, a transplanted Italian who rules his domain with unquestioned, if velvety, authority. Chef Daniel Boulud is French, and the menu reflects both influences. Sirio insists that he invented *pasta primavera,* a dish so good it has become a cliché. In a show of currently fashionable menu rustication, the otherwise plebeian *pot au feu* is brought to new heights of perfection. Desserts are splendid, and the final reckoning is no more staggering than at the few other restaurants with which Le Cirque can be fairly compared.

CITÉ *French/International*
120 W 51st St. (near 7th Ave.), NY 10019
☎*956-7100. Map 5N3* ▥ *to* ▥ ⌷ ■■
▨ ◉ ◍ ▦ *Main room closed Sat and Sun lunch; grill open daily.*

This midtown extravaganza was a hit from the day it opened its doors. Apparently, however, business faltered, and the original concept of a Manhattan version of a Parisian brasserie has been re-thought. Clever advertising has now positioned it as a kind of Gallic steakhouse; less pretentious, if not much less expensive. There is still much to compel a visit, not least their proximity to the theater district and the possibility of a snack or a meal any time from 11am to 2am. The main room is a dual-level Art Deco phantasmagoria with giant chandeliers and crimson velvet banquettes; the adjoining grill is quieter and less conspicuously decorated. Chicken, fish, and steak in their less complicated guises are safest. To get out of the door with your bank account nearly intact, consider the big rich crock of onion soup in the grill, which is accompanied by a basket of five honorable chewy breads. It will bring back memories of Les Halles.

CONTRAPUNTO ✿ *Italian*
200 E 60th St. (1st Ave.), NY 10022
☎*751-8616. Map 6N5* ▥ ⌷ ▨ ◉ ◍
▦ *Open daily.*

The minimalist quasi-Milanese setting is on the second floor overlooking lively Third Avenue, next door and upstairs from **Arizona 206**. Very bright track lighting, wooden chairs, a perky espresso machine, and glass tops over white tablecloths are the extent of the decor. Concentrate on the food. It is fresh pasta, dressed rather than sauced. Mushrooms of the season are grilled,

peppered, sprinkled with minced garlic and parsley, drizzled with oil — a delicious starter. *Crostini* — sourdough bread piled with roasted peppers, onions and oily sun-dried tomatoes — is good, too. All manner of pasta forms are tossed with lobster and sage, or with tomato and Pecorino cheese, or with exotic fungi, or with Ricotta, grated nutmeg and chopped chives. Italian-style *gelati* are made right here, in such surprising flavors as praline, grapefruit and white chocolate. They don't take reservations, so expect a wait.

LA CôTE BASQUE ⌂ *French*
5 E 55th St. (near 5th Ave.), NY 10022
☎*688-6525. Map 6N4* ▥ ⌷ ■■ ▬ ▨
◉ ◍ ▦ *Closed Sun.*

Henry Soulé introduced serious *haute cuisine* to New York, and his disciples soon began opening places of their own on every midtown block. La Côte Basque was one of the maestro's creations, and he died while working here in 1966. Not long after, it looked as if the restaurant might expire as well, but it was resuscitated by chef-proprietor Jean-Jacques Rachou in the early 1980s. Soulé would be proud of his successor, for Rachou is not afraid to create such familiar fare as *cassoulet* and tarragon chicken, in generous portions that would make the avatars of *nouvelle cuisine* blanch. The disingenuously cozy room even retains its red banquettes and the original Lamotte murals of the Basque coast, flying in the face of the current design school that dictates hard polished surfaces and seating that looks better than it feels. Its resultant popularity with the privileged over-40s set causes traffic jams in the vestibule, especially at lunchtime. Unless known to the management, persons with 1.30pm reservations can expect to wait 15 minutes or more. The flavors of some dishes prove somewhat wan, as in one special appetizer with saffron in its name but none visible in its taste or color. Another irritation is that the menu is only in French, an affectation that deserves prohibition by law. This is New York, not Lyon. However, the staff is gracious and anticipatory, the customers genteel and/or celebrated, and the prices, although high, are not unreasonable. Good-to-excellent wines are served by the glass, the way to go, given the steep prices of bottles from the extensive cellar. The lunch menu is up to 40 percent cheaper than dinner.

DAWAT ♣ Indian

210 E 58th St. (between 2nd Ave. and 3rd Ave.), NY 10022 ☎355-7555. Map 6N5 ▢ to ▢ ▭ ▰ AE ⊡ ⊙ ▨ *Closed Sun lunch.*

In a city with a burgeoning number of restaurants of Indian and allied subcontinental persuasions, Dawat surpasses the genre. Count it among the best of any kind, and go for lunch to get a bargain in the process. The three special noon meals cost less than a couple of hamburger platters at far less distinguished eateries. The "light" fish lunch, for one, arrives in bowls and little copper pans — one with curried tilefish, another with gingered cauliflower, a third with rice and vegetables, plus salad, mango chutney, yogurt, and a superb *nan* bread. At dinner, a similar spread, with drinks, wine, and dessert, can race toward the ▨ price band. Service is, if anything, *too* attentive. Decor is restrained, with carved heads spotlighted on salmon-pink walls.

L'ÉCOLE French

462 Broadway (Grand St.), NY 10013 ☎219-3000. Map 3S4 ▢ ▰ ▬ ▰ AE ⊡ ⊙ ▨ *Closed Sun.*

On the seedy SE edge of SoHo, an airy light-filled ground-floor space stops passers-by in their tracks. It is a vision of understated elegance, with French country chairs, spinning overhead fans, and a small wine bar. Despite appearances, it is a classroom for students in the respected French Culinary Institute. The ambitious menu changes monthly. There are glitches in service and presentation, as charitable patrons will understand, but the overall performance is admirable. Besides, the fixed-price lunches and dinners are considerably cheaper than can be expected else-

where for food of equally high intent. The wine card features several bottles a day, at retail prices, not the usual 100- or 200-percent markup. Go to give the kids a chance to show what they've learned. In a few years, you'll have to pay a lot more for their services.

ELAINE'S Italian

1703 2nd Ave. (near E 88th St.), NY 10028 ☎534-8114. Map 8K5 ▨ ▭ AE *Closed Sat and Sun lunch.*

Luminaries of the literary world and, by mutual attraction, from show business and politics, make this saloon-restaurant their own. The proprietress takes care of them, saving their favorite tables and shooing away *paparazzi* and gawpers. There is no reason to believe they come for the listless food, which may account for the fact that no one shows up before 10pm.

ELDORADO PETIT ⌂ Spanish

47 W 55th St. (bet. 5th and 6th Aves.), NY 10019 ☎586-3434. Map 6N4 ▨ to ▨ ▭ ▬ AE ⊙ ▨ *Closed Sat lunch; Sun.*

Very much in the Post-Modernist Catalan spirit, Eldorado Petit looks as if it had been transported whole from the chi-chi Eixample district of Barcelona. A peachy glow is imparted to the two cave-like dining rooms, by pinlights aimed straight down at tables and images of seashells projected on walls. Taped classical guitar solos undergird the desired mood. After an early, ill-advised effort at an indifferent "continental" menu, the kitchen returned to its roots: the *nueva cocina* interpretations of the wondrously resourceful Catalan cooking that were pioneered by older Eldorado Petits back in the homeland. *Tapas* of fat shrimp or grilled squid quell appetites while decisions are made from the ample menu. *Mar i muntanya* ("sea and mountain") joins lobster and chicken, and *arrosejat de fideus* (thin noodles sautéed in garlic and oil) demonstrates the Catalan mastery of pasta. An "Olympic Menu" was introduced in 1992, each of its healthful offerings analyzed for number of calories and grams of fat.

FISHIN EDDIE ✿ *Eclectic American*
73 W 71st St. (Columbus Ave.), NY 10023
☎874-3474. Map 7M3 ▦ ▭ ▇ AE ◉
◎ ▨ *Open dinner.*

Another, younger version of VINCE & EDDIE'S, it too was a virtually instant success. The formula is the same — unfussy preparations of simple ingredients at moderate prices. Fishin Eddie is a little more conspicuously decorated, with a deliberately casual selection of Shaker chairs and wood tables left bare or with blue-and-white oilcloths. A peaked glass skylight covers most of the large back room, visually alleviating the rather cramped seating. The emphasis is on seafood, even among the inevitable pastas. Grilled salmon, swordfish, tuna, red snapper and others are served with ratatouille and polenta cakes. Platters for two include the fish stew *cioppino* and a heap of airily crisp *fritto misto*. The appreciative clientele includes oldsters, families, and a noticeable number of men with ponytails and women with brush cuts.

FOUR SEASONS △ ▥ *International*
99 E 52nd St. (Park Ave.), NY 10022
☎754-9494. Map 6N4 ▦ ▭ ▇ ▅ AE
◉ ◎ ▨ *Closed Sun.*

Lunch is the main event here, and the **Grill Room** is the arena. Publishers soothe and stroke brand-name authors and their agents in a daily ritual in which every change of table or occupant is duly charted. Unknowns are hustled up and out of sight into the Grill Room Siberia, a small room with a portrait of James Beard to compensate for being away from the action. At dinner, the locus shifts to the **Pool Room**, with its floral bounty and marble-bound pool. It is a vaulted space three stories high, at the base of the Seagram Building. Some find it rather arctic, but the tables are comfortably spaced, and much of the artwork is rotated four times a year. Officially designated a landmark space, it is the first restaurant in New York to be so honored. The food, usually of the highest quality, is almost worth the prices. The scope is broad enough to qualify for the catch-all "continental"

label, with chocolate cake the preferred dessert. The superior cellar highlights American vintages. Fixed-price pretheater dinners are a way to sample these delights at lower cost.

GAGE AND TOLLNER ▥ *Southern American*
372 Fulton St. (near Borough Hall),
Brooklyn, NY 11201 ☎*(718) 875-5181.*
Map 4V7 ▦ ▭ ▅ AE ◉ ◎ ◎ ▨ Closed Sat lunch; Sun.

This is an officially designated landmark, handy to Brooklyn Heights. The gaslit Gay Nineties atmosphere is authentic, because it opened in 1879. It hasn't changed much since, and some of the staff look as if they might have been around as long. They wear emblems attesting to their years of employment. Seafood has always been its *raison d'être,* and the bisques and soles and snappers are all good, in some cases surpassingly so. Of late, the food has taken a turn toward the American South, with Carolina she-crab soup, catfish stew, and barbecued ribs all worth a try.

THE GINGER MAN ✿ *American/ International*
51 W 64th St. (near Broadway), NY 10023
☎399-2358. Map 7M3 ▦ ▭ ▅ AE ◉ ◎
▨ *Open daily.*

Sustenance, not amazement, is the function of the hamburgers and full dinners in this cozy, crowded tavern-restaurant directly across Broadway from the Lincoln Center. The patrons, after all, are either anticipating or savoring the ballet or opera or concert they will attend or have just left. In that frame of mind, a profound culinary experience would be wasted, even if it were available. Serviceability is therefore the keynote, and simplicity the greater virtue. Choose from the menu accordingly. From 6-8pm and from 10pm until closing, it is jammed, from the glass-enclosed sidewalk room all the way to the back. Keep in mind the possibility of a quiet breakfast in the grill-room snuggery, especially when it's cold enough outside for a fire within.

RESTAURANTS A TO Z

GOLDEN UNICORN ♣ *Chinese*

18 E Broadway (Catherine St.), NY 10038
☎941-0911. Map 2T5 ▢ to ▢▢ 🅰🄴
🅾 🆅 *Open daily.*

A flashy building just E of Chatham
Square heralds the presence of a much-
noted new Hong Kong restaurant. Enter
to find a young woman at a podium
taking names of supplicants. She is in
brisk communication with a colleague
upstairs by walkie-talkie. Then join the
rest of the would-be diners milling in
the lobby. It feels like a snowed-in airport lounge, but it doesn't take long to
be summoned forth and sent aloft in the
two elevators. After all, they can seat
600 people up there. (Diners express-
ing a willingness to share a table with
strangers will get up there faster.) The
second floor is gaudy and raucous, the
third, plain and raucous. Splendid *dim
sum* spark the joyful din, especially at
lunch. Solemn young women in white
tuxedo jackets rattle by pushing trolleys
laden with goodies, pausing at each
table and explaining what is on offer
with varying levels of fluency in English. Be patient, because more than 50
types of *dim sum* are available. Full
Cantonese meals are also available and
patrons exclaim over the inventive seafood specialties, in particular. To make
the most of it all, go with a gang of four
or more dedicated eaters. An uptown
branch has been opened in the WAL-
DORF-ASTORIA (see HOTELS).

GOTHAM BAR AND GRILL *Eclectic American*

*12 E 12th St. (5th Ave. and University
Place), NY 10003* ☎620-4020. Map 3R4
▥ to ▥▢ ▆ 🅰🄴 🅾 🅾 🆅 *Closed Sat
and Sun lunch.*

Despite the folksy name, there is little
that is self-effacing about this high-rise
monument to contemporary American
cooking. It is large, bustling, and,
abetted by New Age music on the stereo, inevitably loud at peak dining
hours. The food is testimony to the
puissance of relentless culinary invention, each dish one step ahead of cliché:
warm skate salad, duck *terrine,* goat
cheese ravioli, veal *carpaccio,* and, of

course, pasta with almost anything. In
less capable hands, it could be dismissed as all flash and fad, but Alfred
Portale is a master, not a follower.
Allowing for the occasional breakdown
behind the swinging doors, a meal here
is almost certain to be memorable. The
head chef's trademark towering presentations — pyramids of food in imminent
danger of collapse — help to imprint a
visual, as well as gustatory, impression.
(Freud might have something to say
about Portale's edible edifice complex.)
If anything is lacking at Gotham, it is
that sense of playfulness that reminds
us that a meal is not a benediction, but
something we will have to do again in
a few hours.

GREENE STREET CAFÉ *Eclectic American*

101 Greene St. (near Prince St.), NY 10012
☎925-2415. Map 3S4 ▥ ▢ 🍸 ♪ 🅰🄴
🅾 🅾 🆅 *Open daily.*

An all-inclusive drinking-dining-enter-
tainment center, its interior expands beyond the SoHo norm, with walls of
brick and groves of palm trees and
other greenery within a towering cube
of space modified by balconies and
staircases. The young and uniformly attractive servers are capable of reeling
off numbingly long lists of daily specials. A playful global cuisine is the inclination of the busy kitchen, with a
New American orientation. Most preparations are well above par, and prices
are surprisingly fair. It is easy to start
with early evening cocktails in the active front bar and stay past midnight.
Piano or chamber music usually accom-
panies dinner (allowing for the latest
enthusiasm of the hyperactive owner,
Tony Goldman) and there is jazz most
nights at 11pm (for which there is a
cover charge and a two-drink minimum
for non-diners). It is essential to make a
reservation. Next door is an allied enterprise, the **SoHo Kitchen and Bar,**
(#103 ☎*925-1866, map 3 S4),* its featured attraction a huge Cruvinet that can
serve glasses of wine from more than
100 bottles. The simpler fare of burgers
and pizzas doesn't distract.

203

HATSUHANA *Japanese*
17 E 48th St. (between 5th Ave. and Madison Ave.), NY 10017 ☎ *335-3345. Map 604* ▨▢▭▨▣▣▨ *Closed Sat lunch; Sun.*

The idea of ingesting raw fish was once daunting to Americans. Now, *sushi* and *sashimi* are just two more food categories among ever-expanding dining options. Hatsuhana helped to foster this acceptance, and still remains a heavy favorite of enthusiasts. It is authentic, the close quarters make it easy to strike up a conversation, dieters can save calories, and a full meal is light enough to precede 2 hours in a theater seat. Young Japanese adroitly slice quiveringly fresh tuna and shrimp, wrap them in sheets of kelp, top with salmon eggs and arrange them artistically on lacquered trays of vinegared rice, all within inches of the diners at the two long narrow pine counters. Most customers eat at the *sushi-sashimi* bars, where they can see their food prepared. But there are tables, too. This and the other, slightly younger branch *(237 Park Ave.* ☎ *661-3400, map 6N4)* are by now looking a little ragged from heavy use, in this case a sign of continued popularity rather than of neglect.

HUDSON RIVER CLUB ⌂ *Eclectic American*
4 World Financial Center, 250 Vesey St. (West St.), NY 10281 ☎ *786-1500. Map 1U4* ▨▰▭▨ *Closed Sat lunch.*

Dining out in the Wall St. area can use all the help it can get, and this, the flagship restaurant of the dazzling WORLD FINANCIAL CENTER, provides it. Overlooking the marina, the river, ELLIS ISLAND, and the STATUE OF LIBERTY, it complements the view with the most sophisticated food to be found s of TriBeCa. In keeping with the setting, the kitchen highlights the game, dairy products, and wines of the surprisingly productive Hudson Valley. Seating is comfortable and tables set well apart, ideal for high-level business lunches or, with the addition of candlelight, hand-holding sunset dinners. Here is the place to try New York State duck *foie gras,* blue

crab, rabbit, sweet corn and a wide selection of local wines, red and white, that deserve to be more appreciated.

ISABELLA'S ❧ *Eclectic American*
359 Columbus Ave. (77th St.), NY 10023 ☎ *724-2100. Map 7L3* ▨▭▨▨▣ ▨ *Open daily.*

There are several dining possibilities behind the American Museum of Natural History, but none more worthy than this prototypical Columbus Avenue contemporary bistro. The French doors all around the corner location are opened in warm weather, when 18 tables are set out on the sidewalk. Inside are two levels with marble floors and raffia safari chairs pulled up to tables with vases of fresh flowers. At midday, working women and ladies of a certain age lunch on imaginative sandwiches and salads. Dinner brings couples and such modish victuals as fried calamari with two sauces, grilled Portobello mushroom salad, baby lamb with rosemary, roast Cornish hen with garlic-mashed potatoes. Young servers bring loaves of warm bread after taking orders; they're efficient and pleasant enough, although this seems to be just a brief detour off their chosen career paths.

JANE STREET SEAFOOD CAFÉ *American Seafood*
31 8th Ave. (Jane St.), NY 10014 ☎ *243-9237. Map 3R3* ▨▭▭ ♈ ▨▣ ▨ *Open daily, dinner only.*

A hint of spare and salty New England in the NW corner of Greenwich Village. The ceiling is low and made of molded tin, the walls exposed brick, tables are bare wood, and there is even a fireplace — with a fire, when weather dictates. Wear comfortable clothes, arrive in a patient mood, since there will be a wait, and eventually settle in to a meal composed of produce fresh from the market. Everyone raves about the bread, the coleslaw, the chowder, but those are merely starters. Little that follows will disappoint. Steamed lobster, for one example, is done as well as it can be. No advance reservations are accepted, but the bar in front is convivial.

JOJO ♣ *French*
*160 E 64th St. (near Lexington Ave.), NY
10021* ☎*223-5656. Map 8M4* ▥ ▭ ▣
▣ ▣ ▥ *Closed Sun.*

Chef-Proprietor Jean-Georges Vonge-
richten (known to his chums as JoJo)
was a star at **Lafayette**, the honored
dining room of the Drake Hotel. He still
is, now in his own deliriously successful
bistro. JoJo knows his trends, and in-
genious food in filling portions at
reasonable prices is the gastronomic
mantra of the early 1990s. For that
promise, patient patrons put up with
the noise and being crammed into the
cubbyhole front bar while the clock
ticks past the hours they reserved days
before. When they do get seated on one
of the wool crimson banquettes in the
main room, they are briskly handed
menus in plain, non-hyperbolic English
that give little hint of the delights in
store. From the kitchen, which looks as
crowded as the Paris Metro during rush
hour, come rhapsodically flavored
ragouts and terrines that take those
humble bistro dishes to new heights.
Salmon arrives with a tiny rosemary tree
and an underlying sauce of black beans,
corn and scallions; lobster is poached in
sauternes and orange juice. The chocolate cake is a stunner. Among your
fellow diners are more than a few familiar faces from large and small screens
and many of the chef's colleagues sniff-
ing out his latest techniques and inno-
vations.

JOUR ET NUIT *French*
337 West Broadway (Grand St.), NY 10013
☎*925-5971. Map 3S4* ▥ *to* ▥ ▭ ▣
▣ ▣ ▥ *Open daily.*

SoHo is fertile ground in which to plant
a hip new bistro. It can also become
inhospitable quickly, for there are always other entrepreneurs ready to cast
their own seeds. The Europeans who
own this hot bistro may defy the statis-
tics, even though they are surrounded
by avid competitors. Their food is
simple, yet often twists the tail of convention. *Pot au feu,* for one, is unusually tangy, with the chunks of sirloin
cooked separately and no more than

medium rare. Rabbit on toasted tri-
angles of polenta was equally satisfying. Chewy sourdough bread makes
up for the thin and acidic house wines.
Oil paintings are in the style of Matisse
and Chagall without being copies. In
good weather, walls open out to the
street, where irritable drivers emerging
from the Holland Tunnel lean on their
horns. Those who care know that here,
at least, the *upstairs* room is socially
preferable, another switch on the norm.
Since its denizens in stretchy black legg-
ings and minidresses wouldn't dream of
dining before 9pm, it is often possible
to get a table without a reservation if
you are willing to show up at 7pm.

LA KASBAH ♣ *Kosher Middle Eastern*
70 W 71st St. (Columbus Ave.), NY 10023
☎*769-1690. Map 7M3* ▥ *to* ▥ ▭ ▰
▣ ▣ ▣ ▥ *Closed Sat-Thurs lunch; Fri.*

No one need know a thing about the
kitchen's *glatt* kosher cooking rules to
appreciate these five tasty versions of
couscous, mounded with chicken,
lamb, or vegetables. Given the size of
the portions, appetizers, although available, aren't really necessary. The setting
isn't the Middle Eastern seraglio that
might be imagined. Tables are snugly
spaced, in peach-colored rooms with
aqua trim. Lamb is the most expensive
item, of course, but even that will not
spoil the pleasant surprise of the
reckoning. Early-bird specials are available Monday to Thursday until 6pm, at
even lower prices.

K-PAUL'S *Creole-Cajun*
622 Broadway (Houston St.), NY 10012
☎*460-9633. Map 3S4* ▥ ▭ ▰ ▣ ▣
▥ *Dinner only. Closed Sat.*

With his famous New Orleans restaurant and an influential cookbook,
Paul Prudhomme was almost single-
handedly responsible for thrusting
Cajun cooking into the national consciousness. His signature recipe for
blackened redfish once threatened to
put that creature on the endangered
species list. Eventually, he brought his
formidable reputation and exceedingly
robust self to New York, presumably on

the theory that you haven't really "made it" unless you have prevailed in the Big Apple. It was intended to be simply a road trip, but the lines immediately formed along lower Broadway, so K-Paul's is now a permanent presence. Here is the place to see what Cajun "popcorn" (batter-fried crayfish) and gumbo are all about. Fortunately, Mr. Prudhomme has relented on his "no reservations" policy. *Un*fortunately, he commutes between his two enterprises, and there is a perception that the kitchen doesn't perform as well in his absence. It's still the best place in town to sample America's most distinctive regional cuisine. Some of his most recent creations have been crawfish etouffée with dirty rice and fried catfish with hush puppies.

LOLA ✿ *Caribbean/Southern*
30 W 22nd St. (near 6th Ave.), NY 10010
☎675-6700. Map 6Q4 ▥ ▭ Æ ◉ ▨
Closed Sat lunch.
There is not a glum customer to be found inside these doors. Every last one enjoys the experience, typically at the top of his or her lungs. This accounts, in some part, for the decibel level, which roughly equals that of an overworked steel mill. The tumult is abetted by an utter lack of sound-baffling drapes and carpets and rounded out by spirited combos playing jazz, reggae, calypso or, at Sunday brunch, gospel music. So go in a party mood and have reservations, for this is one of the hottest tickets in town. One reason is the spectacularly flavorful food, usually described as Caribbean, but incorporating Southern and Creole elements.

The fried chicken is perhaps the best you'll ever eat, unimaginably tender beneath the incomparable crust, and with a hint of vinegar and a nosegay of spices. Huge appetizers cry out to be shared, especially the mountains of fried calamari and onion strips. Rum drinks such as Planter's Punch prevail, but many patrons choose the "Lola," a frozen slush of brandy, triple sec, lemonade, and grenadine. The desserts justify the extra time on the exercycle. Lola

herself has departed, by the way, but it is interesting to note that the present head chef, the sous chef, and the pastry chef are all women, something that is rare in a profession still largely dominated by men.

LUTÈCE ⌂ *French*
249 E 50th St. (near 2nd Ave.), NY 10022
☎752-2225. Map 605 ▥ ▭ ▬ Æ ◉
◉ ▨ *Closed Sat and Mon lunch; Sun.*
Lutèce was long the standard against which any American restaurant that aspired to French cuisine was measured. Hardly half a dozen establishments in New York approach its mark. While to dine here is very nearly an honor — reservations must be secured at least 3 weeks in advance — no one is made to feel less than an eagerly anticipated guest. Rank, class, prominence and frequency of visits have no discernible bearing on treatment at the hands of the staff. That is the way it should always be, of course — especially at these prices — but too rarely is. The captains contrive to be attentive but not unctuous, friendly but not familiar, helpful but never patronizing. This exquisite balance, which carries from reception to appetizer to entrée to coffee, is orchestrated by chef-proprietor André Soltner and his wife Simone, who functions as *maîtresse d'*. They have been here more than 30 years, and he is one of the few men in America whom the great chefs of France acknowledge as their equal. He emerges from the cramped narrow kitchen periodically, geniality personified in his unsoiled whites, circulating among his patrons to make suggestions and answer questions. Human endeavor can only aspire to perfection, however, and there are quibbles. The famous **Garden Room** is a trifle too unassuming for such a grand reputation, and some waiters are too avuncular and off-handed, especially with customers for whom this is a once-in-a-blue-moon event. Those grumbles aside, simply stab at the card, or attend to the captain's recitation of the specials. The cellar is a library of great vintages of Bordeaux and Burgundy, usually at breathtaking

prices. A secondary list of serviceable wines offers rational substitutes, and white wine is served by the glass.

MIMOSA ♣ Mediterranean
1354 1st Ave. (72nd St.), NY 10021
☎988-0002. Map 8M5 ▥ ▢ AE ◉ ◐
▥ *Closed Sat lunch; Sun lunch.*
Near-rave reviews have kept Mimosa in deep clover since its opening day, which wasn't very long ago. The reasons are fair prices and the gratifying creations of chef Marilyn Frobuccino. She has put in time in the respected kitchens of **Arcadia** and **Arizona 206**, preparation that stands her in good stead. Her lovely yet informal presentations are part of the story, as with crispy striped bass fillets bedded on kale, with a flourish of grapes or grilled mahi-mahi, lying atop a puddle of polenta framed with *haricots verts*. The rooms are attractive and somewhat noisy, the staff ingratiating and sometimes distracted. Most of the main courses are below $20 and decent wines can be ordered by the glass.

MONTRACHET French
239 West Broadway (between Walker St. and White St.), NY 10013 ☎219-2777.
Map 1T4 ▥ *to* ▥ ▰ ▢ ▰ AE *Closed Mon-Thurs lunch; Sat lunch; Sun.*
For years, this TriBeCa outpost was known nearly as much for its stark minimalism as for its often superb food. The walls were neutral, empty of embellishments. There were no flowers on the tables. The staff was dressed in black from chin to toe. Ownership finally took note of the loud hints by hanging abstract art, installing mirrors, and giving the staff less glum outfits to wear. What appears on the plate remains excellent, as always. Unlike many chefs, who burn themselves out on appetizer fireworks and then slide quickly into banality, Debra Ponzek lengthens her patrons' attention span with main courses and desserts every bit as arresting as her starters. The daily game and seafood specials demand consideration, and the soufflés and praline ice cream with bananas are special.

Meals this good rarely come at prices so reasonable, at least for the lower two of the three fixed-price meals that are always available. When entering a cab uptown for the journey to TriBeCa, by the way, make sure to specify *West* Broadway, where there is a cluster of restaurants, and not just Broadway, where there are none. Reservations are necessary — jacket and tie are not.

MORTIMER'S International
1057 Lexington Ave. (75th St.), NY 10021
☎517-6400. Map 8L4 ▥ ▢ ♈ AE ◉
◐ ▥ *Open daily, dinner only.*
The ingredients of success cannot be isolated, otherwise everyone would do it. What wizardry transforms a restaurant with indifferent food at middling-high prices in unremarkable surroundings into a *de facto* semi-private club for powerhitters, trendsetters, and their eager followers? Probably even the owners of Mortimer's don't know, and utter small prayers that they don't unwittingly jar the composition out of balance. Apparently, so far they haven't, for their success no longer has to do with the fashion of the moment. Mortimer's has crossed over into the status of an institution. To witness the phenomenon at flood stage, drop in after 11pm. A parade of lovelies and their attendants, some of them celebrated, fill the big bar and modest dining room. If they choose to eat, it is from a conventional continental menu featuring such items as gravlax and *paillard* of chicken. Considering the floor show, prices are reasonable.

IL MULINO Italian
86 W 3rd St. (Bleecker St.), NY 10012
☎673-3783. Map 3R4 ▥ ▢ ♈ AE
Closed Sat lunch; Sun; July.
Italian restaurants in the Village used to mean checkered tablecloths, melted candles in old Chianti bottles and watery sauces on overdone spaghetti. Il Mulino is a good deal more ambitious, and its efforts have paid off. Limousines and expensive foreign sedans line drab W 3rd St. on weekend nights, and often reservations for Saturday evening must

be made 3 weeks ahead. Except for those nights, the welcome is gracious and the service is deft and knowledgeable. A dish of nibbles arrives with cocktails and the menu. Have the *prosciutto* with ripe figs, and the soft-shell crabs when they're available. Otherwise, you won't go wrong with any of the various pasta offerings, the fish or shellfish, all in hefty helpings. The value received is greater than at most of the posh Italian eateries of the Upper East Side, and at no sacrifice in ambience. Go for lunch to avoid the crowds. Men should wear jackets.

NICE ♧ *Chinese*
35 E. Broadway (near Catherine St.), NY 10002 ☎406-9776. Map 2T5 ▥ ▰ ▱
▨ *Open daily.*
The giant GOLDEN UNICORN, across the street, siphons off hundreds of seekers of *dim sum*. But if the wait there begins to seem like Friday night in an emergency ward, pop over here for a friendlier welcome and even lower prices. Women with only slight command of English trundle carts of those tasty nibbles around the room, identifying them as "gort" and "skood." Never mind, just point at what looks intriguing. Choices that turn out less than expected can be set aside, since no one dish costs much. The variety isn't as great as at their larger rival, but the quality is equal. Each item is toted up on a card, so point and eat until full. In all probability, you'll be sharing a large table with other diners, nearly all of them Chinese. Some will be able to identify what rolls by.

ODEON *Eclectic American*
145 West Broadway (Thomas St.), NY 10013 ☎233-0507. Map 1T4 ▥ ▱ ▨
▣ ▨ *Open Sun-Fri noon-3pm, 7pm-2.30am; Sat 7pm-2.30am.*
This is an Art Moderne cafeteria of World War II vintage, left pretty much as it was, with a speckled marble floor and chrome tubular chairs with leatherette upholstery. Some customers wear studded leather and green hair, others Wall Street pinstripes. Most, however,

are the jeans-and-tweeds sorts of the TriBeCa-SoHo community, who come for semi-*nouvelle* dishes of brook trout with mint and almonds, gingered roast duck, chilled black bean soup, or whatever the chef has devised that night. Steak au poivre and roast chicken with mashed potatoes are comforting counterpoints to the jazzier entries. Full dinners are served until 12.30am, light suppers until 2.30am, and the clientele grows more entertainingly bizarre as the night wears on.

OYSTER BAR AND RESTAURANT
Seafood
Grand Central Terminal (42nd St. and Vanderbilt Ave.), NY 10017 ☎490-6650. Map 6O4 ▥ ▱ ▰ ▨ ▣ ▨ ▨ *Closed Sat; Sun.*
Reclaimed from oblivion in the late 1970s, this venerable 1913 fishhouse is better than ever. The cavernous vaulted space is sheathed in beige tiles, its high arches echoed by pinlight traceries. When seasons and shipments overlap, the menu is crammed with more than 120 items, changed daily according to availability. The day's catch can include such rarities as *loup de mer*, shark, sea urchin, sand dab and ray. Up to ten types of oyster are usually on hand, along with chowders, pan roasts, stews, lobsters and crabs. Lake sturgeon, salmon and trout are smoked on the premises. Nearly everything is superfresh, not too surprising in a place with this high volume. The simplest preparations are best. Service is speedy, without any flourishes. There is an excellent list of California white wines. Since they do not close between lunch and dinner, unhurried pre-theater meals are possible. To avoid the lunchtime cacophony of the main room, ask for a table in the adjoining "Saloon." Otherwise, the greatest deficiency is the churlish attitude of certain members of the staff.

PALIO △ *Italian*
Equitable Center, 151 W 51st St. (near 7th Ave.), NY 10010 ☎245-4850. Map 5N3 ▥ *to* ▥ ▱ ▰ ▾ ▰ ▨ ▣ ▨ ▨
Closed Sat lunch; Sun.

Vivid expressionist murals by Sandro Chia surround the striking horseshoe marble bar inside the entrance. Snacks called *sfiziosi* are available here all the time, just right as an appetite-assuager before the curtain rises. To the right is an elevator that carries the sleekly turned-out crowd to the restaurant proper, one floor up. Wide aisles permit easy passage for diners and waiters, an amenity to be cherished, given the cost of floor space in Manhattan. Despite that room to maneuver, service can get a trifle confused at times, perhaps because most of the staff is more comfortable with Italian than English. Food is of the *nuova cucina* variety, often brought out at excessively long intervals and a little too light for those accustomed to heartier fare from the land of its origin. Infelicities are constantly scoured away, however, and this continues to be an excellent choice for business meals by day and dressy couples at night. Try to get to the bar before 6pm, and always reserve ahead for meals. Men are expected to wear a jacket and tie.

THE PALM *Steakhouse*
837 2nd Ave. (near E 45th St.), NY 10017
☎687-2953. Map 605 ▥ ▢ ☒ ☒ ☒
▨ Closed Sat lunch; Sun.

Beef is the reason for The Palm, and for its annex across the street, **Palm Too** (☎697-5198). Admirers of precisely seared slabs of unadorned prime cow flesh are a manly lot, it would appear, impatient with the fancy rituals of those swishy French places. Giant steaks or lobsters are what they want, and they get them here, with loaves of hashed brown potatoes, preceded by shrimp and followed by cheesecake, all of them in stupefying portions. (Split portions to keep the total cost down.) There is sawdust on the floor, faded cartoons line the walls and ceiling, and women are mostly decoration, preferably silent. The bored and/or sullen waiter recites the menu, for none is written, and there isn't all that much to remember. Those inclined to stoking up in such places insist that this is one

of the three best steakhouses in New York, and are willing to pay for the privilege. Reservations are taken for lunch, none for dinner.

PAMIR ♣ *Afghan*
1437 2nd Ave. (near 75th St.), NY 10021
☎734-3791. Map 8M5 ▢ to ▥ ▢ ▰
☒ ☒ ▨ Open daily, dinner only.

Another way to shave expenses with ethnic food? Try Afghan, and try it here, for it is packed with satisfied wallet-watchers every night. It conjures up a central Asian club of the sort Indiana Jones laid waste, with its red ceiling, guttering candles, and Oriental rugs on walls and floor. Staff members are eager to please, explaining every dish. They are especially attentive to children, but all ages are represented, partly because nothing too weird arrives on the plate. *Kabobs* are favorites, lamb dishes are expectably pervasive, and the heady scents of cilantro and cardamom drift lightly on the air. There is a newer branch with the same name at 1065 1st Ave. (☎694-9158, *map6N5)*, but opinion is mixed on whether its food matches that of the original.

PARK BISTRO *French*
414 Park Ave. S (near 29th St.), NY 10016
☎689-1360. Map 6P4 ▢ to ▥ ▢ ▰
☒ ☒

One of the more recent districts to undergo gentrification is lower Park Ave., and this still-hot bistro has made the most of it. It only hints at its humble inspiration, however, with cheeky compilations that don't ignore culinary inventions of recent years. There have been, among the oft-changed items, sautéed skate wing in vinegar sauce with cabbage, *terrine* of rabbit, roasted monkfish with fennel and tomato *coulis*. As usual, lunch is the time to keep costs within reason. Always reserve; men usually wear jackets. The same owners opened another, similar place nearby to sop up the spillover. **Les Halles** *(411 Park Ave. S* ☎*679-4111, map6P4)* looks as if it was transplanted from the erstwhile Parisian market district; it is every bit as crowded and clangorous as its older cousin. It is advisable to reserve.

PÉTROSSIAN *International*

182 W 58th St. (7th Ave.), NY 10019
☎245-2214. Map 7N3 ▥ ☐ ■■ ▣ ◉
◉ ▦ *Open daily.*

The famed Parisian firm of Pétrossian provides sustenance for those who can't get through the week without periodic infusions of *foie gras* and fish eggs. To showcase their products in the New World, they opened this upmarket bistro-takeout-boutique in an appropriately grand Beaux Arts building. Immediately inside the entrance are glass cases filled with such essential edibles as duck and goose terrines, truffles, smoked silver eel and Scottish trout, *mousselines* and Russian caviar. For those who intend to make a habit of such delectables, sterling silver *présentoir* sets are for sale. A right turn leads into the restaurant, a snug Art Deco setting with marble floors and nudes etched on the mirrors behind the angled bar. The tables are already set with Champagne flutes, should any patrons miss the thrust of the enterprise. Deft young waiters bring copies of the aforesaid *présentoirs*, heaped with caviar, or impeccably arranged plates of the several "Pétrossian Teasers," such as roulades of smoked sturgeon with wild mushrooms or bouquets of shrimp with smoked cod roe. Main courses are half *nouvelle*, half classical French. The vodka is Russian, of course, and the house champagnes are available by the glass. This outpost of the good life has experienced ups and downs of late, with repeated changes in the kitchen, but the *prix fixe* luncheons and weekend brunches are still bargains.

THE QUILTED GIRAFFE ⌂ *International*

15 E 55th St. (near Madison Ave.), NY 10022 ☎593-1221. Map 6N4 ▥ ■■ ▰
▣ ◉ ◉ ▦ *Closed Sat lunch; Sun; Mon.*

The owners, a husband-and-wife team by the predestined name of Wine, are a peripatetic pair. Testing themselves at a restaurant in upstate New York, they brought their act to the big town on the crest of the early enthusiasm for *nouvelle cuisine*. Many thought they were too hot not to cool down. In a way, they were right. The Wines have matured and achieved a steadier hand at the controls. Excessively innovative dishes, some of which bordered on the simply silly, were removed from the menu; the original decor of ceramic and stuffed giraffes departed the premises. Soon enough, the establishment was deemed to have joined **Lutèce** and **Le Cirque** at the tip of the pyramid. Then, ever restless, they moved to the AT&T BUILDING, in a room of brushed steel, marble, and gray leather banquettes, the chilly post-industrial effect of which is moderated by sprays of flowers. While innovation is still important to Mr. Wine, it does not supersede all other considerations. His passion is tempered by an apparent entrancement with the culinary arts of Japan, filtered through an obviously boundless imagination. It is evident in the ingredients, all top of the bin and many of them shipped daily from their upstate farm. The most delicate of touches show themselves in the fabrications that appear on the plate, drawing every last wisp of natural flavor from fish and vegetable. Wine himself delivers the dishes to the table when anyone orders the highest-priced *Kaiseki* dinner. (He's the one in kitchen whites who looks a little like Dan Quayle.) His staff is as precisely trained in all nuances of service as any to be found. There is no point in mentioning specific dishes, for they don't remain long on the menu. Suffice it to say that disappointments are few. Very few. Save this for a landmark birthday, a silver anniversary, or the conclusion of a major business deal. Whether even those events are worth the cost of monthly sustenance for a family of four is an issue to be resolved in the heart of each patron.

LE RELAIS *French*

712 Madison Ave. (64th St.), NY 10021 ☎751-5108. Map 8M4 ▥ ☐ ■■ ▱ ▣
A beneficiary of the present bistro craze, Le Relais is thriving well beyond the lifespan that might easily have been

predicted for it more than 10 years ago. The food, which is no better than adequate, is not central. The crowd is. They gather on velvet banquettes, beneath walls crowded with framed mirrors and etchings, gaggles of East Siders seated haunch to denimed haunch, and aproned waiters who remain calm and cogent despite the clamor. The short menu is adjusted to seasonal availabilities, but might include sorrel soup, bass cloaked in seaweed, tender softshelled crabs and rosy-centered lamb. Save it for a warm day, when tables are set out on the sidewalk and the interior is less claustrophobic.

LA RÉSERVE ⌂ French
4 W 49th St. (near 5th Ave.), NY 10020 ☎247-2993. Map 604 ▥ ▭ ◼ ▰ ▱ ◉ ◍ ▨ Closed Sat lunch; Sun.
There are people who have no need to agonize over which Manhattan restaurant to select for the big splash — they simply rotate. **Lutèce** on Tuesday, **Le Bernardin** on Wednesday, **La Côte Basque** on Thursday and La Réserve on Friday. At least, they *look* like the same crowd, with their immaculately coiffed hair, winter tans, and flares of gold at wrist and throat. Two large rooms are illuminated by chandeliers of Venetian glass and decorated with large murals of game preserves. The china is Limoges and the balloon-shaped goblets allow the proper savoring of a Château Laffitte. The food is *haute,* with an up-to-date concern for presentation. Mediocrity is not permitted, nor is novelty for novelty's sake. Tables are closely placed, but not oppressively so, and service is efficient, if not warm. The pre-theater dinner, which must be ordered between 5.30-6.45pm, is a less expensive way to sample the kitchen's wares. Although it can take several weeks to reserve a table at others of this class, 2-3 days' notice is usually sufficient here.

RIVER CAFÉ ⌂ Eclectic American
1 Water St., Brooklyn, NY 11201 ☎522-5200. Map 476 to ▥ ▭ ≪ ▰ ▰ ↑ ▱ ◉ ◍ ▨ Open daily.

The breathtaking views of the Manhattan skyline from this remodeled barge beneath the Brooklyn Bridge more than compensate for the frequent changes of the guard behind the stoves. One celebrity chef after another first came to wide attention for his work here before moving on: Larry Forgione (**An American Place**), Charles Palmer (AUREOLE), and, most recently, David Burke (PARK AVENUE CAFÉ). Depending upon who is cooking at the moment, the culinary mix is usually part Gallic conceit, part chauvinistically native produce. Ingredients are Key West shrimp, Smithfield ham, California snails, New Jersey pheasants — resolutely American — but the twin sauces, aspics and *terrines* cry out their Old World origins. Furnishings are agreeable — bamboo, bentwood and portholes — but the decor is the vista, which stretches from the STATUE OF LIBERTY to the EMPIRE STATE BUILDING. The most atmospheric time to be there is at dusk, when lights are kept low. A piano is played, and tables are set out on the terrace in summer. Sunday brunch is popular, and reservations are always essential.

ROSA MEXICANO Mexican
1063 1st Ave. (58th St.), NY 10022 ☎753-7407. Map 605 ▥ ▭ ▱ ◉ ◍ ▨
The fever for Mexican food came later to New York than to other parts of the country, so its converts are often unschooled in that great cuisine. Hybrid Tex-Mex and New Southwestern variations confused the issue, and the management here feels compelled to specify on the menu that "you may not find some of the Americanized dishes associated with Mexican food." Authenticity aside, these dishes are singularly satisfying. In a city of rubbery, shop-bought tortillas, Rosa Mexicano makes its own, fresh daily. In contrast to the usually vapid yuppie Margaritas, these are concocted with fresh lime juice and premium tequila, and are deceptively benign. Given the difficulties of obtaining proper ingredients (there are scores of different chilies used in Mexican cooking, from mild to incendiary) this

kitchen so carefully replicates south-of-the-border recipes that patrons are transported to Veracruz and Cuernavaca. Duck comes in a creamy green pumpkinseed sauce with a hint of serrano; raw bay scallops are marinated in lemon juice, chili, and coriander. Off-menu specials often feature recipes from one or more of Mexico's regional cuisines, such as Yucatán's shredded peppery pork, slow-baked in banana leaves. Lovers of guacamole are in for a treat — it's made to order at tableside with cilantro and zingy jalapeño peppers. Even the mango ice cream is made on the premises. The wine list is adequate, but this food cries for real Mexican beer — Corona or Dos Equis. Reservations are essential, even for such celebrity regulars as Placido Domingo.

THE RUSSIAN TEA ROOM *Russian*

150 W 57th St. (near 7th Ave.), NY 10019 ☎ *265-0947. Map 5N3* ▦ ⊂⊐ ▬ ▣ ◉ ◉ ▨

Restaurants where celebrities gather are notorious for indifferent food, but a number of eccentricities endear the Tea Room to Woody Allen, Jackie O, Rudolf Nureyev, Liza Minnelli, Joseph Heller and Max von Sydow (to drop the names of some regulars). There is the fact that it really does serve Russian food, rare in these parts. Its vividly painted exterior of aqua, crimson and white is a festive hint of the interior, where Christmas decorations wreathe the light fixtures — all year. No two of the many clocks have the same time. And perhaps most of all, as violinist Isaac Stern said, the Tea Room is "a private professional club where the public is allowed." Noncelebrated folk with the wherewithal to afford attendance are not, however, permitted to approach the stars, which helps to assure their frequent return. While gazing upon each other, they dip into borscht, dine on salmon *kulebiaka* or lamb *shashlik,* and rhapsodize over the finest grades of caviar, especially in concert with *blinis.* Lately, there have been some signs of decline, but in all probability the Tea Room will sail majestically into the next century, its slogan intact — "Slightly to the left of Carnegie Hall."

SABOR ✿ *Cuban*

20 Cornelia St. (near Bleecker St.), NY 10014 ☎ *243-9579. Map 3R3* ▦ ⊂⊐ ▦ ▣ ◉ ▨

Cuban food is direct and unassuming, a blending of dishes from the Iberian homeland with the ingredients and tang of the Caribbean. There isn't a better place in the city to make its acquaintance than Sabor. The setting is a narrow former storefront on a tatty side street in the Village, the principal decorative element of which is a 19thC stamped tin ceiling. Start with a birdbath-sized Margarita, made with fresh lime. Move on to plump, tender mussels dressed in a saffron-tomato sauce, or to *escabèche* (a cool, firm piece of fish hidden beneath a blanket of crisp pickled vegetables). *Pollo con comino* is boneless baked chicken breast marinated in lime juice, cumin and garlic, accompanied by strips of onion and sweet pepper. Don't be put off by the implications of *ropa vieja* — "old clothes" — for this Cuban classic is in fact shredded beef tossed in a piquant sauce of tomato, cloves and cinnamon. Expect not a whiff of pretension on the menu or in the staff.

SAM'S *American*

152 W 52nd St. (near 7th Ave.), NY 10019 ☎ *582-8700. Map 5N3* ▦ to ▦ ⊂⊐ ▣ ◉ ◉ ▨ *Closed Sun.*

Actress Mariel Hemingway is "Sam," and this is her second restaurant. *(The first is at 1406 3rd Ave. ☎ 988-5300, map 8L5).* Landlords at the Equitable Building wisely invited her to open here as an informal and far less expensive alternative to **Le Bernardin** and **Palio,** both securely ensconced just a few yards away. The huge interior is reasonably attractive, with a lower noise level than might be expected. Hamburgers with chewy shoestring potatoes equal any to be had, and the juicy pork chop with blue cheese sauce is an understandable favorite. At night, the kitchen is somewhat more ambitious, which doesn't necessarily mean better. Simple grills, pastas, and pizzas are the safest choices, shunning the trickier items. Only those who choose to have two or three courses, dessert, and the top wine in the cellar will receive a bill that edges into the expensive range. Sam's is ideally situated for before or after the theater.

THE SEA GRILL *Seafood*

19 W 49th St. (near 5th Ave.), NY 10020
☎246-9201. Map 604 ▥ �¤ ⊡ ■ ᴁ
⊡ ⊙ ▨

When the skating rink at the foot of the GE BUILDING in the ROCKEFELLER CENTER was overhauled, it was the management's intent to upgrade the eating places that bordered the popular arena. They didn't have to reach too high, given the feeble performances of a succession of previous occupants. The fact that the Sea Grill turned out to be better than required was a surprise to many. The decor is neither flashy nor dowdy, with comfortable leather chairs allowing views of skaters (in winter) twirling outside, and cooks flashing knives and spatulas over the open grill. It is an atmosphere in which both businesspeople and adult tourists feel at ease. The menu leans toward regional American dishes, an elastic rubric that incorporates grilled fish, chowders, oysters Rockefeller, charred *pompano* and chicken, and the San Francisco invention, *cioppino* (seafood stew). Most of it is competent, and, truth to tell, rather ordinary. Entrance to the restaurant is from the glass bubble on 49th St. Reservations are recommended, particularly at lunchtime. There is outdoor dining in good weather. The companion restaurant across the rink is the **American Festival Café** *(20 W 50th St.* ☎*246-6699, map 6O4)*. With its broader menu and lower prices, this may be a better choice for families.

THE SHARK BAR ♣ *Southern*

307 Amsterdam Ave. (between 74th and 75th Sts.), NY 10024 ☎874-8500. Map *7L3* ▥ ᴁ ⊡ ⊙ ▨ *Open daily.*
Short of the renowned **Sylvia's,** up in Harlem, there is no more accomplished purveyor of Southern soul food than this lively newcomer. A mixed crowd of yuppies and boomers, both Black and White, testifies to this, drawn by the reasonable prices and party-time atmosphere. Steps up from the packed front bar is a dining room a-chatter with people digging into crawfish cocktails, seafood gumbo, blackened catfish, blackeyed peas, honey-dipped fried chicken, and sweet potato pie. Service is affable, but often overworked, especially at the popular Saturday gospel brunches. There is live music Tuesday evenings, too, at 11. Dinner is served until after midnight, and they deliver within a limited area.

SHUN LEE *Chinese*

43 W 65th St. (near Broadway), NY 10023
☎595-8895. Map *7M3* ▥ to ▥ ⊡ ■
ᴁ ⊡ ⊙ ▨ *Open daily.*
One of a small group of restaurants that brought high style to Chinese restaurants back in the 1970s, this was a happy improvement upon the quiche-and-burger emporia that long dominated the Lincoln Center area. One might even go there simply to eat, rather than to fuel up for an evening of Puccini or Bach. The black-and-white decor is enlivened at the entrance and in the lounge by *papier mâché* dragons and monkeys with glowing red eyes. Spicy Szechuan and Hunan cuisines were introduced to New Yorkers by the original owners, and the chili oil is shaken with a generous hand, if requested. Among the resulting winners are pan-fried pork dumplings, crispy Hunan sea bass and sliced duckling with young ginger root. When a full meal might rest too heavily on the stomach during a night at the opera, the *dim sum* at the adjoining **Shun Lee Café** *(43 W 65th St.* ☎ *769-3888, map 7M3)* are just the ticket. The Café is open for dinner only from Monday to Friday, for lunch and dinner on Saturday and Sunday.

SOLERA *Spanish*

216 E 53rd St. (between 2nd and 3rd Aves.), NY 10022 ☎644-1166. Map *6N5*

▭ to ▭ ▭ ▬ 𝐴𝐸 ⊡ ▭ ▭ *Closed Sat lunch; Sun.*

The brief enthusiasm for Spanish *tapas* never really caught fire this side of the Atlantic, but several restaurants still serve them. Truth to tell, they are often more skillfully wrought here than in the mother country. That's the case at Solera, which serves them at the long bar just inside the front door. A changing blackboard menu lists about twelve *tapas* each night, often including the sturdy potato-and-egg omelet called a *tortilla,* and fried squid rings or white beans tossed in vinaigrette with strips of sweet peppers and salami. Two or three choices shared by a couple constitute a light, relatively inexpensive meal. The surroundings are pertinent, with quarry tiles on the floor, tables with red-veined marble tops and models of galleons on shelves. In the dining rooms in back and upstairs, such regional specialties as *paella,* salt-cod salad and monkfish medallions with black olive purée are carefully prepared by the American chef, who has put in time at some of the city's finest restaurants.

SPARK'S ⌂ *American*

210 E 46th St. (near 3rd Ave.), NY 10017 ☎687-4855. Map 605 ▭ ▭ ⇉ 𝐴𝐸 ⊡ ▭ ▭ *Closed Sat lunch; Sun.*

This is one of the best of the classic Manhattan steakhouses, its huge chops and lobsters as succulent and overpriced as any in town. If anything, it has pulled ahead of most of its increasingly smug competition. What makes it even more notable is that few restaurants of any category can match its inventory of fine wines. European wine buffs can here test the virtues and vintages of California, from Mondavi to Mirassou and dozens of other vintners. There are French, Spanish and Italian bottles, too. Between sips, dig into sublimely simple sirloins and filet mignons or any of a half dozen types of fish, all cooked precisely to order. "Steak fromage" is about as fancified as things get. The masculine room, with its dark wainscotting and landscapes in gilded frames, is hosting more women these days, with careers,

not time to kill. It helps if they have fat expense accounts as well, for the double-thick veal chops and four-pound lobsters don't come at hot dog prices. Service is solemn and correct, with covered plates and debris rolled silently away on trolleys and fresh tablecloths unfolded between the main course and dessert. The laundry bill must be stupendous.

TAKE-SUSHI *Japanese*

71 Vanderbilt Ave. (near 46th St.), NY 10017 ☎867-5120. Map 604 ▭ ▭ ▬ ▤ ⅄ 𝐴𝐸 ⊡ ▭ ▭ *Closed Sat lunch; Sun.*

Sushi and *sashimi* — raw fish with and without rice — have for some time now been sufficiently commonplace to draw distinctions between their purveyors. Many *sushi* chefs pursue their craft with the fierce solemnity of a *ninja.* That can be offputting, especially for a neophyte diner who would welcome a little advice along with the showy knifemanship. Friendliness is a hallmark of this branch of a growing family-owned chain, from the barman in the bamboo-and-slate vestibule to the kimonoed waitresses and the chefs themselves. While their command of the English language runs from not bad to unintelligible, they go out of their way to instruct gently on the niceties of this specialized sort of eating. They might urge that you begin with the unadorned, buttery-soft "fatty tuna," or that you stir a little horseradish in your dish of soy sauce, or that the yellowtail rolled with rice in seaweed sheets is best eaten with the fingers, not chopsticks. This results in a far more gratifying evening of culinary theater than you will find at one of those places where the eating of uncooked fish is regarded as a mystic ritual. Don't accept a table upstairs.

TAVERN ON THE GREEN *American/International*

Central Park W (67th St.), NY 10023 ☎873-3200. Map 7M3 ▭ ▭ ▬ ▦ ▬ 𝐴𝐸 ⊡ ▭ ▭ *Open daily.*

Tavern On The Green is one of those places that must be mentioned simply because it is there and everybody knows about it. Once a barn for the sheep that wandered in the adjacent meadow, it has been a restaurant for much of the current century. Successive managements have consistently fallen short in matching the dining experience to the promise of the building and the park surroundings. The latest to try — successfully — is a Mr Leroy, an apostle of the "eat-with-the-eyes" theory of restaurateurship. His version is visually provocative, crammed with carved plaster, etched mirrors, and a profusion of brass, crystal and copper ornamentation. The trees outside are strung with thousands of pinlights, seen from blocks away. Some describe the experience as "festive"; others call it noisy, disorganized, and pretentiously cute. The food can be good, but it is impossible to predict which dishes at what hours. Service is erratic. Despite all this, out-of-towners and many New Yorkers love it. Maybe you'll agree. To find out, try the relatively inexpensive pretheater dinner.

THAILAND ✿ Thai
106 Bayard St. (Mulberry St.), NY 10013 ☎ 349-3132. Map 3T4 ▮▯ ▭ ▰ Closed Mon.
It might seem sacrilegious to venture into Thai food while you are in Chinatown, for a year of uninterrupted consumption would not exhaust the Szechuan, Mandarin, Cantonese and Hunan cuisines to be sampled in its perhaps 200 restaurants. But this admittedly seedy little place across from Columbus Park deserves consideration, with prices as low as any in the neighborhood. The menu is bewilderingly comprehensive, with nearly 100 listed items. A party of four can take advantage of the variety.

TRATTORIA DELL'ARTE Italian
900 7th Ave. (57th St.), NY 10019 ☎ 245-9800. Map 5N3 ▮▯ ▭ ▰ ▦ ▣ ▤ ▩ Open daily.
Some people are pained by the decor, which features outsized representations of body parts — a nose, lips,

ear, breast — and Renaissance drawings of same. If you're apt to find that offensive, don't go, but you'll miss super pizzas and pastas and a most tantalizing antipasto bar. (Single diners can sit at the marble counter around that delectable array, pointing and eating until buttons pop.) Most members of the multinational staff haven't been any closer to Rome than Little Italy, but they're a cheerful lot who move through their tasks with alacrity. The Italian touch is brought to Saturday and Sunday brunch with polenta pancakes, fruit foccaccia and cappuccino. Some of the main courses fall short, but all in all, this is just the spot for a meal or snack before or after performances at CARNEGIE HALL, directly across the street.

TRIBECA GRILL Eclectic American
375 Greenwich St. (Franklin St.), NY 10013 ☎ 941-3900. Map 1T4 ▮▯ ▭ ▦ ▣ ▤ ▩ Closed Sun.
It can be assumed that the owners of this fashionable eatery had much to do with pulling in the hordes that have squeezed into it since day one. One of them is Robert De Niro, after all, and this is to be one element of a planned film-performance-and-arts center. (It already features "dinner and a movie" every Friday night). Were the possibility of seeing a famous face or two the only reason for attending, it wouldn't be worth the trek to the far edge of TriBeCa. But Bobby and his buddies were smart enough to call in the man who put the laudable **Montrachet** on the map, and he has more than measured up to his billing. In the middle of the cavernous room is the grand old bar salvaged from the near-legendary **Maxwell's Plum**, now departed. Large semi-abstract figurative canvases hang on the brick walls. Grills, roast chicken and pastas prevail on the menu, hardly an astonishment, but all is admirably professional in execution and prices are fair. Brokers in shirtsleeves and braces and artists in T-shirts and jeans mingle merrily, with lots of hugging and laughing going on, and the gatekeepers display no favoritism.

21 (TWENTY-ONE) CLUB *American*
21 W 52nd St. (near 5th Ave.), NY 10019
☎582-7200. Map 6N4 ▥ ▄ ⊏⊐ AE ●
● ▥ *Closed Sat (in summer); Sun.*

Once a Prohibition-era speakeasy, "21" went on to become a sanctuary for the power elite. Celebrities are often on view, but the carefully tonsured and garbed regulars who frequent the place are more often senior partners in important law firms, executives of multinational corporations, or the men who decide who will be permitted to run for political office. It is not a club in the sense of excluding the general public, but strangers are granted no more than distant courtesy. Under new management, the food has been up and down, but currently appears to be on the ascendancy. Prices are staggeringly high, however, and many people settle for a manly martini in the colorful bar and go elsewhere to eat.

UN DEUX TROIS ♣ *French*
123 W 44th St. (near Times Sq.), NY 10020
☎354-4148. Map 5O3 ▥ ⊏⊐ ▄ AE ●
▥ *Closed Sat and Sun lunch.*

This restaurant's allegiance to the brasserie archetype is not slavish, but with its vast ramshackle room, paper tablecloths and hearty rather than delicate victuals, the point is made. At lunch, its clients run to executive sorts, but at nightfall, a disco-theater crowd prone to spiky hair and violet cheekbones mingles with specimens of the Concorde Set. Most of the servers are exactly what they appear to be — actors, singers, dancers. One host was a tenor who "aged from Vivaldi to Mozart" during his tour of duty. No one raves about the food, but compromises are made for moderate prices and convenience to Broadway theaters. Selections from the regular menu — roast chicken, steak au poivre — are usually preferable to the daily specials.

UNION SQUARE CAFÉ ♣ *French/Italian/American*
21 E 16th St. (near 5th Ave.), NY 10003
☎243-4020. Map 6Q4 ▥ to ▥ ▄ ⊏⊐
▄ ▄ AE ● ▥ *Open daily.*

If this writer could eat in only one Manhattan restaurant for the rest of his days, he would choose the Union Square Café. That assumes, of course, that they don't change a thing. Certainly not the welcome, by a host who appears so delighted to see you that you hardly notice he is steering you to the worst table in the house. Not the bubbly, knowing waiters (hunky) and waitresses (dishy), who convey the impression, however untrue, that they wouldn't mind if they never made it to the Broadway stage as long as they could keep working here. Not the food, the very model of pan-oceanic eclecticism, with myriad flavors that explode in the mouth at every bite. And definitely not the prices, about half what uptown emporia charge for eats of comparable quality. It couldn't start to take itself too seriously, either. Keep such whimsical notes as the yellowfin tuna "burger," served on a seeded roll. And don't touch the big expressionistic murals of floating nudes, or alter the composition of the crowd, which seems, for a change, less interested in "making the scene" than in enjoying itself. Even solo diners are not set adrift, especially if a platter of iced oysters and a flinty Chardonnay at the mahogany bar satisfies their notion of lunch. Put this beguiling place on the must-list, right up there with the Metropolitan Museum of Art and the Empire State Building.

VINCE & EDDIE'S ♣ *Eclectic American*
70 W 68th St. (between Columbus Ave. and Central Park W), NY 10023 ☎721-0068.
Map 7M3 ▥ ⊏⊐ ▄ AE ● ● ▥ *Open daily.*

Winters, a fire crackles in the raised fireplace; summers, the back opens to a small terrace. In between, this mightily successful eatery strives to resemble a Kansas farmhouse. Its close quarters contain mis-matched chairs and oilcloth on the tables, antique picture frames and old tools on the walls. The food fits the setting — hearty soups and stews, roast chickens, fried oysters, memorable lamb shank with mashed potatoes. Weekend brunches get a

Continental touch, with baked mussels, seafood crepes and fried calamari among the selections. Hugely popular in the evenings and on weekends, it is often easiest to gain entrance at lunchtime. A little more polish might be asked of the service staff, but they work with breathy earnestness. That's probably Vincent behind the bar while Eddie works the room, both of them confident, fatherly presences who want you to be happy.

WINDOWS ON THE WORLD *International*
1 World Trade Center, NY 10048
☎*938-1111. Map 1U4. Three restaurants,*
all ▭ ■■ ▰ ▣ ▣ ▣ ▨ *The Cellar in the Sky* ▥ *dinner only, closed Sun. The Hors d'Oeuvrerie* ▥ ◁ ↑ *The Restaurant* ▥ ◁ *closed Sun dinner.*

There are three distinct eating places under the **Windows On The World** umbrella, all of them in the N tower on the 107th floor. Enduring the wait at the reception desk of **The Restaurant** can be a chore, but persevere, for it justifies the temporary aggravation. Surely there is no more stunning urban vista anywhere — sparkling spires, bands of winking sapphires, silvered waters and webs of bridges. All is made available to view from tiered tables in a muted spaceship environment. As is usual in rooftop restaurants, competence on the plate proves elusive, but the fixed-price dinner at least eases the fiscal bite. The premise of **The Hors d'Oeuvrerie** is to make entire meals of appetizers, a gimmick that was overdue. The starter dishes of different countries — Chinese *dim sum,* Italian *antipasti,* Spanish *tapas* — are featured on a rotating monthly basis. Jazz performers are on duty from 4.30pm until closing. Reservations are unnecessary. **The Cellar in the Sky** has no views, but attempts to compensate with ambitious 7-course meals enhanced by five different wines. They have only a single sitting each evening (dinner only) for a maximum of 36 diners.

Reservations are essential for **The Cellar** and **The Restaurant**, often at least 2 weeks in advance. Avoid the hectic Sunday buffet and brunch. Wines available at the complex are often superb, and are reasonably priced.

WOO CHON ♣ *Korean*
8-10 W 36th St. (5th Ave.), NY 10018
☎*695-0676 Map 6P4* ▭ *to* ▥ ▭ ■■
▰ ▣ ▣ ▨ *Open 24 hrs.*

A glance at the signs up and down this seedy street w of 5th Ave. confirms that this is "Little Korea," far smaller than Chinatown, but growing. Right in the middle is this shining example of how good an ethnic restaurant can be without pandering to the uninitiated. Its two floors are fancier than might be expected, with a mock waterfall downstairs, and busy at literally any hour with mostly Korean and other Asian patrons. The long menu includes sushi, sashimi, and other Japanese dishes, but the star attractions are the several barbecued items. Immediately upon seating, one waiter pours glasses of hot tea and another brings small bowls of *kim chee.* There are reportedly more than 100 varieties of these pickled vegetables and seafood — bean sprouts, squid rings, cucumbers, turnip — from mild and vinegary to potent and peppery. (In Korea, some recipes call for *kim chee* to be fermented in clay crocks buried in the ground for months.) They are just to keep you occupied until the meal arrives. Lunch specials are uncommon bargains. Typical are the compartmented red-and-black lacquered *bento* trays that come with barbecued short ribs, tempura shrimp with dipping sauce, a green vegetable, mixed salad and rice, with a bowl of miso soup on the side. All this can be had for under $10, and there are several other combinations. Color photographs show what you're getting, and the staff is helpful to the limits of their respective commands of English.

ZARELA ♣ *Mexican*
953 2nd Ave. (between 50th and 51st Sts.),
NY 10022 ☎*644-6740. Map 6N5* ▥ ⬧
■■ ▰ ▣ *Open daily, dinner only.*

Fans call it the best Mexican in the city. It isn't (see ROSA MEXICANO above), but who cares? This is a perpetual fiesta in progress, full of tumult and people enjoying themselves. Ceilings are hung with piñatas and loops of colorful paper cutouts, a staircase wall has cubbyholes loaded with south-of-the-border folk art. Plates are plain and white, flatware is stainless steel, the young patrons are casually attired. Among the most ordered dishes are ancho chilies stuffed with beef picadillo, red snapper hash, steak fajitas and cheese enchiladas. Seasonings are mainly on the mild side, with few firebreathers. Margaritas and thirst-quenching Mexican brews are the beverages of choice.

ZEN PALATE ✿ Asian Vegetarian
663 9th Ave. (46th St.), NY 10036
☎*582-1669. Map 503* 🔲 🔲 🎞 🎞 🖾
🖾 🖾 *Open daily.*

Muted cherry woodwork, ocher walls, terracotta floors, and horticultural prints of squash and bok choy set the gentle mood. Friendly servers illuminate the innovative menu items, in which shredded gluten, tofu, and other veggies stand in for chicken, squid and duck.

Apart from the no-alcohol vegetarian stance, there is nothing dogmatic about the recipes. The kitchen borrows from China, Japan, Thailand, Indonesia, with curries and pastas as well as *moo shu* rolls and scallion pancakes. Even dedicated carnivores find this the perfect pre-theater repast, with no danger of nodding off halfway through the first act due to overindulgence in wine or beef. Reservations are a good idea in the evening, but they are rarely necessary for lunch.

Good fast food

It isn't necessary to resort to the ubiquitous representatives of the franchised food chains for a quick snack or a light meal. Here are some inexpensive alternatives.

ATOMIC WINGS
1644 3rd Ave. (92nd St.) ☎*410-3800. Map 8K5.*
Spicy *chicken* wings, that is, the ultimate bar snack.

BENNY'S BURRITOS
113 Greenwich Ave. (Jane St.)
☎*633-9210. Map 3R3.*
Greenwich Village's *numero uno* tortilla joint. These Tex-Mex burritos are about the length and thickness of a man's forearm, with many tempting choices of fillings.

BROOME STREET BAR
363 West Broadway (Broome St.)
☎*925-2086. Map 3S4.*
Salads, sandwiches and "pub grub" in SoHo.

CAFÉ BEL CANTO
1991 Broadway (between 67th and 68th

Sts.) ☎*362-4642. Map 7M3.*
Because this is technically a public space, enclosed in winter and open in summer, no one is required to buy food to sit at one of the tables. But if they do, there's a choice of *fritattas,* pizzas and pastas.

DOSANKO
135 E 45th St. ☎*697-2967, map 604;*
423 Madison Ave. ☎*688-8575, map 604;*
329 5th Ave. ☎*686-9359, map 6P4, and other locations.*
No-decor Japanese noodle shops feature cheap, filling soup and fried chicken.

DALLAS BBQ
1265 3rd Ave. ☎*772-9393, map 8M5; 21 University Place* ☎*674-4450, map 3R4, other locations.*
Generous margaritas and copious portions of Texas-style barbecued fare

compensate for the noise and the slap-dash service.

EJ'S LUNCHEONETTE
433 Amsterdam Ave. (between 80th and 81st Sts.) ☎*873-3444. Map 7L3.*
A cut above the average corner diner, offering black bean chili and chef's salad as well as sandwiches — and open daily from early morning to 11pm or midnight.

FINE AND SHAPIRO
138 W 72nd St. (near Broadway) ☎*877-2874. Map 7M3.*
One of the better Jewish delis.

1ST WOK
1374 3rd Ave. (78th St.) ☎*861-2600. Map 8M5.*
One of a growing Szechuan chain.

GREAT JONES
54 Great Jones St. (near the Bowery) ☎*674-9304. Map 3R4.*
Low-cost Cajun.

HAMBURGER HARRY'S
157 Chambers St. (near West Broadway) ☎*267-4446. Map 1T4.*
Imaginative variations on America's favorite sandwich.

JACKSON HOLE
517 Columbus Ave. (85th St.) ☎*362-5177, map 7L3 and 1270 Madison Ave. (91st St.)* ☎*427-2820, map 8K4, other locations.*
Huge burgers, sandwiches, salads.

JOHN'S PIZZERIA
278 Bleecker St. (near 7th Ave. S)
☎*243-1680. Map 3R4.*
Long lines form here for what, by consensus, is New York's top pizza. There's another branch at 408 E 64th St., map **8**M5.

PAPAYA KING
201 E 59th St.(3rd Ave.) ☎*753-2014, map 6N5, and 179 E 86th St. (3rd Ave.)* ☎*369-0648, map 8L5.*
You won't find seats here, but maybe the tastiest hot dogs in town — two of them and a cup of papaya juice for less than a Big Mac. It is not to be confused with others with similar names. No charge/credit cards.

TONY ROMA'S
400 E 57th St. (near 1st Ave.) ☎*308-0200. Map 6N5.*
Northern outpost of Florida barbecue chain. The onion ring loaf is super-sized.

TORTILLA FLATS
767 Washington St. (W 12th St.) ☎*243-1053. Map 3R3.*
Tex-Mex temptations in the West Village.

VESELKA COFFEE SHOP
144 2nd Ave. (9th St.) ☎*228-9682. Map 4R5.*
Honest renditions of Polish and Ukrainian dishes.

WYLIE'S RIBS
891 1st Ave. (50th St.) ☎*751-0700. Map 6O5.*
Good, but not great, Southern barbecue and chili, served with onion loaves as big as bricks.

Open late

When dinner has been deferred to avoid nodding off in the theater or concert hall, it can be distressing to learn that the nearby restaurant takes no orders after 10.30pm. The following places stay open well past midnight. Some of them are described in greater detail in the above section.

BRASSERIE
100 E 53rd St. (near Park Ave.)
☎ *751-4840. Map 6N4.*
Sort-of French, best-known for being open 24 hours.

CARNEGIE DELICATESSEN
854 7th Ave. (near 55th St.) ☎ *757-2245. Map 5N3. Open until 4am. See page 198.*

COLUMBUS
201 Columbus Ave. (69th St.)
☎ *799-8090. Map 7M3.*
Ignore the food and ogle the celebs. One of the owners is Mikhail Baryshnikov. Open until 2am.

CORNER BISTRO
331 W 4th St. (Jane St.) ☎ *242-9502. Map 3R3.*
Greenwich Village chili-burger-and-brew café.

EMPIRE DINER
210 10th Ave. (22nd St.) ☎ *243-2736. Map 5Q2.*
Retro-glitz, often full of bizarrely costumed club-goers. Open 24 hours.

HARD ROCK CAFÉ
221 W 57th St. (near Broadway)
☎ *489-6565. Map 5N3.*
Inspired by London's original. Raucous,

jammed, loud — definitely for younger revelers. Open until 4am.

ODEON
145 West Broadway (Thomas St.)
☎ *233-0507. Map 1T4.*
"New American" in TriBeCa. Open until 2.30am. See page 208

P.J. CLARKE'S
915 3rd Ave. (55th St.) ☎ *759-1650. Map 6N5.*
Tavern food, lively mixed crowd. Open until 4am.

STAGE DELI
834 7th Ave. (near 54th St.) ☎ *245-7850. Map 5N3.*
The Carnegie Deli's closest competition in location and quality. Open until 2am.

WILSON'S
201 W 79th St. (Amsterdam Ave.)
☎ *769-0100. Map 7L3.*
Comfortable pub-eatery, ideal after visiting Lincoln Center. Open until 4am.

WOLLENSKY'S GRILL
205 E 49th St. (between 2nd Ave. and 3rd Ave.) ☎ *753-0444. Map 6O5.*
A cheaper sidecar to Smith & Wollensky's steakhouse. It stays open until 2am.

Sunday brunch

More lunch than breakfast, brunch is an established event in New York. Usually offered in a fixed-price menu, it can be buffet or table service. Informality is the rule, and it is a way to sample the wares of restaurants that can be prohibitively expensive during the week. These are just a few of many. Normal hours are 11am or midday to 3 or 4pm. Reserve ahead.

CAFÉ DES ARTISTES
1 W 67th St. (near Central Park W)
☎877-3500. Map *7M3.*
Very popular, soothing setting.

DARBÁR
44 W 56th St. (near 6th Ave.) ☎*432-7227.*
Map 6N4.
Bargain northern Indian buffet.

LA MÉTAIRIE
189 W 10th St. (W 4th St.) ☎*989-0343.*
Map 3R3.
Somewhat pricey Village French. Try
other branch too *(1442 3rd Ave, near
82nd St., map 8L5).*

PIG HEAVEN
1540 2nd Ave. (near 80th St.)
☎*744-4887. Map 8L5.*
Gimmicky Chinese, featuring pork and
an overdone barnyard theme. Enjoyable, nonetheless.

LE REGENCE
37 E 64th St. (near Madison Ave.)
☎*606-4647. Map 8M4.*
The lovely dining room of the Hotel
Plaza Athénée; very French.

EL RIO GRANDE
160 E 38th St. (3rd Ave.) ☎*867-0922.*
Map 6O4.
Large, yuppie-single Tex-Mex in Murray Hill.

THE RUSSIAN TEA ROOM
150 W 57th St. (near 7th Ave.)
☎*265-0947. Map 5N3.*
Celebrity roost; blinis are the perfect
brunch. Avoid upstairs room. See page
212.

SARABETH'S KITCHEN
423 Amsterdam Ave. (near 80th St.)
☎*496-6280. Map 7L3.*
Serves delectable omelets, waffles and
pancakes. There is another branch too
*(1295 Madison Ave., near 93rd St.,
map 8K4).*

20 MOTT STREET
20 Mott St. (near Pell St.) ☎*964-0380.*
Map 2T5.
Superb, inexpensive *dim sum.* Packed
on weekends.

Nightlife and entertainment

New York by night

On the evidence of what is available, it might reasonably be inferred that half the population of New York never sees the light of day. Following cocktails and dinner, there can be opera, ballet, a symphony or rock concert, or a Broadway musical. After that, they can choose to see the late show at a cabaret or comedy club, or drop in at a disco or jazz loft. Many places stay open until 4am, and most revelers find that's enough. But the hardy and knowledgeable move on to transient after-hours bars, essentially illegal and with the lifespan of a fruit fly. Finally, perhaps, they might decompress with croissants or bagels at a 24-hour Art Deco diner.

Presented with such a banquet of choices, some people can be paralyzed with indecision. There are a number of considerations that help pare away choices. While most visitors will want to experience at least one play or musical, tickets are, need it be said, expensive. There are discounts to be had, as explained on page 223, or an Off-Broadway musical or revue might be substituted.

> Everyone in Manhattan is a star *manqué,* and every flat surface
> in the island is a stage.
> (Quentin Crisp, writer and performer)

Dress is another factor, for many clubs dictate standards of appearance, even if only to prohibit denim clothing. That being the case, it is advisable to plan an evening with an eye on compatible districts and events. For instance, don a dressy outfit and combine a deluxe restaurant with the trendiest of supper clubs on the East Side. For an evening in SoHo-Greenwich Village, jeans and a sweater will do for a pub crawl, dinner and a jazz or rock club. Something in between is suitable for opera or ballet at the LINCOLN CENTER, a post-theater supper and intimate conversation at a piano bar, all on the West Side.

There has been no attempt here to identify bars, clubs, or theaters of hardcore sexual orientation. They soon make themselves apparent, and in any case are too ephemeral for print. It is sufficient to note that all predilections are accommodated. For guidance, check *The Village Voice* and that tasteful journal, *Screw.* Prostitution is illegal, although that does not dissuade its practitioners. While streetwalkers are flamboyantly visible around Times Sq., their sisters who work hotel bars are cautious and less readily identifiable.

Performing arts

A city of tall buildings and people with tall talents...
(Percy E. Sutton, Apollo Theater Investors)

Not even the most avid of culture seekers, blessed with unlimited funds and few encumbrances, could exhaust the groaning board of music, dance and theater the city spreads before us for 12 months of the year. A merely average week sees ten plays and musicals open or in preview, adding to the 80 already showing. The same week will contain at least a dozen ballet companies performing 20 different programs, ten to 20 movie premières and up to 40 concerts, operas and recitals. To this potent cultural mix is stirred in performance art, jazz openings, film festivals, poetry readings, and lectures.

Obviously, this profusion of choices can be quite daunting, and it doesn't hurt to make decisions well before arriving in town. Cost is one way to trim a "want list," especially with top-price tickets for some Broadway musicals flirting with the three-digit stratosphere. But even there, economies are possible, with half-price and lesser discounts available for most types of cultural events, discussed in the appropriate sections below.

The best sources of current information about what's on are the arts and leisure guides appearing in the Friday and Sunday editions of *The New York Times* and the entertainment sections of the weekly magazines, *New York* and *The New Yorker*.

BALLET

There is surely no other city that enjoys ballet in such abundance and variety. In addition to a dozen or more locally-based companies, the troupes of other cities and nations are regular visitors. Here are the principal venues.

BROOKLYN ACADEMY OF MUSIC
30 Lafayette Ave. (downtown Brooklyn), NY 11217 ☎*(718) 636-4100.*
A.k.a. "BAM," the feisty institution in downtown Brooklyn makes room for experimental dance works in its annual Next Wave festival. Frequent appearances are also made by such organizations as the Martha Graham troupe, the Dance Theatre of Harlem and the Pennsylvania Dance Company.

CITY CENTER
131 W 55th St., NY 10019 ☎*246-8989. Map 5N3.*
The Center enjoys an embarrassment of riches, with such troupes as the Joffrey Ballet, the Merce Cunningham Dance Company, Twyla Tharp, the Alvin Ailey Dance Theater, and the Paul Taylor Dance Company all making appearances in recent seasons.

DIA CENTER FOR THE ARTS
155 Mercer St, NY 10012 ☎*431-9232. Map 3S4.*
Experimental dance and poetry readings, sometimes in combination, are presented at this SoHo performance space, not to be confused with the gallery for the visual arts on 22nd St. in Chelsea.

JOYCE THEATER
175 8th Ave., NY 10011 ☎*242-0800. Map 5Q3.*
Modern and avant-garde dance, often by skilled troupes from abroad, and the

permanent home of the Feld Ballets/NY.

MANHATTAN CENTER STUDIOS
311 W 34th St., NY 10001 ☎*279-7740. Map 5P3.*
A new performance space, which has been used by the innovative Mark Morris Dance Group.

METROPOLITAN OPERA HOUSE
Lincoln Center, NY 10023 ☎*580-9830. Map 7M3.*
Host for the American Ballet Theater,

which long had Mikhail Baryshnikov as its artistic director and has seen performances by most of the other famous Russian emigrés.

NEW YORK STATE THEATER
Lincoln Center, NY 10023 ☎*870-5570. Map 7M3.*
Home of the New York City Ballet.

SYMPHONY SPACE
2537 Broadway, NY 10025. Map 7K2.
A hall used for various types of cultural events, including dance.

Other venues
A selection of other places where dance is frequently on view:
Bessie Schönberg Theater   219 W 19th St. ☎924-0077, map **5Q3**
Florence Gould Hall   55 E 59th St. ☎355-6160, map **6N4**
Performance Space   150 1st Ave. ☎477-5288, map **4R5**
St Mark's In-the-Bouwerie   2nd Ave. and 10th St. ☎924-0077, map **4R5**
Soundance Studio   385 Broadway ☎340-8043, map **1T4**
Theatre for the New City   155 1st Ave. ☎254-1109, map **4R5**
Schomburg Center   515 Lenox Ave. ☎465-3458

CINEMA
Films are of profound concern to many New Yorkers, often to the point of reverence. In strong-mindedly rejecting the foolishness of the notorious Cannes event, for example, the **New York Film Festival** *(Alice Tully Hall, Lincoln Center, mid-Sept to early Oct)* overcompensates on the side of solemnity. No prizes are awarded, no starlets drop their bras, and few outsiders notice that anything happened.

Worthwhile films are introduced, nonetheless, some of which go on to limited release. "Art" films — usually foreign-made and of slim domestic appeal — are showcased by managers who no doubt pray for the occasional hit. A few of these do happen. Many are subtitled. Theaters specializing in such films have a distressingly high mortality rate, so check the newspapers or call ahead. Among them:
- **Angelika Film Center**   Houston and Mercer Sts. ☎995-2000, map **3S4**
- **Art Greenwich Twin**   Greenwich Ave. and 12th St. ☎929-3350, map **3R3**
- **Carnegie Hall Cinema**   7th Ave. and 56th St. ☎265-2520, map **5N3**
- **Carnegie Screening Room**   887 7th Ave. (57th St.) ☎757-2131, map **5N3**
- **Cinema 3**   59th St. (near 5th Ave.) ☎752-5959, map **6N4**
- **Le Cinématographe**   15 Vandam St. ☎675-4680, map **3S3**

- **Cinema Village**   3rd Ave. (between 12th and 13th Sts.)
  ☎505-7320, map **3R4**
- **Film Forum**   209 W Houston St. (near 6th Ave.) ☎727-8110,
  map **3S4**
- **Lincoln Plaza**   Broadway (near 63rd St.) ☎757-2280, map
  7M3
- **Paris**   4 W 58th St. (near 5th Ave.) ☎688-2013, map **6N4**
- **The Public Theater**   425 Lafayette St. (near E 4th St.)
  ☎598-7150, map **3R4**
- **Quad Cinema**   13th St. (between 5th and 6th Aves.)
  ☎255-8800, map **3R4**
- **Walter Reade**   165 W 65th St. (Lincoln Center) ☎875-5600,
  map **7M3**

In addition, several movie theaters specialize in revivals, often in "festival" or retrospective form. They can be high-minded or high camp, composed of movies foreign or domestic, anything from 1-50 years old. Such theaters include:

- **Anthology Film Archives**   32-34 2nd Ave.(2nd St.)
  ☎477-2714, map **4R5**
- **Cinema Village**   33 E 12th St. (near University Pl.)
  ☎924-3363, map **3R4**
- **8th Street Playhouse**   8th St. (near University Place)
  ☎674-6515, map **3R4**
- **Theater 80**   80 St Mark's Pl. (near 1st Ave.) ☎254-7400, map
  4R5
- **Waverly Twin**   323 Ave. of the Americas (W. 3rd St.)
  ☎929-8037, map **3R4**

Several museums have regular film programs. The most comprehensive is at the **Museum of Modern Art** *(11 W 53rd St. (6th Ave.)* ☎ *956-7070, map 6N4)*. Also try the **Museum of the Moving Image** *(35th Ave. and 36th St., Queens* ☎ *(718) 784-4520)* and the **Museum of Television and Radio** *(25 W 52nd St.* ☎ *621-6600, map 6N4)*.

For general movie showtime information ☎777-3456.

CLASSICAL MUSIC

Avery Fisher Hall *(Lincoln Center* ☎ *875-5020)* is home for the New York Philharmonic and its new German conductor, Kurt Masur. When they are not in residence, all manner of visiting organizations fill the seats, as diverse as the Bulgarian State Female Choir and Royal Liverpool Philharmonic. Chamber orchestras, string quartets and instrumentalists are heard at **Alice Tully Hall** *(Lincoln Center* ☎ *875-5050)*. The National Orchestra of New York and such large out-of-town organizations as the Philadelphia and Cleveland Orchestras play at **Carnegie Hall** *(57th St. and 7th Ave.* ☎ *247-7800, map 5N3)*, while smaller groups and individual artists use the attached **Weill Recital Hall.**

Venues used by classical artists as well as by pop, dance, jazz, and/or rock ensembles include **Merkin Concert Hall** *(129 W 67th St.* ☎ *362-8719, map 7M3)*, **Town Hall** *(123 W 43rd St.* ☎ *840-2824, map 6O4)*, the **Tisch Center for the Arts** of the **92nd Street Y** *(Lexington Ave.*

☎ *415-5440, map8 K4),* the **Brooklyn Academy of Music** *(30 Lafayette Ave.* ☎ *(718) 636-4100)* and **Symphony Space** *(Broadway and 95th St.* ☎ *864-5400, map 7K2).* **Florence Gould Hall** *(55 E 59th St.* ☎ *355-5160, map 6N4)* often showcases French chamber groups and instrumentalists as well as dance.

Check, too, the **Metropolitan Museum of Art** *(5th Ave. and 82nd St.* ☎ *570-3949, map 8L4)* for recitals by individuals and small groups. As is to be expected, the renowned **Juilliard School** for the performing arts has its own theater for music, opera, and dance, at 60 Lincoln Center Plaza (☎ *769-7406, map 7M3).* Tickets must be obtained, but are usually free. That is also the case at the **Manhattan School of Music** *(120 Claremont Ave.* ☎ *749-2802).* New music has a regular outlet at **The Kitchen** *(512 W 19th St.* ☎ *255-5793, map 5 Q3).*

A service similar to "TKTS" (see page 231) offers half-price day-of-performance tickets for opera, classical music and dance events. A modest service charge is added. Look for the booth in Bryant Park on 42nd St., near 6th Ave., map 6O4 (☎ *382-2323 after 12.30pm; open Tues, Thurs, Fri noon-2pm and 3-7pm; Wed, Sat 11am-2pm and 3-7pm, Sun noon-6pm).* They also sell full-price tickets for future performances. To charge tickets by phone for events at LINCOLN CENTER, call **Centercharge** ☎721-6500.

Of special interest is the **Taipei Theater** *(1221 6th Ave.* ☎ *373-1853, map 6 O4),* which produces dramas, operas, and especially music recitals and concerts, starring Chinese artists.

JAZZ

It can be argued that America's purest music should be listed among the smoky cellar clubs and grungy bars in which it is so often heard, not here among the divas and *corps de ballet.* But jazz is surely this continent's most original and exportable art form, its practitioners as profoundly skilled as any who work the operatic and symphonic vineyards. From Benny Goodman to Wynton Marsalis, they cross over to the shores of classical music as readily as to those of pop and rock. **Lincoln Center for the Performing Arts** has belatedly recognized its importance, in 1991 establishing a jazz department charged with producing year-round concerts.

Jazz was born in New Orleans and journeyed up the Mississippi to Kansas City and Chicago, but its ultimate destination was New York. This is where it thrives, as nowhere else. Jazz musicians were not — *are* not — certain of recognition until they were accepted here. One of their number was credited with the invention of that celebrated nickname for the metropolis: "I made it, brother, I'm going to the Big Apple."

Jazz flourished and grew in New York from World War I into the 1950s. It hung on in the face of the onslaught of Elvis, The Beatles and their progeny. And it persists, as vital as ever, available in all its permutations — Dixieland, swing, fusion, mainstream, bop, progressive, and wildly experimental. It is performed in old-line clubs that have been on the scene for 50 years and in fifth-floor "lofts" that are no more settled than Bedouins. Concerts are also held in the halls of colleges and churches all over town, and jazz brunches are often mounted Sundays at restaurants that have no other regular live entertainment.

In June, a city-wide **jazz festival** brings in names and groups as near-mythic as Ray Charles, Dizzy Gillespie, and the late Miles Davis. They perform indoors and out, in clubs and concert halls, and often for free. The festival changes names according to its major sponsor of the moment. At present, that corporation is the JVC electronics firm.

Call **Jazzline** (☎ *(718) 465-7500)* for a daily recorded announcement on jazz events.

ANDIAMO

1991 Broadway (between 67th and 68th Sts.), NY 10023 ☎*362-3315. Map 7M3* ☽ ⇶ ♪ 🆑 🔄 🔄 📟 *Open daily.*
Behind a separately managed streetside café is this large, crisply modern space occupied by arresting sculptures and paintings that don't just fade into the background. Generally good Italian food complements mostly mainstream jazz. On Sunday, there is an all-you-can-eat brunch with live blues groups.

ANGRY SQUIRE

216 7th Ave. (23rd St.), NY 10011 ☎*242-9066. Map 5Q3 ♪ 🆑 🔄 Open daily.*
A pub-tavern that was an early contributor to the Chelsea renaissance, with fittingly British cookery that is at least as authentic as American hamburgers in London. The music is mainstream and hard bop, with champagne weekend brunches. Sit in the bar to avoid the cover charge.

BIRDLAND

2745 Broadway (105th St.), NY 10025 ☎*749-2228. Map 7J2 ⇶ ☽ ♪ 🆑 🔄 🔄 📟 Open nightly.*
The fabled Birdland of the 1940s and 1950s hosted jazz greats Charlie Parker and Dave Brubeck, and others of their prominence. This upper West Side club is far removed from the midtown original and only infrequently signs up stars of that luminosity. Buffs still think it is worth the trek. Lesser-known practitioners such as the capable Jimmy Heath and Paul Ostermayer quartets are the rule, with occasional appearances by such legends as Milt Jackson. As usual, it is less expensive to sit or stand at the bar.

BLUE NOTE

131 W 3rd St. (Ave. of the Americas), NY 10012 ☎*475-8592. Map 3R4* ☽ ⇶ 🎵 ♪ 🆑 *Open nightly.*
Put this at the top of the "must" list. New York's premier jazz showcase boasts a long roster of performers that includes just about every notable performer, past and present, from Nancy Wilson and Joe Williams to Illinois Jacquet and Tito Puente. Naturally enough, with that caliber of musician, it is packed with fans nearly every night. Headliners have two shows during the week, three on Friday and Saturday, and afterwards, a house trio jams on until 4am. On weekends, there are matinees with late brunch. Minimum and cover charges vary , but are never small. To lessen the bite, listen from the bar.

BRADLEY'S

70 University Pl. (11th St.), NY 10003 ☎*228-6440. Map 3R4* ☽ ♪ 🆑 🔄 🔄 📟 *Open daily.*
Bright and bubbling, with conversation drowning out the music early on. The 'burgers are good and the progressive mainstream duos and trios at the end of the long bar even better. They tune up twice nightly, somewhere around 10pm and midnight. Not infrequently, but always late, name musicians drop by to jam. There is no cover charge on Monday or Tuesday.

B. SMITH'S ROOFTOP CAFÉ

771 8th Ave. (47th St.), NY 10036 ☎*247-2222. Map 5O3 ⇶ ☽ ♪ 🆑 🔄 🔄 📟 Closed Sun-Thurs.*
One of those people habitually referred to as a "supermodel" is the canny businesswoman who owns this stylish

new theater-district hot spot. A percentage of her clients routinely show up in tuxedos and evening gowns, and the kitchen nearly lives up to that implied demand. Upstairs, on a stage wrapped in glass, is the combo of the week. As a general rule, they are as cool and contained as their audience. Music on Friday and Saturday only.

THE CAJUN
129 8th Ave. (16th St.), NY 10011 ☎691-6174. Map 5Q3 ⥤ ⥂ ⋔ AE ⊙ ⊙ VISA
Closed Sun.
Creole-Cajun food, more or less, with Dixieland jazz leavened by serious blues. Swing combos are brought in from time to time.

CONDON'S
117 E 15th St. (Irving Place) NY 10003 ☎254-0960. Map 6Q4 ⥤ ⥂ ⋔ AE ⊙ ⊙ VISA *Open nightly.*
The blooming Union Square neighborhood recently added this user-friendly club-restaurant to its slate of enticements. Big names are routinely staged — Ahmad Jamal and Abbey Lincoln, for two examples — and they come from any of several schools, from trad to progressive. There is room for large bands. The food is better than the average for such precincts; cover charges vary according to the reputations of the musicians.

FAT TUESDAY'S
190 3rd Ave. (17th St.), NY 10003 ☎533-7902. Map 6Q4 ⥤ ⥂ ♪ ⋔ AE ⊙ ⊙ VISA *Open nightly.*
Once upon a time, this was **Joe King's Rathskeller**, a magnet for generations of collegians. The main floor hasn't changed, in spirit. Singles mingle, 'burgers are munched, pitchers of beer are quaffed. Downstairs is different. Jazz prevails, largely of the progressive mainstream variety, with increasing Latin intrusions. There is a hefty cover charge, and the minimum is best consumed in liquid form. Sets are usually at 8pm, 10pm and, Friday and Saturday, at midnight, and there are weekend brunches with live music.

GREENE STREET CAFÉ
101 Greene St. (Prince St.), NY 10012 ☎925-2415. Map 3S4 ⥤ ⥂ ⋔ AE ⊙ ⊙ VISA *Open nightly.*
SoHo's perennial party place rarely suffers a quiet moment, not with its several levels, packed bars and imaginative menus. The music reflects the current ardors of the ever-active owner, but most of it has a jazz base, which is often Latin-tinged.

KNICKERBOCKER BAR & GRILL
33 University Place (8th St.), NY 10003 ☎228-8490. Map 3R4 ⥤ ⥂ ⋔ AE ⊙ ⊙ VISA *Closed Mon, Tues.*
No crowding, no cover and a reasonable minimum at tables (none at the bar) make this engaging restaurant-club as attractive as any in the Village. Featured are piano and bass duos and, sometimes, singers.

KNITTING FACTORY
47 E Houston St. (near Lafayette St.), NY 10012 ☎219-3055. Map 3S4 ⥂ ⋔ *Open nightly.*
Quartets and quintets squeeze onto a tiny stage to deliver narratives on improvisation in the modernist mode. Elbow-to-elbow patrons tend to be an attentive lot, who treat the music as the centerpiece, not as a backdrop. While most of the artists are not widely known, some headliners, such as Lee Konitz, are booked. From time to time, there are acoustical folkies, and people who don't fit into pigeonholes. There are usually two sets a night, the first between 8 and 9pm. An admission fee is charged.

RED BLAZER TOO
349 W 46th St. (between 8th and 9th Aves.), NY 10036 ☎262-3112. Map 5O3 ⥂ ♪ ⋔ AE ⊙ ⊙ VISA *Open nightly.*
Forget Bird and Diz. The riffs and rumbles at this jumping after-theater club date back to the epoch between the Volstead Act and V-E Day. From the dawn of the Roaring Twenties, that is, when New Orleans checked into Prohibition Chicago with ragtime and dixie, up to a few years after Goodman

and Krupa had them dancing in the aisles at the old Paramount. *Le jazz hot* hadn't learned to be cool yet. Big bands often take the stand, and there are jazz brunches on Sunday.

SWEET BASIL

88 7th Ave. S (Bleecker St.), NY 10014 ☎242-1785. *Map 3R3* ⊶ ⅄ ▣ ↑ AE ⓒⒹ ⓥⓘⓢⓐ *Open daily.*

Mainstream jazz in an attractive brick-and-wood setting, with such artists as Nat Adderley and Chris Conner. Music starts at 10pm; or show up for Saturday and Sunday afternoon sessions and avoid the cover charge. Meals from lunch through late supper are served; there are music brunches on Saturday and Sunday.

VILLAGE GATE

60 Bleecker St. (Thompson St.), NY 10012 ☎475-5120. *Map 3R4* ⅄ ↑ revue AE ⓒⒹ ⓥⓘⓢⓐ *Open daily.*

Stability is not necessarily a characteristic of jazz emporia, but the "Gate" grooves on, now in its fourth decade. Performers range from good to unsurpassed, their preferences from be-bop to fusion to salsa. They're housed in a large, comfortable, noisy room. Music starts at 10pm. The multilevel complex also puts on comedy acts, revues, theater, chamber music, to name but a few.

VILLAGE VANGUARD

178 7th Ave. S (near 11th St.), NY 10011 ☎255-4037. *Map 3R3* ⅄ ↑ *No cards. Open nightly.*

Landmark cellar club on the scene for over 50 years. Mainstream jazz, mostly, often by large bands of up to 20 musicians and combos the likes of Milt Jackson and Terence Blanchard. Two sets nightly Monday to Thursday, three Friday to Sunday. Monday night, the big house band takes the stage.

VISIONES

125 MacDougal St. (Bleecker St.), NY 10012 ☎673-5576. *Map 3R4* ⅄ ↑ AE ⓒⒹ *Open nightly.*

A Spanish restaurant is perhaps an unlikely venue for jazz, but here it is, in the middle of the Village entertainment district. The groups on stage aren't marquee names, the reason a cover charge isn't charged much of the time. That doesn't mean the performers don't give full measure every night at 9 and 11pm. Late third shows are scheduled Friday and Saturday, with jam sessions Monday night and Saturday afternoon.

ZINNO

126 W 13th St. (near 7th Ave.), NY 10011 ☎924-5182. *Map 5Q3* ⊶ ⅄ ↑ AE ⓒⒹ ⓥⓘⓢⓐ *Closed Sun.*

Duos and trios (there isn't room for more) split themselves between the bar and dining room nightly to tender immaculate versions of blues and mainstream jazz. It's not unlike a party at a friend's house. The bonus is good food — rare at Manhattan jazz showcases — which makes the minimum charge easy to meet. A cover is levied, too. Sets usually start at 8 or 9pm. Reservations are essential if you intend to eat.

Other options

Those are 18 of about 50 possibilities where jazz is the centerpiece. For a night (or brunch) out in which music is primarily a pleasant backdrop or a filler of gaps in conversation, there are many others. A few: **Tavern on the Green** *(Central Park W at W 67th St. ☎873-3200, map 7M3)*, **Café de la Paix** *(Hotel St. Moritz, 50 Central Park S. ☎755-5800, map 6N4)*, **Cameo** *(Columbus Ave. and 69th St. ☎874-2280, map 7M3)*, **Hors d'Oeuvrerie** *(1 World Trade Center ☎938-1111, map 1U4)*, **Honeysuckle** *(507 Columbus Ave. (84th St.) ☎496-8095, map 7L3)*, **Cavaliere** *(108 W 73rd St. (near Columbus Ave.) ☎799-8282, map 7M3)*, and **Vanessa** *(289 Bleecker St. (7th Ave. S) ☎243-4225, map 3R3)*.

OPERA

Full-scale productions are mounted during extended seasons of the Metropolitan Opera Company and the New York City Opera at the **Metropolitan Opera House** *(Lincoln Center* ☎ *580-9830, map 7M3)* and the **New York State Theater** *(Lincoln Center* ☎ *870-5570, map 7M3).* Both theaters host visiting companies. **City Center** *(131 W 55th St.* ☎ *581-7907, map 5N3)* is an important site for smaller touring and regional companies.

Gilbert and Sullivan and Victor Herbert fans support a year-long season at the **Light Opera of Manhattan** *(316 E 91st St.* ☎ *831-2000, map 8K5).*

Singing principals of these and other companies perform in concerts in other venues around the city, including:

* **Alice Tully Hall**   Lincoln Center ☎875-5050, map **7**M3
* **Brooklyn Academy of Music**   30 Lafayette Ave. (downtown Brooklyn) ☎(718) 636-4100
* **Carnegie Hall**   57th St. and 7th Ave. ☎247-7800, map **5**N3
* **Town Hall**   123 W 43rd St. ☎840-2824, map **5**O3

Amateurs and young professionals form the companies of the **Amato Opera Theater** *(319 Bowery* ☎ *228-8200, map 4 S5)* and the **Bel Canto Opera** *(220 E 76th St.* ☎ *535-5231, map 8 L5).*

A source for small-scale contemporary opera (veering over the edge into performance art) is **La Mamma** *(74A E 4th St.* ☎ *956-6047, map 4 R4).* Skilled productions are mounted by the **Juilliard Opera Center**, from the performing arts school of the same name *(155 W 65th St.* ☎ *769-7406, map 7M3).*

THEATER

Doomsayers have been predicting the death of the New York theater since the invention of talking movies. During the boom-and-near-bust cycles of the passing decades, they have almost been proven correct more than once, but the "Fabulous Invalid" survived. As recently as 1990, it looked as if the final curtains might have fallen. Then the '91-'92 season arrived and theatergoers spent more money on tickets than ever before in Broadway history, over $292 million. That result was due in large measure to higher prices — the musical "Miss Saigon" hit the $100-per-ticket plateau. But attendance figures were higher, too, provoked substantially by the resuscitation of the American musical, both original and in revival. There hasn't been a better time in years to plan a Broadway vacation.

Broadway, the avenue, long ago gave its name to Broadway, the theater district. Few of the 36 theaters actually front onto that thoroughfare, however. Rather, they cluster in the side streets around **Times Sq.**, the intersection of Broadway and 7th Ave. Here are the lavish musicals, popular intimate comedies and, against heavy odds, the occasional serious drama.

Economics mitigated against experimentation, so that role was traditionally assumed by what came to be known as "Off-Broadway" —

smaller houses with lower overheads and greater daring. Many of these are found in and near **Greenwich Village**, but they are also located throughout Manhattan. In recent years they have grown somewhat more wary, in effect serving as a pre-Broadway tryout circuit, although few productions manage the long step into the big time. Alternative theater, often raw and wildly avant-garde, is known as "Off-Off-Broadway." These productions — happenings — are mounted in garages, churches, lofts, backrooms of restaurants, galleries, anywhere.

Good seats at a hit musical are extremely expensive; seats are not cheap even at the back of the auditorium. There are ways to reduce the bite, however. Productions nearing the end of their runs issue "twofer" passes to shops and hotels: take these to the box office of the appropriate theater and receive two tickets at a 33-percent discount. Or, visit the **TKTS** booth at the N end of Times Sq. on the day you wish to attend *(Mon-Sat 3-8pm for evening performances; Sun noon-8pm, Wed, Sat 10am-2pm for matinees)*. Last-minute cancellations and unsold seats are made available at substantial discounts, although not for all plays, of course.

There are additional TKTS booths on the mezzanine at 2, World Trade Center *(open Mon-Fri 11am-5.30pm, Sat 11am-1pm)*, and at Court and Montague Sts. in downtown Brooklyn *(Tues-Thurs 11am-2pm and 2.30-5.30pm; Fri 11am-5.30pm; Sat 11am-3.30pm)*. For all locations ☎354-5800.

Many theaters accept telephone or mail orders for tickets to their current productions. Their numbers are listed in the daily "Theater Directory" of the *New York Times*. Have a charge/credit card ready when calling. If there is time, tickets can be mailed; otherwise they are picked up at the box office, usually on the day of performance. There are independent tickets-by-telephone agencies, as well, representing large numbers of theaters and the several sports arenas. Those that have considerable coverage include **Ticketmaster** *(☎ 307-7171)* and **Telecharge** *(☎ 239-6200 or 800-233-3123)*. They take orders 24 hours a day, 7 days a week. A surcharge is added to charge/credit card purchases. There are also **Ticketron** outlets throughout the city and suburbs at which tickets can be purchased for most Broadway and Off-Broadway productions (and concerts and sports events, too). Ticket brokers and hotel concierges can handle requests, but be sure that their handling fee will not exceed the going rate.

Nightlife

New Yorkers are party-hearty, launching into their leisure hours with as much energy and drive as they devote to their careers. The pace is fast, and fashions change in an eyeblink. Not for nothing has the phrase "faster than a New York minute" shouldered its way into the American lexicon.

The recommendations below scratch the surface, and some of them will have sunk into oblivion by the time you arrive in town. Many of these bars and clubs are hardy perennials, though, which have been on the scene for decades. Nearly always, they are surrounded by younger, brasher competitors, so seeking out one is bound to expose others.

Liquor laws are liberal. Establishments serving alcoholic beverages are required to close between 4am-8am (Sunday 4am-noon), although most do not open before 11am, and lock up whenever business is slow. Anyone 21 and over can purchase liquor. (Persons between 16 and 20 years of age are allowed in bars, but cannot order or drink alcoholic beverages.) Some bars and clubs set higher age limits and require two items of positive identification.

Bars and clubs offering live entertainment often fix a "cover" charge that is, in effect, an admission fee; and the range can be considerable, depending on the standard or elaborateness of the show. In dance clubs it tends to rise with the chicness of the place. It might be collected at the door or simply added to the check. Typically, in such places, there is also a "minimum" charge for consumption of beverages and/or food, per person.

Fine food and music are infrequently found in combination, although there has been some improvement on that score. Getting something to eat — a hamburger, a bowl of chili — is nearly always possible, but in general expect no more than alleviation of hunger pangs. Exceptions are such establishments as **The Ballroom** in Chelsea, which serves excellent food and lays on cabaret and dancing, and the **Greene Street Café**, where the owner is determined to create an all-inclusive dining-and-entertainment complex (for these two see RESTAURANTS)

To learn who is appearing where, consult the entertainment listings of the Friday and Sunday editions of *The New York Times,* the weekly magazines *New York* and *The New Yorker,* and, for more offbeat diversions, the weekly newspaper *The Village Voice.* Even then, call ahead for reservations and to inquire about last-minute changes in hours and performers. And, for that matter, to find out if the place still exists.

BARS AND LOUNGES

Passing the night in a bar (or several) is a common diversion and, except when it becomes an addiction, not as decadent as it sounds. Certainly there are hundreds of bars devoted to nothing more elevating than the diligent consumption of alcohol. But the owners know that success lies in distractions. These may be no more than the preservation of antique trappings — stamped tin ceiling, potbellied stove, stained-glass window — but can escalate into exciting meals, collections of imported beers and wines, live music and entertainments of every description, or dancing. Or it may be simply a matter of creating the kind of environment that attracts crowds of like-minded seekers-after-companionship. The roster that follows merely indicates the possibilities. Unless otherwise noted, all bars are open seven days a week, usually from 11am or noon until at least 2am, and serve food.

Fake Tiffany lamps and dark-stained plywood still try to substitute for atmosphere. The real thing still exists, however. **Fanelli's** *(94 Prince St. in SoHo* ☎ *226-9412, closed Sat, Sun, map3 S4)* predates the Civil War, and looks it. Neighborhood working men share it with the recent artistic immigrants. **McSorley's Old Ale House** *(15 E 7th St.* ☎ *473-9148, map 4 R5)* is even older, and did not miss a working day during the 13-year experiment called Prohibition. Only two decades ago did they grudgingly allow women inside the door.

There still isn't a sign to mark **Chumley's** *(86 Bedford St. in Greenwich Village* ☎ *675-4449, map3 R3),* and it retains the Bohemian aura of Edna St Vincent Millay and Eugene O'Neill. Yellowing book jackets of former clients line the walls, and there is a working fireplace in winter. Good 'burgers, too. O. Henry was a regular patron of **Pete's Tavern** *(129 E 18th St.* ☎ *473-7676, map 6 Q4),* which opened in 1864. They have sidewalk tables for warm-weather dining, with mostly Italian food.

Not far away is the 1890s **Old Town Bar** *(45 E 18th St.* ☎ *473-8874, map 6 Q4),* which retains its tile floor and molded tin ceiling. The venerable **P.J. Clarke's** *(915 3rd Ave. at 55th St.* ☎ *355-8857, map6 N5)* remains dark and cobwebby in the corners, with sawdust beneath the feet; an archetypal Irish saloon, but the clientele wears three-piece suits now, and chatters of media campaigns and TV audience shares. The **White Horse Tavern** *(W Hudson St. and 11th St.* ☎ *243-9260, map 3 R3)* was established in Greenwich Village in 1880. Dylan Thomas, Norman Mailer, poet Delmore Schwartz and Brendan Behan gathered there. British pub grub — shepherd's pie, steak and mushroom pie — is on the menu of the 1868 **Landmark Tavern** *(626 11th Ave. at 46th St.* ☎ *757-8595, map5 O2).* Drop in after the theater, but before midnight, or for Sunday brunch.

Bars with shorter histories but as much atmosphere include:

- **Blue Mill Tavern**   50 Commerce St., in Greenwich Village ☎243-7114, map **3**R3, a former Prohibition speakeasy
- **Broome Street Bar**   363 West Broadway, in SoHo ☎925-2086, map **3**S4
- **Harvey's Chelsea**   108 W 18th St. ☎243-5644, map **6**Q4; tavern restaurant
- **The Lion's Head**   59 Christopher St., in Greenwich Village ☎929-0670, map **3**R3 — literary lions, that is
- **Prince Street Bar**   125 Prince St., in SoHo ☎228-8130, map **3**S4

Joe Allen *(326 W. 46th St.* ☎ *581-6464, map5 O3)* looks older than it is, perhaps because of the photos of Leslie Howard, W.C. Fields, and Billie Holliday. The battered bar frequently supports the tailored elbows of stars of the New York-based soap operas. Food was recently upgraded. Serious students of hops and barley malt have a home at the boutique brewery/bar/bistro **The Manhattan Brewing Company** *(40 Thompson St.* ☎ *219-9250, map 3 S4)* and at the **Peculier Pub** *(145 Bleecker St.* ☎ *353-1327, map 3 R4)*, which claims to stock over 250 different brands of beer.

Wine bars, where the titular tipple is the only one available, never quite caught on. Some conventional bars have installed Cruvinets, and have more and better selections than the usual jug wines. Among these are **I Tre Merli** *(463 Broadway* ☎ *254-8699, map 3 S4)*, **SoHo Kitchen and Bar** *(103 Greene St.* ☎ *925-1866, map 3 S4)*, and **Lavin's** *(23 W 39th St.* ☎ *921-1288, map 6 O4)*.

Desperate loneliness pervades hotel bars, and the occupants seem to exude their disinclination to venture more than 100 feet from their bedrooms. Among the dozen exceptions, so engaging that even New Yorkers stop in, is **Bemelman's Bar** in the plush **Carlyle** *(Madison Ave. and 76th St.* ☎ *744-1600, map 8 L4)*. Jazz piano, often played by luminary Barbara Carroll, is the backdrop, and the justification for the cover charge.

The bar of the **Algonquin Hotel** *(59 W 44th St. near 5th Ave.* ☎ *840-6800, map 6 O4)* is still a charmer, burbling with talk of book packages and theatrical contretemps. Bankers' pinstripes dominate at the handsome **Oak Bar** of the **Plaza** *(5th Ave. and 59th St.* ☎ *759-3000, map 6 N4)*, where the principal diversion is the sound of egos colliding.

Very different indeed is **The Whiskey** *(235 W 46th St.* ☎ *819-0404, map 5 O3)*, the lounge of the Philippe Starck-designed **Paramount**. Many people, mostly hip, usually pretty, often famous, sidle up to the mahogany bar and sink into the asymmetrical velvet chairs. Similar in their aggressively post-modernist appeal are the bar of **Charlotte**, the restaurant of the **Hotel Macklowe** *(145 W 44th St.* ☎ *789-7508, map 5 O3)* and **44**, at the **Royalton Hotel** *(44 W 44th St.* ☎ *944-6644, map 6 O4)*.

Strictly for tourists is **The View**, the rotating bar-restaurant of the **Marriott Marquis** *(1535 Broadway* ☎ *704-8900, map 5 O3)*; the free hors d'oeuvres during happy hour are some compensation for the mob scene and steep prices. Quieter, with gentle piano background and less restricted overlooks is **Top of the Tower**, on the 26th floor of the refurbished **Beekman Tower** *(3 Mitchell Place at 49th St.* ☎ *355-7300, map 6 O5)*.

The hope of human contact, of conversation, however brief, is a primary motive for bar-hopping. When it became clear back in the 1970s that increasing numbers of unmarried people were choosing to retain that status, the "singles bar" became an explicit entity. Few unencumbered folk admit to visiting such places, which leaves open the question of why they flourish nevertheless. And, of course, they fall into categories, subject to unpredictable change and fashion.

A note of cautious sobriety has pushed its way into the once superheated sexuality of such places, owing to the spread of herpes, then AIDS. However, that hasn't slowed the quest for commitment nor the inclination to engage in an evening's flirtation. Allegiances shift, but try:

- **Amsterdam's**   428 Amsterdam Ave. (81st St.) ☎874-1377, map 7L3
- **Café Iguana**   235 Park Ave. S (19th St.) ☎529-4770, map **6Q4**
- **Caramba**   684 Broadway (3rd St.) ☎420-9817, map **3R4**
- **Jim McMullen's**   1341 3rd Ave. (77th St.) ☎861-4700, map **8L5**
- **Live Bait**   14 E 23rd St. (near Broadway) ☎353-2400, map 6Q4
- **Lucky Strike**   59 Grand St. (West Broadway) !941-0479, map **3S4**
- **Lucy's Retired Surfers**   503 Columbus Ave. (84th St.) ☎787-3009, map **7L3**
- **Tortilla Flats**   366 W 12th St. (Hudson St.) ☎627-1250, map **3R3**

Clusters of highly social bars pop up overnight like toadstools, for no discernible reasons, along previously dank and drear avenues and in quarters once shuttered by nightfall. A lot of them have gimmicks. **Perfect Tommmy's** *(511 Amsterdam Ave. (85th St.) ☎ 787-7474, map 7L3)* fits those and several other categories. When TV comedian David Letterman put on a Velcro suit and flung himself at a Velcro-covered wall, it was only a matter of time before some entrepreneur made that opportunity available to the general public. Here it is, in a Wednesday night **"Human Fly"** competition. Probably the fad will have passed by the time these words are dry, but who knows?

Nearby **Hi-Life** *(477 Amsterdam Ave. (83rd St.) ☎ 787-7199, map 7L3)* apes an Art Moderne Forties cocktail lounge, with frosted glass sconces and Formica and imitation leather deployed as if they were new wonder materials. Men in baggy jackets and women in black rubber skirts line up outside for a chance at OK food and drinks that don't cost the world. **Bamboo Bernie's** *(Broadway at 82nd St. ☎ 580-0200, map 7L2)* pushes its tropical theme — hard. Thursday and Friday are Hawaiian Luau nights, 32-ounce rum drinks at half price are poured Monday, and margaritas are *free* Tuesday. And after almost half a century as a plain Irish working man's pub, **McAleer's** *(Amsterdam Ave. and 80th St. ☎ 874-8037, map 7L3)* has had to hire door attendants to control the crowds. **Gecko's** *(407 Amsterdam Ave. (79th St.) ☎ 799-0558, map 7L3)* promotes a semi-rowdy sports bar image with free draft beer for "babes under 50" during Monday night football and dancing to records Wednesday to Saturday.

CABARETS AND SUPPER CLUBS
Whether out of boredom with the never ending succession of discos and dance clubs, or nostalgia for the lost glamor of those places once populated on screen by Bogart and George Raft, the nightclub phenomenon of the early '90s is the supper club. The city was never entirely without them, but usually in leaner versions of those of the World War II era. Back then, gorgeous chorines, over-plumed and under-dressed, descended staircases to the strains of Cole Porter, attended by top-hatted, tap-dancing young men. Between shows, patrons in black tie or sequins dined and danced to swing bands. It was assumed that those days were gone forever. Apparently not.

The current resurgence in the genre was heralded by the re-opening of the fabulous **Rainbow!** complex at the top of the GE BUILDING in Rockefeller Center. The imitators cannot hope to be as grand, but they also aren't as expensive, either. For the price of a meal and, perhaps, a cover charge, enjoy live entertainment and dance music at such high-hopes new enterprises as the **SoHo Supper Club**, **Tatou**, **Laura Belle**, **Country Club**, **Rex**, and the just plain **Supper Club**. The food, invariably indifferent or worse in the past, is often not bad, if nothing to frighten serious restaurants. After all, these places are all about play, not about gastronomy.

The new supper clubs join a number of cabarets that have thrived for years. Typically, these feature singers of Broadway tunes and "art" songs, backed by two to five musicians. Variations include small revues or playlets or comedians. In any case, expect cover and minimum charges and no less than middling-high meal prices. Our suggestions:

THE BALLROOM
253 W 28th St. (off 8th Ave.), NY 10001
☎244-3005. Map **5P3** *(sometimes) AE VISA Closed Mon.*
With a tapas bar in front and a restaurant-cabaret in back, an entire cocktail-to-nightcap experience is possible at The Ballroom. Art singers (Karen Akers and Ingrid Caven, for two) are much in evidence, but nostalgia sells, too (Blossom Dearie is a favorite). The singers are accompanied by four or five instrumentalists and on occasion a couple of backup vocalists. On occasion, big bands of 12 to 20 pieces are booked for dancing. Shows are usually staged at 9 and 11pm. (See also EATING AND DRINKING.)

LE BAR BAT
311 W 57th St. (between 8th and 9th Aves.), NY 10019. Map **5N3** *AE VISA Open daily.*
It's a joke, right? Surely no one is serious about this goofy admixture of Polynesia stirred together with skewed visions of an ersatz Indonesia and a departed French Southeast Asia. These several levels are hung with beaded curtains and fake bats with thyroid problems, among many odd details. They are just barely a match for a fun-loving crowd that can get just as bizarre as the surroundings. The food — satays and spring rolls and fried squid and such — is just as gaily confused, some of it good, some not, and no way to predict which. Both bar and dance floor are routinely packed. Leave solemnity at the door.

BARRYMORE'S HIDEAWAY
32 W 37th St. (6th Ave.), NY 10016
☎947-8940. Map **604** *AE VISA Closed Sun.*
Actor John Barrymore lived in this building, explaining the name but not the entertainment. It is handy for theater-goers, before or after the curtains, and there is live music for dancing six nights a week. In winter, fires crackle in the working fireplaces.

BLUE ANGEL
323 W 44th St. (between 8th and 9th Aves.), NY 10036 ☎262-3333. Map **503** *AE VISA Closed Mon.*
For a time, this club-theater presented a fanciful imitation of a Parisian-style show. At this writing, it is hosting a successful musical comedy about beauty contests called *Pageant*. Judges are selected from the audience, assuring a different outcome every night. Evening shows are supplemented by Wednesday and Saturday matinees. A week hence, who knows? Next door is **The Nile** *(327 W 44th St. ☎262-1111)*, which features belly dancers and suspect Middle Eastern food.

CAFÉ CARLYLE
The Carlyle Hotel, Madison Ave. and 76th St., NY 10021 ☎744-1600. Map **8L4**

↑ 🖽 🔲 🔲 🔳 *Closed Sun, Mon.*

Bobby Short has reigned in this warm room for over 25 years. That used to mean he was at the piano and in full silky voice about eight months a year. These days, he's usually around only in May, June, November and December. An eternal favorite with the older strata of local society and the Establishment, his métier is the show tunes of Cole Porter, Rodgers and Hart, and George Gershwin. His renditions of songs obscure and celebrated are as smooth as hot butter on glass. You will pay dearly to hear them. When he is away, performers of similar stature sit in. Among them have been the Modern Jazz Quartet, pianist George Shearing, Eartha Kitt, and singer Dixie Carter, who is better-known as a star of the television sitcom, *Designing Women.*

CAFÉ SOCIETY

915 Broadway (21st St.), NY 10003
☎529-8282. Map 6Q4 ⇛ ↑ ⩔ 🖽 🔲 🔳
Closed Sun.

The name of this club is a reference to the fabled style-setters of the 1930s and 1940s, and the stunning Art Deco interior certainly recalls the era that was immortalized by scores of Hollywood musicals. The Swing Fever Orchestra plays for dancing on Monday and Tuesday, jazz or blues bands perform on Wednesday, impersonators shoot for laughs Thursday, and a disc jockey is on duty Friday and Saturday.

CHIPPENDALES

1110 1st Ave. (61st St.), NY 10021 ☎935-6060. Map 6N5 🖽 ⊠ *Closed Sun-Tues.*

It's only fair: at this "Ladies Only" show, women get to ogle muscular young waiters without shirts, and equally endowed colleagues who take off nearly all their clothes to the accompaniment of thumping music. The male strippers have set routines — cowboy, motorcycle cop, Zorro, whatever — just like their female counterparts. The more daring members of the squealing audience stuff ten-dollar bills into the G-strings of the dancers in expectation of a kiss and an overt squeeze of glistening flesh. Alien males are permitted to enter after 10.30pm.

CLUB 53

New York Hilton, 53rd St. and 6th Ave., NY 10019 ☎261-5853. Map 6N4 ⩔ 🖽 🔲
🔲 🔳 *Closed Sun, Mon.*

Singers on the lofty order of Barbara Cook helped inaugurate this new cabaret room at the Hilton Hotel. How it will evolve is not yet possible to predict. Shows are at 8.45 and 10.45pm.

COUNTRY CLUB

210 E 86th St. (3rd Ave.), NY 10028
☎879-8400. Map 8L5 ⇛ ▢ ⩔ ↑ ⩔ 🖽
🔲 🔲 🔳 *Closed Sun.*

Still another dine-and-dance palace evoking the years of the last good war, this one uses trompe l'oeil paintings of palm trees and a moonlit ocean to set the mood. A striped awning stretches over the bar, which contains a milling crowd of post-college-age men. Music is provided by a game little band. On Wednesday at 10pm there is a cabaret in another room, but go on Friday or Saturday or risk being very lonely.

DUPLEX

61 Christopher St. (7th Ave. S), NY 10014
☎255-5438. Map 3R3 ⩔ ↑ *revue. No cards. Open nightly.*

Cabaret and individual music and comedy acts have been staged at Duplex for more than 20 years. At its old Grove St. location, a couple of blocks away, it was the testing ground for many performers who went on to high-profile careers, including Woody Allen and Rodney Dangerfield. It continues that function, despite the unpredictability of such enterprises. Depending upon the week, the season and the whims of management, any given night might see improvisations and sketches, magicians, jazz combos, revues, singers. A piano bar with an open mike is downstairs, the cabaret one flight up.

EIGHTY EIGHTS

228 W 10th St. (between Bleecker and Hudson Sts.), NY 10012 ☎924-0088.
Map 3R3 ⇛ ⩔ ↑ No cards. Open nightly.

The upstairs cabaret showcases comedians, singers, and revues, with a different act every night. Showtimes are 8 and 10.30pm Sunday to Thursday, 8.30 and 11pm Friday and Saturday. Downstairs is a piano bar, with the inevitable audience participation.

55 GROVE STREET
55 Grove St. (Bleecker St.), NY 10014
☎366-5438. *Map 3R3* ☒ ♪ *No cards.*
Closed Mon-Wed.
Parodists, singers, comics, musical revues and comedies take the floor in the upstairs cabaret.

JEWEL BOX LOUNGE
323 W 44th St. (between 8th and 9th Aves.), NY 10036 ☎262-3333. *Map 503*
☒ ▣ ▣ ▣ ▥ *Closed Mon.*
It first gained attention with "The Fabulous Bud E. Luv," a parodist of the oilier breed of lounge singer. Its future direction is uncertain at this writing, so check the publications mentioned above.

LAURA BELLE
120 W 43rd St. (6th Ave.), NY 10036
☎819-1000. *Map 503* ▤ ▭ ☒ ♪ ☒ ▣
▣ ▣ ▥ *Closed Sun-Tues.*
The Rainbow Room's nearest competition, this does about all it can without being blessed with an authentic Art Deco aerie. It had a good start, however, with an ornate old midtown movie palace and the owner and chef of the heralded RIVER CAFÉ (SEE RESTAURANTS) at the controls. What was the orchestra level is now multi-tiered, with tables and booths around a large dance floor. There is lavish use of marble and velvet and chandeliers overhead. With a 10-piece band as inspiration, there are people twirling around the floor who actually know their ballroom dancing. (The band isn't on duty every night, but a skilled deejay spins Glenn Miller and Tommy Dorsey records when they aren't. Ask when reserving.)

MICHAEL'S PUB
211 E 55th St. (near 3rd Ave.), NY 10022
☎758-2272. *Map 6N5* ☒ ▤ ♪ ▣ ▣ ▣
▥ *Closed Sun.*

In this shadowy chain of rooms, the varied offerings include such comedians as Joan Rivers and Sid Caesar, singers as different as Anita O'Day and Vic Damone, and combos that often favor the swing era. Early in the week, the program shifts to traditional jazz — Dixie, blues, ragtime. Woody Allen is known to sit in on Mondays at the clarinet when he's in the mood. Music starts at 9.30pm.

THE OAK ROOM
Algonquin Hotel, 59 W 44th St. (near 6th Ave.), NY 10036 ☎840-6800. *Map 604*
☒ ▤ ▣ ♪ ▣ ▣ ▥ *Closed Sun, Mon.*
In a renewed tradition, this room in the venerable hotel favored by British actors and Manhattan literati features cabaret singers, usually accompanied only by a piano, such as the ageless Julie Wilson and newcomer Mary Clere Haran, who construct eclectic programs by Sondheim, Kern and other Broadway composers. Nightly shows are usually at 9.30pm Tuesday to Thursday and 9.30 and 11.30pm Friday and Saturday, but scheduling may be adjusted to accommodate performers and the season. Dinners are offhandedly served and, while better prepared than in recent years, not yet likely to distract from the music, which is customarily very engrossing for fans of the genre.

RAINBOW!
30 Rockefeller Plaza (GE Building), NY 10017 ☎632-5100. *Map 604* ▤ △ ▭
☒ ▤ ♪ ▾ ▣ *Rainbow Room closed Sun, Mon.*
The glamor has returned with a vengeance to what was once the premier supper club in Manhattan. Two years and $25 million in renovations were worth it. The famous Art Deco extravaganza **The Rainbow Room**, at the top of the GE Building, once again conjures images of Fred Astaire and Ginger Rogers whirling across the revolving dance floor, beneath hundreds of pinlights. From 7.30pm onward, there is continuous music from the 12-piece dance band, which shares the stand with a similar group that swings to a Latin beat.

Even the food is good, although expensive. (A Sunday *prix-fixe* meal, available from noon to 9pm, takes out some of the sting, and there is a teadance from 4-7pm.) The cover charge is higher on Friday and Saturday. Another new feature is the transformation of the once ordinary bar-lounge. Called the **Rainbow Promenade**, its floor was raised 16 inches (40cm) and the walls opened in banks of glass to take maximum advantage of the most stunning vista in New York. As a bonus, they serve delectable "little meals" that are the ideal pre-theater snack: grilled shrimp, Cajun sausage and three types of caviar are some of the dishes likely to be encountered. Even by itself, the Promenade can be considered as being on a par with the METROPOLITAN MUSEUM OF ART as a "must see" destination in New York.

In another part of the complex is a small supper club with slightly lower tariffs — **Rainbow & Stars** — which offers intimate cabaret entertainment. Tony Bennett was the opening act, but not all performers are of that magnitude. Nostalgia is an apparent factor in the selection here, with the likes of the McGuire Sisters and Rosemary Clooney figuring highly on the bill. Sunday nights at 7 and 9.30 are set aside for more casual cabaret and revues. Men are required to wear a jacket and tie in all areas of the club. Reservations are essential in the main room and in the cabaret.

REX
579 6th Ave. (between 16th and 17th Sts.), NY 10011 ☎741-0080. Map 6Q4 ▬ ▭ ♈ ♫ ➍ 🖭 ➍ 🖭 *Closed Sun, Mon.*
Chelsea is host to dozens of discos and clubs, a subject of some concern to those residents who like to sleep nights. Rex doesn't help them. Recorded music is the background at dinner, with a live band at 11.30 (or when they get around to it.) A young crowd prevails, younger still upstairs in the disco. The food is uneven, due in part to frequent changes in the kitchen, but it is better than it needs to be.

RUSSIAN TEA ROOM
150 W 57th St. (near 7th Ave.), NY 10019 ☎265-0947. Map 5N3 ♈ ▬ ♫ 🖭 ➍ 🖭 🖭 *Open daily.*
Cabaret is a relatively recent innovation at this famous celebrity hangout. So far, performances are only Sunday at 8pm (and, on demand, 10.30) and the first Monday night of each month. Sometimes, comedians are featured, but individual singers and vocal groups prevail.

THE SOHO SUPPER CLUB
492 Broome St. (West Broadway), NY 10012 ☎966-3371. Map 3S4 ▬ ▭ ♈ ♫ ♩ 🖭 ➍ 🖭 🖭 *Closed Sun-Tues.*
A recent attempt to cash in on the current supper club craze, this is at the hub of the SoHo restaurant wheel. Music from the '30s and '40s is played by trios and quartets early in the week, with vocal groups and swing bands at week ends. Food is "old-fashioned Italian," not necessarily a recommendation.

SOUNDS OF BRAZIL
204 Varick St. (Houston St.), NY 10014 ☎307-7171. Map 3S3 ▬ ♩ ♫ 🖭 🖭 *Closed Mon, Tues.*
Familiarly known as "S.O.B.," this colorful and persistently lively club is known more for its Latin American and African dance music than for the merely serviceable Brazilian food. It is frequented by a buoyant cosmopolitan crowd that is not dismayed by the offhanded decor, largely made up of masks and hanging gourds. Dinner is served from 7pm, and the admission charge is lower if you eat there. Shows, mostly of salsa and Afro-jazz, are at 8 and 11pm. Singer Astrud Gilberto is typical of the better-known attractions. Friday and Saturday are the big nights.

STEVE McGRAW'S
158 W 72nd St. (near Broadway), NY 10023 ☎595-7400. Map 7M3 ▬ ▭ ♈ ♩ 🖭 ➍ 🖭 🖭 *Closed Mon.*
Home to one long-running cabaret play, *Forever Plaid*, this popular West Side club also makes room for short-term revues and musical groups. Two shows some nights: call ahead.

STRINGFELLOWS
35 E 21st St. (Park Ave. S), NY 10010
☎254-2444. Map 6Q4 ⇥ 𝖄 🆎 💲 💳
💳 ⊠ *Open nightly.*

This started life as an exclusive disco modeled after a London establishment with the same name. Things change, as former patrons will be startled to learn. Now, it is a leader in a thriving sub-category of the nightclub business — the elegant strip club. The hope is to introduce to these shores a tastefully sexy show along the lines of the Paris *Lido*. The women, who peel down to G-strings and high heels, are uncommonly attractive, and they dance by the dozen. The overwhelmingly male (need it be said) audience dresses in suits and ties. They come for the "gourmet" prime rib and seafood dinners, of course. Between shows, the women circulate among the audience, offering up-close table or "lap" dancing. Tips are tucked into garters. The promoters would have us believe that this is an ideal setting for business meetings.

SUPPER CLUB
240 W 47th St. (near Times Square), NY 10036 ☎921-1940. Map 503 ⇥ 🗀 ▪
𝖄 🍴 ⅊ 🆎 💲 💳 💳 *Closed Sun, Mon.*

Big, it certainly is, with seating for 400 in acres of cobalt-blue paint with white trim and voluminous swags of crimson velvet to fill the vastness. Loud, too, with a 10-instrument band complete with singer, alternating with variety

acts. Old-time LA is the look, the Cocoanut Grove before the fire, maybe. Fortunately, the food is better than that implies, if one enters with the knowledge that no place this large can pretend to be the second coming of *Lutèce*. In its early days, a fair number of middle-aged celebs made the scene here. Maybe they still do. Go late at night and late in the week.

TATOU
151 E 50th St. (between Lexington and 3rd Aves.), NY 10017 ☎753-1144. Map 604 ⇥ 🗀 𝖄 🍴 ⅊ 🆎 💲 💳 💳 *Closed Sun.*

The theater this once was brings with it a fitting cachet — Edith Piaf and Desi Arnez once performed here. It provides a gratifying impression of plush decadence, with velvet swags, carved moldings, spinning mirrored balls, and faded tones of deep peach and tan. Men of a certain age almost feel obliged to drink champagne out of a high-heeled pump. On stage, starting about 8.30pm, easy-on-the-ear jazz combos and Ella Fitzgerald clones perform through the dinner hour. The food is quite respectable, the main courses in servings large enough to make appetizers unnecessary. Service is friendly, if harried. At 11pm, tables are pushed aside and a deejay plays records for dancing. On Sunday, there is a gospel brunch. Now if only the patrons were as stylish as the surroundings . . .

COMEDY AND MAGIC

As an alternative to cabaret or a show, try stand-up comedy. Its most typical manifestation is in the form of showcase clubs, in which parades of would-be comics are given opportunities to test their material before live audiences. Should you attend, don't sit near the stage unless you are prepared to be the object of the performers' jibes. Their language, furthermore, is often scatological. Non-Americans and even non-New Yorkers are apt to find many references obscure.

CAROLINE'S COMEDY CLUB
1626 Broadway (49th St.), NY 10019
☎757-4100. Map 503 𝖄 ⇥ 🎵 🆎 💲
💳 💳 *Closed Mon, Tues.*

This new 275-seat venue on Times

Square is the third for the now-venerable comedy emporium, but selectivity is still the rule. Most of the performers on the bill here are seasoned professionals who have already garnered at least a measure of journalistic or television attention. Since the club's policy is to have just one opening act followed by a headliner, they are given time to develop their material, without the pressure of lines of novice comedians standing anxiously about waiting for their turns. The surroundings are downright opulent, by comparison with others of the breed.

CATCH A RISING STAR

1487 1st Ave. (77th St.), NY 10028 ☎*794-1906. Map 8L5* 🔲 ⚲ 🆎 🆑 *Open nightly.*
Continuous streams of comedians and other entertainers so anxious to perform that they line up every week for auditions. Two masters of ceremonies keep the pace brisk. Some of the performers have already done the late-night TV talk show circuit, but most are unpaid unknowns. Much of their humor is ethnic, very local in origin, and often mystifying to outlanders.

CHICAGO CITY LIMITS

351 E 74th St. (2nd Ave.), NY 10028 ☎*772-8707. Map 8M5* 🍸 🔲 🆑 🎟 *Closed Sun-Tues.*
Improvisational comedy has been associated for decades with the Second City (Chicago). This troupe takes suggestions from the audience for its sketches, some of which are hysterical, some of which fall flat, as is only to be expected. Two shows Friday and Saturday.

COMEDY CELLAR

117 MacDougal St. (near Bleecker St.), NY 10012 ☎*254-3630. Map 3R4* 🔲 ⚲ 🆎 🆑 🎟 *Open nightly.*
This is one of a number of showcase clubs where young comedians can try out their material on a live audience and pray that a producer will be sitting there and be impressed. A few of them actually make it. It is best to arrive early, as performances start around 9.30pm. It is under the **Olive Tree Café**, in the middle of Greenwich Village.

COMIC STRIP

1568 2nd Ave. (81st St.), NY 10028 ☎*861-9386. Map 8L5* 🔲 ⚲ 🆎 🆑 🆑

🎟 *Open nightly.*
One of the younger comedy showcases, with most of the qualities of the others. The emphasis is on fledgling comics, as many as fourteen per night, each doing about ten minutes of material. There are more misses than hits, but that's the nature of the game. Shows begin about 9pm, twice on Friday and Saturday. Sometimes, they bring on comedy revues.

DANGERFIELD'S

1118 1st Ave. (near 61st St.), NY 10021 ☎*593-1650. Map 6N5* 🔲 🆎 🆑 🆑 🎟 *Open nightly.*
Stand-up comic Rodney Dangerfield grew weary of life on the nightclub circuit and decided to open his own place. In the twenty-odd years since doing so, he became popular in the movies and on television, so he almost never works on this stage. Able professional comedians do that, up to eight of them every night. They are typically of the middlebrow Las Vegas stripe. Sometimes, guest comics with bigger names put in surprise turns. There are two shows on Friday, three on Saturday night. On Sunday at 8.45pm, the stage is given to aspiring talents, some them funny.

THE IMPROVISATION

358 W 44th St. (near 9th Ave.), NY 10036 ☎*765-8268. Map 503* 🔲 ⚲ 🆎 *Open nightly.*
The first of the showcase (read "tryout") clubs, and therefore able to boast the longest list of alumni who have gone on to have successful careers as comics and singers. Most of those who now appear are professionals, some of them familiar from TV gigs. The by-play between performers and hecklers can get vicious at times, and it is painful to watch obvious failure. But people crowd in to hear the ones who have true promise.

MOSTLY MAGIC

55 Carmine St. (near Bleecker St.), NY 10014 ☎*924-1472. Map 3R3* 🍽 🍸 🔲 🆎 🆑 🎟 *Closed Sun, Mon.*

The magic here is not of the breathless giant-scale variety where elephants are made to disappear and mountains are split asunder. These performers are funny, or at least attempt to be, and laughs are as important to them as gasps at their illusions. Jugglers, comics, and musicians are on hand, too.

Since most of the acts here are essentially visual, visitors who are less than fluent in English will be able to enjoy themselves.

NEW YORK COMEDY CLUB
915 2nd Ave. (between 48th and 49th Sts.), NY 10017 ☎*888-1696. Map* **605** ☰ ℣ ▣ ▦ ▣ ▣ ▦ *Open nightly.*

Among the many comics who file across this stage are always a few who have been seen on television. One show nightly between Sunday and Wednesday, two on Thursday, three Friday and Saturday nights. The food runs to ribs, fried chicken and the like. Prices are relatively low.

STAND UP NEW YORK
236 W 78th St. (near Broadway), NY 10024 ☎*595-0850. Map* **7L2** ▣ ▦ ▣ ▦ *Closed Sun.*

This is a bare-bones operation, with packed tables, straight-backed chairs, exposed pipes and wiring, and a painted brick wall as backdrop for the performers. However, it is the only comedy club on the West Side, and a few of the comics who have appeared here went on to achieve a modicum of success in more prominent arenas of showbiz.

The usual schedule has three or four comedians performing a night, not counting the master of ceremonies. Often, they return as a group to engage in improvisations based upon code words solicited from the audience. On occasion, stars drop in unannounced. One show nightly from Sunday to Thursday, two on Friday, three on Saturday. Pizza and a variety of other light meals are available.

COUNTRY AND WESTERN
New Yorkers, who prefer to think of themselves as worldly, were the last to adopt this otherwise beloved American genre. Responding some years back to a fad fueled by such movies as the 1980s *Urban Cowboy,* they took to wearing snakeskin boots and pearl-button shirts, and supporting radio stations and clubs that specialized in the heartfelt plaints of Waylon Jennings and Willie Nelson. That fixation faded to a flicker, and although there has lately been still another resurgence in national interest, it remains to be fully rekindled in Manhattan.

A few places carry on for diehards. Foot-stompin' and hootin' by transplanted Texans from Houston and Brooklyn sets the walls trembling from 10pm on at the **Rodeo Bar** *(375 3rd Ave.* ☎*683-6500, map* **6** *Q4).* It's open every night, and there's no cover charge. Business is booming and twanging as well at **The Cowgirl Hall of Fame** *(519 Hudson St.* ☎*633-1133).* The margaritas and serviceable Tex-Mex food attract at least as many customers as the music.

The **Cottonwood Café** *(415 Bleecker St.* ☎*924-6271, map* **3** *R3)* is a little ol' chunk of Texas plunked down in Greenwich Village, but is so friendly and relaxed (if sometimes a little rowdy) that even native New Yorkers fit right in. Distinctions blur at **Eagle Tavern** *(355 W 14th St.* ☎*924-0275, map* **5** *Q3),* for there, country is just one element of a musical menu that picks and chooses among many strains, including bluegrass and various folk musics on different nights. It does not take charge/credit cards.

When the Lone Star Café was down in Greenwich Village, it billed itself as "the biggest and best honky-tonk north of Abilene." Now, as the **Lone Star Roadhouse** *(240 W 52nd St.* ☎ *245-2950, map 5 N3),* and moved to larger quarters in the theater district, it has broader tastes in music. Different bands are on every night, playing just about anything that will get toes tapping — blues, gospel, 1950s rock 'n' roll, and, of course, country. Many of the accouterments of the old Lone Star have been salvaged, along with the better-than-average Texas vittles and brews for which it was known. Loyalties of country purists have now been transferred to **O'Lunney's** *(915 2nd Ave.* ☎ *840-6688, map 6 O5),* still a fair approximation of a Waco beer hall (Waco is a small city in Texas, reputed to represent the "real" Texas), and there is music every night. See also POP/FOLK/ROCK.

DANCE CLUBS

Discotheques nearly disappeared after their 1960s heyday, revived and faded in each of the next two decades, and now seem at least as healthy as they ever were. Just take a late-night stroll around what has been called the Chelsea Discoland and see. It has nearly a score of clubs in just a few square blocks, one of which, the **Sound Factory**, has a capacity of 1,350 mostly gay celebrants. Obviously, predictions on the fate of the clubs are difficult to make. Of those that persist, some are cavernous spaces ablaze with multimillion-dollar special effects that would do credit to *Star Wars;* others are simply cafés that shove aside a few tables after the dishes are cleared away. Most are expensive, with admission or cover charges and stiff prices for drinks.

References to "disco music" are met with sneers by habitués, who insist that "disco is dead." Even if it sounds pretty much the same to the unattuned ear, it is now called "house music," or in the case of its more strident, metallic versions, "acid house." To fogeys over 40 this may be a nuance without a difference. Otherwise, old rules apply. It's still difficult to get into the clubs-of-the-moment, with entrance denied or permitted by hard-eyed centurions at the door. Being appropriately bizarre in dress, or rich, or famous, or in the company of a comely young woman, may help. Or not. It is safest to approach with a firm grip on your ego. After all, this is an experience that has caused a new verb to be invented: "to club."

AU BAR
41 E 58th St. (Madison Ave.), NY 10022
☎ *308-9455. Map 6N4* ⇶ ☿ ⊙ ◗ ⋎ 🆎
Open nightly.
Euro-lemmings of the Concorde Set and their North American counterparts, including sizeable numbers of celebrities from both shores, have made this their temporary home. Very dressy, but not all that difficult to gain entrance to, and no more expensive than its competitors. They open at 9pm for dinner and stay up for breakfast around 4am.

THE CHINA CLUB
2130 Broadway (75th St.), NY 10023
☎ *877-1166. Map 7L2* ☿ ◗ ⋔ ⋎ *No cards. Closed Sun.*
With live bands every night but Monday and a growing reputation as a hangout for celebs — wasn't that Michael Douglas? — this important West Side club

might just beat the odds. Soul, blues, and get-down rock 'n' roll are the sounds of choice.

DANCETERIA

29 E 29th St. (between Madison and Park Aves.), NY 10016 ☎*683-1046. Map 5P4* 🎵 ♪ 📶 🏧 💳 🚇 *Closed Sun-Tues.*

Hot one year, closed the next. Now it's open again, with five pounding floors and a different theme every night — fashion parades, models, live bands, deejays or all of the above, and more. Because of its size, it's easier to gain entrance. Those who arrive before midnight will pay a reduced entrance fee and lower prices for drinks. No food.

MARS

28-30 10th Ave. (13th St.), NY 10014 ☎*691-6262. Map 5Q2* ♦ ♪ 🏧 💳 🚇 *Closed Mon-Wed.*

This 5-story warehouse and meat-packing plant at the edge of the Hudson was transmogrified into a club by a man who specializes in this in-bred form of creativity. Its decor, if such it might be called, is comprised primarily of urban refuse — walls of outdated computer chips, vintage TV sets, lava lamps, African masks, and equipment left over from the building's former function. Dressing right is the key to getting in, apparently interpreted by the rope attendants as lots of leather and/or lots of skin. Each floor has different sounds — house music at painful levels, slightly less loud New Wave, Germanic industrial-synth, and, when the rooftop terrace is open in summer, reggae.

PALLADIUM

123 E 14th St. (between 3rd and 4th Ave.), NY 10003 ☎*473-7171. Map 6Q4* ♦ ♪ 🏧 💳 🚇 *Closed Mon, Tues.*

The creators of **Studio 54** roared back after a brief court-induced absence, to set the night ablaze with still another monument to frivolity. Their 7-story phantasmagoria attracted the positive attention of no less a presence than the architecture critic of *The New York Times*. Elements of the rococo theater this once was are augmented with towering sculptural dividers, vast murals and clusters of TV monitors bouncing with the impressionistic imaginings of experimental video artists. Naturally, every member of — or aspirant to — the international glitterati made the scene. It's far less exclusive now, since the management has to fill more than 10,000 square feet of space.

RED ZONE

440 W 54th St. (between 9th and 10th Ave.), NY 10019 ☎*582-2222. Map 5N3* 🍽 ♦ ♪ 🏧 *Closed Sun-Wed.*

Bucking the recent trend toward smaller, more intimate clubs, Red Zone occupies much of a city block, with a claimed 14,000 square feet. on two floors. Every disco-technology of the last 20 years is employed and updated on the ground floor — lasers, smoke machines, big screen projections, strobes — and *42* loudspeakers. Upstairs is calmer, quieter (as these things go), with a restaurant serving trendy eats. Flamboyant gays, S&M studded leather fans and drag queens constitute much of the crowd, but suits are in evidence and the crowd has taken on a Latino flavor. Have dinner and they will waive the cover charge.

ROSELAND

239 W 52nd St. (near Broadway), NY 10019 ☎*247-0200. Map 5N3* 🍽 🎵 ♪ ♪ 🏧 🚇 *Closed Mon-Wed.*

More than 65 years old and resisting repeated threats to its existence, this grand old ballroom carries on with two orchestras playing 1930s swing and 1940s Latin American rhythms from 2.30 in the afternoon until 11pm Thursday to Sunday. All ages waltz or samba with each other or with professional dance teachers. It has a huge buffet-style restaurant.

ROXY

515 W 18th St. (near 10th Ave.), NY 10011 ☎*627-0404. Map 5Q2* ✡ ♦ 🎵 *No cards. Closed Sun-Tues.*

Step back to the infancy of the twenty-something patrons to find the last (but by no means first) manifestations of this only slightly updated roller-disco. (The skates are of the new-fangled in-line variety.) The space is immense, loud, with regular dancing to house music as well as for skating. Some nights are geared to gays; call for the current schedule. No food. Another of the many Chelsea discos.

Other options

Several clubs have music for dancing on more limited schedules, including these, noted for their torrid salsa beat: **Copacabana** (*10 E 10th St.* ☎ *755-6010, map 3R4*), **Club Broadway** (*Broadway and 96th St.* ☎ *864-7600, map 7K2*), and **El Morocco** (*307 E 54th St.* ☎ *750-1500, map 6N5*). All are open Friday and Saturday, the Copa on Tuesday, as well.

POP/FOLK/ROCK

While most performers in these categories appear in dance clubs and bars of one kind or another, check the publications suggested above for other venues. Or, call any of the following for schedule information:

Paramount at **Madison Square Garden**   7th Ave. and 33rd St. ☎465-6741, map **5**P3

Radio City Music Hall   **6th Ave. and 50th St.** ☎247-4777, map **6**O4

Beacon Theater   **Broadway and 75th St.** ☎496-7070, map **7**L2

Carnegie Hall and its annex **Weill Recital Hall**   7th Ave. and 57th St. ☎247-7800, map **5**N3

Apollo Theater   253 W 125th St. ☎864-0372

Alice Tully Hall   Lincoln Center, Columbus and Amsterdam Aves. ☎875-5050, map **7**M3

Avery Fisher Hall   Lincoln Center, Columbus and Amsterdam Aves. ☎875-5030, map **7**M3

Merkin Concert Hall   129 W 67th St. ☎362-8719, map **7**M3

Joyce Theater   175 8th Ave. ☎242-0800, map **5**Q3

Symphony Space   Broadway and 95th St. ☎864-5400, map **7**K2

Town Hall   123 W 43rd St. ☎840-2824, map **5**O3

92nd St. Y   92nd St. and Lexington Ave. ☎996-1100, map **8**K4

Some of the clubs suggested below have survived decades of changing fashions, but many opened yesterday and will close tomorrow. Always call ahead to learn of scheduled performers, prices, dress code, and present policies.

See also COUNTRY AND WESTERN and CABARETS AND SUPPER CLUBS.

THE BACK FENCE

155 Bleecker St. (Thompson St.), NY 10012 ☎*475-9221. Map 3R4* ☜ ♩ *Open daily.*

A Greenwich Village haunt of more than 40 years standing, it's just the place to recapture whichever segment of that period constituted one's youth. The milling, happy, noisy participants in that quest are suburbanites sliding into their middle years, ageing hippies or their latter-day reincarnations, and graduate students and faculty from nearby New York University. Performers are part of the same spectrum, re-creating golden rock-and-roll oldies and folkie laments from the halcyon days of social protest and flower power.

A few are known to suggest that songs have been written since 1970, but not often. Dress is very casual. There is a two-drink minimum, but bar prices are inexpensive.

THE BITTER END
149 Bleecker St. (near La Guardia Pl.), NY 10012 ☎673-7030. Map 3R4 🞔 🎵 ⅋ *Open daily.*
Since the 1960s, when it showcased Bob Dylan and Joni Mitchell, this has been one of the most influential rooms in New York. It is still snug and plain, but with an unusually good sound system and acoustics. Genres represented run from folk to jazz to rock and their subspecies. Shows are usually at 9pm and midnight.

BOTTOM LINE
15 W 4th St. (near Washington Sq.), NY 10003 ☎228-7880. Map 3R4 🞔 🎵 *Open nightly. No cards.*
Lines form days in advance for tickets to the celebrated acts more likely to appear here than at any other club in the city, those on the order of Lyle Lovett and Charlie Pride. (Not the *really* big names, though, who appear only at the largest theaters and arenas.) One-night stands are the rule for a catholic schedule of highly-regarded performers, leavened with groups judged to be on the way up. Bruce Springsteen and Stevie Wonder played here in their salad days. Any musical persuasion might show up — bluegrass, New Wave, folk, blues, jazz, pop.

CBGB
315 Bowery (Bleecker St.), NY 10012 ☎982-4052. Map 3R4 🍸 🎵 *Open nightly.*
Once the home of imported British punk, this grungy but unintimidating ex-garage now promotes what might be called the second generation of the New Wave, known by such other labels as "alternative" or "gothic" rock. Sometimes, famous alumni return — David Byrne has been one — but most acts are known only to serious fans of this kind of music. For those over 30, a visit now qualifies as a nostalgia trip.

DELTA 88
332 8th Ave. (26th St.), NY 10001 ☎924-3499. Map 5P3 🞔 🎵 ⬛ ⬛ *Open nightly.*
Gustatory sustenance is middling soul food and icy beer, served until midnight or later, and at an all-you-can-eat Sunday evening buffet. Nourishment for the spirit are groups — changing every night — who give their all to gospel, rhythm 'n' blues standards, and occasional butt-kickin' rockabilly.

LIMELIGHT
47 W 20th St. (5th Ave.), NY 10011 ☎807-7850. Map 6Q4 ⬤ ⬛ *Open nightly.*
Years ago, this was the hottest club in town for the usual 6 months. Those days are long past, but the club has managed to survive both bankruptcy and passing fancy. Call ahead to make sure it's still in operation, then go to see what enthralled the night people for so long. It's a converted church, stained-glass windows intact, with seating in side chapels and on upholstered pews. Candles and lasers provide illumination. The androgynous models and celebrities have all but disappeared, but at least mere mortals can get inside the doors. Being shock-proof helps — some strange things go on in all those nooks and crannies.

MANNY'S CAR WASH
1558 3rd Ave. (between 87th and 88th Sts.), NY 10028 ☎369-2583. Map 8K5 🍸 🞔 🎵 ⅋ ⬛ *Open nightly.*
Maybe they actually did wash cars here once, but now they couldn't fit a Matchbox truck inside. It is shoulder-to-shoulder and belly-to-back, which makes for intriguing conversational possibilities. At the far end of the room, beyond the postage stamp dance floor, good-to-super blues bands howl at the night. They don't seem to make their listeners too mournful, though. The music starts at 9pm, half an hour earlier on Sunday.

THE RITZ
254 W 54th St. (Broadway), NY 10010 ☎541-8900. Map 3R4 🞔 🎵 ⅋ *Open nightly. No cards.*

The management cares how their big rock palace looks as well as sounds — it's a restored rococo opera house — but it's uncertain whether the young crowd notices. Some are skinheads, some sport chains and leather, and many are teenagers from suburban fringes trying hard to look *bad*. Although this is primarily a concert venue, serious slam-dancing sometimes erupts, to New Wave, white rap, and classic and underground rock. International bands and performers can be as well-known as Lionel Richie and Iron Maiden , or as obscure as Afghan Whigs and Cleavage. Anyone whose complexion has cleared up will feel like an antique. Kids who can pass for 16 will love it. Seats can be reserved in the balcony, only. No food, no cards, and steep prices for watery drinks.

ROCK 'N' ROLL CAFÉ

149 Bleecker St. (Thompson St.), NY 10012 ☎*677-7630. Map 3R4* ⛾ 🛋 🎴 🎴 *Open nightly.*

Rock of the 60s, 70s, and 80s is played here, but not by the original bands. "Tributes" are the thing, to Springsteen, Led Zeppelin, AC/DC, Van Halen, and so forth, by bands calling themselves things like Mentally Bankrupt and The Great Red Shark. Scruffy, fun bar on a scruffy, fun street in The Village, next to the *Bitter End*.

SWEETWATER'S

170 Amsterdam Ave. (68th St.), NY 10023 ☎*873-4100. Map 7M2* ➡ 🛋 🎴 🎴 🎴

🎴 *Closed Mon.*

This can be just the right place for winding down after a cultural stint at the Lincoln Center. The usual format is a singer backed by a small instrumental group. The thrust is toward a glossy mix of pop, rock and soul, but there is dancing to latin combos Sunday and Wednesday, and Monday is set aside for comedy. Two shows nightly.

TRAMPS

45 W 21st St. (between 5th and 6th Aves.), NY 10010 ☎*727-7788. Map 6Q4* ➡ 🎴 🛋 🎴 🎴 🎴 *Open nightly.*

Tramps has moved to a larger, more comfortable space a few blocks deeper into the Flatiron District, but the music policy is essentially the same. Blues in all its variations is the staple, although jazz, country, zydeco (cajun/creole country music from Louisiana) and experimental rock are all featured from time to time.

WETLANDS

161 Hudson St. (Vestry St.), NY 10013 ☎*966-4225. Map 3S3* ⛾ 🎴 🛋 🎴 🎴 🎴 *Open nightly.*

An ecologically-minded management promotes worthy causes by circulating broadsides and petitions among its patrons. They book music over a wide spectrum to make their points, with any given night showcasing reggae, soul, funk, folk, industrial, hip-hop, and psychedelic rock reminiscent of the Grateful Dead. You can't miss it, just outside the entrance to the Holland Tunnel.

RADIO

Most mid- and higher-priced hotel rooms have AM-FM radios, as do nearly all rental cars. Narrow-format radio stations are the rule, but some employ mixed programming. Since there are over 80 stations to be heard in the metropolitan area, it is useful to know which play what, if only for setting the clock radio. The numbers after each station's call letters below are those to dial on the AM or FM bands.

WABC-AM (770)	Call-in talk shows leaning to the right.
WADO-AM (1280)	Music, talk, and news in Spanish.
WBAI-FM (99.5)	Noncommercial talk, music, with leftist bias.
WEVD-AM (1050)	Talk, nostalgia and Forties band music.
WFAN-AM (660)	Talk and news about sports.

WMCA-AM (570)   Mostly call-in, plus news reports.
WQXR-AM (1560)   Classical music on *New York Times* station.
WQXR-FM (96.3)   Classical music.
WPLJ-FM (95.5)   Top forty popular music.
WOR-AM (710)   Talk and advice, with news, traffic reports.
WPAT-AM (930)   Mostly instrumental sanitized pop.
WPAT-FM (93.1)   More sanitized pop, "easy listening."
WBGO-FM (88.3)   Jazz, usually.
WNEW-AM (1130)   Pop standards of Sinatra stripe.
WNEW-FM (102.7)   Album rock.
WNCN-FM (104.3)   Classical music.
WNYC-AM (820)   News and talk without commercials.
WNYC-FM (93.9)   Commercial-free classical music, some jazz.
WCBS-AM (880)   All news.
WINS-AM (1010)   All news.
WWRV-AM (1330)   Ethnic music, talk.
WWRL-AM (1600)   Gospel music.
WPLR-FM (99.1)   Rock music and comedy tracks.
WNSR-FM (105.1)   Soft pop/rock of the Sixties to the present day.
WYNY-FM (103.5)   Country music.

Shopping

Where to go

All the world's goods pour into Manhattan. There is no material need, and few of the psychic kind, that is not supplied by its shops and stores. Many objects and services are offered at heart-stopping prices, but more often prices are equal to or below those of the countries of origin. From Peruvian folk art to Japanese video recorders, Belgian lace to Colombian emeralds, Florentine leather to Chinese porcelain — if it isn't here, somewhere, it probably isn't worth having. Those who shop as a form of recreation cannot exhaust the possibilities for diversion. Those who regard shopping as a chore can, with prior research, march into a single shop and emerge minutes later with the precise product they require.

At this center of the nation's garment industry, clothing is available in bewildering profusion. Milanese and Parisian couture are represented, of course, often in salons devoted exclusively to the work of a single house. Native designers challenge them on every front, especially in sportswear and ready-to-wear. Part of the success of Calvin Klein, Bill Blass, Geoffrey Beene, Ralph Lauren and Anne Klein is attributable to their willingness to design for broader markets. While custom tailoring is still available, careful sizing in both men's and women's ready-to-wear garments largely eliminates the need. The better shirts, for example, are calibrated in both neck and sleeve size, and dresses are proportioned to body type — petite, junior, misses, women's — as well as size.

Photographic and home electronics equipment is consistently sold below list price. High volume permits this, and heavy competition also requires it. Many camera dealers bypass the US distributors, for example, to purchase directly from Japanese manufacturers, thereby eliminating intermediate price rises.

With more than 90 percent of the nation's publishers quartered here, discounting of new books is widespread, all languages are represented, and rare and out-of-print volumes are quickly located. Specialization reigns, and shops can concentrate exclusively on Marxism, homosexuality, feminism, travel or detective novels. Jewelry and unset gems, musical instruments, kitchenware and fashion accessories are of the highest quality and at accessible prices.

The picture is not entirely blue sky and clear sailing, of course. Objects of substantial age, such as antiques or Oriental carpets, are available in quantity, but are invariably over-priced. Be wary, too, of shops that proclaim in foot-high letters that they are going out of business: some of them have had those signs up for years. Check labels and identifications carefully, especially on watches and electronic equipment. Unknown brands aren't worth the risk, and some are made to look like products of reputable companies, right down to names with only one letter changed. Street vendors peddle scarves, umbrellas, belts, almost anything portable. Their prices are low, but remember that they move about and might not be at the same site tomorrow.

STRATEGIES

Weekday mornings are the best times to shop, lunch hours and Saturdays the worst. The only days on which virtually everything is closed are Thanksgiving *(last Thurs in Nov)*, Christmas and New Year's Day. Other holidays are used as an excuse for sales. Although Sunday is still usually a day off, many large stores now open on Sunday afternoon. As a rule, midtown shops are open from 9.30am or 10am until 6pm, Monday to Saturday, with late closing 8pm or 9pm on Thursday evening.

Elsewhere, the hours reflect the religious convictions or life-styles of the communities. In Bohemian Greenwich Village and SoHo, doors may not open until noon, but close at midnight or later. Jewish-owned businesses of the Lower East Side and elsewhere are closed on Friday afternoons and Saturdays, but are open on Sundays. In the nine-to-five world of the Wall St. area, many shops close on Saturday as well as Sunday.

Sales personnel, being New Yorkers, can be brusque or helpful, irritable or patient. For no obvious reason, assistants in camera stores and luxury clothing emporia are testy and/or indifferent in undue proportions. Generally, however, encounters will be pleasant and informative. While department stores are logical first stops in the quest for two or more unrelated items, they are frequently under-staffed, and the wait can be long at the payment and wrapping counter.

Items of a more specific or unusual nature are more easily found in smaller shops. Their owners, fearing crime, often keep their doors locked, buzzing them open only after making snap judgments of potential clients. On that subject, incidentally, take care never to leave a handbag or wallet on a counter while signing a sales slip or examining goods. They can be snatched in a twinkling.

Charge/credit cards are widely accepted, even in the smallest shops, although a minimum purchase price might be stipulated. Travelers checks are *not* regarded as simply another form of money. Supplementary identification is often required, and checks drawn in another currency are invariably refused. Personal checks from out-of-town banks are not welcomed, but individual managers can sometimes be persuaded to take them, with two or more types of identification, if the customer appears trustworthy.

While diversity prevails, certain streets and neighborhoods have taken on distinct commercial identities, with regard to either cost or similarity of merchandise. Even casual window-shoppers gravitate to the stretch of **5th Ave**. from about 47th St. to 57th St., a half-mile of world-famous clothiers, jewelers, booksellers and purveyors of superior luggage and shoes. The same distinction applies along 57th St., especially between 1st Ave. and 5th Ave. Antique hunters and art lovers will want to explore Madison Ave., from 57th St. to 80th. Tucked between the galleries are scores of boutiques trafficking in leather goods, pet supplies, lingerie, materials for needlework, and clothing geared to expectant mothers, debutantes, urban cowboys and country squires.

Before settling on **Tiffany's** or **Cartier**, stroll both sides of **47th St.** between 5th Ave. and 6th Ave. for a boggling pageant of jewelry and precious stones of every description and price. For art galleries, see A TOUR OF NEW YORK'S GALLERIES on pages 268-71. For discount designer and mass clothing, make the popular pilgrimage to **Orchard St.** on the Lower East Side, but go there *only* on Sunday. For photographic equipment, head for **34th St.** near Herald Sq. or for **Lexington Ave.** between 42nd St. and 52nd St. Crafts and offbeat articles of clothing are apparent on a gallery tour of **SoHo** and along the blocks of **W 4th St.** and **Greenwich Ave.**, just w of 7th Ave. in Greenwich Village. The compilation that follows does no more than sketch the highlights.

Shops are open normal hours (9.30 or 10am-5 or 6pm) unless otherwise stated.

ANTIQUES
If rarity and distinction, not cost, are your criteria, there are dozens of exclusive dealers along 57th St., Madison Ave. and the adjoining blocks. For antique porcelain, silver, jewelry and accessories, look at:

- **A La Vieille Russie**   781 5th Ave. (59th St.) ☎752-1727, map 6N4
- **The Antique Buff**   321 1/2 Bleecker St. (Grove St.) ☎243-7144, map 3R3
- **Chinese Porcelain Company**   822 Madison Ave. (69th St.) ☎628-4101, map 8M4
- **Cobblestones**   314 E 9th St. (2nd Ave.) ☎673-5372, map 4R5
- **Gem Antiques**   1088 Madison Ave. (85th St.) ☎535-7399, map 8L4
- **James Robinson**   12 E 57th St. (near 5th Ave.) ☎752-6166, map 6N4
- **Jean Hoffman/Jane Starr Antiques**   236 E 80th St. ☎535-6930, map 8L5
- **J&P Timepieces**   1057 2nd Ave. (56th St.) ☎249-2600, map 6N5
- **Little Antique Shop**   44 E 11th St. (Broadway) ☎673-5173, map 3R4
- **Maya Schaper Antiques**   862 Lexington Ave. (65th St.) ☎734-0176, map 8M4
- **Sam's Place**   378 Bleecker St. (near Charles St.) ☎633-6791, map 3R3

Fine European and American furniture can be viewed at:
- **Better Times Antiques**   500 Amsterdam Ave. (84th St.) ☎496-9001, map 7L3

- **French & Co.**   17 E 65th St. (near 5th Ave.) ☎535-3330, map **8**M4
- **Kurland-Zabar** 19 E 71st St. (Madison Ave.) ☎517-8576, map **8**M4
- **Old Versailles**   315 E 62nd St. (near Lexington Ave.) ☎421-3663, map **6**N4
- **Gene Tyson**   19 E 69th St. (near 5th Ave.) ☎744-5785, map **8**M4
- **Michael B. Weisbrod**   906 Madison Ave. (73rd St.) ☎734-6350, map **8**M4

Overseas visitors may be more interested in American furnishings, quilts, and folk arts. Among shops focusing on these:

- **American Hurrah**   766 Madison Ave. (67th St.) ☎535-1930, map **8**M4
- **The Gazebo**   127 E 57th St. (near Park Ave.) ☎832-7077, map **6**N4
- **Geoffrey Goodman Antiques**   825 Broadway (13th St.) ☎674-2673, map **3**R4
- **Laura Fisher**   1050 2nd Ave. (near 56th St.) ☎838-2596, map **6**N5
- **Oldies Goldies & Moldies**   1609 2nd Ave. (near 83rd St.) ☎737-3935, map **8**L5
- **Poor Richard's Antiques**   37 W 20th St. (near 5th Ave.) ☎675-6477, map **6**Q4
- **Somethin' Else**   182 9th Ave. (in Chelsea) ☎924-0006, map **5**Q3
- **Speakeasy Antiques**   799 Broadway (11th St.) ☎533-2440, map **3**R4
- **Spirit of America**   269 W 4th St. (in Greenwich Village) ☎255-3255, map **3**R4

The multifloored antique galleries of London and Paris have their counterparts here, too. There can be good buys, somewhat below the stratospheric price ranges of the shops already mentioned. Dealers in silver, enamel, crystal, music boxes, vintage clothing, china, paperweights, brassware and every category of bric-a-brac lease space at:

- **Manhattan Art and Antiques Center**   1050 2nd Ave. (56th St.) ☎355-4400. Map **6**N5. 85 stalls.
- **New York Antique and Flea Market**   145 E 23rd St. (near Lexington Ave.) ☎777-9609. Map **6**Q4. 20 shops.
- **Place des Antiquaires**   125 E 57th St. (near Park Ave.) ☎758-2900. Map **6**N4. Nearly 40 shops.

Antique shows large and small are frequently staged around the city. The most prestigious is the **Winter Antiques Show** at the 7th Regiment Armory *(Park Ave. & 67th St., map 8M4)*, in January. The furniture and objets on display are always beautiful, often unique, and rarely cost less than several thousand dollars.

No collector, serious or casual, should miss **Newel Galleries** *(425 E 53rd St. ☎ 758-1970, map 6N5)*. Its six floors of antiques of every type and period constitute a virtual museum.

AUCTION HOUSES

Auctions are a source of enlightenment and entertainment even for those who have no intention of bidding.

CHRISTIE'S

502 Park Ave. (near 59th St.), NY 10022 ☎*546-1000. Map 6N4.*

Closest in stature to **Sotheby's**, Christie's is also a British house and nearly as comprehensive in its offerings. It has another branch, **Christie's East** at 219 E 67th St. *(*☎*606-0400, map 8M4).*

SOTHEBY'S

1334 York Ave. (72nd St.), NY 10021 ☎*606-7000. Map 8M5.*

This result of a merger of British and American firms continues to hold center stage. They deal in snuff boxes, folk arts, antiquities, Oriental carpets, Impressionist paintings, toys, Judaica, Art Nouveau — everything.

BEAUTY PARLORS AND HAIRDRESSERS

Once the exclusive province of women, both skin-care centers and hairstylists now cater to men as well. The former retain their markedly feminine decor and emphasis, despite the fact that as much as 40 percent of their clientele is male.

Facial treatments typically take an hour to an hour and a half. Inevitably, there are soft-sell efforts by attendants to sign you up for repeat sessions and costly creams and lotions. Advance reservation is essential. Many salons serve both men and women.

- **Elizabeth Arden**   691 5th Ave. (54th St.) ☎407-1000, map 6N4. The one and only. Five packages of services are available. Book at least a week in advance.
- **Michael Kazan**   16 E 55th St. (near 5th Ave.) ☎688-1400, map 6N4
- **Borja and Paul**   805 Madison Ave. (67th St.) ☎734-0477, map 8M4
- **Kenneth**   19 E 54th St. (5th Ave.) ☎752-1800, map 6N4
- **Georgette Klinger**   501 Madison Ave. (52nd St.) ☎838-3200, map 6N4, and 978 Madison Ave. (76th St.) ☎744-6900, map 8L4
- **Lia Schorr**   686 Lexington Ave. ☎486-9670, map 6N4, open Sunday. Half the clients are men.
- **Christine Valmy**   767 5th Ave. (58th St.) ☎752-0303, map 6N4

At the following hairstylists, appointments are not always required, but call ahead for hours and rates.

- **Larry Matthews**   536 Madison Ave. (54th St.) ☎246-6100, map 6N4
- **Nardi**   143 E 57th St. (3rd Ave.) ☎421-4810, map 6N5
- **Vidal Sassoon**   767 5th Ave. (near 58th St.) ☎535-9200, map 6N4

In a category all its own is **Astor Place Hair Designers** *(2 Astor Place, near Broadway* ☎ *475-9854, map3 T4).* It's a haircutting assembly line, with *100* barbers on three floors. They'll do anything for anyone's hair, male or female, including, but not restricted to, shaving a Batman or

Mercedes-Benz logo on the back of heads. Tom Cruise might be in the next chair, and prices are moderate.

BOOKS AND MAGAZINES

At the center of publishing in North America, the city has bookstores to suit every taste. Booklovers may want to coordinate a trip with the "Book County" street fair in mid-September, when publishers set up open-air booths along 5th Ave. from 48th St. to 57th St.

ARCHIVA

944 Madison Ave. (75th St.), 10028 ☎*439-9194. Map 8L4* 🆎 🔘 💳 *Closed Sun.*

Art, architecture, interior design, and landscape books.

BARNES & NOBLE

105 5th Ave. (18th St.), NY 10003 ☎*675-5500. Map 5Q4* 🆎 🔘 💳 *Open daily.*

One of a chain of 12 shops, all in Manhattan, concentrating on recent books at substantial discounts. At most outlets, the selection is limited, but the 5th Ave. and 18th St. location has been called by Guinness the "world's largest bookstore." There are many bargains, with 10 percent off for paperbacks and up to 30 percent off for bestsellers. They sell tapes, records, and magazines, too. The principal uptown branch is at 5th Ave. and 48th St. *(map 6 O4).*

B. DALTON BOOKSELLER

666 5th Ave. (52nd St.), NY 10019 ☎*247-1740. Map 6N4* 🆎 🔘 💳 *Open daily.*

The substantial stocks include more than 300,000 titles on every imaginable subject at this flagship store of a chain of 800 outlets nationwide. They also carry computer software programs. There is an even larger branch at 396 6th Ave. *(* ☎ *674-8780, map 3 R4).*

BOOKS & COMPANY

939 Madison Ave. (75th St.), NY 10028 💳 *Open daily.*

Classic bookstore, with creaking floors, piles of books sitting about in organized disorder, and hardly a bestseller in sight. Occasional poetry readings are another attraction.

DOUBLEDAY

724 5th Ave. (57th St.), NY 10019 ☎*397-0550. Map 6N4* 🆎 🔘 🔘 💳 *Open until midnight (Mon-Sat).*

Large three-level shop. Every category is covered, with a marked emphasis on the performing arts. It sells records, too.

GOTHAM BOOK MART

41 W 47th St. (near 6th Ave.), NY 10036 ·☎*719-4448. Map 6O4* 🆎 🔘 💳 *Closed Sun (usually).*

The founder of this revered bookstore was working in the shop on her 100th birthday, 68 years after she first opened these doors. Frances Steloff has passed on, but the stock remains comprehensive and iconoclastic, with particular strength in poetry and classic and experimental fiction.

HOTALING'S NEWS AGENCY

142 W 42nd St. (bet. 6th & 7th Aves.), NY 10036 ☎*840-1868. Map 5O3. Open daily.*

This newsstand, near Times Square and an X-rated peep show, has been here for almost 90 years. It sells hundreds of newspapers and periodicals from other American cities and foreign countries in uncounted numbers of languages.

MURDER INK

271 W 87th St. (near West End Ave.), NY 10024 ☎*362-8905. Map 7K2* 🔘 💳 *Open daily.*

Deals exclusively in crime mysteries.

THE MYSTERIOUS BOOK SHOP

129 W 56th St. (near 6th Ave.), NY 10019 ☎*765-0900. Map 5N3* 🔘 💳 *Closed Sun.*

Mysteries, as the name implies, with abundant selections from publisher backlists.

NEW YORK BOUND BOOKSHOP
50 Rockefeller Plaza (near 5th Ave.), NY 10019 ☎245-8503. *Map 6N4. Closed Sun.*
Specializing in out-of-print books and recent titles about New York, it also attracts clients for its old prints and for axonometric maps of midtown Manhattan, on which buildings are reproduced right down to the stairs and construction cranes.

PAN AM NEWSTAND
200 Park Ave. (45th St.), NY 10017. Map 6O4. Open daily.
If this shop on the main floor of the Pan Am Building doesn't have the latest copy of every magazine and periodical published in the civilized world, it's not for want of trying. There are more than 2,000 titles here, attesting to the diverse interests of the tens of thousands of readers who pass the shop daily. To find it, take the escalators up from the main hall of Grand Central Terminal and bear right, past the new **Tropica** restaurant.

RAND McNALLY
150 E 52nd St. (near Lexington Ave.), NY 10022 ☎758-7488. *Map 6N4* 🆎 💿 🎴
Maps and atlases, of course, as well as language books, travel guides and videos, and children's games.

RIZZOLI
31 W 57th St. (near 5th Ave.), NY 10019 ☎759-2424. *Map 6N4* 🆎 💿 💿 🎴 *Closed Sun.*
The New York outlet of the prestigious Italian publisher, with books in several European languages, and classical background music in keeping with its studied elegance. There is another branch at 454 West Broadway, in SoHo *(map 3 S4).*

SPRING STREET BOOKS
169 Spring St. (near West Broadway), NY 10013 ☎219-3033. *Map 3S4* 💿 🎴 *Open daily.*
Books and magazines reflecting the interests and tastes of the SoHo surroundings.

STRAND
828 Broadway (12th St.), NY 10003 ☎473-1452. *Map 3R4* 🆎 💿 🎴 *Open daily.*
Shelf after shelf of mostly used books, in a gratifying clutter that ensnares book lovers for hours. Reviewers sell off their advance copies here at discounted prices.

CAMERAS AND ELECTRONICS EQUIPMENT
Cameras and photograpic supplies are here in great profusion, but most of these shops deal in all manner of electronic gadgets — camcorders, cellular phones, computers, stereos, televisions, calculators, fax machines. Sales and discounts are the rule in this enormously competitive field. Check the full-page ads in the Sunday *New York Times* before setting out. Profit margins are slashed to the bone, which makes some floor managers irritable when you inquire if they will match the lower price for the same lens or projector at a shop down the street. Ask anyway. When making a purchase, be certain it is handed over in a sealed factory carton.

Most shops listed below are open seven days a week, and take major charge/credit cards.

BROTHERS
466 Lexington Ave. (45th St.), NY 10017 ☎986-3323. *Map 6O4.*
Some of the sales people come on pretty strong, so don't be rushed into a hasty purchase. Selection is wide; there's another shop at 52nd St. and Lexington Ave. *(map 6 N4).*

CAMERA WORLD
104 W 32nd St. (near 6th Ave.), NY 10001 ☎563-8770. *Map 6P4.*

This shop is nearly as well-stocked as **Willoughby's**, and it holds frequent sales. It makes a point of carrying electrical products in foreign voltages. A branch at 885 6th Ave. *(map 6 P4)* specializes in audio products.

47th STREET PHOTO
67 W 47th St. (near 6th Ave.), NY 10036 ☎260-4410. *Map 6O4*

Everyone was surprised when the owners filed for protection from bankruptcy in 1992, for this always appeared to be a thriving operation. At this writing, it endures, and the selection is still substantial. Arrive knowing exactly what make and model you want, since you'll get little advice, just low prices. The Orthodox Jewish owners close from 2pm Friday until 10am Sunday.

GRAND CENTRAL CAMERA
420 Lexington Ave. (near 44th St.), NY 10017 ☎986-2270. *Map 6O4*.

The personnel here have proved consistently helpful, and prices are good for laptops and fax machines, point-and-shoot cameras and personal stereos.

HIRSCH PHOTO
341 Madison Ave. (44th St.), NY 10017 ☎867-9280. *Map 6O4.*

Prides itself on its attentiveness to individual needs.

WILLOUGHBY'S
110 W 32nd St. (near 7th Ave.), NY 10001 ☎564-1600. *Map 5P3.*

Although known primarily as a camera shop, Willoughby's has substantial inventories of computers and other electronic appliances. They accept trade-ins and telephone orders, and members of the staff speak several languages.

THE WIZ
12 W 45th St. (near 5th Ave.), NY 10017 ☎302-2000. *Map 6O4.*

No doubt aided by the demise of Newmark & Lewis, its similar multi-outlet rival, The Wiz continues to expand, with almost 40 branches in the metropolitan area. Their stock is substantial, including both office and home electronics of every kind. They guarantee to undercut their competitors' printed prices.

CRAFTS

A city of immigrants and compulsive travelers is compelled to gather and display the treasures of its homelands and voyages. Folk arts of many countries are available for purchase, but given the prevailing demographics, they tend to be African or Latin American in origin. Here is a short list:

- **Craft Caravan**   63 Greene St. (near Spring St.) ☎431-6669, map 3S4. African masks, baskets, artifacts, fabrics, stools.
- **Luna d'Oro**   66 Greene St. (near Spring St.) ☎925-8225, map 3S4. Molas from Panama, milagros from Mexico, crafts from 15 countries.
- **Pan American Phoenix**   Citicorp Center, 153 E 53rd St. (Lexington Ave.) ☎355-0590, map 6N4. A wealth of Mexican handicrafts, especially fabrics and garments.
- **Mythology**   370 Columbus Ave. (near 77th St.) ☎874-0774, map 7L3. Mostly Mexican crafts, at fair prices.
- **Objects of Bright Pride**   455A Columbus Ave. (near 81st St.) ☎721-454579, map 7L3. Carvings and jewelry of Eskimos and Pacific Northwest Indians. Closed Wednesday.

And, make a point of passing the sidewalk merchants who display their wares on the N side of 53rd St., near 6th Ave., not far from the AMERICAN CRAFT MUSEUM. While there can be no guarantee of authenticity, many of their African tribal masks and carvings are quite handsome.

DEPARTMENT STORES

The departure of Alexander's and Gimbel's from the local retail scene, and the fiscal difficulties of **Macy's** and **Bloomingdale's**, have some savants predicting the end of the department store era. Perhaps, but the survivors are still good places to reconnoiter pricesa and the availability of desired products and services. Some are open Sunday afternoons.

ABRAHAM & STRAUSS

420 Fulton St. (Hoyt St.), Brooklyn 10001
☎ *718-875-7200. Map 4V7.*

Known as "A&S," this is Brooklyn's largest and best-stocked department store. Although somewhat low profile outside its home borough, it is comparable to **Macy's** in the breadth and price range of its offerings. That competition has grown sharper with the new eight-floor branch near Herald Sq. *(map 6P4).*

BARNEY'S

7th Ave. and 17th St., NY 10011 ☎ *929-9000. Map 5Q3* 📼 🆎 💿 *Open Sun.*

Within the memory of many of its customers, Barney's was an out-of-the-way discount house that drew them to inconvenient Chelsea with promises of bargains. Those low-priced days are gone, but now men and women of every shape, height and girth come for the unrivaled range of garments in all sizes and fashions. They have at their disposal a café in which to ponder over meatloaf and chicken salad whether the Wall St., Rue de Rivoli or Via Condotti look is for them. A midtown branch is due to open in 1993 at 60th St. and Madison Ave. *(map 6N4).*

HENRI BENDEL

10 W 57th St. (near 5th Ave.), NY 10019
☎ *247-1100. Map 6N4* 📼 🆎 💿 📼
Closed Sun.

While it avoids the flashy, Bendel's is at the forefront of fashion trends, at least among department stores. A step inside the door of its new building reveals an atrium several stories high, goods spilling out from what amounts to a vertical mall of boutiques. A peek at size labels reveals that the cautious and/or amply proportioned shopper would best spend time elsewhere. Clothes, stationery, table linens, shoes, cosmetics, and housewares are the main categories.

BERGDORF GOODMAN

754 5th Ave. (57th St.), NY 10022
☎ *752-3000. Map 6N4* 🆎

On what is perhaps the most glamorous corner in New York, Bergdorf's follows through with unrivaled service and products. Furs, lingerie, fragrances, linens are of the highest order. To a degree, the store is shelter to the glossy boutiques of Givenchy, Halston, St-Laurent and their like. Men who can afford the tariffs are drawn to the new annex recently opened just for them across the street. Prices are high at both locations, which shouldn't come as a surprise.

BLOOMINGDALE'S

1000 3rd Ave. (59th St.), NY 10022
☎ *355-5900. Map 6N5* 📼 🆎

Multitudes of New Yorkers and suburbanites slavishly follow the dictates of the great guru Bloomie, denying all the while that their living rooms are replicas of those in the store, that they dress like the models in the newspaper ads, that the food they eat imitates the delights of the gourmet stores on the first floor. They need not be defensive, for they could hardly find a better model to follow. In the evening and on Saturday they are as likely to drop in just to meet people similarly afflicted as to buy anything. A welcome innovation for foreign visitors is the new currency exchange booth, next to the American Express office on the Metro level. Don't miss the 6th floor restaurant, **Le Train Bleu**, a replica of a luxurious dining car.

CURACAO EXPORT

20 W 57th St.(near 5th Ave.), NY 10019
☎ *581-6970. Map 6N4* 🆎 💿 📼

It doesn't really belong in this category, but this is the first stop for in-the-know Europeans seeking a variety of products that are far more expensive back in Milan or Munich. In fact, *only* shoppers with non-US passports can buy here. They are after Levi's jeans and jackets, Ray Ban sunglasses, Nike athletic shoes, Sony radios, Swatch watches, and Timberland shoes (said to routinely outlive their owners.)

LORD & TAYLOR
424 5th Ave. (39th St.), NY 10016 ☎*391-3344. Map 6O4* 🆎 *Closed Sun.*
Whether you want a cashmere sweater or a chair, curtain fabric or a crystal bowl, buy it here and it will remain a classic until its natural demise. That might be later than your own, for Lord & Taylor has been around well over a century, and it has no intention of alienating coming generations. Known mainly for sportswear, it also employs interior decorators to advise on renovations both modest and ambitious. Decisions can be made over soup and salad in one of the store's three cafés.

MACY'S
Broadway and 34th St., NY 10001 ☎*971-6000. Map 6P4* 🆎 *Open also Sun.*
Macy's occupies the area between the bland middle ground and the snappy upper-middle ground represented by **Bloomingdale's**. One of its most admired departments is the repository of kitchenware and gourmet foods called **The Cellar**. The largest store in the world occupies an entire city block, its several floors containing something for everyone, from antiques to puppet shows. Its recent filing for protection from creditors hasn't visibly affected service (which was never all that good anyway) or its wide range of goods and services. There are seven places in which to eat a snack or a full meal.

SAKS FIFTH AVENUE
611 5th Ave. (50th St.), NY 10022 ☎*753-4000. Map 6O4* 📍 🆎 *Closed Sun.*
Scrupulously choreographed and relentlessly edited, Saks contrives to retain its conservative image without descending into dowdiness. Clothes are its strength, from sports to formal wear, as delineated by Bill Blass, Oscar de la Renta and their colleagues — for women, men, teenagers, and children. Eight floors.

FASHION
With ready access to the creations of the famous American designers — Bill Blass, Oscar de la Renta, Donna Karan, Perry Ellis/Marc Jacobs, Anne Klein *et al,* — and most of their European and Japanese compeers, New Yorkers are among the most fashionable of Americans. Whether they choose the near-timeless elegance of garments and accessories purveyed by shops that have been on the scene for a century or more, or the kicky, highly perishable fads of the newest downtown clubs, they set standards of taste for the world.

Some shops thought to have a feminine identity carry men's clothing, as well. Check, also, the department store listings above.

Clothing and shoes for women
Most of the famous American designers choose to make their creations available through the major department stores rather than in their own salons. An exception is Ralph Lauren, who has taken over the impressive Rhinelander mansion on Madison Ave.

EMPORIO ARMANI
110 5th Ave. (16th St.), NY 10011 ☎*727-3240. Map 6Q4* 🆎 💳 💳 *Closed Sun.*
High-end ready-to-wear clothing is moving south, or at least that's the prediction now that Armani has made the jump from the Upper East Side. Both

sexes — and children — are served in this spacious loft building, with suits, sportswear, shirts, and jeans. Prices? Figure the equivalent of two nights in a luxury uptown hotel for a silk blouse. For gear that most regular people can afford, Armani has opened a budget branch in SoHo, **A/X** *(568 Broadway (Prince St)* ☎*431-6000, map 3S4).* Most of the jeans and T-shirts there are under $100.

GALERIES LAFAYETTE

Trump Tower, 725 5th Ave. (56th St.), NY 10022 ☎*355-0022. Map 6N4* AE *Open Sun.*

The opening of this, the first North American branch of the Parisian fashion landmark, burnished the image of the glittery Trump Tower. A number of French designers are represented by the impeccable collection of coats, suits, dresses, lingerie, accessories and shoes.

GUCCI

683 5th Ave. (54th St.), NY 10022 ☎*826-2600. Map 6N4* AE ⬤ ⬤ VISA *Closed Sun.*

Despite the (sadly, not-unwarranted) reputation of the sales staff for sullenness, flocks of moneyed patrons storm these four exclusive floors daily *(not Sun).* They are men and women who admire fine Italian craftsmanship in leather goods — shoes, belts, handbags and luggage — and don't mind wearing someone else's initials: the famed double G.

CHARLES JOURDAN

725 5th Ave. (56th St.), NY 10022 ☎*644-3830. Map 6N4* AE ⬤ ⬤ VISA

Imported shoes of frolicsome panache — wispy sandals, shoes in frothy hues that are lighter than air but remarkably long-lived. There are men's shoes, too, but they are much more traditional. All are expensive, of course, but not unspeakably so.

NORMA KAMALI

11 W 56th St. (5th Ave.), NY 10022 ☎*957-9797. Map 6N4* AE ⬤ VISA

One of the country's hottest designers has herself a 6-story showcase in a grandly refurbished old building just off 5th Ave. She covers the female form from beach to disco, office to dinner party, and throws in equally inventive clothing for children.

POLO/ RALPH LAUREN

867 Madison Ave. (72nd St.), NY 10021 ☎*606-2100. Map 8M4* AE

Make an excuse to visit this stunning four-floor specialty shop even if the price tags make most shoppers blanch. America's most admired designer of the loose, classic look has outfitted the 1895 mansion to reflect every element of his wide-ranging interests. Antique furnishings and accessories are arranged in rooms authentic to the last detail, settings for the maestro's clothing for women. It also stocks items for men and children.

YVES ST-LAURENT/ RIVE GAUCHE

855 Madison Ave. (near 70th St.), NY 10021 ☎*988-3821. Map 8M4* AE ⬤ ⬤ VISA

From the striking front to the metal-and-leather interior, this boutique sizzles with the products of the restless mind of the celebrated French designer. Shirts, trousers, shoes, dresses, suits, belts are at the leading edge of fashion. One pays dearly to participate.

SCREAMING MIMI'S

22 E 4th St. (Lafayette St.), NY 10012 ☎*677-6464. Map 3R4* ⬤ VISA

Everything old is new again. Just for fun, or if you truly want to regress to the Disco Seventies, take this detour off Washington Sq. Here they are: platform shoes, lace-up boots with chunky heels, flared pants, and bric-a-brac that might have furnished a situation comedy of the era.

SUSAN BENNIS/ WARREN EDWARDS

22 W 57th St. (near 5th Ave.), NY 10022 ☎*755-4197. Map 6N4* AE ⬤ VISA

Superb quality pumps and low-heels of impeccable craftsmanship and exquisite materials, mostly imported. And as the billionaire said to the millionaire, if you have to ask the price, you can't afford it.

UNIQUE CLOTHING WAREHOUSE
718 Broadway (Washington Pl.), NY 10003 ☎674-1767. Map *3R4* ⚏ ⚏ ⚏ *Open Sun.*

As an antidote to the jasmine-and-musk air of the 5th Ave. boutiques, or simply because it's Sunday, drop down to Greenwich Village. This repository of rugged working-man's apparel and military uniforms was the first, it is said, to recognize the inherent chic of such things. A few years later, the Parisian and Milanese couturiers were turning out their own versions for the Côte d'Azur. The prices are good, but the quality is variable, so it is wise to choose very carefully.

VALENTINO
823 Madison Ave. (68th St.), NY 10022 ☎744-0200. Map *8N4* ⚏ ⚏ ⚏

The legendary Valentino permits us to gaze on his trend-anticipating lines of dresses, sweaters and separates, and to marvel at fabrics and sartorial details that can be had only at very high prices. Saleswomen speak several European languages.

Clothing for men

Some shops thought to have a feminine identity carry men's clothing, as well, including Armani and Ralph Lauren. Check, also, the department store listing on pages 257-8.

ALAN FLUSSER
14 E 52nd St. (near 5th Ave.), NY 10022 ☎888-7100. Map *6N4* ⚏

Since he outfitted Michael Douglas for his role as an ethics-free financier in the movie, "Wall Street," Flusser has attracted clients from that milieu. They pay substantial sums for the honor, his suits of approximate English cut, but of softer construction. He has other outlets downtown at 50 Trinity Place *(map 1 U4)* and in the District of Columbia.

BANCROFT
363 Madison Ave. (45th St.), NY 10017 ☎687-8650. Map *604* ⚏ ⚏ ⚏

While it sells a complete line of haberdashery, Bancroft may be best known for its wide selections of dress shirts in cottons and blends, and in unusual sizes not usually stocked by other shops. Moderate prices and frequent sales prevail.

BERGDORF GOODMAN MEN
5th Ave. & 58th St., NY 10022 ☎753-7300. Map *6N4* ⚏ ⚏ ⚏

Essentially an annex to the main store (for women) across the street, this doesn't stint on names, either: Armani, Hermès, Turnbull & Asser, and their exclusive compeers.

BROOKS BROTHERS
346 Madison Ave. (44th St.), NY 10017 ☎682-8800. Map *604* ⚏

In an aberrant world, it is comforting to know that there is still Brooks Brothers. Tradition cleaves to its stately spaces. This is the 170-year-old home of the natural-shoulder suit that has long been the preferred wear of American business leaders and those who aspire to succeed them. Their conservative detailing has been altered somewhat in recent years, in deference to current taste and the fashion for physical fitness. But the trenchcoat purchased in 1970 is remarkably similar to the one that was bought yesterday.

CUSTOM SHOP SHIRTMAKERS
555 Lexington Ave. (50th St.), NY 10022 ☎759-7480. Map *604* ⚏ ⚏ ⚏ ⚏

Men of proportions that don't quite fit off-the-shelf shirts — thick neck, short arms; thin neck, long arms — can stop here for made-to-measure cottons and cotton blends that cost not much more than readymades, depending on fabric and collar style. There is a minimum order of four, but first-time customers get a substantial discount. Custommade suits are also available. There are five branches.

THE GAP

145 E 42nd St. (near 3rd Ave.), NY 10017
☎*286-9490. Map 6O4* 🔲 🔳 *Open daily.*
This and several other branches
throughout Manhattan purvey jeans in
every style, color and size — but from
reputable manufacturers, not over-
priced bootleg merchants. The signature Gap pocket T-shirt has become a
fashion statement for both men and
women.

HARRY ROTHMAN

*200 Park Ave. S (near Union Sq.), NY
10010* ☎*777-7400. Map 6Q4* 🔲 🔳
Discounts up to 50 percent on mid-level
suits and furnishings. There is a better
selection of large, tall, and unusual sizes
than is the rule.

PAUL STUART

Madison Ave. and 45th St., NY 10017
☎*682-0320. Map 6O4* 🔳 🔲 🔲 🔳
Closed Sun.
For the mid-Atlantic look, Paul Stuart
has suits and sports jackets in a subdued
palette of checks, herringbones, flan-
nels and twills. The arm-holes are
higher than those of the equally traditional **Brooks Brothers**, the shoulders
are squared, the waists ever-so-slightly
more suppressed. Most are of natural
fibers, but there are some blends. Shirts
come in an unusually broad range of
sizes. There is a small women's department. The prices are high, but not out
of sight.

A. SULKA

430 Park Ave. (57th St.), NY 10022
☎*980-5200. Map 6N4* 🔳 🔲 🔲 🔳
Made-to-measure silk shirts are the ultimate luxury in this exclusive shop, but
there are also suits, coats and accessories of comparably high standard.
Monogrammed handkerchiefs make an
affordable gift; custom cashmere bathrobes do not.

SYM'S

42 Trinity Pl. (near Rector St.), NY 10006
☎*791-1199. Map 1U4.*
One of the more prominent discount
men's shops by virtue of its insistent
advertising, Sym's takes a center path in
fashion and delivers decent value. The
original list price is followed on the tag
with Sym's price. Those willing to
examine carefully three floors of racks
and counters can emerge with twice as
much clothing as the same expenditure
would obtain midtown.

VICTORY SHIRT COMPANY

96 Orchard St. (Broome St.), NY 10002
☎*677-2020. Map 4S5* 🔳 🔲 🔲 🔳
Closed Sat.
This shop is a real boon to the odd-sized
man or woman who doesn't care to pay
for custom tailoring. Victory makes 100-
percent cotton shirts of made-to-
measure quality at ready-made prices.
Some sweaters and ties are available, all
in natural fibers. Telephone orders are
accepted.

FOOD AND KITCHENWARE

New Yorkers have always been interested in food and cooking, if only
to reproduce the cuisines of their homelands. The recent enthusiasm
for gourmet cookery has intensified that concern, and these shops are
booming. Try to avoid Saturdays. Unless otherwise noted, these are all
open seven days a week.

BALDUCCI'S

424 6th Ave. (9th St.), NY 10011 ☎*673-
2600. Map 3R4* 🔳
Enter Balducci's immediately after a
large meal, or your eyes will grow
round as billiard balls and you will be
seized with a compulsion to sweep up

heaps of everything in sight. You will
be in competition with milling throngs
anxious to get their hands on the very
same cheeses, pastries, choice vegetables, thick slabs of prime meats, rin-
glets of homemade sausages, smoked
fish, or lobsters.

BRIDGE KITCHENWARE

214 E 52nd St. (near 2nd Ave.), NY 10022
☎688-4220. Map 6N5 💳 📠 *Closed Sun.*
The shelves are packed with quality
utensils for the serious cook. Pick
through stainless carbon knives by several manufacturers, food processors,
graters, coffee grinders, bowls of steel
and ceramic, copper molds, crystal. The
prices are neither exorbitant nor low:
they are simply fair, which helps make
up for the grumpy sales staff.

CAVIARTERIA

*29 E 60th St. (near Madison Ave.), NY
10022* ☎759-7410. Map 6N4 📧 💳 📠
Closed Sun.
Unprepossessing inside and out, this
small shop is easy to dismiss. But it deals
in the essentials of a calculated seduc-
tion or a dinner designed to impress.
The caviar is Iranian, Russian and
American. The last is an increasingly
successsful undertaking, and at half the
price of the imports. They also stock
smoked salmon and related delicacies,
and enjoy a substantial mail order trade.

DEAN & DELUCA

560 Broadway (Prince St.), NY 10012
☎431-1691. Map 3S4.
Expensive, yes, but not unconscionably
so, and the mark-up is justified merely
by the aroma encountered at the front
door: coffee, freshly baked bread,
cheeses, fresh produce all contribute.
White walls and marble floors are the
minimalist setting for 10,000 square feet
of exotic mushrooms, pâtés, terrines,
produce, cheeses, smoked fish, pastas,
an extraordinary selection of herbs,
honeys and jams. There are also racks
of kitchen utensils, including whisks,
cast-iron pans and oven-usable stone-
ware. Drink it all in with a cappuccino
at the handsome coffee bar near the
front door, perhaps with a fresh muffin
or pastry. Dean & Deluca is an obligatory stop for New York's legion of
foodies.

E.A.T.

1064 Madison Ave. (81st St.), NY 10028
☎772-0022. Map 8M4 📧

Prepared dishes and baked goods are
made on the premises, from sourdough
and raisin bread to pâtés to complete
meals. Teas, jams, salmon and cheeses
are imported. Prices are as eye-popping
as the food.

FAIRWAY

2127 Broadway (near 75th St.), NY 10023
☎595-1888. Map 7L2 💳 📠
Unlike most of the shops on this list,
quality of produce and other items at
Fairway is high, *but* prices are almost
reasonable. Crimson rhubarb is heaped
next to indigo Japanese eggplants, next
to stacks of Portobello and Shitake
mushrooms. Cheeses, pastas, and sausages are excellent. It is open from 7am
until 11pm or midnight, and packed
with shoppers for almost every hour of
that schedule.

GRACE'S MARKETPLACE

3rd Ave. & 71st St., NY 10021 ☎737-
0600. Map 8M5 💳 📠
Upper Eastsiders needn't journey
across Central Park for their approximation of *Zabar's:* here it is, steep prices
and all. Pastries are special, and the air
is filled with seductive aromas from prepared dishes, fresh produce, and
cheeses. Breads come in bewildering
variety, including wholewheat croissants, blueberry scones, eight-grain ba-
guettes, walnut raisin loaves ...

ZABAR'S

2245 Broadway (80th St.), NY 10024
☎787-2000. Map 7L2 📧 💳 📠 *Open
daily, Sat until midnight.*
Balducci's and **Zabar's** are perennial
contenders for the throne of gourmet
stores, but Zabar's may have pulled
ahead by virtue of its second-floor expansion for kitchenware. Absolute
kitchen essentials — fish poachers and
duck presses — take their place among
food mills and copper pots. On the first
floor, cheese, coffee, caviar, smoked
fish, prepared terrines and entrees,
pumpernickel bread, ice cream, coffee
cake, chopped liver, herring, and other
intoxicating sights and aromas battle for
attention.

HOME FURNISHINGS

Assuming that most visitors are reluctant to deal with the purchase and shipping of looming chifferobes and four-poster beds, there are any number of shops selling smaller items that can enhance what they already have at home. Here are a very few, most of them closed on Sunday.

CERAMICA

59 Thompson St. (Spring St.), NY 10012
☎*941-1307. Map 3S4* ▣ ▣
Colorful Mediterranean ceramics in profusion — hand-painted and glazed terracotta jugs and vases and amphoras and bowls — are on offer at good prices. Italian, Portuguese, and Moroccan products dominate.

CONRAN'S HABITAT

Citicorp Center, 53rd St. & Lexington Ave., NY 10022 ☎*371-2225. Map 6N4* ▣
▣ ▣
The British Habitat chain gained much experience in Europe before coming to these shores to promote its founder's vision of the moderately-priced good life. Furniture occupies much of the space, but many smaller, transportable items of similar spirit are available — area rugs, crockery, glassware, and kitchen utensils, among many. There are additional branches at Broadway and 81st St. *(map 7L2)* and at 2 Astor Place, in Greenwich Village *(map3 T4)*.

THE GAZEBO

127 E 57th St. (near Park Ave.), NY 10022
☎*832-7077. Map 6N4* ▣ ▣ ▣
Quilts, handmade and bountiful, are the focus. There are also braided rag rugs and appliquéd curtains and pillow covers.

MAXILLA & MANDIBLE

451-5 Columbus Ave. (81st St.), NY 10024
☎*724-6173. Map 7L3* ▣ ▣
This doesn't quite belong under this heading, but then, it's difficult to fit anywhere. Why? Because what we have on sale here are bones. Skulls, animal and human. Skewered butterflies and beetles. Hippo teeth. Antlers. It sounds grisly, but it is, in fact, fascinating, and, on reflection, beautiful. It occupies an appropriate location, only steps away from the AMERICAN MUSEUM OF NATURAL HISTORY.

PAVILLON CHRISTOFLE

680 Madison Ave. (62nd St.), NY 10021
☎*308-9390. Map 6N4* ▣ ▣ ▣
Silver and crystal are the raison d'être of this Parisian firm, founded in 1830. The designs it sells are exquisite and often highly contemporary, without being at all stuffy. A range of porcelain is also available.

SÉGRIÈS A SOLANÉE

866 Lexington Ave. (65th St.), NY 10021
☎*439-6109. Map 8M4* ▣ ▣ *Closed Sat in summer.*
Glassware, pottery, linens in the style of *haute* Provence. Full dinner services, platters and tureens, quilts, and even a selection of Provençal furniture are on hand.

JEWELRY

From the waiting limousines to the understated window displays and the hushed, almost ecclesiastical interiors, **Cartier, Harry Winston, Tiffany & Co.** and **Van Cleef & Arpels**, the Titans of the retail trade in gold, gems, silver and watches, breathe an ever-tasteful opulence. Dress for the occasion. All of them have a well-crafted trinket or two at relatively modest cost for recipients back home who will be impressed by the name on the gift box.

Department-store marketing techniques are used by **Fortunoff**, and its stock is supplemented with fine jewelry and watches, antique silver and flatware. There are four floors, and prices are reasonable, as these things go.

While all these shops are within a few steps of each other, true comparison shopping is best undertaken along 47th St., between 5th Ave. and 6th Ave. Every imaginable sort of jewelry is on hand in shoulder-to-shoulder (and floor-upon-floor) shops that sell nothing else. Start at the **International Jewelers Exchange**, with its dealers installed in 84 cubicles, then work w along 47th St., crossing to the opposite side and returning E. Prices are often negotiable, so it's best to delay purchase until several trays of the desired object have been examined.

- **Cartier**   5th Ave. and 52nd St.   ☎753-0111, map **6**N4
- **Michael C. Fina**   580 5th Ave. (78th St.)   ☎869-5050, map **8**L4
- **Fortunoff**   681 5th Ave. (near 54th St.)   ☎758-6660, map **6**N4
- **International Jewelers Exchange**   5th Ave. and 47th St. ☎869-1528, map **6**O4
- **Tiffany & Co.**   5th Ave. and 57th St.   ☎755-8000, map **6**N4
- **Van Cleef & Arpels**   5th Ave. and 57th St.   ☎644-9500, map **6**N4
- **Harry Winston**   718 5th Ave. (56th St.)   ☎245-2000, map **6**N4

MUSEUM STORES

Cultural curiosity and the acquisitive impulse are handily combined in the gift and bookstores of all the major museums and most of the smaller ones. While selections naturally reflect the concerns of the museums in which they are located — seafaring motifs at the **South Street Seaport**, folk art at the **Brooklyn Museum** — they interpret their missions with broad strokes. Given their auspices, trashy merchandise rarely slips onto the shelves. For the same reason, expect fair prices but no bargains. See individual entries in SIGHTS AND PLACES OF INTEREST for addresses and telephone numbers.

Predictably, the shop in the **Metropolitan Museum of Art** is largest, with excellent reproductions of many items in the collections, notably jewelry and carvings, as well as art books and illustrated catalogs. The **Museum of the American Indian** has handcrafted "squash-blossom" necklaces, silver belt buckles, "concha" belts, and Navajo rugs. Reproductions of Egyptian jewelry and authentic Latin American ceramics and dolls are the specialty of the BROOKLYN MUSEUM.

Books and posters once dominated at the **Museum of Modern Art**, but its new design shop, on the opposite side of the street from the museum, has a greatly expanded inventory of exquisite glassware, pottery, flatware, cigarette lighters, garden shears and clocks.

At the **Jewish Museum**, even Gentiles are drawn to the brass candlesticks and *menorahs, mezuzah* boxes, and the jewelry. At the **Cooper-Hewitt Museum**, Christmastime brings out the tree ornaments and toys. There are quilts and crafts, antique and contemporary, at the **Museum of American Folk Art**.

Garments of Latin American Indian textiles, exotic jewelry, and stuffed toy animals fill the two shops of the **American Museum of Natural History.**

PHARMACIES

Despite their fanciful European imitations, not all American drugstores resemble supermarkets. Most concentrate on the sale of cosmetics, perfumes, toiletries, assorted sickroom and surgical devices and, of course, prescription and nonprescription medicines. Be sure to bring along your doctor's prescription. Foreign visitors should also bear in mind that certain drugs that can be bought without prescription at home require one here. Two of the oldest pharmacies in New York are **Caswell-Massey** (established 1752) and **Bigelow Pharmacy** (established 1838). The **Duane Reade** chain, with locations all over town, is noted for its discounts.

- **Bigelow Pharmacy**   414 6th Ave. (near 8th St.), NY 10011 ☎533-2700. Map **3**R4. Still in its original quarters, and open every day.
- **Caswell-Massey**   518 Lexington Ave. (near 48th St.), NY 10017 ☎755-2254. Map **6**O4. Closed Sunday. Caswell-Massey blended soaps and colognes for George Washington and Sarah Bernhardt, and its products make good souvenirs.
- **Kaufman Pharmacy**   Lexington Ave. and 50th St., NY 10022 ☎755-2266. Map **6**O4. Open 24 hours a day, seven days a week.

RECORDS AND TAPES

Music is a constant in the city, on streets and in theaters, nightclubs and homes. That is evidenced by the thousands of glassy-eyed residents bobbing to silent rhythms drilled into their heads by earphones from the ubiquitous personal radios. While it can be assumed that the sounds they choose are primarily pop, rock and rap, no musical form is neglected in the shops and megastores that service this insatiable need.

BLEECKER BOB'S GOLDEN OLDIES

118 W 3rd St. (near 6th Ave.), NY 10012
☎*475-9677. Map 3S4* 🔲 🔲 *Open daily.*
This Village institution has enough endearing quirks to amuse any audiophile. It doesn't open until noon, but doesn't close until 1am *(3am Sat, Sun).* The huge inventory concentrates on rock in its many forms, but has recordings of other musical persuasions, too. Head down to Bleecker Bob's if you must have that one hit record by the doo-wop group that disappeared forever in 1956.

HMV MUSIC

72nd & Broadway, NY 10023
☎*721-5900. Map 7M2* 🔲 🔲 🔲 *Open daily until midnight.*
New and large, with three floors of CDs and audio and video cassettes, as well

as a **Ticketmaster** booth for the purchase of tickets to Broadway shows.

SAM GOODY

666 3rd Ave. (E 43rd St.), NY 10017
☎*986-8480. Map 604* 🔲 🔲 🔲 🔲 *Open also Sun noon-5pm.*
Records and tapes in all categories, and at a discount. Audio equipment, musical instruments and sheet music are also on sale. Additional branches at 51 W 51st St., map **6**N4; 901 6th Ave., map **6**P4; 575 5th Ave., map **6**O4; and 42nd St. and 2nd Ave., map **6**O5.

TOWER RECORDS

4th St. and Broadway, NY 10012 ☎*505-1505. Map 3R4. Open daily* 🔲 🔲 🔲 *Open daily.*
California-style merchandizing techniques are applied to the sale of rec-

ords, tapes and videos in a manner that was a revelation to Easterners. Tower is *the* place to search for obscure titles, imported and domestic, as well as the latest pop hits. Both of its Manhattan branches are huge, claiming to stock as many as 50,000 different recordings in all formats. The downtown shop also has a classical music annex and bookstore, at 4th St. and Lafayette St., map 3R4. The discounted prices are good-to-excellent.

SPORTS AND CAMPING EQUIPMENT

Ever-competitive New Yorkers relieve stress and relive their youth on dozens of tracks, courts, and playing fields around the city. The fitness enthusiasm has led many of them to take up hiking, skiing, and rock-climbing, activities that often lead to an interest in such related pursuits as flyfishing and camping. No enthusiasm is denied, and discounting of list prices is widely practised.

- **Athlete's Foot**   16 W 57th St. (near 5th Ave.), NY 10022 ☎586-1936. Map 6N4. Runners stop here, or at one of its six branches, for its full line of footwear and warm-up suits.
- **Eastern Mountain Sports**   20 W 61st (Broadway), NY 10023 ☎397-4860. Map 5N3. Camping and hiking are emphasized.
- **Herman's**   Midtown branches at 135 W 42nd St. (near Times Sq.), NY 10036 ☎730-7400. Map 5O3. Also 845 3rd Ave. (near E 51st St.), NY 10022 ☎688-4603. Map 6N5. One of the largest general sporting goods stores; everything from camping to skiing.
- **Hudson's**   97 3rd Ave. (13th St.), NY 10003 ☎473-0981. Map 3R4. Open daily. For camping and outdoor equipment.
- **Paragon**   867 Broadway (near E 18th St.), NY 10003 ☎255-8036. Map 6Q4. Open daily. Huge stock of general sporting goods.
- **Spiegels**   Nassau St. and Ann St., NY 10005 ☎227-8400. Map 2T4. Closed Saturday in summer. For all sports goods in lower Manhattan, at discounted prices.

TOYS

It is tempting to begin and end with **F.A.O. Schwarz**, but there are other shops too. All of them will wrap and ship.

- **F.A.O. Schwarz**   767 5th Ave. (58th St.), NY 10022 ☎644-9400. Map 6N4. Open also Sunday. A wonderland of fantasies even for the most cynical adult, it qualifies as a not-to-be-missed sight. Ten-foot-high stuffed giraffes, storybook villages complete with dogs and street lamps, child-sized cars that really work, marionettes, electric trains and, of course, a vast selection of dolls, books and games... three floors of them.
- **Childcraft Center**   150 E 58th St. (Lexington Ave.), NY 10022 ☎753-3196. Map 6N4. Focuses on sturdy educational toys.
- **Penny Whistle**   1281 Madison Ave. (near 91st St.), NY 10028 ☎369-3868. Map 8K4. Young patrons are actually encouraged to play with the dolls and games. Other branches in SoHo *(132 Spring St., map 3 S4)* and on the West Side *(448 Columbus Ave., map 7 L3).*

- **Toy Park**   112 E 86th St. (near Amsterdam Ave.), NY 10024
  ☎427-6611, map **7L3** and 626 Columbus Ave. (near 90th St.), NY
  10024 ☎769-3880, map **7K3**. Extra-large toy emporia, with a play
  area for children so grownups can shop.
- **Toys "R" Us**   1293 Broadway (Herald Square), NY 10018
  ☎594-8697. Map **6P4**. Another outpost of the highly successful
  and unfortunately named chain, this has 45,000 square feet of
  heavily advertised Barbie dolls, Tonka trucks and Nintendos.

WINES AND LIQUOR

Equidistant from the vineyards of France and California, New York
samples the vintages of Old World and New. Special sales are frequent,
sometimes of wine from unexpected countries — Lebanon, Chile,
Yugoslavia. Their advantage is price, of course. Choices can be bewildering, but the salespeople at the following shops are generally helpful, and their wares are exemplary for price and/or variety.

All are closed on Sunday; most accept charge/credit cards and make
deliveries.

- **Astor Wines & Spirits**   12 Astor Pl. (near Lafayette St.)
  ☎674-7500. Map **3T4**.
- **Embassy Liquors**   796 Lexington Ave. (near 61st St.)
  ☎838-6551. Map **6N4**.
- **Morrell & Co.**   307 E 3rd St. (near 2nd Ave.) ☎688-9370. Map
  4R5.
- **Sherry-Lehmann**   679 Madison Ave. (E 61st St.) ☎838-7500.
  Map **6N4**.
- **67 Wines & Spirits**   179 Columbus Ave. (W 67th St.)
  ☎724-6767. Map **7M3**.
- **SoHo Wines & Spirits**   461 West Broadway (Prince St.)
  ☎777-4332. Map **3S4**.

A tour of New York's galleries

In this volatile playground of creativity, gallery-hopping is a cherished pastime of culturally aware New Yorkers. Although the galleries are in the business of selling art, browsers are welcome. Most galleries are open from Tuesday to Saturday, usually 10am-5pm or 6pm, and a few are open on Monday as well. Summer is the slow season, with various closing periods, often July or August, or both. The galleries cluster in three principal areas. While 57th St. and Madison are still very active, the focus has shifted dramatically to SoHo.

Walking tours, as those laid out below, are the practical way to get to know the galleries. Since they move and close with the unpredictability of discotheques, however, the ones mentioned here are only samplings. There are many more, and following these routes will take walkers past buildings that house equally prominent dealers. They gather in substantial numbers under single roofs, so many buildings are de facto mini-museums. Those are the locations emphasized.

Caveat emptor

The galleries' pricing policies bear striking resemblances to those of Middle Eastern rug merchants, amalgamating artists' reputations, what the market might bear, overhead costs and informed and/or wishful thinking. Bargaining is expected, even on very expensive artworks.

One way for those of limited means to begin a fine art collection is to buy graphic art prints. The pitfalls, though, are many. A true print is made by several methods: silk-screen, lithography, and engraving or etching on wood or metal. Most of these leave slight elevations or depressions on the paper surface. Prints are run in editions, usually under the supervision of the artist. Editions or runs might have five copies or as many as 300 or more. A notation such as "14/120" refers to the 14th print of an edition of 120. The value of a print is enhanced, of course, when it is signed by the author.

Excellent photographic reproductions, sometimes with the faked signature of the artist, are hard to detect, and unscrupulous or ignorant dealers might term these "artists' prints." Avoid those shops blazoned with such signs as "Fine Art Liquidations — 50 percent off!" Obtain both a **receipt** of sale and a **certificate of authenticity** on gallery notepaper, signed by the dealer.

57TH ST.

Start on the w side of Fifth Ave., walking n toward 57th St.

724 Fifth Ave. *(map 6N4)*

- **Grace Borgenicht** ☎247-2111. The New York School and movements that followed.
- **Krausharr** ☎307-5730. Recent sculpture.
- **Holly Solomon** ☎757-7777. Moderns.

Turn w (left) on 57th St., walking along the s side.

24 W 57th St. *(map 6N4)*

Among many:

- **Arras** ☎265-2222. Multimedia works by living artists.
- **Marian Goodman** ☎977-7160. Living Americans.
- **Grand Central Galleries** ☎867-3344. Realists.
- **Multiples Inc.** ☎977-7160. Serigraphs, lithographs, etc.
- **Reece** ☎333-5830. Contemporary sculptures and paintings.
- **Suzuki Graphics** ☎582-0373.
- **Jack Tilton** ☎247-7480. New paintings and sculpture.

40 W 57th St. *(map 6N4)*

- **Kennedy** ☎541-9600. American graphics and figurative paintings since 18thC.
- **Marlborough** ☎541-4900. 19th and 20thC works in many styles and media.

50 W 57th St. *(map 6N4)*

- **Terry Dintenfass** ☎581-2268. Recent representational work.
- **Frumpkin/Adams** ☎757-6655. Figurative artists.
- **Lillian Heidenberg** ☎586-3808. Impressionists and Post-Impressionists.
- **Luise Ross** ☎307-0400. Recent paintings and sculpture.
- **Robert Schoelkopf** ☎765-3540. Contemporary painting and sculpture.
- **Tatistcheff** ☎664-0907. Young Americans.

Cross to the N side of 57th St. and walk E.

41 W 57th St. *(map 6N4)*

- **Tibor de Nagy** ☎421-3780. A range of modern paintings and sculpture.
- **Sherry French** ☎308-6440. Recent landscapes and figurative paintings.
- **Schmidt-Bingham** ☎888-1122. Landscapes and representational images.
- **Brewster** ☎980-1975. Modern masters, American, European and Mexican.

41 E 57th St. *(map 6N4)*

The **Fuller Building** has 25 galleries, including:

- **ACA** ☎644-830. Contemporary American and European painting and sculpture.
- **Andre Emmerich** ☎752-0124. Paintings and sculpture since the 1950s.
- **James Goodman** ☎593-3737. Calder, Hepworth and other 20thC masters.
- **Jan Krugier** ☎755-7288. Specializes in Picasso and other

20th-century European masters.
* **Marisa del Re**   ☎688-7019. Postwar Europeans.

MADISON AVE.
Many of these galleries are on side streets, but near Madison. Start at 63rd St. and walk N.
* **19 E 64th St., map 8**M4   Wildenstein ☎879-0500, 17th-20thC paintings, sculpture and furniture.
* **23 E 67th St., map 8**M4   Blumka II ☎879-5611, eclectic holdings of largely European antique art.
* **19 E 70th St., map 8**M4   Knoedler ☎794-0550, prominent dealer in American vanguardists.
* **21 E 70th St., map 8**M4   Hirschl & Adler ☎535-8810, British and American 20thC art.
* **19 E 71st St., map 8**M4   Kovedsy ☎628-6886, Eastern European 20thC artists. Prakapas ☎737-6066, photography.
* **23 E 73rd St., map 8**M4   Mary-Anne Martin ☎288-2213, Latin American painters.
* **922 Madison Ave., map 8**M4   Jane Kahan ☎744-1490, important 20thC Americans and Europeans.
* **956 Madison Ave., map 8**M4   Avanti ☎628-3377, contemporary Americans from 1960s forward.
* **984 Madison Ave., map 8**L4   David Findlay ☎249-2909, primarily figurative paintings.
* **988 Madison Ave., map 8**L4   Weintraub ☎879-1195, mostly sculpture, by Henry Moore, Calder, Giacometti *et al.*
* **1014 Madison Ave., map 8**L4   Graham ☎535-5767, 19th and 20thC Americans.
* **18 E 79th St., map 8**L4   Acquavella ☎734-6300, French Post-Impressionists and American abstractionists.

Cross to the E side and walk S.

* **1035 Madison Ave., map 8**L4   Sindin ☎288-7902, European, Latin, and North American masters since 1900.
* **959 Madison Ave., map 8**M4   Solomon & Co. ☎737-8200, 19th and 20thC sculptors and painters.
* **851 Madison Ave., map 8**M4   Hirschl & Adler Folk ☎988-3655, American folk artists. Hirschl & Adler Modern ☎744-6700, living artists.

SOHO
Once the exclusive arena of wildly avant-garde artists working beyond esthetic and ideological boundaries, SoHo is now the principal art marketplace in New York. Established painters and sculptors mingle with young turks, causing an often dismaying tangle of the unimaginable and the familiar.

The galleries are concentrated, if not contained, in the area bounded by Houston St. on the N, Grand St. on the S, West Broadway and Broadway (four blocks apart in downtown's scrambled geography.) Those mentioned here are an arbitrary sampling, largely of buildings with three or more galleries. Remember that even prominent dealers move to new quarters without warning. Walk s on West Broadway from Houston St.

- **429 West Broadway, map 3S4**   Nancy Hoffman ☎966-6676.
- **420 West Broadway, map 3S4**   Sonnabend ☎966-6160.
  Marilyn Pearl ☎966-5506. 49th Parallel ☎925-8349. Cowles ☎925-3500. Castelli ☎431-5160.
- **417 West Broadway, map 3S4**   Mary Boone ☎431-1818.
- **415 West Broadway, map 3S4**   Stephen Haller ☎219-2500.
  Gimpel/Weitzenhoffer ☎925-6090. Witkin ☎925-5510. Helander ☎966-9797. Staempfli ☎941-7100. Davidson ☎925-5300.

Turn E on Spring St.

- **155 Spring St., map 3S4**   Laurie Rubin ☎226-2161.
  Lieberman & Saul ☎431-0747. Stux ☎219-0010.

Turn N on Broadway.

560 Broadway *(map 3S4)*

Among many:
Wolff   ☎431-7833.
Jack Shainman   ☎966-3866.
Max Protetch   ☎966-5454.
David Nolan   ☎925-6190.
Diane Brown   ☎219-1060.
Paula Allen   ☎334-9710.
Perlow   ☎941-1220.

568 Broadway *(map 3S4)*

A total of 22 galleries, including:
Damon Brandt   ☎431-1444.
Phoenix   ☎226-8711.
Crown Point Press   ☎226-5476.
Fawbush   ☎966-6650.
John Gibson   ☎925-1192.
Lang & O'Hara   ☎226-2121.

583 Broadway *(map 3S4)*

New Museum of Contemporary Art   ☎219-1222, multiple simultaneous exhibitions.

Turn W on Houston St., then s on Mercer St.

164 Mercer St. *(map 3S4)*

Morningstar   ☎334-9330.
Pleiades   ☎226-9093.
John Szoke Graphics
☎219-8300.
Cutler   ☎219-1577.
Blom & Dorn   ☎219-0761.

Turn W on Prince St., then N on Greene St.

142 Greene St. *(map 3S4)*

Sperone Westwater   ☎431-3685.
John Weber   ☎966-6115.
Pace   ☎421-3292.

Recreation

New York for children

From boat trips to zoos, New York is a city packed with interest for young people. The "CUE" section in the back of the weekly magazine *New York* lists current activities for children, and *The New York Times* has a "For Children" page in its Friday editions. The following are some of the most enticing and popular possibilities.

BOAT TRIPS
Circle Line   Pier 83, W 43rd St. ☎563-3200, map 5O2. 3-hour trips around Manhattan Island may be a trifle long for the very young, but there are few dull moments for everyone else. Cruises depart at least 10 times daily *(Apr-Nov 9.45am-5.30pm)*, weather and demand permitting. Half-price for under 12s.

Ellis Island Ferry   Battery Park, Lower Manhattan ☎269-5755, map 2V4. Ferries cross to the famous old immigrant processing center *(daily May-Nov at 9.30am, 11.45am, 2pm and 4.15pm)*. Schedules are adjusted according to season and demand, so call ahead for up-to-date information. The fare includes a 1-hour guided tour of the poignant national monument.

Seaport Line Harbor Cruise   South Street Seaport, Pier 16 ☎385-0791 or 233-4800, map 2U5. Three boat tours leave repeatedly from the SOUTH STREET SEAPORT, but this one has an hour-long sunset cruise that just fits young attention spans. The children can have soda pop while watching Miss Liberty float by, and their grownups can relax with a cocktail below deck. Schedules vary with the season, so it is wise to call first.

Staten Island Ferry   Battery Park, Lower Manhattan ☎248-8097, map 2V4. The double-decker ferry leaves Whitehall St. pier every 20-30 minutes. It passes the Statue of Liberty and provides unparalleled views of bridges, harbor traffic and an imposing skyline. Note that the terminals and ferries are shelter for numbers of homeless people, a perhaps unsettling, but rarely threatening circumstance.

Statue of Liberty Ferry   Battery Park, Lower Manhattan ☎269-5755, map 2V4. Spectacular views from the crown of the famous lady, as well as the ride from the city, are included in the fare. Usually, however, there's a long wait, more than many children and teenagers can bear.

CHILDREN'S THEATER

• The **Courtyard Playhouse** *(39 Grove St., near 7th Ave. S ☎ 765-9540, map 3 R3)*, usually has two performances daily on Saturday and Sunday. • Excellent fare is offered by the **Little People's Theater Company**. Admission is inexpensive; reservations are essential. • **First All Children's Theater** *(37 W 65th St., near Central Park W ☎ 873-6400, map 7 M3)*. Musical productions with casts of children, usually from October to May on Saturday and Sunday only; more frequent performances during the school vacations. • **Hartley House Theater** *(413 W 46th St., near 9th Ave. ☎ 666-1716, map 5 O3)*. • The **On Stage** company mounts several plays a year, including such classics as *Charlotte's Web*. Ordinarily, there are two shows on Saturday, one on Sunday. Moderately expensive admission; reservations necessary.

• **Jan Hus Playhouse** *(351 E 74th St., near 2nd Ave. ☎ 772-9180, map 8 M5)*. Plays, magic shows, and musicals are presented on an irregular schedule, sometimes two in an afternoon. Admission is inexpensive. • **Mostly Magic** *(55 Carmine St. at Bleecker St. ☎ 924-1472, map 3 R4)*. Magicians leaven their illusions with laughs and puns, often assisted by recruits from the audience. Best for under-10s. Shows are on Saturday afternoons; reserve. • **New Media Repertory Company** *(512 E 80th St, near 1st Ave. ☎ 734-5195, map 8 L5)*. Unpredictable entertainments performed by child actors on Saturdays during the school year. Aimed at 3-7s; inexpensive. • **Open Eye Theater** *(270 W 89th St at West End Ave. ☎ 769-4143, map 7 K2)*. Excellent stagings of original and classic productions, usually with music and dancing and aimed at various age groups. Prices are low to moderate; reserve ahead.

• **Promenade Theater** *(2162 Broadway at 76th St. ☎ 240-8202 or 677-5959, map 7 L2)*. • The **Theaterworks/USA** troupe puts on plays and musicals, often based on the lives of historical and mythical figures, and all short enough for a child's mind not to wander. Afternoon shows from September to June, Saturdays and Sundays. • **13th Street Repertory Company** *(50 W 13th St., near 5th Ave. ☎ 675-6677, map 6 Q4)*. New plays with music, based on children's stories. Usually, two shows on Saturdays and Sundays, all year. Inexpensive, but you must reserve.

• At **Pixie Judy's Musical Theatre**, they offer lunch before, and a dance party after, the musical about a circus family. With all that, admission isn't too expensive. • **Theatre East** *(211 E 60th St. ☎ 838-8528, map 6 N5)*. • **The Paper Bag Players** are a veteran entertainment group that have appeared in numerous settings over their many years. They are worth seeking out. One venue they have used is **Symphony Space** *(Broadway and 95th St. ☎ 864-5400, map 7 K2)*. • **Tada**, a children's theatrical company, stages musicals on Friday evenings at 7.30 and on Saturday and Sunday at 1 and 3.30pm *(Tada Theater, 120 W 28th St. ☎ 627-1732, map 5 P3)*.

CHRISTMAS DECORATIONS

The luxury shops and large department stores are ablaze with holiday lights and window-dressing from late November to late December, and midtown **5th Ave.** is a glorious spectacle. The centerpiece is the **70-foot tree** with myriad winking lights looming above the skating rink at the foot of the GE BUILDING; the **Channel Gardens** that lead into ROCKE-FELLER CENTER from 5th Ave. are transformed; **shop windows** and interior displays of invariable delight are those of **Lord & Taylor** *(38th St., map 6 O4)*, **Saks Fifth Avenue** *(50th St., map 6 O4)*, and **F.A.O. Schwarz** *(58th St., map 6 N4)*.

Elsewhere in Manhattan, a Christmas tree is framed within **Washington Arch** in GREENWICH VILLAGE, wreaths encircle the necks of the lions outside the **42nd St. Library**, an elaborate tableau of castles and elves fills the lobby of the MUSEUM OF THE CITY OF NEW YORK, and a tree in the Medieval Hall of the METROPOLITAN MUSEUM OF ART emphasizes the spiritual origins of the holiday, supplemented by a panorama of 200 18thC figures gathered about the birthplace of the Christ child. Down at **South Street Seaport**, carolers arrange themselves into a living Christmas tree while they sing.

COMEDY AND REVUE

Several nightclubs have afternoon or early evening sessions, in some cases specifically for children. But inevitably clubs change policy and others close, so always telephone for schedules and prices. Remember that profanity is not uncommon in many comic acts that are not directed at youngsters, and children under 16 usually must be accompanied by parents.

• The **Comic Strip** *(1568 2nd Ave., near 81st St.* ☎ *861-9386, map 8 L5, Sat 5pm, Sun 5.30pm)* has spotlighted professional stage youngsters appearing in current TV and stage shows. • Periodic early shows have been presented by **Chicago City Limits** *(351 E 74th St.* ☎ *772-8707, map 8 M5)*, where no alcohol is served and by **Improvisation** *(358 W 44th St., near 9th Ave.* ☎ *765-8268, map 5 O3)*, one of the oldest comedy clubs in town. • **Stand-up New York** *(236 W 78th St.* ☎ *595-0850, map 7 L2)* brings on a clown and a magician, Sunday at 2pm. • Saturday at 1pm is the time for children's cabaret at **Steve McGraw's** *(158 W 72nd St.* ☎ *595-7400, map 7 M3)*. • A similar event, performed by children for children, is held each Saturday noon at **The Duplex** *(61 Christopher St.* ☎ *769-9180, map 3 R3)*.

CONCERTS FOR YOUNG PEOPLE

The **American Symphony Orchestra** and the **New York Philharmonic** give irregularly scheduled concerts of classical music directed at ages 6-16. Most are performed in the fall and winter at **Carnegie Hall** *(*☎ *247-7459)* or **Avery Fisher Hall** *(*☎ *874-2424)*. Check newspapers for full details.

EVENTS AND ENTERTAINMENTS

Big Apple Circus: New York's very own one-ring circus in a tent, modeled after the intimate European troupes that have no other equivalent in the US. Clowns cavort, aerialists execute the fabled triple somersault, elephants dance, and jugglers and acrobats twirl and tumble. Prices are low at this not-for-profit enterprise; operation is most likely in summer and the Christmas season. A frequent site is **Damrosch Park** in the LINCOLN CENTER, but it moves through all the boroughs.

Citicorp Center *(Lexington Ave. and 53rd St.* ☎ *559-4259, map 6N4):* the atrium has free entertainment most days, but Saturday afternoon is for children, with music, magic, jugglers and puppets.

July 4th (Independence Day) festivities: an awesome fireworks display is put on by Macy's Department Store, set off over the East River. Among the better vantages are the **South St. Seaport** and the **Brooklyn Heights Promenade**. Be there by 9pm. The **"Old New York"** celebrations take place at BATTERY PARK in lower Manhattan, with street performers and suitable ceremonies from noon-dusk.

Storytelling: at the **Hans Christian Andersen Memorial** *(near 5th Ave. and 72nd St., map 8M4),* stories are read *(May-Sept, Sat at 11am)* to children, some of whom sit in the bronze lap of the master. An excellent children's bookstore, **Eeyore's** *(2212 Broadway at 79th St.* ☎ *362-0634 and 25 E 83rd St.* ☎ *988-3404, map 7L2)* has story hours most Sundays at 11am at the West Side store and at 12.30pm at the East Side store *(except July-Aug)*. Ages 3-6. Call ahead to confirm.

Radio City Music Hall *(6th Ave. and 50th St.* ☎ *632-4041, map 6O4):* Christmas and Easter Shows featuring the precision dancing Rockettes are geared to families, as are such special appearances as **Walt Disney's World On Ice**. Pre-teen and older children might enjoy the backstage tour, conducted several times daily. Just the up-close look at the giant Wurlitzer organ is almost worth the time.

Madison Square Garden *(7th Ave. and 33rd St.* ☎ *563-8300, map 5P3):* The venerable **Ice Capades** show, featuring recent Olympic and world champion figure skaters and a lot of feathers and sequins, appears annually. They keep it up-to-date with music by current Top Forty pop and rock groups. In January. Another child-pleaser is **The World's Toughest Rodeo**, if only for the fearless clowns that lure the rampaging bulls away from their fallen riders. Calf roping, steer wrestling, barrel racing; usually in November. Also at The Garden, every April, is that hardy perennial, the **Ringling Bros. and Barnum & Bailey Circus**.

HOTELS

Various discounts and incentives help keep costs within reason when children are in tow. Some hotels permit children under 12 (or 14, or even 17) to stay with their parents for free. Most will bring in an extra bed or cot at a small additional charge, making a substantial saving over the cost of separate rooms.

Alternatively, a suite sleeping 3-4 is often cheaper than two rooms. Reception desks or concierges normally have lists of **baby-sitters**.

Swimming pools are an important feature for children, and the following Manhattan hotels and motels have them: MARRIOTT FINANCIAL CENTER, HOLIDAY INN CROWNE PLAZA, PARKER MERIDIEN, RAMADA INN, SHERATON MANHATTAN, UN PLAZA-PARK HYATT, PENINSULA, and the NEW YORK VISTA. These are listed under WHERE TO STAY (pages 162-86).

MUSEUMS AND EXHIBITIONS

Belvedere Castle *(in Central Park, near 79th St. and s of the Great Lawn* ☎ *772-0210, map 7L3. Hours vary* ☒*).* Kids are delighted by the miniature castle itself, commanding a small hill beside a pond. Despite the forbiddingly titled series of programs held inside the "Central Park Learning Center," more play than work goes on, and a wide variety of experiences is provided. At Christmas, children might make their own tree ornaments; in summer, there are nature walks and outdoor games related to the park. Call for details, and to reserve places.

Brooklyn Children's Museum *(145 Brooklyn Ave., between Eastern Parkway and Atlantic Ave.* ☎*(718) 735-4400, open Mon, Wed-Fri 2-5pm; Sat, Sun 10am-5pm* ☒*).* The oldest (1899) children's museum in the US is in a new building. Exhibits cover basic technologies, social and natural history, and handling and participation are encouraged. Several levels support a steam engine, water-wheels, ladders, a windmill, hydraulic devices, plants and animals. There are thousands of objects and displays.

Uris Center for Education of the Metropolitan Museum of Art *(5th Ave. and 82nd St.* ☎*879-5500, ext. 351, map 8L4, open Tues 10am-8.45pm; Wed-Sat 10am-4.45pm; Sun and hols 11am-4.45pm).* Somehow it manages to be intellectually accessible to children under 12 without patronizing them. Exhibits, from the permanent collections and outside sources, introduce the arts and inspire a thirst for further exploration in the galleries upstairs. There is also a lively program of workshop demonstrations, films, and gallery tours.

Children's Museum of Manhattan *(212 W 83rd St., near Amsterdam Ave.* ☎ *721-1234, map 7L2, open Tues-Fri 11am-5pm; Sat noon-5pm* ☒*).* This increasingly ambitious museum emphasizes hands-on participation in games, displays and workshops concerned with natural history, conservation, culture and society. Puppetry and mask-making also take place.

In addition to the four museums mentioned above, many of the city's other museums also have presentations that are of interest for children. For addresses and opening times, and fuller details, see individual entries throughout SIGHTS AND PLACES OF INTEREST.

American Museum of Natural History: the reassembled dinosaur skeletons, and dioramas of mounted animals and birds in simulated habitats are long-time favorites; but more vivid are the detailed depictions of the peoples and cultures of Asia, Central America and Africa. Several rooms are set aside for schoolchildren, to increase their awareness of the museum through participatory exhibitions, games, performers, films, story hours and guided tours.

The **Hayden Planetarium** is part of the facility, and on Saturday during the school year (October-June) mounts a "Young People's Sky Show," which includes realistic overhead projections of galaxies and constellations, accompanied by music and narration.

Aunt Len's Doll and Toy Museum: hundreds of antique toys, dolls and miniature houses crowd every inch of space in this refreshingly informal museum; visits by appointment only.

Brooklyn Museum: programs on Saturday and Sunday introduce youngsters aged 6-12 to the collections through talks and demonstrations that do not abuse attention spans; art workshops are another feature.

Guinness World Records Exhibit Hall: excess fascinates, and this set of tableaux of the longest, highest, shortest, fattest, oldest, youngest and most bizarre creations of man and nature never fails to grab attention.

Intrepid Sea-Air-Space Museum enthralls youngsters, the deck of the decommissioned aircraft carrier crowded with rockets, planes, and weaponry.

Museum of Television and Radio: children can enjoy tapes and kinescopes of radio and TV shows of the "olden times"; adults are usually just as intrigued.

Museum of the City of New York: puppet shows *(Nov-Apr, Sat)* are the incentive to join in various "please touch" demonstrations of objects related to the history of the area; on Sunday, there are concerts to which children over 10 are invited; and the gallery of toys and dolls on the third floor is fascinating.

New-York Historical Society: a scale-model of a Noah's Ark, populated by 300 animals, dominates the collection of vintage toys and dolls on the second floor; storytelling, too.

South Street Seaport Museum: the authentic tall ships of this open-air museum are diverting for all ages, and there is a theater designed for children; youngsters can take part in lectures, and browse in shops concerned with toys, ships' models and games with a nautical bent.

OBSERVATION DECKS ◁€

Empire State Building *(350 5th Ave., near 34th St.* ☎ *736-3100, map 6P4; open daily 9.30am-midnight; closed Christmas and New Year's Day; children under 12 half-price);* there are two decks, on the 86th and 102nd floors.

World Trade Center *(2 World Trade Center, Lower Manhattan* ☎ *466-7377, map 1 U4; open daily 9.30am-9.30pm; children 6-12 about half-price* ▣ *under 6).* An enclosed deck is on the 107th floor, an open deck on the 110th. On a clear day, it is easy to imagine that you can see the curvature of the earth.

Closer to sea-level (and free) is the pedestrian walkway of the **Brooklyn Bridge**, as well as the **Brooklyn Heights** promenade.

In addition, there are several restaurants with excellent views, sky-high or from the ground. As long as one can afford not to inspect the bill too closely, the following can be pleasant: **The River Café** *(1 Water St., Brooklyn, map 4 U6),* **The Water Club** *(500 E 30th St, map 6P5),* **The Hors d'Oeuvrerie** *(1 World Trade Center, map 1 U4),* **Rainbow Promenade** *(GE Building, map 6 O4),* **The Terrace** *(Butler Hall, Columbia University),* **Windows on the World** *(1 World Trade Center, map 1 U4).*

PARADES

For youngsters, the big one is the **Macy's Thanksgiving Day Parade** *(last Thurs in Nov),* with its huge floating balloons of comic-book heroes. The longest and most eagerly anticipated is the **St Patrick's Day Parade** *(Mar 17)*, but that can be rowdy, with its roving bands of intoxicated teenagers. Most months have a parade of some kind in some part of the city, but 5th Ave. has several events in fall.

See CALENDAR OF EVENTS on pages 47-51.

PLAYGROUNDS

Numerous conventional playgrounds dot New York. But the ones suggested below are described as adventure playgrounds, with stacked wooden blocks, rope nets, sections of concrete tubes, and comparable combinations of imagination-provoking shapes and materials.

Central Park • Central Park West and 68th St. • Central Park West, near 85th St. • 5th Ave. and 85th St. • 5th Ave. and 71st St.

Battery Park City • West St., s of Vesey St.

Greenwich Village • Washington Square Park, between 5th Ave. and University Pl. • Abingdon Square Park at Hudson St. and Bleecker St.

Upper East Side • 1st Ave. near 67th St. • East End Ave. and 84th St.

Upper West Side • W 45th St. near 10th Ave. • W 90th St. near Columbus Ave.

PUPPETS AND MARIONETTES

• The famous toy store **F.A.O. Schwarz** *(5th Ave. and 58th St.* ☎ *644-9400, map 6N4)* has free puppet shows *(Mon-Fri at 2.30pm)*.
• **Heckscher Puppet House** *(Central Park, 59th St.* ☎ *397-3162, map 6N4)* has two performances Monday to Friday, for elementary-school children and their younger siblings. Reservations essential; ask about suitable age group when calling.

• **Museum of the City of New York** *(1220 5th Ave. at 103rd St.* ☎ *534-1672, map 8J4. Shows Oct-Apr, Sat at 1.30pm):* admission inexpensive. • **Puppet Playhouse** *(555 E 90th St.* ☎ *369-8890, map 8K5; Oct-May, two shows each Sat and Sun):* past performances have brought Winnie the Pooh and other favorites to life. The stage is occupied by visiting puppeteers of considerable skill. Inexpensive; reserve ahead.
• **South Street Seaport Museum** *(16 Fulton St. at South St.* ☎ *766-9020, map 2U5):* shipboard puppet shows and related entertainments on Sunday at 2pm. • **Swedish Cottage Marionette Theater** *(81st St. and Central Park West* ☎ *988-9093, map 7L3; performances Sat, Sun, some weekdays; call ahead for times):* inexpensive; reservations required.

• **Papageno Puppet Theater** *(173 W 81st St.* ☎ *874-3297, map 8L3):* the long-established group usually has two shows on Saturday and Sunday, but its schedule varies and it has appeared at other locations, so call first. Inexpensive; reserve ahead. • **The Puppet Company** has mounted marionette musicals at the **Metropolis Café** *(31 Union Square W* ☎ *741-1646, map 6Q4).* Check to see if they're in residence.

RESTAURANTS

Apart from their prohibitive cost, the shrines of *haute cuisine* set children squirming and are unlikely to have available the simple fare they prefer. There are many moderately-priced restaurants catering to families, however, with special children's menus, high-chairs, and speedy service. The following tend to be large and rather touristy, but they go to considerable lengths to amuse young patrons.

America *(9 E 18th St.* ☎ *505-2110, map 6 Q4)*. In a room the size of an aircraft hangar and with the noise level of a 747 starting up, there is ample opportunity for audiovisual diversion. Up to 400 people mill about beneath its neon canopy, ordering from a 200-plus-item menu of fast food and yuppie drinks. Portions are large, prices relatively low, the clientele a vivacious cross-section of tourists and the striving classes.

Benihana *(47 W 56th St.* ☎ *581-0930, map 6 N4, and 120 E 56th St.* ☎ *593-1627, map 6 N4)*. Diners sit in groups of 6-8 around a horseshoe counter that encloses a sizzling grill. A cook in *toque blanche* arrives and, with a showy clatter, swoops over piles of shrimp, zucchini and beef, slicing, flipping, sautéing, serving. It may not be Japanese, but it is theatrical.

Caribe *(117 Perry St.* ☎ *255-9191, map 3 R3, no cards)*. This West Indian outpost in far west Greenwich Village hops around the islands for its culinary inspirations, from Martinique to Cuba to Jamaica. Kids will find some of the preparations "icky" — oxtail stew, perhaps — but others quite to their liking — deviled turkey leg, say. Ask about the degree of spiciness before ordering. There are so many potted plants that a guide is almost required to find a table. Go early, since it can get a little raucous as the evening wears on.

Carmine's *(2450 Broadway* ☎ *362-2200, map 7 K2)*. Everyone loves Italian food, children especially, assuming it isn't too spicy. This large, friendly, family-style eatery on the West Side actually welcomes kids and caters to their needs. Their parents have food prepared to adult tastes, and the bill doesn't spoil their appetite.

Ed Debevic's *(661 Broadway* ☎ *982-6000, map 3 S4)*. Most kids couldn't care less about parental memories of how things were in the "old days" — the decade of the Fifties roughly imitated here. They'll enjoy just about everything else, though. It looks like a roadside diner of that time, with recorded music by Sinatra and Elvis. Employees break into the twist and bunny-hop with little provocation. Weighty, comforting fare such as meatloaf and mashed potatoes clog the menu.

Hamburger Harry's *(145 W 45th St.* ☎ *840-2756, map 5 O3)*. Designer burgers are the obvious fare, in variations unseen elsewhere and usually satisfying to adults as well as youngsters. A counter around the open grill adds to the fun. Menu alternatives include *fajitas,* chicken and chili. It's a good choice for a quick meal before the theater. The original branch is in TriBeCa *(157 Chambers St.* ☎ *267-4446, map 1 T4)*.

Hard Rock Café *(221 W 57th St.* ☎ *459-9320, map 5 N3)*. Parents are almost obligated to take their progeny, aged 6-16, to this New World version of the London original. The wait is long, under the "awning" of the rear end of a finned 1950s Cadillac, the noise level inside almost painful. Rock memorabilia decorates the walls; good burgers and chocolate malts adorn the tables. A Hard Rock T-shirt will be a teenager's proudest memento of the trip to New York.

John's Pizzeria *(278 Bleecker St.* ☎ *243-1680, map 3R4, and 408 E 64th St.* ☎ *935-2895, map 8M5).* All arguments about New York pizza start over who is in *second* place, for most everyone agrees that John's is number one. Beware of imitators and assorted frauds with similar names, and if possible, get to the Greenwich Village branch. Expect a wait.

Mickey Mantle's *(42 Central Park S* ☎ *688-7777, map 5N3).* Every Little League third-string outfielder has heard of The Mick, even though his brilliant career with the New York Yankees belongs to the Dark Ages — the 1960s. Lots of baseball memorabilia and TV sets within sight of every table will keep the little ones interested through the decent burgers 'n' fries. Besides all that, the slugger himself shows up regularly and submits to autograph requests.

SPORTS AND OTHER ACTIVITIES
See SPORTS on pages 282-7 for information on **Bicycling**, **Boating**, **Horseback riding**, **Ice-skating** and **Swimming**.

MODEL BOATS
Miniature boats both humble and elaborate, radio-controlled or sail-powered, are seen nearly every day of the year on the **Conservatory Pond** *(in Central Park, near 5th Ave./72nd St., map 8M4).*

TELEVISION SHOWS
A number of game shows and variety specials originate in New York. Children between the ages of 6 and 18 must be accompanied by an adult. Tickets are free, and sources are:

American Broadcasting Company   1330 6th Ave. ☎581-7777, map **6**N4

Columbia Broadcasting System   51 W 52nd St. ☎581-4321, map **6**N4

National Broadcasting Company   30 Rockefeller Plaza, ☎664-3055, map **6**O4

New York Convention and Visitors Bureau   2 Columbus Circle, ☎397-8222, map **5**N3

ZOOS AND AQUARIUM
For addresses and opening times, see individual entries in SIGHTS AND PLACES OF INTEREST.

Bronx Zoo   The new Children's Zoo, within the larger park *(open Apr-Oct),* has gentle animals for petting, and camels and pony carts for riding. Kids also enjoy the monorail that circles the "Wild Asia" preserve, the aerial tram that glides over the re-created "African Plains," and the tractor train that tours the entire park.

Central Park Zoo *(Open 7 days a week, all year round)*. Next to the 64th St. entrance is a merry-go-round, and inside are pony rides and a seal pool. To the N is the **Children's Zoo**, on a triangle of land on 5th Ave. between 65th St. and 66th St. It has been undergoing renovation, however, and may not have re-opened; check before going.

New York Aquarium There are performances *(May-Oct)* by dolphins, whales and sea-lions. Most winter in Florida, but there are still indoor tanks featuring fish that resemble floating flowers and others, even stranger, that inspire shudders.

Prospect Park Zoo This compact zoo also features pony rides, and a section of small farm animals set aside for children.

Staten Island Zoo The comprehensive reptile collection is the big attraction, supplemented by a children's zoo and pony rides. Admission is free on Wednesday.

Sports and activities

The following guide to sports and leisure activities in and around New York offers ideas for both spectators and participants.

Spectator sports

ARENAS AND STADIUMS

Baker Field *(W 218th St. and Broadway* ☎ *567-7423)*. American football as played (usually poorly) by Columbia University, one of the "Ivy League" of prestigious colleges; September to November.

Byrne Arena *(Meadowlands Sports Complex, E Rutherford, NJ)*. Opened in 1981, this is the venue for the professional basketball team, the **Nets** *(*☎ *(201) 935-3900)* and the **Devils** hockey squad *(*☎ *(201) 935-6050)*, as well as rock concerts, circuses, college basketball, and other events. You can get there by bus from the Port Authority Bus Terminal on 8th Ave.

Giants Stadium *(Meadowlands Sports Complex, E Rutherford, NJ)* Crowds fill the superb arena on Sunday afternoons from late August to December to watch professional football with the **Jets** *(*☎ *(516) 838-6600)* and the **Giants** *(*☎ *(201) 935-8111)*; tickets for regular-season games are nearly impossible to obtain. Repeated experiments with professional **soccer** have failed, but the 1994 World Cup competition in the US should renew interest, and some of those games are to be played in this stadium. On that occasion, real grass will replace the artificial turf.

Madison Square Garden *(8th Ave. and 33rd St.* ☎ *563-8300, map* **5***P3)*. Among its many guises, it is the home of **New York Rangers** ice hockey *(Oct-Apr)*, **Knicks** basketball *(Oct-Apr)*, and college basketball *(Nov-Apr)*. Also boxing and wrestling matches and such special events as the circus, the Ice Capades, track and field, dog and cat and horse shows, and rock concerts.

Nassau Coliseum *(Uniondale, Long Island* ☎ *(516) 794-4100)*. Special musical and entertainment events are presented at the Coliseum, as are the ice hockey games of the once highly successful **Islanders**.

National Tennis Center *(Flushing Meadows-Corona Park, Queens* ☎ *(718) 271-5100)*; site of the US Open Championships *(early Sept)*.

Shea Stadium *(126th St. and Roosevelt Ave., Queens)*. The professional baseball **Mets** *(*☎ *(718) 507-8499)* play here *(Apr-Sept)*.

Yankee Stadium *(River Ave. and W 161st St., The Bronx* ☎ *293-6000)*. Home base *(Apr-Oct)* of the **Yankees**, who have often been champions and are one of the oldest teams in professional baseball.

AUTO RACING

Despite misgivings about its tobacco company sponsorship, the **Marlboro Grand Prix of New York** was approved for June 1993. Whether it will be the first and only or the first of many remains to be seen. The race is over a 1.3-mile track around the WORLD TRADE CENTER.

RACETRACKS

For horse-racing results ☎976-2121. Bets can be placed at nearly 100 Off-Track-Betting parlors (OTB) throughout the city. One of the most convenient is on the main floor of GRAND CENTRAL TERMINAL.

Aqueduct *(108th St. and Rockaway Blvd., Queens* ☎*(718) 641-4700)*. The "Big A" features thoroughbred flat racing *(Jan-May and Oct-Dec; for routes and fares* ☎*(718) 330-1234)*. It can be reached by subway.

Belmont Park *(Belmont, Long Island* ☎*(718) 641-4700)*. Thoroughbred racing *(May-July, Sept-Oct)*. The **Long Island Railroad**, departing from Penn Station, has special trains and fare-admission packages *(* ☎ *739-4200 for information)*.

Meadowlands *(Meadowlands Sports Complex, E Rutherford, NJ* ☎*(201) 935-8500)*. Most of the grandstands are enclosed at this relatively new track, permitting comfortable viewing of thoroughbreds *(Sept-Dec)* and of trotters *(Jan-Aug)*. Evening races can be watched from the **Pegasus** dining-room.

Roosevelt Raceway *(Westbury, Long Island* ☎*(516) 222-2000)*. Evening trotters go through their paces *(Jan-Mar, June-Aug, Oct-Dec)*. Package fares on the **Long Island Railroad** from Penn Station (see above) include bus transfers and track admission.

Yonkers Raceway *(Yonkers, NY* ☎*(914) 968-4200)*. Easily accessible off the Gov. Thomas E. Dewey Thruway, N of The Bronx. The track is devoted to trotting races *(Mar-Apr, June-July, Sept-Oct and Dec)*. Special **buses** leave from the Port Authority Bus Terminal on 8th Ave *(map 5 O3)*.

Participant sports

BASEBALL

The national game is played on fields all over New York. "Pick-up" teams come together for a few innings whenever a sufficient number of enthusiasts gather. If you are interested, contact the **Heckscher Ballfields** *(Central Park, E of Central Park W at about 64th St.* ☎*408-0213, map 7M3)*.

BASKETBALL

There are basketball courts within a few blocks of nearly every address in Manhattan. These are usually occupied by local youngsters, or aging executives who take the game very seriously *(* ☎ *360-8111 for the closest court)*.

Branches of the **YMCA** have gymnasiums *(215 W 23rd St.* ☎ *741-9220, map 6 Q4; 224 E 47th St.* ☎ *755-2410, map 6 O5; and 5 W 63rd St.* ☎ *787-4400, map 7M3)*, but there is a stiff fee for one-time use by nonmembers. Visitors who can present a membership card from a hometown "Y" can usually gain entrance for a limited number of times and for smaller fees.

BICYCLING

Shops in most neighborhoods rent bicycles by the hour, day, or week — consult the Yellow Pages under *Bicycles*. City streets can be intimidating, so consider CENTRAL PARK, since some of its roads are closed to cars at midday, during weekday evenings and throughout the weekends. The **Loeb Boathouse in Central Park** (☎861-4137, *map 8M4*) has bicycles for rent.

BOATING AND SAILING

Rowboats are available for rent at the **Loeb Boathouse in Central Park** (☎517-2233). Rentals by the hour to anyone over 16. Children may go, if accompanied by an adult.

Sailing instruction is offered by the **New York Sailing School** (*City Island, The Bronx* ☎864-4472).

BOWLING

All the boroughs have bowling emporia, but the only one still in business in Manhattan is the 44-lane **Bowlmor** (*110 University Place* ☎255-8188, *map 3R4*) in Greenwich Village. It's open every night until at least 1am.

CRICKET

Immigrants from the what was the British West Indies keep the imperial heritage alive, on pitches in **Flushing Meadows-Corona Park** in Queens (☎(718) 520-5900), and in **Van Cortlandt Park** in The Bronx (*W 250th St. and Broadway* ☎430-1825).

DIVING

Instruction in SCUBA is given by the **Aqua-Lung School of New York** (*1089 2nd Ave.* ☎582-2800, *map 6N5*), **Atlantis II** (*498 6th Ave.* ☎924-7556, *map 6Q4*), and **Scuba Plus** (*201 E 34th St.* ☎689-0035, *map 6P4*), all in Manhattan. They also arrange diving trips for qualified divers. There are a number of intriguing wrecks in offshore waters.

FISHING

Anglers over 16 must obtain a license to use the freshwater lakes and rivers of New York City and State. These are readily available for a small fee at many sporting goods stores. Anyone can fish in salt water without a permit. Lakes within **Central Park, Prospect Park** (*Brooklyn*), and **Van Cortlandt Park** (*The Bronx*) contain such gullible species as catfish, bluegills and carp. Charters and party boats (each passenger pays a fare) are available at **City Island** (*The Bronx*) and **Sheepshead Bay** (*Brooklyn*).

GOLF

There are no golf courses in Manhattan, but there are 13 in outlying boroughs. For information: **The Bronx** ☎822-4711; **Brooklyn** ☎(718) 965-6511; **Queens** ☎(718) 520-5311; **Staten Island** ☎(718) 422-7640.) Expect to wait for a tee-off.

There is an alternative for the most avid of golfers, those who descend into fairway deprivation in January. It is the **Midtown Golf Club** *(7 W 45th St.* ☎ *869-3636, map 6 O4)*, and it is indoors. What are offered are simulators, using computer-driven video screens to project dream courses from Pebble Beach to St. Mellions. Tee off, watch the ball hit the floor, but see an imaginary ball continue on the screen on its pre-destined arc. A solo round of the simulated course takes about an hour.

HANDBALL
New York City has more than 2,000 handball courts *(☎ 397-3100 for the location of the nearest city-owned court in Manhattan).*

HORSEBACK RIDING
Instruction and rent-by-the-hour are available at: **Claremont Riding Academy** *(175 W 89th St.* ☎ *724-5100, map 7K3)*, classes for children, too; **Clove Lake Stables** *(1025 Clove Rd. Staten Island* ☎ *(718) 448-1414);* **Van Cortlandt Park Stables** *(Broadway and W 254th St., The Bronx* ☎ *549-6200).*

The trails for the **Claremont** wind through Central Park; it has an indoor ring, as well.

ICE-SKATING
The rink at the base of the **GE Building** in the Rockefeller Center has a constant crowd of spectators and so is used primarily by skilled and/or exhibitionist skaters. Central Park has two outdoor rinks: **Lasker** *(near 5th Ave. at 110th St.* ☎ *397-3106, map 8J4)* and **Wollman** *(near the Zoo, 5th Ave at 61st St.* ☎ *517-4800, map 6N4)*. All are open from November to April. The **Sky Rink** *(450 W 33rd St.* ☎ *695-6555, map 5P2)* is large, indoors and on the 16th floor. Open all year, it has disco skating on Friday and Saturday nights.

Skating is also permitted on natural lakes and ponds when there is safe ice cover, but it is wise to stick to the artificial rinks.

RACQUETBALL AND SQUASH
So popular it threatens to eclipse tennis as an amateur sport, racquetball is normally available only at membership clubs. Hotels often have arrangements with nearby clubs; check with the concierge. A few clubs are open to the public on a courts-available basis. Daily rates aren't *too* steep.

Among these are:
Grand Central Racquetball Club   25 Vanderbilt Ave. ☎883-0994, map 6O4
Manhattan Plaza Racquet Club   45 W 45th St. ☎594-0554, map 6O4
Manhattan Squash & Racquetball Club   41 W 42nd St. ☎869-8969, map 6O4
Park Avenue Squash & Racquet Club   3 Park Ave. ☎686-1085, map 6Q4
Park Place Squash Club   25 Park Place ☎964-2677, map 1T4

All are usually open 7 days a week, 7am-midnight. They sell or rent equipment, and charge/credit cards are accepted. Reserve well ahead.

Hotels that have courts include the **Parker Meridien** and the **New York Vista**.

RUNNING

New York runners are a hardy breed, seen on every street, at all hours, in any weather. A morning jog or a serious 10-mile effort can follow any route, but certain areas and pathways are favored because of their even road surfaces, lack of vehicles and crowds, and relative freedom from air pollution.

CENTRAL PARK has 30-plus miles of roads, providing substantial variety in distances and difficulty. Suggested routes:

- The fenced reservoir slightly N of the mid-point of the park has two cinder tracks. Enter the park at **Engineer's Gate**, at 5th Ave. and E 90th St. The inner track is 1.57 miles (1km) long.
- Slightly S of the reservoir is **The Great Lawn Oval**, with a measured circumference of half a mile and markers at 220-yard (200m) intervals.
- A 6-mile loop follows the main drive around the perimeter of the park. Cut E or W for runs of 1, 2 or 4 miles. Enter at **Engineer's Gate**, or at W 66th St. beyond the Tavern On The Green restaurant, or just beyond the Zoo.

Less crowded parks are **Fort Tryon**, **Prospect** *(Brooklyn)*, **Riverside**, and **Van Cortlandt** *(The Bronx)*. The NEW YORK BOTANICAL GARDEN *(also in The Bronx)* is an ideal place for runners, and is a worthy destination by itself.

For river vistas, try **Riverside Park** *(between 72nd and 96th Sts., map 7M2-K2)* and the promenades along the East River, with easy access S from **Carl Schurz Park**.

Road races of varying lengths are held every month in the city. For dates, times and registration details, contact the **New York Road Runners Club** *(9 E 89th St.* ☎ *860-4455, map 8K4)*. There are indoor tracks at: **McBurney YMCA** *(215 W 23rd St.* ☎ *741-9224, map 6Q4)*; **92nd St. YMHA** *(1395 Lexington Ave.* ☎ *427-6000, map 8K4)*; **West Side YMCA** *(5 W 63rd St.* ☎ *787-4400, map 7M3)*.

SKIING

Cross-country skiing, on rolling terrain with gentle slopes, is available in **Prospect Park** *(Brooklyn* ☎ *965-6511)* and at **Van Cortlandt Park** *(The Bronx* ☎ *543-4595)*. Equipment rental, instruction, tours to upstate and New England ski centers are all available from **Scandinavian Ski Shop** *(40 W 57th St.* ☎ *757-8524, map 6N4)* and **Sportiva Sporthaus** *(145 E 47th St.* ☎ *421-7466, map 6O4)*.

SWIMMING

Municipally-owned pools in the five boroughs are open from late May to early September. They tend to be shabby, crowded, and rowdy. Visitors are likely to prefer the indoor pools at the following hotels, some of which are open to outsiders as well as guests: **Holiday Inn Crowne Plaza**, **Marriott Financial Center**, **Parker Meridien**, **Sheraton Manhattan**, **UN Plaza-Park Hyatt**, **Ramada Inn**, **New York Vista**, and the **Peninsula** (see WHERE TO STAY on pages 162-86).

Jones Beach State Park *(on the s side of Long Island)* has the finest public beach and related facilities in the region, and is less than an hour by car *(via Southern State Parkway, exiting s on Wantagh State Parkway)* or special bus from the Port Authority Bus Terminal. Municipal beaches are nearly always crowded, and the color of the water is often suspect, even when certified safe for swimming, but most are within reach by public transportation. CONEY ISLAND beach *(S Brooklyn)* is best known, but **Rockaway Beach**, to the E, is three times as long, with a tenth of the humanity. **Orchard Beach** *(near City Island in The Bronx)*, and **Great Kills Park** *(Staten Island)* are also popular.

TENNIS

Commercial tennis clubs usually have equipment shops, lounges, instructors, and lockers available. Many also have saunas, air conditioning, swimming pools, weekend brunches and evening parties. There are indoor courts at:

Crosstown Tennis   14 W 31st St. ☎947-5780, map **6**P4
Columbus Racquet Club   795 Columbus Ave. ☎663-6900, map **7**J3
HRC Tennis   East River piers at end of Wall St. ☎422-9300, map **2**U5
Manhattan Plaza Racquet Club   450 W 43rd St. ☎594-0554, map **5**O2
Sutton East Tennis Club   488 E 60th St. ☎751-3452, map **6**N5
Tower Tennis Courts   1725 York Ave. ☎860-2464, map **8**K5
Turtle Bay Tennis & Swim Club   1 United Nations Plaza ☎355-3400, map **6**O5
USTA National Tennis Center   Flushing, Queens ☎(718) 271-5100
Village Courts   110 University Place ☎989-2300, map **3**R4

These are normally open 7 days a week from 7am-midnight; always call ahead to reserve a court and, if alone, to arrange a game. All boroughs have municipal courts, with more than 100 in Manhattan alone, but permits are required, and red tape slows the process. Most accessible is the 24-court **Central Park Tennis Center** *(near Central Park W, between 94th and 96th Sts. ☎397-3190, map 7K3)* Fanatics should take note of the **Stadium Tennis Center** *(11 E 162nd St. in The Bronx ☎293-2386, open Oct-May 24hrs a day)*.

Excursions

Environs of New York

Unlike the capitals of Europe, New York has no medieval cathedrals or ancient university towns within easy reach. Beyond the inner ring of bleak smaller cities, however, the countryside is dotted with hamlets of Colonial serenity, inviting inns, dairy farms and vineyards, mock châteaux and castles and a remarkable number of grand estates. These are found in a great variety of natural settings, from hushed valleys to surf-pounded shores. For the following tours a car is essential.

A TASTE OF NEW ENGLAND

105 miles round trip NE. One day, preferably with an overnight stop.

Leave the city via the West Side Highway, which goes through several name changes and two toll booths. After the second toll, take the first exit onto the Cross Country Expressway. This merges eventually with the Hutchinson River Parkway, heading toward Connecticut. Leave it at Exit 27, turning left, N, on Route 120 *(Purchase St.)*. This was long a community of large estates of the very wealthy. It still is, in part, but corporate and collegiate campuses now stand behind the high walls and towering shade trees. That's Manhattanville College beyond the IBM installation on the left.

At the next traffic signal, turn right, E, on Anderson Hill Rd. There are several restaurants along this road, the Doral Arrowwood resort and conference center, and the entrance to the State University of New York at Purchase. On campus is the **Neuberger Museum**, with an important collection of 20thC painting and sculpture. The public is welcome *(🎦 closed Mon ☎ (914) 251-6000)*.

Follow Anderson Hill Rd. to the next intersection, Route 120A *(King St.)*. Turn left, N. Continue past the traffic light at the entrance to the Westchester County Airport on the left. The next street on the right is Cliffdale Rd. — turn into it. It winds down a steep hill into a bosky gorge with a tumbling brook, and leads on through a neighborhood of luxurious homes. After a mile, Cliffdale Rd. ends at Route 433 *(Riversville Rd.)*. Turn left, N.

At the intersection with John St., about a mile farther on, is the tall, chunky steeple of the **N Greenwich Congregational Church**, erected in 1896. On the opposite corner is an **Audubon Center**, with nature trails open daily to the public (🏞). Continue N on Route 433 to the first traffic signal, and turn right on Route 22. Just beyond a large canary yellow furniture store is **Smith's Tavern**. Built at the time of the Revolutionary War, it is now a modest museum of such items as antique dollhouses and quilts. Due to a shortage of volunteers, it cannot keep regular hours; to arrange a tour ☎273-4510. Behind the museum are three other historic buildings, including a blacksmith's stable and a Quaker meeting house.

Route 22 rolls on, across undulating hills, past country clubs and examples of residential architecture dating back 300 years. Eventually there is **Bedford Village**, settled in 1680 by pioneers from New England. At the fork in the road, park near the tiny schoolhouse (1829), which is now a museum of local history *(open Wed-Sun 2-5pm; often closed from Christmas to mid-Feb)*. Across the street is a white clapboard **Methodist Church** (1806), which is now the headquarters of the Bedford Historical Society *(☎ (914) 234-9328)*. The adjacent burial ground was first established in 1681.

Bedford deserves an exploratory stroll. Around the triangular village green are the **Bedford Free Library** (1807), the **Courthouse Museum** *(1787 — open Wed-Sun 2-5pm)*, and **Post Office** (1838). Side streets have homes of the Dutch Colonial and Greek Revival styles. Most date from after 1779, when a British commander burned all but one of the then existing houses, in retribution for rebel resistance. Some of the historic buildings are open to the public *(usually open Wed-Sun 2-5pm)*, but they are dependent upon volunteers, so they can open and close at unpredictable times.

You will soon have an opportunity to picnic, and a tasty spread can be assembled at the **Bedford Gourmet** take-out store, opposite the movie theater. They specialize in cheeses and coffees and have an array of artfully composed salads and sandwiches.

Return to the car and continue through the village on Route 22. Just beyond, bear right at the junction on Route 121, N. This eventually passes the Cross River Reservoir, part of New York City's water system.

Just before the junction with Route 35 is the entrance to the **Ward Pound Ridge Reservation** (▨) — 4,750 acres (1,900ha.) of hiking trails and campgrounds. If you do decide on a picnic, this is the place, but take time picking a spot. There are several picnic areas, with tables, stone barbecues, and fields in which to fling Frisbees. Drive carefully, for the reservation is home to many deer, most of them unafraid of cars and humans in this sanctuary. They graze by the side of the roads and may bolt suddenly across your path. In winter, cross-country skiing is popular. A small **museum** *(open Wed-Sun 9am-5pm)* has mounted specimens of wildlife known to inhabit the area, including hawks, racoons, and an occasional coyote. Return, after lunch or a look around, to Route 35. Turn right (E). The nearby **Yellow Monkey Antiques** store rewards a visit.

Soon, 35 crosses into Connecticut and the town of **Ridgefield**. On the left are the **West Lane Inn** and the **Inn at Ridgefield**, both of which offer lodgings, with lunch and dinner daily at the second establishment. Turn left on **Main St.**, (Route 33), an avenue of great spreading trees and splendid 19thC homes. On the right is the **Aldrich Museum of Contemporary Art** *(open Tues-Sun 1-5pm ▨)*. Sculptures monumental and whimsical are placed about the lawn and are on view every day. They, and the works within, are primarily by Americans since 1945. A large new wing allows the new director to bring in provocative temporary exhibitions. A visit is a must.

Continue N through the village on Main St. Eventually, Route 33 merges with 116 as the road re-enters New York State.

≈ At the intersection with Route 121 is the deceptively humble-appearing **Auberge Maxime** *(☎(914) 669-5450; closed Wed* ▥*)*, which is widely regarded as one of the finest restaurants in the region. It is often possible to obtain a table without notice at lunch or even dinner during the week, but reservations are essential on weekends. Duck comes in five delectable versions, the bouillabaisse is memorable, soufflés are supernal. Window tables in back look out over rolling hills and meadows.

After dining, drive s on 121, passing several fair-sized horse farms. Stay with it until it intersects with Route 138, turning right (W) toward Goldens Bridge. There, pick up the 684 highway, which connects with the Hutchinson River Parkway back to the city.

STATELY HOMES OF THE HUDSON

250 miles round trip N. Minimum one overnight, preferably two nights and three days.

Travel N on the West Side Highway, which becomes the Henry Hudson Parkway and then the Saw Mill River Parkway after it crosses the city line into Westchester County. It is designated Route 9A all the way. Continue through the city of Yonkers and the town of Hastings-on-Hudson, taking exit 17 in Dobbs Ferry, W on Ashford Ave. until it joins with Broadway *(Route 9)*. Turn right, N, and drive on past the commercial district of the village of Irvington.

Four blocks beyond Main St., turn left, W, on Sunnyside Lane. At the end, just before the railroad tracks and the Hudson, is **Sunnyside** *(▨ open Wed-Mon 10am-5pm Apr-Dec; Sat, Sun only Jan-Mar)*, the home of Washington Irving (1783-1859), an author, diplomat and scholar. Although well-traveled — he was once a diplomatic attaché to Spain — Irving always returned to this region, which he called "Sleepy Hollow" in his novels and stories. His house, gardens and outbuildings have been scrupulously restored, with guides dressed in appropriate 19thC garb. This is part of the Historic Hudson Valley restorations, a group of historic buildings that includes **Philipsburg Manor**, **Van Cortlandt Manor** and **Montgomery Place** (see page 295). Combination tickets can be purchased for all four, at a substantial saving. Less expensive grounds passes, which don't include house tours, are also available.

Return to Route 9 *(S Broadway)* and go N, to reach a Gothic Revival mansion called **Lyndhurst** *(☎(914) 631-0046 ▨ open May-Oct, Wed-Sun 10am-5pm)*. It was constructed in 1838 by a mayor of New York and purchased by the railroad tycoon Jay Gould in 1880. Many of Gould's furnishings are in place, complementing the vaulted ceilings and stained-glass windows. There are well-attended summer concerts on the grounds. Picnicking is permitted.

Back on Route 9, proceed N two miles beyond the Dewey Thruway, watching for signs to **Philipsburg Manor** (■ *open as Sunnyside, above*). Frederick Philipse, a late 17thC Dutch immigrant, was a businessman and entrepreneur of exceptional acumen. This bustling complex of dam, gristmill, granary, bakery, stockyards, shipping wharf and farmland was only part of his holdings, which at one time totaled 90,000 acres (36,000ha.) on both banks of the Hudson. Costumed attendants give demonstrations of Colonial cooking, millwork, weaving, and agricultural trades and crafts. There is a guided tour, beginning with a short film and then visiting the farmhouse, mill and barn, with its live cows and sheep. The **Old Dutch Church**, across the street and slightly N on Route 9, was built by Philipse in 1697. Washington Irving is buried in the nearby cemetery.

Leaving the parking lot of Philipsburg Manor, turn right, up the hill to the traffic light. Turn left on Bedford Rd. (Route 448). Soon, the presence of high green chain-link fences announce the presence of the Rockefeller estate, **Kykuit**. The 40-room mansion in which four generations of one of America's wealthiest families lived is being readied for visits by the public in 1994. Information and transport will be available from Philipsburg manor.

At the stop sign E of the estate, turn left, still on Bedford. This is **Pocantico Hills**, a lovely Brigadoon of a village that looks as if it had been lifted intact from the mountains of northern Vermont. Shortly, on the right is the small stone **Union Church**. It, too, was a beneficiary of Rockefeller largesse, which purchased the **stained glass windows**, designed by Marc Chagall. The church is locked up much of the time, but do stop for a look if it's open, which it usually is on weekends.

Bedford Rd. continues through the village and between large pastures with grazing cattle. A cowboy wrangler on horseback is sometimes seen tending to his charges. It is difficult to believe you are only 25 miles from Times Square. Too soon, the road emerges at the traffic light on Route 117. Turn right and stay in the left lane. At the next light, turn left down the ramp onto Route 9A. The next few miles aren't especially beguiling, but 9A then merges with Route 9, beside the Hudson. After they cross the Croton River, entering the village of Croton-on-Hudson, take the first exit after the bridge. Turn right at Croton Point Ave., continue to the first traffic signal, and turn right again on S Riverside Ave.

Van Cortlandt Manor *(open as Sunnyside, above),* another part of the Historic Hudson Valley organization, is about 100 yards down the road. The main house began as a modest lodge erected in the late 1600s and was expanded to its present size by subsequent generations of the wealthy Van Cortlandt family, who lived on this land for more than 260 years. The original 86,000 acres (34,400ha.) have now vastly shrunk, but those that remain are well-tended, and the manor has been restored to its 18thC splendor.

Down by the river, past flourishing gardens and fruit trees, is the **Ferry House**, an inn of the same period, which served passengers of the ferry across the Croton River operated by the Van Cortlandts. At that time, the river was much wider and deeper, before a dam was built upstream in the 1840s. In the early days of this century, a stretch of it served as a setting for the first *Tarzan* movie. This close to the big city, the river is brackish and tidal, rising and falling three feet every six hours. George Washington visited the Van Cortlandts frequently, as did many other prominent figures of the Revolutionary War period. As at the other Historic Hudson Valley restorations, appropriately attired guides and craftspeople give demonstrations of home and farm skills. Frequent special events include a Christmas Candlelight Tour and the Fall Crafts and Tasks Festival.

Return to Route 9 and continue N (Route 9A soon branches off once again, but stay on 9). Beyond the city of Peekskill, turn W on Route 6, following it around the traffic circle and on toward the Bear Mountain Bridge. The road ascends, curling around the mountain face, with an excellent observation point overlooking the Hudson at the top, on the left. Continue down toward the Bear Mountain Bridge, now in view. But instead of crossing the bridge, drive N on Route 9D.

About eight miles from the bridge, on the left, is the **Boscobel Restoration** *(☎ (914) 265-3638 ✉ open Apr-Oct Wed-Mon 9.30am-5pm; Nov, Dec, Mar 9.30am-4pm).* The centerpiece is the 1804 Federalist mansion reached after a walk through an apple orchard and rose garden. Now painted a creamy mustard with white trim, the restored structure was moved here from its original location and opened to the public in 1961. And what a site it is, with an unblemished vista of the Hudson Highlands, to the S. Concerts by the Hudson Valley Philharmonic are held on the lawn in summer, an excuse to take a picnic and drink in that view.

The mansion itself functions as a **museum of the decorative arts** of its period, featuring furnishings by the renowned cabinetmaker, Duncan Phyfe. Christmas candlelight tours are held here, too. At the exit, continue in the same direction on Route 9, turning left at the traffic light onto Main St., into **Cold Spring**. Six blocks of the street, with many 19thC houses, are on the National Register of Historic Places. It descends to the edge of the river. Swans make their year-round home here, and in summer, pleasure boats and windsurfers dart across the swiftly flowing water. Opposite looms **Storm King Mountain**, the tallest peak in these Hudson Highlands. Down to the left (S) is seen the fortress-like **US Military Academy**, the officers' training college that is better known as **West Point**.

✿ ⇌   **Hudson House** *(▥ 2 Main St. ☎ (914) 265-9355),* opposite the bandstand at river's edge, is open all year and has a dining room and a number of plain but comfortable rooms. Better choices, though, might be the **Vintage Café** *(▥ 91 Main St. ☎ (914) 265-4726),* for its whimsical pastas and fish dishes, the brick oven pizzas of **Riverview** *(▥ 45 Fair St. ☎ (914) 265-4778)* and the fetching rustic rooms and savory breakfasts of **Pig Hill Inn** *(▥ 73 Main St. ☎ (914) 265-9247).* Half of the eight rooms at Pig Hill are equipped with fireplaces and private baths.

Another lodging possibility is the **Old Post Inn** *(▥ 43 Main St. ☎ (914) 265-2510),* but its chief attractions are the jazz groups that jam in the basement bar Friday and Saturday nights.

Main St. is lined with diverting cafés, bakeries, and gift and antique stores, including **The Country Goose** (#101), with its assortments of gourmet foods and kitchenware. Cold Spring causes people to linger longer than they intended.

When ready to leave, go up Main St., straight ahead through the traffic light. This is Route 301, heading E. Before long, it enters **Clarence Fahnestock State Park** *(open all year)*. Boats are rented at the shed on the left, and there are picnic grounds a little farther on the right. Shortly, take the entrance to the Taconic State Parkway, N. While a pleasant enough route, this detour's primary purpose is to avoid the often crippling traffic produced by the several large shopping malls that line Route 9 between Fishkill and Poughkeepsie. Exit the Taconic on Route 55 heading W toward the river city of Poughkeepsie. Turn left, S, on Route 49. This is Titusville Rd. It soon crosses County Road 31.

✍ Turn left on Red Oaks Mill Rd., bearing right at the next fork to the entrance to **Inn at the Falls** *(▥ 50 Red Oaks Mill Rd. ☎(914) 462-5770)*. Opened in 1985, it is admittedly short on personality, but makes up in creature comforts. Rooms and suites are large, in varying decors, with room safes, bathroom scales and phones, remote cable TV and terry robes. Twelve rooms have unstocked mini-fridges; most look out on Wappingers Creek. Breakfast is included in the reasonable room rates.

🍽 The inn has no restaurant, but there are several satisfactory choices within short drives. Some are located in the downtown district of Poughkeepsie, which is not, sad to say, an especially good place to wander at night. A less chancy possibility is **Le Pavillon** *(▥ 230 Salt Point Turnpike ☎(914) 473-2525)*, with such familiar but well-executed French comfort foods as coarse country pâtés and *coq au vin*. It's as if the cuisines *minceur* and *nouvelle* had been repealed.

If it is summer and still light at dinnertime, two other possibilities are **Mill House Panda** *(▥ 289 Mill St. ☎(914) 454-2530)* for commendable Chinese fare and **Angelisa** *(▥ 15 Collegeview ☎(914) 454-6332)*, known for contemporary seafoods and pastas. Both have outdoor patios.

Keep Angelisa in mind for lunch the next day, for it is located at the edge of the **Vassar College** campus, which can occupy part of a morning if time and interest permit. From the Inn at the Falls, turn right, then right again on Route 376, which bears right in a little over two miles and enters the campus on Raymond Ave. One of the first institutions of higher education for women (opened 1865) and a member of the prestigious "Seven Sisters" group, Vassar turned co-educational in 1968.

On Raymond is the **Vassar College Art Gallery** *(▣ open Wed-Sat, 10am-5pm; Sun noon-5pm ☎(914) 437-5235)*. Located in Taylor Hall, the large collection includes works by artists of the Hudson River School, America's first native-born landscape painters. A stroll across the 1,000-acre (405ha.) campus might also take in the college chapel, with its Tiffany glass windows.

Afterwards, drive N on Raymond, turning left (W) on Routes 44 and 55. Travel toward the downtown Civic Center, turning N on Washington Ave., which soon merges with Route 9 N. The buildings here are part of Marist College.

Hyde Park is next, a village rich in associations with historical figures. On the left is an unusual educational institution sometimes called "the other CIA," **The Culinary Institute of America** *(☎(914) 471-6608)*.

Graduates of the demanding 21-month program staff many of the finest kitchens in the US. Its student-chefs operate four restaurants, all open to the public. Many people feel they rival the best of Manhattan, and at half the cost. The problem for the casual visitor is that the three best-known rooms — the **American Bounty**, **Escoffier**, and the **Catherine de Medici** — are booked up for weeks, even months, in advance. The fourth, **St Andrew's Café**, is the best chance for walk-in diners, but they shouldn't be disappointed if every last chair is taken.

Continuing N, on the left is the entrance to the **Franklin Delano Roosevelt National Historic Site** *(☎ (914) 631-0046 ☒ open daily Apr-Oct 9am-5pm; Nov-Mar Thurs-Mon 9am-5pm)*. Parts of the house date from 1826, and it enjoys unobstructed views of the Hudson from the south lawn. F.D.R., the 32nd president and the only one elected for four terms, was born there in 1882. He and his wife Eleanor are buried in the rose garden.

The unpretentiously furnished house is as worn as comfortable old slippers and hardly what might be expected of one of the Valley's wealthiest families. Walking through, it seems as if the celebrated former occupants will be back any minute. There are fresh flowers in vases, magazines of the period scattered about, Roosevelt's wheelchair, and his dressing gown waiting on the bed.

The **FDR Library** is also in the grounds, an initiative followed by every president since. For true Roosevelt buffs, Eleanor's personal hideaway, **Val-Kill**, is a short drive away, following Route 40A E and 9G N. It is closed from late November through February.

A little farther N on Route 9, again on the left, is the **Vanderbilt Mansion** *(times as FDR home, above)*. Frederick W. Vanderbilt was a financier by virtue of the inheritance handed down by his famous grandfather, "Commodore" Cornelius Vanderbilt, a railroad and shipping magnate of the mid-19thC. Far more lavishly appointed than the FDR home, the 54-room Beaux Arts mansion was designed by the fashionable McKim, Mead & White firm and cost $660,000 to build in 1898. Most of the works of art and furnishings in it are original. The mansion perches astride a bluff with still another magnificent panorama of the river, the land behind it studded with giant specimens of over 40 varieties of trees. Leaving by the marked exit drive, turn left (N) on Route 9.

The **Catskill Mountains** now come into view, rising beyond the west bank of the river. **Rhinebeck** is the next village, and one of the most attractive in the entire valley. It is still evolving from a rural market center to the sporadically gentrified retreat of permanent and weekend refugees from the city downriver. It has enough of the latter to support a cinema specializing in art and revival films, as well as antique stores and galleries and several passable-to-good eating places.

🍴 An enjoyable stop for lunch is **La Parmigiana** *(🏠 37 Montgomery St. ☎ (914) 876-3228)*, housed in a deconsecrated Baptist Church. They specialize in semi-designer pizzas baked in wood-fired ovens.

🛏🍴 At center stage, however, is the **Beekman Arms** *(🏠 meals and rooms; Routes 9 and 308 ☎ (914) 876-7077; open all year)*. There has been an inn at the site since at least 1766, and probably earlier, the basis for the declaration that it is the oldest inn in continuous operation in the US. Others contest that claim, and the structure has been expanded and remodeled so often that it would be difficult to find a joist or floorboard predating the Civil War. But never mind. It is a welcoming place with many inviting public spaces, including an atmospheric tap room and a greenhouse dining area, as well as 60 bedrooms in five buildings and annexes.

The most beguiling of these is the 1844 **Delmater House**, a block away. A notable example of the Carpenter Gothic style, it has a few large rooms off a central foyer. Other rooms are ordinary motel style, and not all have TV and/or air-conditioning. Inquire when booking. There is a two-night minimum stay on weekends from May 15 to October 31 and holiday weekends throughout the year. The inn's food service operations were recently taken over by Larry Forgione, a celebrity chef known for his **An American Place** restaurant in Manhattan. Sunday brunch is particularly popular, and reservations are obligatory for all weekend meals.

Should the next day be a Saturday or Sunday *(June-Oct only)*, there are airshows featuring vintage planes at the **Old Rhinebeck Aerodrome** *(☎(914) 758-8610 to check times)*, reached by driving N on Route 9, and right on Stone Church Rd. for about a mile. History buffs aren't the only spectators who enjoy the aerial acrobatics and simulated dogfights between restored planes of the Great War and the 1920s.

Returning to Route 9, turn N, toward Red Hook. In the center of that village, turn left on Route 199. If it's mealtime, there is a comely café on the right, **Green & Bresler** *(▣ closed Wed and occasionally dinner; 29 W Market St. ☎(914) 758-5992)*. Dishes are adapted from many cuisines, with perhaps an edge for those of Asia.

Pick up Route 9G N, which goes through orchard country, some of them pick-your-own operations. In two miles, there is a juncture with Annandale Rd., on the left. Take that road, following its bend to the left and arriving at the gate of **Montgomery Place** *(☎(914) 631-8200 ▨ open Nov, Dec, Mar, Sat and Sun; Apr-Oct daily 10am-pm, closed Jan, Feb)*. The latest acquisition of the Historic Hudson Valley organization dates from 1804, remodeled in the 1860s in the prevailing Classical Revival mode. Antiques and crafts shows are among the scheduled events in July and August. And, there are more of those river views from great sweeps of lawn.

Go back to 9G and turn left (N). In a little over two miles, an amusing (and entirely optional) detour can be made by turning left (W) on Route 199. This soon arrives in the hamlet of Tivoli. At first, it appears to be nearly deserted, but then signs of reawakening appear — an old church turned into a mini-mall and an out-of-place but capable Tex-Mex restaurant, **Santa Fe** *(▣ dinner only, closed Mon; 52 Broadway ☎(914) 757-4100)*. Back on 9G, keep driving N. Antique stores are even more in evidence now.

After crossing the line into Columbia County, look for the left turn onto County Route 6. This enters **Clermont State Park**, and eventually leads to the mansion of the influential Livingston family. The large white house was first built in 1730, torched by the British in 1777 in retaliation for the family's openly rebellious sentiments, and rebuilt after the Revolution. The patriarch at that time was one of the drafters of the Declaration of Independence, a minister of foreign affairs for the new nation, and a principal in the negotiation of the Louisiana Purchase from France. His descendants occupied the estate until 1962. Many picnic tables on the grounds take advantage of the riverside setting.

Back to 9G, left toward Germantown. The terrain is far less scenic after that village, but persevere. There is just one more suggested stop, and in some ways, it is the most compelling of the entire trip. Watch for the entry road to the **Olana State Historic Site** (☎ *(518) 828-0135* 🔲 *for house* 🔳 *for grounds; closed Mon and Tues Nov-mid-Apr).* It makes a long upward loop to the top of a high rounded knob of hill, where a vision of an imagined Arabian Nights stands majestically against the sky. The "castle" was designed by and built for Frederic Edwin Church, a painter of the 19thC Hudson River School. Obviously, he was most successful at his craft; he had to be to afford this Oriental palace, with its great halls, bell tower, and layer upon layer of intricate patterns inside and out. He dug his own lake on the 250-acre (100ha.) property and planted thousands of trees on its slopes.

Best of all, though, is the **view** from the front of the house, one that surpasses even those already encountered on this tour. On clear days, three neighboring states can be seen. Straight out and down, the silvered Hudson flows toward the Atlantic, the blue Catskills at one side, both mountains and waters disappearing over the far horizon. The grounds are open all day, all year, so no one need be denied this climactic event in an exploration of one's of America's most storied rivers.

To return to New York, continue N on Route 9G a short way, to Route 23 E. This leads, after a change in designation to Route 82, to the Taconic State Parkway. It is less than three hours from there back to the city.

Farther afield

SHAKERS AND BERKSHIRES
290 miles NE. Minimum two days.
There are numerous opportunities for swimming, hiking, and picnicking along this route, so dress and pack accordingly.

Leave Manhattan via the West Side Highway. This becomes the Henry Hudson Parkway, which joins the Saw Mill River Parkway. Follow the latter to Hawthorne Interchange, transferring to the Taconic State Parkway, N, which passes through a sparsely settled countryside of meadows, groves, and green and tawny land with folds like a rumpled quilt. Leave the Parkway at the Route 44 exit, following signs E toward **Millbrook**. Watch for the junction with Route 82. About one mile beyond is Tyrrell Rd. Turn right, S, down that narrow, winding road. In a little over a mile is **Innisfree Garden** (🔳 ☎ *(914) 677-8000, open May-Oct Wed-Sun 10am-4pm),* the creation of a painter by the name of Walter Beck. A stone house with a slate roof stands at the gate, containing a gallery with a selection of Beck's paintings.

Return to Route 44 and turn right, E. Almost immediately, on the left, is a turn onto Route 44A. Take that, and, in slightly less than a mile, watch for the 1817 brick house that is the visitor center of the **Mary Flagler Cary Arboretum** (⬛ ☎ *(914) 677-5359, open May-Sept Mon-Sat 9am-6pm, Sun 1-6pm; Oct-April Mon-Sat 9am-4pm, Sun 1-4pm).* The arboretum is an educational facility of the Institute of Ecosystem Studies of the New York Botanical Garden, but hardly as dry as that association might suggest. There are walking trails and drive-through roads, a **perennial garden** and a **lilac collection.**

After a visit, return to Route 44 and follow it into the pleasant village of **Millbrook.** This has long been a retreat for the horsey set, testified by the numerous grand estates, both active and abandoned, that are to be viewed along the way. The most eerily dramatic of these is the vacant and decaying **Halcyon Hall,** a rambling Tudor-style manse with an astonishing 200 rooms. It is at the intersection where Route 44 turns left into the village. In recent years, Millbrook has become a heaven for antique hunters.

Continue on Route 44, noting at the intersection with the other end of 44A the amusingly overblown stone **gatehouse** for an unseen manor. About seven miles from that point is the intersection with County Road 83, on the left, opposite a sign directing up that road to the **Cascade Mountain Farms Winery** (▥ *914-373-9021).* Follow 83 through prosperous farmlands devoted primarily to the raising of sheep, horses, and dairy and beef cattle. In 2.8 miles, pick up County Road 5 (straight ahead when 83 bends left), and after another 1.3 miles, turn right on Morse Hill Rd. In a little over one-half mile, pick up Huckle Berry Road. (This route is also posted with signs displaying symbolic clusters of grapes.)

Shortly, on the right, is the Cascade Mountain Farms Winery. One of over a score of wineries in the mid-Hudson Valley region, its owners are more skilled than most at public relations. They offer a brief self-guided tour of its wine-making operation, followed by free tastings. Their pressings frequently win state awards, but they thankfully don't take themselves *too* seriously — one of their best efforts is simply called "A Dry White Wine." Upstairs in the same building is a cheerful **restaurant** serving satisfying lunches of soups, smoked fish, pâtés, cheese platters, chicken salads and fruit tarts *(open July-Oct Fri-Mon noon-3pm; Nov-June Sat and Sun noon-3pm.)*

Leaving the winery, turn right, then right again, on dirt-surfaced Flint Hill Rd. This soon ends at County Road 83. Turn left, returning to Route 44 and continuing E. In about two miles is Amenia. Once there, proceed E on Route 363.

❧   Off this road is **Troutbeck** (▥ ☎ *(914) 373-8581),* an exemplary inn that serves as a conference center during the week, with tennis courts, pool and a trout stream meandering through the property. Private guests are accepted from Friday afternoon to Sunday evening. Weekend packages are expensive, but include all meals. Reservations are essential.

Continue on Route 363 into **Sharon,** there taking Route 4 two miles SE to the **Northeast Audubon Center** (⬛ ☎ *(203) 364-5826, open Mon-Sat 9am-5pm; Sun 1-5pm),* a wildlife sanctuary with miles of nature walks, a museum, and a herb garden. When you leave, return to Sharon and turn N on Route 41, passing through the center of the town of white clapboard frame houses and sheltering elms and maples. Route 41 soon arrives in **Lakeville**. Just before 41 joins with 44 is a sign pointing to **Holley Place** (▥ ☎ *(203) 435-2727)*, behind the fire house. A 19thC cutlery factory has been turned into a rustic-contemporary setting for the serving of such Austrian favorites as bratwurst, schnitzel and *roesti,* augmented by pastas and substantial salads. After lunch, continue N on Route 41, which goes through the heart of contiguous **Salisbury**.

☜☰ Many travelers choose to stop for lunch or the night at the **White Hart Inn** (▥ to ▥ *Route 41 and 44, Salisbury, CT 06039* ☎ *(203) 435-0030)*. It closed for a while in the late 1980s, the apparent victim of changing public tastes. Now it has been restored and upgraded, a landmark once again, and with a much improved kitchen.

Route 41 soon crosses the state line into Massachusetts. Turn right on Route 23, which curls through the pretty hamlet of **South Egremont**. This is antiques country, too, and among the roadside bed and breakfasts encountered is the **Weathervane Inn** (☎ *(413) 528-9580* ▥). Before long, Route 23 connects with Route 7. Turn left, N, through **Great Barrington**. Once the home of fabric mills, as were so many settlements along the Housatonic River, the town is now a shopping center for the southern Berkshire Hills.

Stay on Route 7 through to **Stockbridge**, 8 miles farther. On most counts a quintessential New England village, Stockbridge stops well short of touristy clutter, despite its considerable popularity with summer renters and weekenders. Turn right, E, into Main St. (Route 102).

☰ At that corner is the **Red Lion Inn** (☎ *(413) 298-5545* ▥ *108 rms, advance reservations essential)*. The dining room serves three meals daily, and there is a convivial tap room downstairs with live music most evenings at 8 or 9pm.

The revered illustrator Norman Rockwell lived in Stockbridge much of his life, and many of his paintings are on view at the **Norman Rockwell Museum** (▨ *open daily, 10am-5pm except major holidays and last two weeks in Jan; shorter hours Nov-Apr)*, just down the street. Two blocks in the other direction, W, is the **Mission House** (☎ *(413) 298-3383* ▨ *open late May-early Oct, Tues-Sat 10am-5pm)*, built in 1739 and maintained as a museum of domestic Colonial life, including a garden. The **Chesterwood** estate of the sculptor Daniel Chester French is 2 miles away, N on Route 102, then S on Route 183. French created the moving sculpture of Abraham Lincoln in Washington, DC's Lincoln Memorial. There are daily guided tours of the house and studio (▨ *open late May-early Oct 10am-5pm)*.

The southern Berkshires host a multitude of cultural activities every summer. In Stockbridge, the **Berkshire Playhouse** presents classics and some pre-Broadway try-outs *(June-Oct)*. The **Boston Symphony Orchestra** and other musical ensembles perform at **Tanglewood**, an open-sided "shed" on spacious grounds in nearby Lenox. The town of **Lee** is known for the annual **Jacob's Pillow Dance Festival**, in a theater created by Martha Graham and Ted Shawn. In winter, there are several popular ski resorts, including **Bousquet, Brodie,** and **Jiminy Peak** near Pittsfield and **Butternut Basin** near Great Barrington. Plan to spend at least one night in the area — more, if possible — but remember that from June to early October is the peak season for visitors. Although the summer crowds are large, they are rarely unruly, given the nature of the attractions. Lodging reservations are mandatory on weekends in July and August and during the fall foliage season, roughly the two weeks either side of Columbus Day, October 11.

There are a score of inns in Lenox alone, and at least that many combined in adjoining Stockbridge, West Stockbridge and Lee. At the end of the last century, Lenox rivaled Saratoga and Newport as the summer resort of the pre-income tax wealthy. Their legacy was dozens of fabulous estates, "cottages" of at least twenty rooms on thirty acres or more. Lavishly appointed with furnishings and materials imported from all over the world, many of them have survived to take on new lives as inns and restaurants.

Notable among these is **Canyon Ranch** *(☎ 1-800-726-9900 ▥),* the eastern branch of the famous Arizona spa. It is ensconced in the Italianate *palazzo* Bellefontaine, built in 1897. **Blantyre** *(☎ (413) 637-3556 ▥, open May-Oct)* is a Tudor mansion inspired by a Scottish castle; **Wheatleigh** *(☎ (413) 637-0610 ▥)* was a wedding present to a woman who married a European aristocrat and maintains an appropriate level of grandeur in price, if not always in attention. Several inns cluster along Walker St. in the center of Lenox.

Gateways Inn *(☎ (413) 637-2532 ▥)* is known as much for its accomplished kitchen and dining room as for its elegant appointments; **The Gables Inn** *(☎ (413) 637-3416 ▥ to ▥)* is a unintimidating version of The Gilded Age; and **The Candlelight Inn** *(☎ (413) 637-1555 ▥)* has a busy restaurant and tavern as well as middling rooms. These are highly visible and are apt to fill up weeks in advance.

Two quieter but no less agreeable "cottages" are found in a neighborhood a few minutes away from the busy main part of town, at #25 and #76 Cliffwood St. They are **Cliffwood Inn** *(☎ (413) 637-3330 ▥ to ▥)* and **Underledge** *(☎ (413) 637-0236 ▥ to ▥).* The first is notable for its many antiques and pool, the second for its uncommonly spacious rooms, most with working fireplaces. Advance deposits and minimum stays apply at most Berkshires inns.

Most of the inns mentioned above have restaurants that welcome diners who are not staying overnight. For a more casual experience, the **Church Street Café** *(69 Church St., Lenox ☎ (413) 637-2745 ▥)* has surprisingly imaginative American fare served in summer on two outdoor decks. Another full-service inn, the **Federal House** *(Main St., South Lee ☎ (413) 243-1824),* is celebrated for its high-style meals at refreshingly reasonable prices. In the past, appetizers have included the likes of cornmeal blini with nubbins of smoked trout topped by teaspoons of two caviars. It's on Route 102, a few miles E of Stockbridge.

When you are ready to leave for New York, drive N on Route 7 to Pittsfield. This is in parts a garish commercial strip, unusual for the Berkshires, and traffic can be heavy. But it isn't far to Route 20, in downtown Pittsfield. Turn left (W). Five miles from the center of Pittsfield is **Hancock Shaker Village** *(☎ (413) 443-0188, open daily May-Oct 9.30am-5pm; daily Apr and Nov 10am-3pm for guided tours only ▩).* This was one of the former settlements of the celibate Shaker religious sect, founded as an offshoot of the Quakers in the 18thC. In accordance with their beliefs, their houses and furnishings were crisp and exquisitely simple. This painstakingly restored village, with its trademark round stone barn, illustrates Shaker crafts and trades, from cookery to herb cultivation to "spirit painting," with admirable clarity. Don't miss it.

There is an excellent gift store in the new visitors' center, which also has a lunch room.

Drive w on Route 20, then turn left, s, on Route 22. After a dull stretch, the bordering landscape grows interesting once again approaching Hillsdale.

At the juncture with Route 23 is **L'Hostellerie Bressane** (☎ *(518) 325-3412 ▥ no cards),* an long-heralded restaurant of classical Provençal leanings. The owner conducts cooking classes during the day, and so serves only dinner. He closes at unpredictable times. There are a few modest, inexpensive bedrooms upstairs.

Continuing down Route 22, the next interesting stopover is Millerton. Turn left into the village on Route 44. If it is mealtime, look for **New Yorker** (☎ *(518) 789-6293 ▥),* about one mile out, on the left. The pubby bistro is owned by a French chef who straddles two-fisted steaks and such Continental whimsies as escargot and wild mushrooms on angel hair pasta. Afterwards, return on 44.

In town, on the right, is **Simmon's Way Village Inn** (☎ *(518) 789-6235 ▥),* a refurbished Victorian charmer that has appeared on the cover of *New York* Magazine. The featured room, with bay windows and a queen-sized bed with antique iron bed, is #5.

Continuing w, look for **McArthur's Smokehouse**, beside the old railroad station. It sells superior homemade sausages and smoked meats and cheeses.

From Millerton, drive s and w on Route 44. Four miles beyond Millbrook is the entrance to the Taconic State Parkway, for the return to New York City.

Index

Page numbers in **bold** type refer to main entries. *Italic* page numbers refer to the illustrations and plans. See also the LIST OF STREET NAMES on page 313.

List of street names

All streets mentioned in this book that fall within the area covered by our maps are listed below. Map numbers are printed in **bold** type. Some smaller streets are not named on the maps, but the map reference given below will help you locate the correct neighborhood.

Albany St., **1**U3-4
Amsterdam Ave., **5**N2-7I3
Ann St., **2**T4
Astor Pl., **3**T4
Ave. of the Americas *see* 6th Ave.

Barclay St., **1**T4
Barrow St., **3**R3
Battery Pl., **1**U4
Bayard St., **2**T4-5
Bedford St., **3**R3
Beekman Pl., **6**O5
Bleecker St., **3**R3-4
Bond St., **3**R4
Bowery, The, **3**R4-4T5
Broad St., **2**U4
Broadway, **7**I2-3U4
Brooklyn Bridge, **2**T5
Brooklyn-Queens Expressway, **4**V6-U7
Broome St., **3**S4-4S6

Canal St., **3**S3-4S5
Cannon's Walk, **2**U5
Carmine St., **3**R4
Catherine St., **2**T5
Central Park S, **5**N3-6N4
Central Park W, **7**N3-I3
Chambers St., **1**T3-2T4
Charles St., **3**R3
Chatham Sq., **2**T5
Christopher St., **3**R3
Church St., **1**T4
Clark St., **4**U6
Clinton St., **4**U6
Coenties Alley, **2**U4
Coenties Slip, **2**U4
Columbia Heights, **4**U6-V6
Columbus Ave., **7**M3-J3

Columbus Circle, **5**N3
Commerce St., **3**R3
Cooper Sq., **3**R4
Cornelia St., **3**R3
Court St., **4**V6

Delancy St., **4**S5-6
Doris C. Freedman Plaza, **8**M4
Dover St., **2**T5

East End Ave., **8**L5-K5
East Broadway, **2**T5-S5
Exchange Pl., **2**U4

FDR Drive *see* Roosevelt Drive
Foley Sq., **2**T4
Franklin St., **1**T3-2T4
Front St., **2**U4-5
Fulton St., **1**U4-2U5
Fulton St.(Brooklyn), **4**V7

Gay St., **3**R3
Grace Court Alley, **4**V6
Grand St., **3**S4-5
Great Jones St., **3**R4
Greene St., **3**S4
Greenwich Ave., **3**R3
Greenwich St., **3**R3-T4
Grove St., **3**R3

Hanover Sq., **2**U4
Henry Hudson Parkway, **7**M2-I2
Henry St., **4**T5-S6
Henry St.(Brooklyn), **4**V6
Herald Sq., **6**P4
Hester St., **3**S4-4S5
Hicks St., **4**V6

Holland Tunnel, **3**S2
Houston St., **3**S4-4R6
Hoyt St., **4**V7
Hudson St., **5**Q3-T4
Hunt's Lane, **4**V6

Irving Pl., **6**Q4

Jane St., **3**R3
John St., **1**U4-2U5

Lafayette St., **3**T4-R4
LaGuardia Pl., **3**R4
Leonard St., **1**T4-2T4
Leroy St., **3**S3-R3
Lexington Ave., **6**Q4-8I4
Liberty St., **1**U4-2U4
Lincoln Sq., **7**M3

MacDougal Alley, **3**R4
MacDougal St., **3**R4
Madison Ave., **6**Q4-8I4
Madison Sq., **6**Q4
Maiden Lane, **2**U4
Manhattan Bridge, **4**T5-6
Mercer St., **3**S4-R4
Middagh St., **4**U6
Mitchell Pl., **6**O5
Montague St., **3**V6-U6
Montague Tce, **4**V6
Morton St., **3**S3-R3
Mott St., **3**S4-4T5
Mulberry St., **2**S4-T5
Murray St., **1**T4-2T4

Nassau St., **2**U4-T4

Old Fulton St., **4**U6
Orange St., **4**U6
Orchard St., **4**S5

Park Ave., **6Q4-8I4**
Park Dr., **7M3-8M4**
Park Pl., **1T4**
Park Row, **2T4**
Pearl St., **2U4-5**
Peck Slip, **2T5-U5**
Pell St., **2T5**
Perry St., **3R3**
Pierrepont St., **4U6**
Prince St., **3S4-4S5**

Queens-Midtown Tunnel, **6O5-6**
Queensboro Bridge, **6N5-6**

Rector St., **1U4**
Remsen St., **4V6**
Riverside Dr., **7M2-I2**
Rockefeller Plaza, **6O4**
Roosevelt Drive (FDR Drive), **6Q6-8L6**

St Luke's Pl., **3S3**
St Mark's Pl., **4R5**
Schermerhorn Row, **4V6**
Sniffen Court, **6P4**
South St., **2V4-T5**
Spring St., **3S3-4**

State St., **1U4-2V4**
Stone St., **2U4**
Sullivan St., **3S4-R4**
Sutton Pl., **6N5**

Thomas St., **1T4**
Thompson St., **3S4-R4**
Times Sq., **5O3**
Tobin Plaza, **1U4**
Transverse Rd., **7L3-8L4**
Trinity Pl., **1U4**

Union Sq., **6Q4**
United Nations Plaza, **6O5**
University Pl., **3R4**

Vandam St., **3S3-4**
Vanderbilt Ave., **6O4**
Varick St., **3S3-4**
Vesey St., **1T4**
Vestry St., **3S3**

Walker St., **1S4-2S4**
Wall St., **2U4-5**
Washington Sq., **3R4**
Washington Mews, **3R4**
Washington Pl., **3R3-4**
Washington St., **3R3-T4**
Water St., **2U4-T5**

Water St. (Brooklyn), **4U6-T6**
Waverly Pl., **3R3-4**
West End Ave., **7M2-I2**
West Broadway, **3T4-S4**
West St., **1S3-U4**
White St., **1T4-2T4**
Whitehall St., **1U4-2V4**
William St., **2T4**
Willow St., **4U6**
Worth St., **1T4-2T5**

York Ave., **8N5-K5**

Numbered Avenues
1st Ave., **4R5-8I5**
2nd Ave., **4R5-8I5**
3rd Ave., **3R4-8I5**
4th Ave., **3R4-6Q4**
5th Ave., **3Q4-8J4**
6th Ave., **3S4-6N4**
7th Ave., **3R3-5N3**
8th Ave., **3R3-5N3**
9th Ave., **5R3-M3**
10th Ave., **5Q2-N2**
11th Ave., **5Q2-M2**
12th Ave., **5P2-O2**

Numbered streets

Numbered streets in Manhattan run from east to west across the island. Above 14th St., streets are called W to the left of 5th Ave. and E to the right. 5th Ave. runs from north to south, along the right-hand edge of Central Park. Above 136th St., streets called E are across the Harlem River, in The Bronx.

1st-9th St., **3R4-4R6**
10th-13th St., **3R3-4R6**
13th-25th St., **5Q2-6Q5**
26th-37th St., **5P2-6P5**

38th-49th St., **5O2-6O5**
50th-62nd St., **5N2-6N5**
63rd-74th St., **7M2-8M5**
75th-86th St., **7L2-8L5**

87th-98th St., **7K2-8K5**
99th-110th St., **7J2-8J5**
111th-115th St., **7I2-8I5**

Clothing sizes chart

LADIES
Suits and dresses

Australia	8	10	12	14	16	18	
France	34	36	38	40	42	44	
Germany	32	34	36	38	40	42	
Italy	38	40	42	44	46		
Japan	7	9	11	13			
UK	6	8	10	12	14	16	18
USA	4	6	8	10	12	14	16

Shoes

USA	6	$6\frac{1}{2}$	7	$7\frac{1}{2}$	8	$8\frac{1}{2}$
UK	$4\frac{1}{2}$	5	$5\frac{1}{2}$	6	$6\frac{1}{2}$	7
Europe	38	38	39	39	40	41

MEN
Shirts

USA, UK Europe, Japan	14	$14\frac{1}{2}$	15	$15\frac{1}{2}$	16	$16\frac{1}{2}$	17
Australia	36	37	38	39.5	41	42	43

Sweaters/T-shirts

Australia, USA, Germany	S	M	L	XL
UK	34	36-38	40	42-44
Italy	44	46-48	50	52
France	1	2-3	4	5
Japan		S-M	L	XL

Suits/Coats

UK, USA	36	38	40	42	44
Australia, Italy, France, Germany	46	48	50	52	54
Japan	S	M	L	XL	

Shoes

UK	7	$7\frac{1}{2}$	$8\frac{1}{2}$	$9\frac{1}{2}$	$10\frac{1}{2}$	11
USA	8	$8\frac{1}{2}$	$9\frac{1}{2}$	$10\frac{1}{2}$	$11\frac{1}{2}$	12
Europe	41	42	43	44	45	46

CHILDREN
Clothing

UK

Height (ins)	43	48	55	60	62	
Age	4-5	6-7	9-10	11	12	13

USA

Age	4	6	8	10	12	14

Europe

Height (cms)	125	135	150	155	160	165
Age	7	9	12	13	14	15

CONVERSION FORMULAE

To convert	Multiply by
Inches to Centimeters	2.540
Centimeters to Inches	0.39370
Feet to Meters	0.3048
Meters to feet	3.2808
Yards to Meters	0.9144
Meters to Yards	1.09361
Miles to Kilometers	1.60934
Kilometers to Miles	0.621371
Sq Meters to Sq Feet	10.7638
Sq Feet to Sq Meters	0.092903
Sq Yards to Sq Meters	0.83612
Sq Meters to Sq Yards	1.19599
Sq Miles to Sq Kilometers	2.5899
Sq Kilometers to Sq Miles	0.386103
Acres to Hectares	0.40468
Hectares to Acres	2.47105
Gallons to Liters	4.545
Liters to Gallons	0.22
Ounces to Grams	28.3495
Grams to Ounces	0.03528
Pounds to Grams	453.592
Grams to Pounds	0.00220
Pounds to Kilograms	0.4536
Kilograms to Pounds	2.2046
Tons (UK) to Kilograms	1016.05
Kilograms to Tons (UK)	0.0009842
Tons (US) to Kilograms	746.483
Kilograms to Tons (US)	0.0013396

Quick conversions

Kilometers to Miles	Divide by 8, multiply by 5
Miles to Kilometers	Divide by 5, multiply by 8
1 meter =	Approximately 3 feet 3 inches
2 centimeters =	Approximately 1 inch
1 pound (weight) =	475 grams (nearly $\frac{1}{2}$ kilogram)
Celsius to Fahrenheit	Divide by 5, multiply by 9, add 32
Fahrenheit to Celsius	Subtract 32, divide by 9, multiply by 5

KEY TO MAP PAGES

1-2 DOWNTOWN MANHATTAN
3-4 DOWNTOWN TO UNION SQ
5-6 9TH ST TO 66TH ST
7-8 60TH ST TO 116TH ST

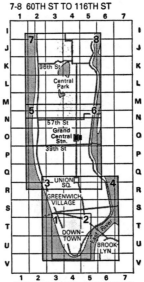

KEY TO MAP SYMBOLS

▨	Place of Interest or Important Building
▨	Built-up Area
▨	Park
† †	Cemetery
†	Church
✡	Synagogue
⊞	Hospital
ℓ	Information Office
⊠	Post Office
☞	Parking Lot
Ⓜ	Subway
→	One-way Street
5	Adjoining Page No.

```
0    200   400   600   800yds
├─────┼─────┼─────┼─────┤
0    200   400   600   800m
```

(Scale bar for use with
maps 3-8 only)

CANAL STREET

DESBROSSES ST
VESTRY ST
LAIGHT ST
3-4 HOLLAND TUNNEL EXIT
ST JOHN'S LA.
LISPENARD ST
WALKER
WHITE
HUBERT ST
GREENWICH ST
WASHINGTON ST
MOORE
ERICSON PL.
FRANKLIN
TRIBECA
NORTH ST
FRANKLIN ST
HUDSON ST
LEONARD
WORTH ST
HARRISON ST
JAY ST
THOMAS ST
CHURCH STREET
BROADWAY
Independence Plaza
DUANE PARK
DURNE ST
READE ST
CHAMBERS
STREET
WARREN ST
MURRAY ST
NORTH
WEST STREET HIGHWAY
MURRAY ST
WEST STREET
PARK PLACE W
PARK PLACE
END AVE
BARCLAY ST
Woolworth Building
VESEY ST
VESEY ST
St.Paul's Chapel

T
U

World Financial Center
North Tower
South Tower
World Trade Center

North Cove

LIBERTY ST
CEDAR
ALBANY ST
ALBANY ST
CARLISLE ST
TRINITY PLACE
BROADWAY
RECTOR PL
Trinity Church
HUDSON RIVER
BATTERY PARK CITY
SOUTH END AVE
WASHINGTON ST
GREENWICH ST
RECTOR ST
W. THAMES ST
FINANCIAL
BATTERY PL
3RD PL.
2ND PL.
South Cove
BOWLING GREEN
1ST PL.
BATTERY
U
V
BATTERY PARK

Castle Clinton

0   100   200   300   400   500yds
0   100   200   300   400   500m

3 4

Statue of Liberty Ferry

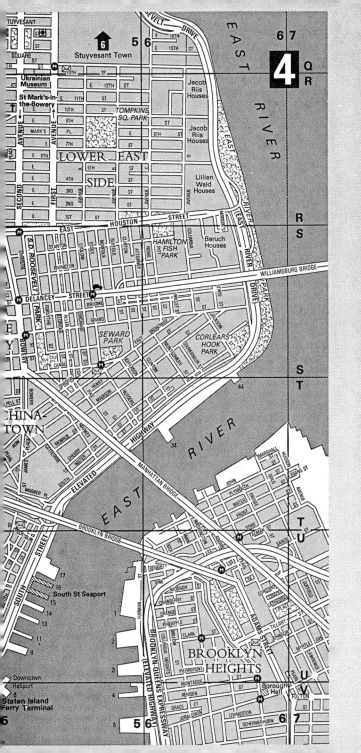

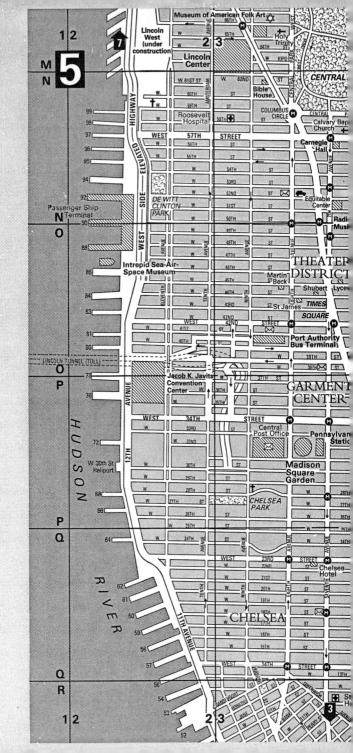

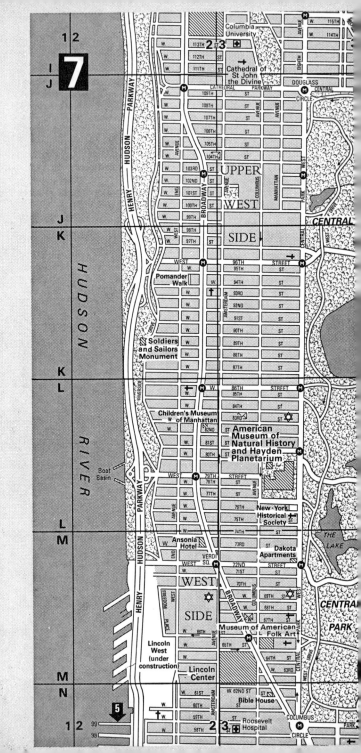

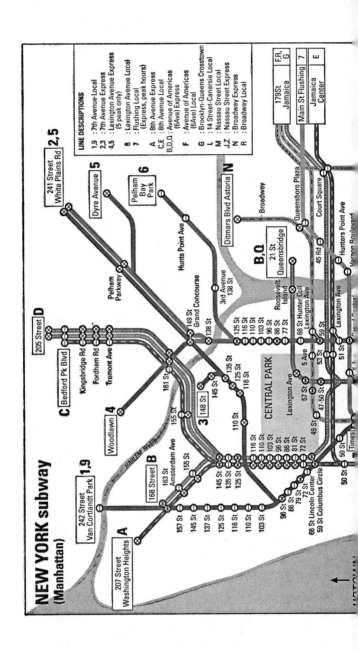

NEW YORK subway
(Manhattan)

LINE DESCRIPTIONS

1,9 : 7th Avenue Local
2,3 : 7th Avenue Express
4,5 : Lexington Avenue Express
        (5 peak only)
6 : Lexington Avenue Local
7 : Flushing Local
        (Express, peak hours)
A : 8th Avenue Express
C,E : 8th Avenue Local
B,D,Q : Avenue of Americas
        (6Ave) Express
F : Avenue of Americas
        (6Ave) Local
G : Brooklyn-Queens Crosstown
L : 14 Street-Canarsie Local
M : Nassau Street Local
J,Z : Nassau Street Express
N : Broadway Express
R : Broadway Local

DOWNTOWN →

EAST RIVER

to Ellis & Liberty Islands
to Staten Island

Rockaway Parkway — L

Metropolitan Ave/Jamaica Center — M, J, Z

Stillwell Ave/Brighton Beach — B,D, N,Q
Lefferts Blvd — A

Bay Parkway — B,M
95St Ft Hamilton — R
Flatbush Ave — 2,5
New Lots Ave/Utica Ave — 3, 4
Smith 9St — G
Stillwell Ave — F

Lorimer St
Bedford Ave
Metropolitan Ave
Grand St
1st Ave
3 Ave
Union Sq
14 St Union Sq
Astor Place
8 St
*
Bleecker St
Delancey St
East Broadway
Essex St
2 Ave
Bowery
Grd St
Canal St
Broadway/Nassau St
Fulton St
York St
Jay St
Hoyt St
Wall St
Court St
Clark St
Brooklyn Hts
Borough Hall/
Court St
JZ Broad St
Whitehall St
Bowling Green
Wall St

34 St
28 St
23 St
Penn Station
Herald Sq
Union Sq Broadway
14 St Union Sq
8 St NYU
West 4 St Washton Sq
Prince St
Spring St
B way
Canal St
Canal St
Chambers St
Bklyn Br. City Hall
6
City Hall
Cortlandt St
World Trade Center
E
Fulton St
Rector St
South Ferry
1,9

34 St
28 St
23 St
6 Ave
14 St
Christopher St
Sheridan Sq
Houston St
Canal St
Franklin St
Chambers St
Park Pl
Cortlandt St
(World Trade Center)
Rector St
Greenwich St

14 Street L

Map authorised user number D/CAS/WW/AM/1013

KEY
━━━ 1,2,3,9
━━━ 4,5,6
━━━ 7
━━━ A,C,E
━━━ B,D,F,Q
━━━ G
━━━ L
━━━ M,J,Z
━━━ N,R

⦵ Local stop
⊗ Express stop
⦵ Local and Express stop
⊶ Free transfers between lines
4 Woodlawn Line and terminating station
* Transfer in downtown direction only

©TCS Designed by R.Woods

What the papers said:

• "The expertly edited American Express series has the knack of pinpointing precisely the details you need to know, and doing it concisely and intelligently." (*The Washington Post*)

• "*(Venice)* ... the best guide book I have ever used." (*The Standard* — London)

• "Amid the welter of guides to individual countries, American Express stands out...." (*Time*)

• "Possibly the best ... guides on the market, they come close to the oft-claimed 'all you need to know' comprehensiveness, with much original experience, research and opinions." (*Sunday Telegraph* — London)

• "The most useful general guide was *American Express New York* by Herbert Bailey Livesey. It also has the best street and subway maps." (*Daily Telegraph* — London)

• "...in the flood of travel guides, the *American Express* guides come closest to the needs of traveling managers with little time." (*Die Zeit* — Germany)

What the experts said:

• "We only used one guide book, Sheila Hale's *Amex Venice,* for which she and the editors deserve a Nobel Prize." (Eric Newby, London)

• "Congratulations to you and your staff for putting out the best guide book of *any* size *(Barcelona & Madrid)*. I'm recommending it to everyone." (Barnaby Conrad, Santa Barbara, California)

• "If you're only buying one guide book, we recommend American Express...." (*Which?* — Britain's leading consumer magazine)

What readers from all over the world have said:

• "The book *(Hong Kong, Singapore & Bangkok)* was written in such a personal way that I feel as if you were actually writing this book for me." (L.Z., Orange, Conn., USA)

• "Your book *(Florence and Tuscany)* proved a wonderful companion for us in the past fortnight. It went with us everywhere...." (E.H., Kingston-on-Thames, Surrey, England)

• "I feel as if you have been a silent friend shadowing my time in Tuscany." (T.G., Washington, DC, USA)

• "We followed your book *(Los Angeles & San Francisco)* to the letter. It proved to be wonderful, indispensable, a joy...." (C.C., London, England)

• "We could never have had the wonderful time that we did without your guide to *Paris.* The compactness was very convenient, your maps were all we needed, but it was your restaurant guide that truly made our stay special.... We have learned first-hand: *American Express — don't leave home without it.*" (A. R., Virginia Beach, Va., USA)

• "Much of our enjoyment came from the way your book *(Venice)* sent us off scurrying around the interesting streets and off to the right places at the right times". (Lord H., London, England)

• "It *(Paris)* was my constant companion and totally dependable...." (V. N., Johannesburg, South Africa)

• "I could go on and on about how useful the book *(Amsterdam)* was — the trouble was that it was almost getting to be a case of not venturing out without it...." (J.C.W., Manchester, England)

• "We have heartily recommended these books to all our friends who have plans to travel abroad." (A.S. and J.C., New York, USA)

• "Despite many previous visits to Italy, I wish I had had your guide *(Florence and Tuscany)* ages ago. I love the author's crisp, literate writing and her devotion to her subject." (M. B-K., Denver, Colorado, USA)

• "We never made a restaurant reservation without checking your book *(Venice).* The recommendations were excellent, and the historical and artistic text got us through the sights beautifully." (L.S., Boston, Ma., USA)

• "We became almost a club as we found people sitting at tables all around, consulting their little blue books!" (F.C., Glasgow, Scotland)

• "This guide *(Paris)* we warmly recommend to all the many international visitors we work with." (M.L., Paris, France)

• "It's not often I would write such a letter, but it's one of the best guide books we have ever used *(Rome)* — we can't fault it!" (S.H., Berkhamsted, Herts, England)

American Express Travel Guides

spanning the globe....

EUROPE
Amsterdam, Rotterdam
  & The Hague
Athens and the
  Classical Sites ∗ ‡
Barcelona, Madrid &
  Seville #
Berlin, Potsdam &
  Dresden ∗ (‡ as Berlin)
Brussels
Dublin
Florence and Tuscany
London
Moscow & St Petersburg ∗
Paris
Prague #
Provence and the
  Côte d'Azur ∗
Rome
Venice #
Vienna & Budapest

NORTH AMERICA
Boston and New
  England ∗
Los Angeles & San
  Diego
Mexico #
New York
San Francisco and
  the Wine Regions
Toronto, Montréal and
  Québec City #
Washington, DC

THE PACIFIC
Cities of
  Australia
Hong Kong
  & Taiwan
Singapore &
  Bangkok ∗ ‡
Tokyo

∗ Paperbacks in preparation   # Paperbacks appearing August 1993
‡ Currently available as hardback pocket guides

*Clarity and quality of information, combined
with outstanding maps — the ultimate in
travelers' guides*